THE TELLING TRUTH

EVANGELIZING POSTMODERNS

BANNOCKBURN INSTITUTE
for Christianity & Contemporary Culture

This book is a project of Bannockburn Institute for Christianity and Contemporary Culture, an international educational institute located just north of Chicago, Illinois, in the United States of America. The Institute endeavors to bring Christian perspectives to bear on particularly important aspects of contemporary culture. It pursues this task, in part, by establishing Centers that address specific arenas such as bioethics, public education, personal and relational growth, and family life. It also carries out broader initiatives, such as the examination of postmodernism reflected in the current volume. The Institute and its various centers produce a wide range of educational resources (including books, audios, videos, web sites, Internet services, newsletters, journals, and a variety of other printed and computer-based resources) and hold conferences and workshops in various parts of the world.

For more information about Bannockburn Institute or its various Centers, contact:

Bannockburn Institute
2065 Half Day Road
Bannockburn, IL 60015
Phone: 847.317.8164
Fax: 847.317.8153
E-mail: bi@biccc.org

Information is also available on the Institute's internet web site:
http://www.biccc.org

TELLING

THE

TELLING THE TRUTH

TRUTH

EVANGELIZING POSTMODERNS

TELLING THE TRUTH

D. A. CARSON
GENERAL EDITOR

ZondervanPublishingHouse
Grand Rapids, Michigan

A Division of HarperCollins*Publishers*

Telling the Truth
Copyright © 2000 by D. A. Carson and the Bannockburn Institute

Requests for information should be addressed to:

⛪ZondervanPublishingHouse
Grand Rapids, Michigan 49530

Library of Congress Cataloging-in-Publication Data

Carson, D. A.
    Telling the truth : evangelizing postmoderns / D. A. Carson, general editor.
      p.   cm.
    Includes bibliographical references and index.
    ISBN: 0-310-23432-8
    1. Evangelistic work—Congresses.   2. Postmoderism—Religious aspects—Christianity—
Congresses.   I. Carson, D. A.
    BV3795.T45 2000
    269'.2–dc 21

                                                          00–039262
                                                               CIP

This edition is printed on acid-free paper.

Interior design by Amy E. Langeler

Printed in the United States of America

00 01 02 03 04 05 /❖ DC/ 10 9 8 7 6 5 4 3 2 1

TABLE OF CONTENTS

PART 1: OPENING PLENARIES

PART 2: THE CHALLENGE

PART 3: CRITICAL TOPICS

128423

PREFACE

This book is one of the outcomes of a conference held at Trinity Evangelical Divinity School May 13–15, 1998. Around nine hundred people attended, about half of them pastors and church workers, and half of them university workers. Enthusiasm was so high that we made the decision to publish the papers. An added incentive was that the schedule allowed conference participants to attend all the plenaries but only nine seminars. To preserve the material in this way will allow much wider dissemination of content that is too useful to be lost. Most of the presentations from that conference are here.

I should make two things plain right away. First, although Trinity was the primary sponsor of the conference, the cosponsors were InterVarsity Christian Fellowship, Campus Crusade for Christ, the Navigators, the Billy Graham Center Institute of Evangelism, and the Bannockburn Institute for Christianity and Contemporary Culture. These organizations contributed time, planning, resources, and personnel. Some of the papers in this book tell us, in effect, what these organizations are doing in the sphere of evangelizing postmoderns. Certainly we at Trinity could not have mounted this effort by ourselves.

Second, a great deal of planning was carried out by a small group consisting of John Nyquist, Harold Netland, and me. Since the other two have more experience, I was privileged to coordinate things and learn from them. Logistical planning was ably chaired by John Kilner of the Bannockburn Institute. The Director of the conference, Roland Kuhl, managed to be ubiquitous and untangled all the knots with charm and courtesy.

Early on we made a few crucial decisions. We decided that anyone invited to speak at the conference must be actively engaged in evangelism. This was not the sort of conference where we wanted mere theoreticians, no matter how capable. We also decided that we needed not only to hear thoughtful cultural analysis but also to probe some of the most important turning points of biblical theology, to listen to the experiences of those who are proving fruitful in contemporary evangelism, and to glean something from those who are thinking hard both strategically and practically.

I want to thank each of the people who contributed to these pages. They responded quickly to my inquiries and reminders, and produced a remarkable collection of papers. Anyone interested in evangelism in the Western world will read these chapters with delight and profit. Where particular priorities or perspectives seem a little removed from where you sit, you will find more than adequate stimulation from the rest of the book.

Finally, my heartfelt thanks go to my graduate assistants, Tom Wood and Sigurd Grindheim, and to my secretary, Judy Tetour, for countless hours of labor discharged with good cheer and wonderful efficiency. It has been a pleasure to work with them.

Soli Deo gloria.
D. A. Carson

CONTRIBUTORS

Michael P. Andrus is senior pastor of the First Evangelical Free Church of St. Louis, Missouri. The church, a spontaneous church plant to which he was called as the first pastor in 1984, has grown from sixty to an average attendance of eighteen hundred. He has also seen the establishment of six other Free Churches in St. Louis. Andrus was educated at Calvary Bible College, Kansas City, Missouri (B.A. with highest honor in preministerial, 1966), Southern Methodist University, Dallas, Texas (M.A. in philosophy, 1969), Dallas Theological Seminary (Th.M. with highest honor in historical theology, 1971), and Trinity Evangelical Divinity School, Deerfield, Illinois (D.Min., 1994).

Don Bartel is codirector of the U.S. community ministries of the Navigators and coordinator of the Scriptural Roots of Ministry study processes. He also serves on the steering committee of the Coalition of Urban Pastors in Philadelphia. He has, over the years, pioneered campus and community ministries while training others to reach those without Christ in their natural spheres of influence through the use of mission outpost concepts.

Ron Bennett is director of the Strategic Resource Group for the Navigators Church Discipleship Ministry. This group develops materials and services for churches interested in becoming intentional in the disciple-making and evangelism process. He received his B.A. in aerospace engineering from Iowa State University in 1967 and worked for Boeing Aircraft in Seattle, Washington. He has been on staff with the Navigators for twenty-seven years and has led ministries on campuses, military bases, and in the community.

Walter L. Bradley is professor of mechanical engineering at Texas A&M University, a position he has held since 1976. He also has been an associate staff member of Campus Crusade for Christ since 1968, working with students and faculty on campus. He received his B.S. in engineering science from the University of Texas in 1965 and his Ph.D. in materials science and engineering in 1968. He has coauthored one book, *The Mystery of Life's Origin: Reassessing Current Theories*, and has written chapters in several other books, including *The Creation Hypothesis*, on the origin of life. He has also spoken on more than sixty campuses in the U.S. and abroad on the topic of scientific evidence for an intelligent designer.

Andrea Buczynski is the national staffed campus director of Campus Crusade for Christ, a position she has held since 1993. She has been a staff member of Campus Crusade for Christ since 1977. She received her B.S. in chemistry from Penn

State University in 1977 and was trained at the Institute of Biblical Studies in Fort Collins, Colorado, in the summers of 1977, 1978, and 1980. Other ministry positions she has held include regional staffed campus director of the Great Lakes region for Campus Crusade for Christ, associate area director for Wisconsin and for Indiana for Campus Crusade for Christ, and associate campus director of Campus Crusade for Christ on the campuses of Indiana University, University of Wisconsin-Madison, and the University of Wisconsin-Stevens Point.

D. A. Carson is research professor of New Testament at Trinity Evangelical Divinity School. He has been at Trinity since 1978. He received the B.Sc. in chemistry from McGill University, the M.Div. from Central Baptist Seminary, and the Ph.D. in New Testament from Cambridge University. His areas of expertise include biblical theology, the historical Jesus, postmodernism, pluralism, Greek grammar, and questions of suffering and evil. He has written or edited more than forty books, including *The Gagging of God: Christianity Confronts Pluralism* (Zondervan), which won the 1997 Evangelical Christian Publishers Association Gold Medallion Award in the theology and doctrine category.

Peter Cha is a permanent part-time instructor of practical theology at Trinity Evangelical Divinity School and pastor of an Asian-American church that he helped to plant in the Chicago area, which primarily ministers to young adults. He received his M.Div. and Th.M. from Trinity Evangelical Divinity School and is currently a Ph.D. candidate in religion in society and personality at Northwestern University. His writings have been published in *Ethos: Proceedings of the Center for Ethics, Bridges: A Cross-Cultural Quarterly,* and *Korean Americans' Religion and Society.* He recently contributed a chapter to a book on discipling Asian-Americans, *Following Jesus without Dishonoring Our Parents* (InverVarsity, 1998).

Robert E. Coleman is director of the School of World Mission and Evangelism and a professor of evangelism at Trinity International University in Deerfield, Illinois. He also serves as director of the Billy Graham Institute at Wheaton, Illinois, and dean of the International Schools of Evangelism. He is a graduate of Southwestern University in Texas, of Asbury Theological Seminary, and of Princeton Theological Seminary, and he received his Ph.D. from the University of Iowa. He is the author of twenty-one books, including *The Master Plan of Evangelism, The Great Commission Lifestyle,* and *The Coming World Revival.* His ministry centers on lifestyle evangelism and discipleship. He frequently lectures at colleges and seminaries and regularly speaks in conferences around the world.

Keith A. Davy is associate director of research and development for Campus Crusade for Christ. In this capacity he has worked on several projects, including spearheading the national research and development effort of CCC's U.S. campus ministry for effective campus ministry among this generation's college students. He also leads the Effective Evangelism Project, which is an ongoing project seeking to devlop new strategies, tools, and training to more effectively reach today's student, and is developing the Evangelism Leadership Model, which is presently giving a framework for national campus leadership to set direction in outreach. He received a B.A. (with honors) in speech communications from the University of Nebraska in 1976, was trained at the Institute of Biblical Studies in San Bernardino, California, in the summers of 1976 and 1977, and received an M.Div. from Trinity Evangelical Divinity School (magna cum laude) in 1984.

CONTRIBUTORS

Mark E. Dever is pastor of Capitol Hill Baptist Church, where he has been serving since 1994. He received his B.A. (magna cum laude) from Duke University, his M.Div. (summa cum laude) from Gordon-Conwell Theological Seminary, his Th.M. from the Southern Baptist Theological Seminary, and his Ph.D. in ecclesiastical history from Cambridge University. Since his ordination in 1985 he has served on the pastoral staff of four churches. He has also taught for the faculty of divinity at Cambridge University while serving as associate pastor of Eden Baptist Church. He is a frequent conference speaker all over the world and feels a deep burden for student ministry.

Ajith Fernando is national director of Youth for Christ/Sri Lanka, a position he has held since 1976. He also serves as visiting lecturer in New Testament at Colombo Theological Seminary and as visiting professor at several seminaries in the U.S. and Canada. He has a worldwide ministry as a Bible expositor. His education includes a B.Sc. from Vidyalankara University of Ceylon, an M.Div. from Asbury Theological Seminary, and a Th.M. from Fuller Theological Seminary. He has written nine books in either English or Sinhala, including *Crucial Questions about Hell* (Crossway), *The Supremacy of Christ* (Crossway), and *NIV Application Commentary* on Acts (Zondervan).

Greg Ganssle has served on the staff of Campus Crusade for Christ for twenty-one years. He graduated from the University of Maryland in 1978 and earned an M.A. in philosophy from the University of Rhode Island (1990) and a Ph.D. in philosophy (1995) from Syracuse University, where his dissertation on God's relation to time won a Syracuse University Dissertation Award. He has taught philosophy at Syracuse and is currently faculty at the Rivendell Institute for Christian Thought and Learning, which is part of the ministry of Campus Crusade for Christ at Yale. He is editing *Four Views of God and Time* for InterVarsity Press and coediting an anthology of philosophical essays on God and time for Oxford University Press.

Mark Gauthier is national director for staffed campus ministries, U.S. campus ministry of Campus Crusade for Christ. He is a graduate of Colorado State University with a degree in industrial technology. He previously served for nine years in Boston directing the student ministry at Harvard and on other campuses in the Boston area. There he and a team helped pioneer new methods to reach the 300,000 students of Boston.

Charles Gilmer has served since 1992 as the national director of intercultural resources for the campus ministry of Campus Crusade for Christ. He is the director of the Impact Conferences, national gatherings of African-American college students. He graduated from the University of Pennsylvania with a bachelors of applied science in 1981. He writes and speaks on the topics of racial reconciliation and African-American apologetics. He travels extensively, speaking to college students and assisting campus ministries in their outreach. He is the author of the articles, "Let's Give the Dream New Life" and "The Truth about Jesus."

Susan Hecht has been a staff member with Campus Crusade for Christ since 1985. As a member of the Communication Center, she speaks at conferences, trains Christians in evangelistic speaking skills, and is involved with research and development for the campus ministry. She graduated from Duke University (cum laude) with a B.S. in botany. She also functions as the project director for *LifeSkills,* an evangelistic strategy designed to introduce non-Christian college students to biblical truth.

Jon Hinkson has been a staff member of Campus Crusade for Christ since 1985. He and his wife together work with CCC on the campus of Yale University. He attended the United Nations School in Vienna, Austria, and then Princeton University, where he earned a B.A. in European history in 1985. He has also received the M.Phil. degree in divinity from Cambridge University in England (1995). During his time in England he served as a student worker at Eden Baptist Chapel in Cambridge. He and his wife are also among the founders of the Rivendell Institute for Christian Thought and Learning.

Greg Jao is a second generation Chinese American, currently serving as an InterVarsity staff worker at the University of Chicago, his alma mater. He was educated as an attorney, and he also serves as a lay leader at Parkwood Community Church and travels widely, speaking at different Asian-American churches and campus ministry groups. He recently contributed to a book on discipling Asian-Americans, *Following Jesus without Dishonoring Our Parents* (InverVarsity, 1998).

Phillip D. Jensen is currently Anglican chaplain to the University of New South Wales, Australia, and rector of St. Matthias Anglican Church, Centennial Park. During his twenty-three-year ministry, he has been in constant demand as evangelist, church planter, Bible teacher, pastor, lecturer, author, publisher, preacher, and church leader throughout Australia as well as overseas. He leads a large ministry team working on the university campus and in the parish ministries. His ministries include Campus Bible Study, the Bible Talks, Sunday Meetings, Greek Bible Fellowship, the Korean Bible Fellowship, the Fellowship of Overseas Christian University Students, the Ministry Training Scheme, and Matthias Media.

Keith E. Johnson has served with the campus ministry of Campus Crusade for Christ for thirteen years. Keith is a frequent speaker on college campuses engaging non-Christian audiences on the topic "Comparative Religions: Do All Paths Lead to the Same Destination?" He has also written an evangelistic article on this topic. For eight years he served as field staff with Campus Crusade at Northwestern University. Presently Keith gives leadership to the theological education of Campus Crusade staff and also teaches graduate courses on apologetics and Bible study methods. He has an M.A. from Trinity Evangelical Divinity School.

Jimmy Long is regional director of InterVarsity Christian Fellowship in the Blue Ridge Region. He has been a staff member since 1975. He received his B.S. in social work from Florida State University in 1972 and his M.Div. in 1975 and D.Min. in 1995, both from Gordon-Conwell Theological Seminary. His ministry is currently on more than thirty-five campuses, with a staff team of fifty-two working with close to 3700 students in three states. He is also a part of a national team of staff that authored the *Small Group Leader's Handbook* (InterVarsity, 1995) and the *Small Group Leader's Handbook: The Next Generation* (InterVarsity, 1995). He has also recently authored *Generating Hope: A Strategy for Reaching the Postmodern Generation* (InterVarsity, 1997).

Kelly Monroe is chaplain to graduate students at Harvard University. She wrote her master's thesis on "The Gospel in the Information Age." She began the Harvard Veritas Forum to bring people together from diverse cultures and disciplines who want to explore Truth—*Veritas*—as understood by the founders of Harvard. She reveals a picture of Christian faith in a secular intellectual setting in her book *Finding God at Harvard* (Zondervan). She presents the testimonies of faculty members, former students, and distinguished orators at Harvard that serve to explode the myth that

Christian faith cannot survive a rigorous intellectual atmosphere. Currently, she advises the Veritas Forum as it emerges in many universities around the world.

Harold A. Netland is associate professor of philosophy of religion and mission, director of the Ph.D. in intercultural studies, and Naomi A. Fausch chair of missions at Trinity Evangelical Divinity School. He received his B.A. in biblical studies and history from Biola College and his M.A. and Ph.D. in philosophy from Claremont Graduate School, where he studied under John Hick. He has done postdoctorate work at the International Christian University (Tokyo), where he studied Japanese language and culture, and at Fuller Theological Seminary, where he studied theology and missions. He has served as a missionary in Japan, and has taught at Biola College and Talbot Theological Seminary. His published works include *Dissonant Voices: Religious Pluralism and the Question of Truth* as well as numerous articles on missions, religious pluralism, and apologetics.

John W. Nyquist is associate professor of mission and evangelism and director of mission and evangelism internship program at Trinity Evangelical Divinity School. He has been on the faculty of Trinity since 1982. Prior to that he was a visiting professor for five years teaching evangelism. He received a B.A. in music and physical education and an M.A. in music performance from California State University in Los Angeles. He earned an M.Div., an M.A. in New Testament, and a Ph.D. in intercultural studies from Trinity Evangelical Divinity School. Before coming to Trinity, he served in a number of roles with Campus Crusade for Christ. His areas of expertise include cross-cultural evangelism, discipleship, New Testament studies, European culture, and the Roman Catholic Church.

Tony Payne is the editorial director of Matthias Media (the publishing company that has grown out of the ministry of Phillip Jensen and St. Matthias Church in Sydney). He is well-known throughout Australia and the United Kingdom as a gifted author of articles, books, and Bible studies.

James W. Sire is senior editor for InterVarsity Press and Campus Lecturer for InterVarsity Christian Fellowship. He has also taught English, philosophy, and theology at a number of universities. He received his B.A. in chemistry and English from the University of Nebraska, his M.A. in English from Washington State University, and his Ph.D. in English from the University of Missouri. He is the author of several books, including *The Universe Next Door, Scripture Twisting, Discipleship of the Mind, Chris Chrisman Goes to College,* and *Why Should Anyone Believe Anything at All?* He addresses groups of students and faculty with talks on the arts, humanities, social science, natural science, and technical fields.

Colin S. Smith is senior pastor of the Arlington Heights Evangelical Free Church in Arlington Heights, Illinois. He is committed to expository preaching and believes that the central tasks of a senior pastor are to preach, pastor, and lead. He received his B.A. in theology from London Bible College and his M.Phil. from Brunel University (for the thesis on "Calvin's Doctrine of Justification in Relation to the Sense of Sin and the Dialogue with Rome"). He has also served as senior pastor of the Enfield Evangelical Free Church in London for sixteen years. While there, he was very active in the Fellowship of Independent Evangelical Churches in England and has served as the fellowship's president.

Mike Tilley is national director for Catalytic (expansion) ministries with Campus Crusade for Christ. He has done graduate work at Trinity Evangelical Divinity School and the International School of Theology and completed his M.Div. at Reformed

Theological Seminary in Orlando, Florida. His team of one hundred fifty Catalytic staff has the responsibility of pioneering new campus ministries through church partnerships, Metro Strategies, and Student LINC (distance consulting).

Ravi Zacharias is a major speaker and Christian leader, and is well versed in subjects such as comparative religions, cults, and secular philosophies. Ravi Zacharias International Ministries was founded in 1984 for the purpose of reaching the thinker and the professional person in the major cities of the world and to aid in leadership development. He graduated from Ontario Bible College and received his graduate degree from Trinity Evangelical Divinity School. He held for three and a half years the Chair of Evangelism and Contemporary Thought at Alliance Theological Seminary in Nyack, New York. He is licensed and ordained by the Christian and Missionary Alliance. Issues pertaining to cross-cultural ministry and to modern professionals and thinkers form crucial parts of his thinking and ministry.

PART ONE

Opening Plenaries

CHAPTER 1

AN ANCIENT MESSAGE, THROUGH MODERN MEANS, TO A POSTMODERN MIND

Ravi Zacharias

In April 1981 Daniel Yankelovich, a social analyst, wrote a very insightful article in *Psychology Today*. His principal thrust was to analyze how Americans were thinking about life and where we were headed should such ideas go uncriticized. It was a warning to the West. In his opening remarks, he defined the role and the imperative of culture. Quoting sociologist Daniel Bell, he said, "Culture is the effort to provide a coherent set of answers to the existentialist situations that confront all human beings in the passage of their lives" (Yankelovich 1981, 36).

To define culture even in these terms may well be outdated now. Some months ago I was lecturing at one of the universities in the country when a student stormed up to the microphone and bellowed, "Who told you culture is a search for coherence? Where do you get that idea from? This idea of coherence is a Western idea." I replied by reminding her that all I had done in that instance was to present a sociologist's definition that culture sought coherence. "Ah! Words! Just words!" she shouted back.

"Let me ask you this then," I pleaded. "Do you want my answer to be coherent?" Some laughter rippled through the auditorium. She herself was stymied for a few moments. "But that's language, isn't it?" she retorted.

I asked her if language has anything to do with reality. "Must words not point to a referent? If you are seeking an answer that must be coherent, but culture itself does not have to be, from whence do you get this disjunction?" One could sense the turmoil within her. Indeed, later on I was told that this individual was a rather outspoken person whose lifestyle was radically aberrant from the normal. Her struggle for coherence was rooted in her very physiological dissonance.

This student may well be the quintessential postmodernist. Our bodies and proclivities are defining our reason for being. That is how intense I believe this struggle is becoming. Friedrich Nietzsche and Michel Foucault—both brilliant yet tragic figures—can be seen as the definitive bookends of the twentieth century. Foucault, of course, was a leading French intellectual who, owing to a very promiscuous life, died of AIDS at the age of fifty-eight. He was a lover of the writings of Nietzsche, who, ironically, had died at age fifty-four in the wake of his pitiful bout with venereal disease and insanity.

So even as we look for our cultural moorings and try to understand the radical shifts that have disrupted the shared meanings of the past, attempting a coherent answer becomes a prohibitive challenge.

Walter Truett Anderson humorously gives us an insight into this in his book *Reality Isn't What It Used to Be*. He reflects on our predicament by presenting an analogy from baseball. A premodern baseball umpire would have said something like this: "There's balls, and there's strikes and I call 'em as they are." The modernist would have said, "There's balls and there's strikes, and I call 'em as I see 'em." And the postmodernist umpire would say, "They ain't nothing until I call 'em" (quoted in Middleton and Walsh 1995, 132–33). In brief, all reality is subject dependent. The postmodernist frames reality by naming aspects at his or her whim.

You and I have in some ways been so influenced by this culture that we too cannot get ourselves completely outside of it. We are locked into this postmodern mindset, or at least some elements of it. Perhaps the most radically affected of all are our children. If you talk to your teenager after a movie that your son or daughter wanted you to see, you suddenly hear comments such as, "I'm sorry, Dad, but I hadn't noticed all the bad language until you were sitting next to me." It is almost as if they live in that world, and they don't even notice it anymore until somehow, someone with a counterperspective is sitting next to them. And then they mutter, "Oh-oh. I've blown this one." The disorientation is thus double-edged, both external and internal. Reality is redefined, and our own thinking is unwittingly reshaped.

THE CENTURY OF CHANGE

How did we get where we are today? I perceive that five major shifts in this century have brought us to where we are. No doubt there are others.

The first major shift was *the popularization of the death of God movement*, the bequest of Nietzsche. Remember how poignantly he talked about the madman running with a lantern, looking for God and unable to find him? That parable stabbed at the heart of reality, offering a different way of looking at things. Then Nietzsche says, "Indeed, this has been such an enormous shift, even as the philosopher's blade has dug into the heart of theism." He warns his readers of the disorientation that would ensue: "Who gave us a sponge to wipe away the horizon? What sacred games will we need to invent? Is there any up or down? Must not lanterns have to be lit in the morning hours? Are we not straying through an infinite nothing? Can we not feel the breath of empty space?" He writes of this radical shift that has come about—there is no up; there is no down. New lights have to illuminate our path. New sacred games need to be invented. Finally, he concludes that the shock is too staggering to immediately gain a footing. "Maybe my time has not yet come," he says. "It takes time for ideas to completely take hold in the mindset of a culture" (Nietzsche 1954, 125).

Nearly one hundred years later, his time has come. There is a popularization of the death of God. The idea of God's nonexistence now either explicitly or implicitly permeates almost every major discipline in secular universities. In fact, a parent recently told me of his daughter's initial orientation at a prestigious university not far from here. In their video presentation, the closing testimonial to the university's intellectual strength was given by a young graduate. Borrowing from Richard Dawkins, she looked into the lens of the camera and said, "One of the best things this university has done for me is that it allowed me to become an intellectually fulfilled atheist." Imagine promoting a very sophisticated university with a testimonial of atheism to prospective students.

The second major shift is the disorienting blow of *religious pluralism,* principally within the context of Western culture. In 1893 at the Chicago Conference on World Religions, one of India's renowned philosophers, Swami Vivekenanda (who incidentally was not one of the program speakers), got up from his chair and went up to the podium. He said this:

> We who come from the East have sat here on the platform day after day and have been told in a patronizing way that we ought to accept Christianity because Christian nations are the most prosperous. We look about us and see England, the most prosperous Christian nation in the world, with her foot on the neck of 250 million Asiatics. We look back into history, and we see that the prosperity began with the invasion of Mexico. Christianity wins its prosperity by cutting the throats of its fellow men. At such a price, the Hindu will not have prosperity. I have sat here today, and I've heard the intolerance. Blood and sword are not for the Hindu whose religion is based on the laws of love.[1]

I am not questioning whether he was right or wrong. His facts clearly were tendentious and at least equally offensive to those he was charging with discourtesy. But beyond the polemics, this is the reigning perspective in the way the Middle Easterner and the Far Easterner think about Christianity. I have spoken in some of the toughest settings in the Middle East. In two rare opportunities, I had the privilege of addressing audiences in Damascus, Syria. Half of the challenge is removing the prejudice of Christianity's baggage across the centuries. But as a result of the infusion of those worldviews into North American, the same prejudices have taken hold in the West. You soon begin to realize how disorienting this has been to Western culture, which has borrowed from Christianity's capital but does not know how much it has borrowed. Now, in numerous academic settings, the most vitriolic attacks upon religion are leveled almost exclusively against the Christian faith.

The third shift is *the power to inform through the visual and the blurring of reality and imagination.* The visual has changed the way people arrive at truth. Is it not interesting that every previous movie production of the sinking of the *Titanic* sent the audience away feeling sorry for what had happened and very shaken up by the tragedy but that in this latest production, the plastic heroes have surfaced to the top from the sinking ship? The romance of the arts through the eye gate has sunk reality and glamorized the artificial personalities of stage heroes. In fact, now the *Titanic* is to be rebuilt and will set sail in 2002, ninety years to the day from the original voyage. Some will pay hundreds of thousands for the best suites, even as this is now branded "The Ultimately Unsinkable." Reality has crossed swords with imagination and lost. William Blake warned of the peril of the eye: "This life's dim window of the soul / Distorts the heavens from pole to pole / And goads you to believe a lie / When you see with and not through the eye."[2]

We are intended by God to see through the eye, but with the conscience. Now we see with the eye, devoid of a conscience. The English journalist Malcolm Muggeridge tells of the time he was in Biafra and some prisoners were about to be executed. The guards lined up the prisoners, and the officer shouted the countdown: "Ready, aim—" Just then a photographer for one of the major networks shouted, "Cut! My battery is dead!" The execution was momentarily suspended until he could get a fresh battery pack. Then the countdown resumed: "Ready, aim, fire!"—*bang, bang*—and the prisoners lay dead. Muggeridge wondered what some future generation would say of the barbarism and where it lay. Would they blame the viewers? Would they castigate the cameraman? He said, "I strongly suspect somebody may plump for the cameras" (1977, 64). Muggeridge may have a point. The medium does become the message, and this blurring between the real and the imagined is really locked into the medium itself.

The fourth shift is *the lost center of cultural molding*. There is a vacuum at the heart of our culture. Saul Bellow argued in his 1976 Nobel Laureate lecture:

> The intelligent public is waiting to hear from art what it does not hear from theology, philosophy and social theory and what it cannot hear from pure science. A broader, fuller, more coherent, more comprehensive account of what we human beings are, who we are, and what this life is for. If writers do not come into the center, it will not be because the center is pre-empted; it is not. (Quoted in Smith 1992, 2)

There is no center to hold things together. Or to put it differently, there is no metanarrative to life, no overarching story by which all the particulars can be interpreted. But while no story is dominating our culture, the means to knowing have taken over as the ends of knowledge. In *Beyond the Postmodern Mind*, Huston Smith makes this comment: "If modern physics showed us a world at odds with our senses, postmodern physics is showing us one that is at odds with our imagination. We have made peace with the first of these oddities, but the problem of the new physics cannot be resolved by refinements in the scale" (1992, 7). How do you measure the imagination? There is no scale.

If I were to identify a handful of fearsome realities, this would be near the top. The pursuit of knowledge without knowing who we are or why we exist, combined with a war on our imaginations by the entertainment industry, leaves us at the mercy of power with no morality.

On several occasions while I was driving and listening to music, every now and then a piece would come on that I found either unmusical or jarring. I would shut the radio off. But then one day I was taken to see a play called *The Phantom of the Opera*. Suddenly I realized that some of the music I had not quite enjoyed was from this play. I was amazed at the difference knowing the story made, whenever I heard the music subsequently. In fact, the music in some portions is utterly magnificent. The love songs, the discourses, even the arguments make sense when you know the story. Life needs a story to understand the details. Life needs to hold together at the center if we are to reach to distant horizons. But our culture neither owns a story nor holds at the center.

The final significant change is *the shifting of power to a younger world*. I have heard it said that over sixty percent of this world's population is under age twenty-four. If you talk to a Hollywood mogul today, he will tell you that in producing films, if one can win the following of an eighteen-year-old male, it will be a block-buster hit. Teenage girls will go to see a movie that their boyfriends want them to see, but the reverse does not hold. The extraordinary economic power of this younger generation increasingly defines cultural priorities.

THE EPISTEMOLOGICAL IMPACT

What, then, have been the results of these shifts? I will underscore just five of them.

The first is philosophy's move to the existential. The power of a Jean Paul Sartre or an Albert Camus was significant in the decade of the 1960s and 70s. Historian Paul Johnson points out the devastating impact of Sartre on the intellectuals of the Angka Loeu movement in Cambodia that destroyed the lives of hundreds of thousands in that "Gentle Land"[3] Indeed, a tremendous power was unleashed as philosophers, through drama and literature, hand-cuffed the intellect of society's power brokers. Stories were introduced to tell us that "man is the measure of all things," but they never told us about the entailments of evil men and women who wrested power and developed the means to destroy their own people. Sartre's recantation on his own deathbed notwithstanding, the fact of the matter is that philosophy's shift to the existential cut a wide swathe in our world.

The second result is the artist's move to the sensual. When God created humanity, two very clear sanctities were imparted. One was the sanctity of life itself; the other was the sanctity of sexuality. Artists are creative people. When they lose the vision of the grand Creator, the greatest artist of all, they will attack the very things that he branded sacred—life and sexuality. With such surrogate creators now in full expression, what do we see? The celebration of violence and eroticism. The desacralizing of the human body has mangled life, and our culture slides pitifully into indulgence of the erotic and the perverse. A repeated, painful refrain in numerous conversations is a mother who is trou-bled about finding erotica in her young teenage son's possession. The prolif-eration of erotic material—from books to magazines and now to the internet—has undermined this generation. Recently in England mothers have been outraged because teen magazines are peddling sexual topics, and they argue that this material is making their daughters "sex-mad." Foucault's death from AIDS moves one between compassion and confusion when we realize that it was the willful embodiment of a philosophy that drove him there.

The third result is religion's move to the mystical. Buddhism has become one of the most popular religions of our time because of the widespread interest in spirituality; feelings are constructed into techniques and aphorisms. Buddhism is a classic example of "how to be good without having God"—how to be ethical without having absolutes.

A fourth result is education's move to the skeptical: "You can't believe anything anymore." "You can't be sure of anything anymore." From fuzzy logic to relativism, the homeless mind has moved to the homeless idea. To argue for truth today is to stir an immediate debate, as if a heresy of devilish proportions has been invoked. The so-called death of God spelled the death of theology, but the morticians of the Absolute were not content to stab God-talk. Inevitably God's undertakers were marching to their own funeral, with all of knowledge being pronounced dead.

Here we see our fifth result—the individual's move to the transcendental. That is, he is his own divine being. The reader is sovereign over the author. As you read anyone else's story, you deconstruct it and reshape it to your own interpretation. Philosopher Richard Rorty says in his *Contingency, Irony, and Solidarity*: "[The Nietzschean self] would seek consolation, at the moment of death, not in having transcended the animal condition but in being that peculiar sort of dying animal who, by describing himself in his own terms, had created himself" (quoted in Lundin 1995, 30). Here is self-deification in the making.

A Divided World

How, then, have East and West responded to these phenomena? If I were to draw a continuum, I would put the Western world on the left and the Eastern world on the right, based on the following generalizations. In the West, Christianity has become marginalized, and in some cases even ridiculed. In the East, Western religion is criticized and Eastern religion is protected. In the West, Christianity struggles with higher education and trends in academia. In the East, there is a resurgence of aggressive pride in ancient wisdom.

In the West, theology has been replaced by religion. In the East, religion has always been seen as a pursuit and thus continues. In fact, one of my colleagues who works with us in India says that India never moved from premodern to modern to postmodern. India just leap-frogged over modern, moving from the premodern to the postmodern. In the West, objective truth has been displaced, and there is nothing to replace it. In the East, displacement of objective truth was not felt because the cultural focus was elsewhere.

Some time ago I was addressing men and women from the bar association of a major city. I knew it would be a challenging audience because words and arguments are their daily fare. I began by recounting a television news item I had just witnessed. A major network had as their first item of news a survey asking people if words meant anything specific at all. Do words such as *affair* and *adultery* have particular public meanings, or could the person speaking fuse them into his or her own private meaning? In our salvation-by-survey culture, the journalists asked people if anything meant anything anymore. Having concluded that there were significant variances in the way people used words, they next inquired if morality was purely a personal matter, or if there were indeed absolutes. Every person interviewed on the street answered the same way: "No! There is no objective morality; we have to define it in our own terms." First item: *Were words subject to the user?* Second item: *Was morality a personal matter?* Having settled on a confused answer that left the individual lord over reality, the newscaster went on to discuss a third item on the news—a warning to Saddam Hussein. If he did not stop playing his word games, we were going to start bombing Iraq. How ironic, I thought. We arrogate to ourselves moral authority and deny referents to words, except when we deal with others who play the same game. It was fascinating to see the expressions of those in the audience change and to see them recognize that communication is impossible if we do not grant univocal meaning to our words.

WINDOWS OF OPPORTUNITY

If this is our culture, where does that leave us? The challenge, as I see it, is this: How do we communicate the gospel to a generation that hears with its eyes and thinks with its feelings?

First, postmodernism may be one of the most opportune thought patterns presented to us for the propagation of the gospel because, in a sense, it has cleared the playing field. All disciplines have lost their "final authority." The hopes that modernity had underscored, the triumph of "Reason" and "Science" that many thought would bring in utopia, have failed in almost every respect. With all of our material gains, there is still a hunger for the spiritual. In virtually every part of the world, students linger long after every session to talk with me and plead for answers to their barren lives. All the education one gets does not diminish that search for inner coherence and a story line for one's own life. I can picture many of their faces as I read hundreds of letters that come, confessing to spent lives and bankrupt hearts.

As much as postmodernism has confused language and definitions, there is a yearning that the postmodernist's own cavalier attitude does not diminish.

But our response becomes more difficult because of what I call the "Vietnamization" of the conflict. Classical techniques don't work anymore. There is no front line or single column to attack; the conflict is on many fronts. Maybe postmodernism is a legitimate child of the confusion of the 1960s. But I assure you that it has cleared the playing field.

In February of this year I spoke at the University of Sheffield. When I walked into the auditorium the opening night, the place was packed to capacity. At the end of the forum, one student came to me and said, "I came in here straddling two worlds. I cannot leave the same way. Can you help me?" What a joy to observe a young Sheffield student give his life to the Lord. Indeed, there is still an openness. Postmodernism may not be as daunting as we may sometimes portray it.

Second, there is just enough of the modern worldview left so that reason still has a point of entry. But we have to use this knowledge wisely. We cannot give an overdose of argumentation.

Third, there is a tremendous search in the postmodern mind for community. Only in the gospel message that culminates in worship is there coherence—which in turn brings coherence within the community of believers, where both individuality and community are affirmed. "Worship," says Archbishop William Temple, "is the submission of all of our nature to God. It is the quickening of conscience by his holiness, nourishment of mind by his truth, purifying of imagination by His beauty, opening of the heart to His love, and submission of will to His purpose. All this, gathered up in adoration, is the greatest expression of which we are capable" (quoted in Watson 1976, 157). The worship of the living God is what ultimately binds the various inclinations of the heart and gives them focus. And a worshiping community binds the diversity of our culture, the diversity of our education, the diversity of our backgrounds, and brings us together into a corporate expression of worship. One of the most powerful appeals to the postmodern mind is a worshiping community.

Fourth, we must be observant of God's sovereign intervention in history. When Princess Diana died, the whole world was hearing with its eyes. A few days later when Mother Teresa passed away, the world was again listening with its eyes. One was a woman who despite having everything lived with rejection in her innermost being. The other, having nothing, spent her life taking care of the rejected of this world. I think these are sovereign moments in history. I remember being in the Czech republic a year ago and being told how when the power of Soviet ideology was broken, the churches suddenly became full. People came expectantly, but somehow, there was nothing there. That moment was squandered.

And last, we are living at a time when G. K. Chesterton's dictum has proven to be true. Meaninglessness does not come from being weary of pain, but meaninglessness comes from being weary of pleasure. We have exhausted ourselves in this indulgent culture.

I began by telling of Yankelovich's description of the titanic changes that are underway. He said in his article that the stakes in such changes are high. He conducted some case studies of numerous couples to see where we are headed and arrived at an astounding conclusion. This is what he said about one of those couples, whom he called Abby and Mark:

> If you feel it is imperative to fill all your needs, and if these needs are contradictory or in conflict with those of others, or simply unfillable, then frustration inevitably follows. To Abby and to Mark as well self-fulfillment means having a career and marriage and children and sexual freedom and autonomy and being liberal and having money and choosing non-conformity and insisting on social justice and enjoying city life and country living and simplicity and graciousness and reading and good friends and on and on. The individual is not truly fulfilled by becoming ever more autonomous. Indeed, to move too far in this direction is to risk psychosis, the ultimate form of autonomy. . . . The injunction that to find one's self, one must lose one's self, contains the truth any seeker of self-fulfillment needs to grasp. (1981, 36, 50)

What an opening to lead to the cross of Jesus Christ!

The most dramatic truth about the gospel is that it contradicts us in the way we experience ourselves as alive and compels us to redefine drastically what we mean by life. Jesus contradicts our routine in the way he contradicted the first disciples, even while he was heading toward the cross. They were the ones marked out for death; he, "the dead one," was really the living.

With all that the cultural terrain presents to us, the dictum that "to find one's self, one must lose one's self" contains a truth any seeker of self-fulfillment needs to grasp. This the church must keep in mind too. The windows of opportunity are momentous. He who has ears, let him hear what the Lord has provided for us.

References

Johnson, David L. 1985. *A Reasoned Look at Asian Religions.* Minneapolis: Bethany House.

Lundin, Roger. 1995. "The Pragmatics of Postmodernity." In *Christian Apologetics in the Postmodern World*. Edited by Timothy R. Phillips and Dennis L. Okholm. Downers Grove: InterVarsity Press.

Middleton, J. Richard, and Brian Walsh. 1995. "Facing the Post-modern Scalpel: Can the Christian Faith Stand Deconstruction?" In *Christian Apologetics in the Postmodern World*. Edited by Timothy R. Phillips and Dennis L. Okholm. Downers Grove: InterVarsity Press.

Muggeridge, Malcolm. 1977. *Christ and the Media*. London: Hodder & Stoughton.

Nietzsche, Friedrich. 1954. "The Gay Science." In *The Portable Nietzsche*. Edited by Walter Kaufman. New York: Viking.

Smith, Huston. 1992. *Beyond the Postmodern Mind*. Wheaton, Ill.: Quest Books.

Watson, David. 1976. *I Believe in Evangelism*. Grand Rapids: Eerdmans.

Yankelovich, Daniel. 1981. "New Rules in American Life: Searching for Self-fulfillment in a World Turned Upside Down." *Psychology Today* 15 (4): 35–91.

CHAPTER 2

THE TOUCH OF TRUTH

Ravi Zacharias

My challenge in this second address is to underscore the points of contact we still have in this desensitized culture in which we live. I have selected as my text the twenty-fourth chapter of the book of Acts. Paul is on his way to Rome. But here he stands before Felix to make his defense. Tertullus the lawyer has finished with his prosecutorial speech and thrown down the gauntlet. Paul makes his response and assures Felix that he has not violated either the law of the land or the Law of God. He is sure that the real reason for his accuser's opposition is that he has become a follower of the resurrected Jesus Christ. Felix then makes his pronouncement on what he has heard:

> Then Felix, who was well acquainted with the Way, adjourned the proceedings. "When Lysias the commander comes," he said, "I will decide your case." He ordered the centurion to keep Paul under guard, but to give him some freedom and permit his friends to take care of his needs.
>
> Several days later Felix came with his wife Drusilla, who was a Jewess. He sent for Paul and listened to him as he spoke about faith in Christ Jesus. As Paul discoursed on righteousness, self-control and the judgment to come, Felix was afraid and said, "That's enough for now! You may leave. When I find it convenient, I will send for you." At the same time he was hoping that Paul would offer him a bribe, so he sent for him frequently, and talked with him. (vv. 22–26)

Many of you may have read the following poem in one commentary or another, or seen it in some devotional book. Unfortunately there is uncertainty as to who authored these lines. That aside, it may be rightly inferred that they

RAVI ZACHARIAS

were penned either by someone in Christian ministry or by someone very close to someone in ministry:

When God wants to drill a man, and thrill a man, and skill a man;
When God wants to mold a man to play the noblest part;
When He yearns with all His heart to create so great and bold a man
That all the world might be amazed;
Watch His methods, watch His ways.
How He ruthlessly perfects whom He royally elects.
How He hammers and hurts him, and with mighty blows converts him,
Into trial shapes of clay which only God understands,
While his tortured heart is crying and he lifts beseeching hands.
How he bends but never breaks, when his good He undertakes.
How He uses whom He chooses and with every purpose fuses him,
With mighty acts induces him to try His splendor out.
God knows what He's about.

The longer I have been in ministry, the more I have reflected on the extraordinary ways in which God molds and shapes his chosen instruments. An old adage says: "He who shapes the back for the burden, also shapes the burden for the back." The Scriptures are filled with narratives of God's shaping process. He raised Joseph in a desert in order to use him in a palace. He raised Moses in a palace in order to use him in a desert. In that glorious passage in Luke's third chapter we read: "In the fifteenth year of Tiberius Caesar— when Pontius Pilate was governor of Judea, Herod tetrarch of Galilee, his brother Philip tetrarch of Iturea and Traconitis, and Lysanias tetrarch of Abilene—during the high priesthood of Annas and Caiaphas, the word of God came to John son of Zechariah in the desert." Did you hear that? There were seven larger-than-life characters punctuating the historical landscape, yet the word of the Lord came to a rather strange man wearing strange clothes and eating strange food, appointing him to stand before the Herods of his time.

Billy Graham was once asked by a press reporter, "How is it that there are so many more educated and more capable preachers in this world but God has chosen you to become the evangelist to the world?" Out of the overflow of his own humility, Billy Graham said, "When I get to heaven that is going to be my first question." Every one of us who has been called into the privileged role of vocational Christian ministry will have the same question for God. You know the glorious sensation every time God uses you. You walk away wondering how this is even possible—that he has taken such a weak, stumbling vessel and somehow brought something good through you. Paul, I believe, saw himself that way. He describes himself in his conversion as one abnormally born, almost prefiguring what C. S. Lewis said of his own conversion as one dragged into the kingdom kicking and screaming, "the most … reluctant convert in all of England" (1955, 228–29). The apostle Paul, as one commentator paraphrases him, describes it in more visceral terms: "I was torn, wrenched away from my mother's womb, the most feisty convert in all of Palestine." And yet God raised him up.

Paul's biographical background helps put in perspective the shaping process begun long before this moment in front of Felix. He was born a Hebrew. He was a citizen of Rome. He lived in a Greek city. At his commission, God said of him, "This man is my chosen instrument to carry my name before the Gentiles and their kings and before the people of Israel. I will show him how much he must suffer for my name" (Acts 9:15–16). One might well ask what was in him that was so unique. From his pen flowed a third of the New Testament. Through his dogged determination and answer to God's call, the Gentile world was to hear the grand news of the gospel. Better still, what is it that God poured into him? And how do we understand the methods that he used from which we can borrow in our time as well?

New Testament scholar William Barclay suggests that when Jesus ascended into heaven, Christians were possibly outnumbered by about one to thirty thousand. Some scholars challenge the exact number, but none suggests that the disparity was anything less than humanly insurmountable. Not only were the numbers staggeringly disproportionate, but the cultural animosities ran deep and passionate.

While we live in this postmodern era characterized by such strident uprooting of shared meanings from the past, let us remind ourselves that it was not any easier in Paul's time. He faced an immense challenge too, particularly in Corinth. The temple of Aphrodite spilled out its prostitutes by the hundreds every night; indeed, Corinth was a byword for sensuality and debauchery. Rome's erratic and erotic self-indulgence speaks volumes even in the fallen stones of Pompeii visible to this day. The arrogance of Greek learning punctuates landmarks in philosophy. Into this discord came Paul, and now he stands before Felix. I present this man as a model because he had both theological integrity and methodological genius. He did not put asunder what God had joined together. Here is the setting as described in the words of one commentator:

> What a contrast. On the throne sat Felix, the faded and withered pagan. A
> former slave. He became a favorite of Claudius, and by that emperor was exalted
> to high rank. Greed, cruelty and lust were stamped upon his countenance. His
> administration as procurator of Judea had been marked by injustice, extortion

and violence. By his side sat the lovely Jewess Drusilla, a daughter of Herod Agrippa. She had first married a Gentile, who to please her, had become a Jew. Then Felix, with the aid of a sorcerer's incantations, had won her from her husband and was living with her in sin and shame. All that was dishonorable in mankind was represented by that combination of Felix and Drusilla as they sat on the throne awaiting the address by Saint Paul. Before them, with chains on his arms and his body scarred with the marks of his sufferings for Christ's sake, and his coarse garment, which his own hands had woven, contrasting with the velvet and purple of Felix and his paramour, stood the lonely ambassador for Christ. (Macartney 1974, 142)

I cannot help but think of a similar moment when Mother Teresa stood before the leaders of our time and addressed the attendees at the Presidential Prayer Breakfast in Washington. This diminutive woman, just four feet and a few inches tall, stood in front of an audience of luminaries from around the world and fearlessly pleaded for the protection of babies in their mothers' wombs. She called for leaders to take pity on the weakest and to show compassion on the little ones. "How," she asked, "can we speak out against violence when we are the most brutal with the most defenseless?" Numerous media elite reported on that awkward moment for the president, the vice president, and their wives, as this meek and selfless person spoke with conviction. The "weak" of this world confounded the "strong." Such was the scene centuries ago when Paul stood before Felix.

The first thing he did as he discoursed before Felix was to broach the theme of righteousness. In short, he found some common ground as a point of reference. Os Guinness contends that there are at least four stages that we have to bear in mind for effective communication: identification, translation, persuasion, and justification. First, the communicator identifies with the listener. Some point of resonance must be struck with the listener. Then, one must make sure that the content of communication is within the idiom of the one to whom the communication is made. This is the step of translation. Next, the ideas being transmitted must have a persuasive element to them. Finally, there must be justification, answering the question of why the ideas presented are worthy of being accepted over against any variation or contradiction of them.

In that first step of identification, it is critical that we find a point of reference and common ground. After being on campuses now for a few years trying to communicate the beauty and the cogency of the gospel, I have noticed some trends. There was a time when the *cosmological argument*—arguing from causality and the First Cause to this present universe—was an extremely powerful argument. There is no doubt that the argument is still valid and even needed, but the receptivity to such an argument has been dulled over the years and pompously blunted by naturalistic scientists. From the misuse of David Hume's arguments to a Big Bang mysticism, skeptical cosmologists mock even its legitimate use. They themselves assume causality in all matters of effect, but when it comes to the universe's existence, they ignore causality and do not ask questions of the Big Bang that they would ask of any other bang—*What caused it?* In many academic settings, therefore, one comes to a dead end, arguing against a prejudice that refuses to change.

We move then to the *teleological argument,* the argument from purpose and design to Designer and Creator. But talking about the specified complexity and the intelligibility in this universe only brings the inevitable challenge as naturalists constantly blur the distinction between aesthetic design and intelligent design. Arguing for a Creator is John Polkinghorne from Cambridge University, in his book *The Quantum World,* and Michael Behe, who in his book *Darwin's Black Box,* shows us the irreducible complexity of the human cell, which biological evolution cannot explain. Behe's expertise in biochemistry prompts him to state unequivocally that biochemically, macroevolution is impossible. To that assertion, atheistic thinkers like Richard Dawkins respond with the charge of "intellectual laziness." Convinced of a "Blind Watchmaker," they argue that somehow, sometime, they will find out how design is actually just random—that anything would look like design if you pulled it out from a myriad of possibilities. Not only do they argue against their opponents, but in effect they argue against their own assumptions in life. Nevertheless, they have worked hard to neutralize the design argument just as they did the cosmological argument.

Where then does one go to find common ground? I refer to the *moral argument,* which argues for God from morality. This issue captures the interest of most minds, and even the postmodernist struggles with it and finds himself hard-pressed to escape from its clutches. Naturalists are trying valiantly even as I speak to show how even our moral sense has evolved. New articles are being written on the biogenesis of ethics. But the point I want to make is that no matter where you go across the globe, when you get into the throes of the moral argument, people are listening. Whether you're in Bombay or Nottingham, whether you're in Harvard or Princeton, students listen carefully when this subject is addressed. In last month's issue of *Atlantic Monthly*, an ethicist attempted a full hit at our moral sense and said we can now completely explain ethics on the basis of biology. A feeble attempt to be sure, but it is a desperate move to take away the last argument that throbs within the human frame. They try hard to formulate in their minds a response to the question of

RAVI ZACHARIAS

how objective ethics can somehow exist without a transcendent reality. They struggle with it, and that struggle is evident.

A few years ago I was speaking at the Center for Geopolitical Strategy in Moscow. It was a very difficult three-hour session. I sat with seven generals around me. My wife was with me, along with one of my colleagues, and around us were atheists systematically and intensely throwing their questions at me. When one walked into the building, one felt dwarfed because of its size—eight stories above ground, four stories below ground. But more than its size was its story of a nation. This is where the mind of the former Soviet Union was forged. Anybody who was a great name in the country had graduated from there.

We sat with faculty members as grim in countenance as imagination had conjured up through pictures. Their pointed questioning seemed relentless and unwavering. But then a break came. In an effort to disarm them from their official self-exaltation, I asked them why their young people were in such a hopeless state if their ideology was as effective as it was pretending to be. Why is it, I asked, that they were unable to harness the heart with respect for life after decades of indoctrination in egalitarianism? Then, as I shared my own conversion story from a bed of suicide, it was as if the scales began to fall from their eyes.

That night my wife and I had dinner with the chief historian. We sat in a very meager-looking restaurant having a meal together. I leaned over and said, "General, I have a question for you, sir. Have you ever read the story of Joseph Stalin? As you know, he was once a seminary student, and then abandoned his faith in God and decided to knock God out of his people entirely."

I then told him the following story: "Stalin was having dinner with a woman who was a visitor from overseas. In the course of their conversation, she asked him how long he expected his people to follow him while he tortured them so relentlessly. Stalin did not answer her. He asked the waiter to bring a live chicken; he clutched the live chicken under his arm as he proceeded to defeather the bird. He completely denuded it and placed that bird on the floor. Then he picked up a piece of bread and moved away. The chicken hobbled over to him and nestled between his trouser legs. He bent down with the bread in his hand, and the chicken started to peck away at that bread. Stalin looked at the questioner and said, 'Madame, have you seen this? I inflicted such pain on this chicken. It'll follow me for food the rest of its life. People are like that chicken. You inflict pain on them, and they will follow you for the rest of their lives.' What do you think of that story, General?"[1] I paused and endured the silence.

He could not fight back the tears that flooded his eyes, and his lips quivered as he nodded his head. He knew what he had seen in his country. In these seven decades, the bequest of a philosophy that masqueraded as one for the common man had reduced life to that of refuse. Is it not intriguing, though, that even in an atheistic nation, the moral law still stabbed like a hatpin in the heart, which bleeds in silence. Even while one may want to fight it, there seems a paucity of words.

When Mother Teresa finished her talk in Washington, the entire audience of hundreds rose to their feet in a standing ovation. The president, the vice president, and their wives did not stand because the issue was very clearly a challenge to their views. And so they stayed seated on the platform as the audience rose to its feet. Philip Yancey, who interviewed the president after it was over and he was in the presidential limousine, made this comment: "Just before we bade good-bye to the President, I said, 'President Clinton, what did you think of what Mother Teresa had to say today?'" President Clinton paused, and said, "It is very difficult to argue against a life so beautifully lived."

It is vitally important in the last moments of this century, when only vestiges remain of moral law, that somehow we reach into what remains to find common ground. Paul shows us how and why he held on to this as his first point of entry. Paul is obviously reasoning with an unrighteousness man about righteousness. He is talking to a Roman. He knows that some perspectives on morality were not the same. But think with me for a moment about how he probably presented the issue.

Paul was a Hebrew by birth, a citizen of Rome living in a Greek city. For the Hebrews, the ideal was symbolized by light: "The Lord is my light and my salvation." "This is the light that lights every man that comes into the world." "The people that sat in darkness have seen a great light." For the Hebrews, that was the epitome of every ideal. For the Greeks, the ideal was knowledge—*episteme*—from which we get *epistemology*, to know, to understand the truth. Their legacy is the academy. Philosophy, the love of wisdom, is rooted in Greek thought. For the Romans, the ideal was the pursuit of glory. Rome was the city of which it was said that it was not built in a day, that it was a city to which all roads converged—the glory of Rome. It was the city over which Augustine wept as the barbarians scaled its walls and ransacked it. From that destruction of what he had thought was an eternal city, he penned his immortal *City of God*. For the Hebrews—light; for the Greeks—knowledge; for the Romans—glory.

Here stands a man, a product of these three cultures. How does he engage all three? Writing to the church at Corinth, he says this: "For God, who said, 'Let light shine out of darkness,' made his *light* shine in our hearts to give us the light of the *knowledge* of the *glory* of God in the face of Christ" (2 Cor. 4:6, italics added).

A face. A face bearing the focus of all that the best of human ideals could have pursued. The light of light, the source of all truth, and the supreme glory.

When I was growing up in India, we had a man working in our home. He came from a village, and city life with all of its offerings was quite foreign to him. One day my mother gave him some money to go and see a movie. He'd never seen a movie. She instructed him on how to purchase the ticket and that there would be an usher to help him find a seat. He got all dressed up, polished his shoes and off he went. He got there late, bought the ticket and entered through the front door. Everything was dark and all he could see were beams coming in through the back wall. He stood there for a few moments enthralled with the particles of light emerging through little openings in the wall. He thought this was wonderful, and indeed it kept him entertained for a few fleeting moments until he thought the sound was coming from the opposite side. So he decided to turn around, and suddenly he saw the screen filled with a face and a scene that matched the sound and told the story. He let out a shout of glee of Archimedean proportions. In fact, he caused such a disturbance that one of the ushers had to come and commandeer him to his seat.

That is, to me, a perfect illustration of human pursuits—thinking we have found it in our tiny little specks of information. But then all of our efforts, exploits, and yearnings are like beams of light, finding a consummate expression upon a face: *the face of Jesus Christ.* For Paul, righteousness was no longer an idea or an attainment, as much as it was an embodiment and an imputation that followed such a recognition. How much we need to learn from this message.

All around us we hear thundering forth the word *morality.* Yes, we must be a moral people. But morality is a fruit, not a tree. The tree is rooted in Christ's righteousness from whom the nourishment comes to produce the fruit of moral purity. I challenge you: when you are preaching righteousness, when you are calling a people to goodness, do not stop with morality alone, because a nation can be morally lost just as easily as immorally lost. What you have to point to ultimately is the centerpiece of righteousness, our Lord Jesus Christ. Righteousness or morality is still a point of reference, but the word is vacuous without Christ as the referent. Incidentally, that is why C. S. Lewis has been one of the most powerful apologists of this century. He well understood that the unshakable moral sense within every culture only made sense by invoking the "Lion of the Tribe of Judah."

Paul moves from a point of reference to a point relevance. He talks to Felix about self-control. Do you think Felix needed to hear about self-control? Living with a sixteen-year-old, whom he had procured through a sorcerer's incantations, he was hardly a man whose passions are well ordered. She was another man's wife when Felix orchestrated this steal. He himself had been married several times. With the power of a king, he still lived with the mind enslaved by sensuality and power. With honor and genius, Paul talked to him about self-control, a point of relevance for him.

The Holy Scriptures are filled with such points of relevance whenever God speaks to a nation or to individuals. A few days ago, along with my wife and some friends, I was seated on the hillside of ancient Laodicea in Turkey. We opened the Bible and read from Revelation 3. Laodicea was known for three or four things. The city was a wealthy one, and its inhabitants bragged of their riches. The textile and garment industry flourished. They were known for an eye ointment that they had manufactured and sold to many parts of the world. It was a popular spot for visitors because of the nearby hot springs at Hierapolis. Known for their wealth, their textiles, their eye ointment, and their hot springs—what does the Word of God say to the Laodiceans through John's Revelation? He says, "You think you are rich, but actually you are very poor. Come and buy gold off me so I can clothe you in white linen, and anoint your eyes that you may see, for you are neither hot nor cold." You think they understood what that meant? The relevance!

With the same kind of relevance, God spoke to Sardis, which had been conquered while its soldiers were asleep. God said to the church at Sardis, "Stay on your watch! Stay on your watch!"

Where is the point of relevance in our time? I believe it is the hunger for love. Even one as cerebrally intimidating as Bertrand Russell said that love was an unsatisfied hunger in his life. Bear in mind that as I say this, my ministry often takes me into the arena of argumentation. I am often forced to deal with arguments and counterarguments. But now, after two and a half decades in the ministry, there are some truths that emerge more clearly, more beautifully, more persuasively in my own mind. We as Christians make a staggering claim: we lay claim to truth that is exclusive. In a society that not only does not believe in a metanarrative or in exclusivity but also rejects the notion of objective truth, ours is a monumental claim. We proclaim one way to God—Jesus, the Way, the Truth, and the Life. When we lay claim to truth in such radical terms, it is imperative that such truth be undergirded by love. If it is not undergirded by love, it makes the possessor of that truth obnoxious and the dogma repulsive. I believe it is vital that we understand this.

RAVI ZACHARIAS

Two years ago when my wife and I went to Honolulu to be alone for a few days, I recalled the story of the famed missionary Joseph Damien, known as Damien of Molokai. That island is one of the most beautiful parts of the world. But Damien, who was Belgian by birth, left his homeland, not because he sought an Edenic setting, but because he wanted to minister to the inhabitants of that island who were expelled to that spot for having leprosy. All of the Hawaiian islands spilled out their lepers into Molokai, for people feared contagion and knew nothing of a cure. Here in a land of great beauty those decimated by this dreaded disease were imprisoned by the world's tallest sea cliffs. To this very day, although the numbers now are few because of a cure, visitors may not just arrive on impulse. Special permission needs to be obtained, and we were able to receive it. What a memorable day that was!

In this setting Joseph Damien poured his life into those people. He embraced them. He loved them. He literally gave his life for them. One morning as he was pouring some boiling water into a cup, the water swirled out of the cup and fell onto his bare foot. He was rudely awakened to the fact that when the boiling water fell on his foot he did not feel it. He took some more boiling water, poured it onto the other foot, and there was no sensation at all. He was terrified of the ramifications. He got ready that morning, went behind the pulpit, and nobody there knew why he changed his opening line. He always began his sermon by saying, "My fellow believers." This morning, however, he began by saying, "My fellow lepers." He was now one of them.

Before we left, we walked into the bookstore and saw the picture of a beautiful young woman on the cover of a book. Her name was Olivia. The book was her story. I turned through the pages and saw how over the years the disease had marred and deformed her body. It was a terrible thing to see. My eyes were drawn to a letter she had written to the well-known actor Alan Alda. She wrote in words to this effect: "In my lonely, wretched life here I enjoy a few things. One of them is watching your program M*A*S*H. But, Mr. Alda, I was very troubled this evening watching today's episode. In one of those attempts at humor you looked at your colleagues, and commenting on the mess in the room, you said, 'What do you think you are? A bunch of lepers living in a leper colony?' Mr. Alda, please don't ever say anything like that again. Those of us who have leprosy are not lepers. We are people who happen to have leprosy."

As we were leaving, I looked at the woman who was showing us around, and I said, "I see a marker here for Joseph Damien's grave. Is Damien buried here?"

"No, sir. Damien is buried back in his home country in Belgium," she said. "The government demanded that his body be flown back." But the people from here wrote and pleaded with them to please send the body to Molokai, for they were the people who found life because of him. Yet the Belgium government saw him as one of their great heroes and wanted to keep his body there. The people wrote back, saying, "Would you consider sending some part of his body, some memory of his physical presence, that we can bury him here?" The authorities cut off the right arm from his corpse, and it is buried in Molokai. That was the arm that reached out to these people who were discarded from life's mainstream.

As we boarded the small plane to leave, I said to my wife, "Isn't it a telling illustration? Leprosy desensitizes you to the sensation of touch. But it did not desensitize them to the reach of love."

It is of enormous interest to ask recent converts to Christ—converts from one of the world's major religions, why, humanly speaking, they were drawn to Christ. The answer is commonly one of two predictable replies. Either there was a supernatural intervention within their lives, or a Christian cared enough to reach out to them by life and example. The miraculous, interestingly enough, "works" within their philosophical worldview of angelic messengers. The reach of love works within their frame of existential need. To many of them, strangely enough, apologetics works *after* their conversion as they are challenged by those who wish to accuse them of surrendering to a "false system of belief."

With all of the proclamation, let us not stop loving the people to whom we minister. One of the things I've learned is that the antagonist will thank you for being patient and kind, not for being hostile or attacking. The audiences listen to you in courtesy because they long for a point of relevance in a world where many hunger to belong and to experience love. Postmodernism has been categorized by some as "a structure of feeling," and this characterization provides the church with both a predicament and a solution. God himself speaks in emotionally laden terms.

The felt need cannot be ignored, but it is important that having met on common ground, we rise to the higher ground of truth, not just emotion. To that end, there is a narrative behind the love. Love does not come without either a story behind it or a story ahead of it. The story is a gripping point of contact. But it is a story grounded in truth. I am not at all surprised that in numerous encounters, Paul pauses to tell his own story because it pointed to the gospel story. The true story, the narrative, the illustration may unlock more suppressed emotions and bring translation to a person better than any argument could.

Paul guides us from a point of reference through a point of relevance to a point of disturbance. His final challenge to Felix comes when he reminds this petty potentate that there is a judge of all the earth. Os Guinness, in the book

No God but God, which he coauthored with John Seel, says: "It is truth that gives relevance to 'relevance', just as 'relevance' becomes irrelevant if it is not related to truth" (1992, 169). That is an important caution to remember, the more so in this postmodernist mind-set when truth is displaced by "relevance." There was no compulsion in Paul to avoid the hard part of his message. He could have stayed with the more palatable aspects of the gospel. But for this chosen instrument, the gospel had the uninviting dimension of judgment as well.

Properly understood, the prospect of judgment forms an important part of rescuing us from our own self-destructiveness. Recently I received a letter from a new Christian studying at a sophisticated university overseas. She stated that whenever she read of the cross, it brought her to her knees, and she would weep thinking about the love of Christ. But whenever she read of hell, it made her angry with God. How fascinating, I thought. Reading about the cross without seeing the hell of it is not understanding the cross at all.

So we are reminded again that all of Paul's genius in method did not rob him of the responsibility of theological integrity. But then, we might well ask, why this approach? Why this track on which to come to Felix? Why righteousness, self-control, and judgment? Was it because they are the tenses of the Christian faith? The *past* of every person's sin countered with the righteousness of Christ? The *present* of temptation responded to by the strength of self-control within the believer? The *future* of judgment secured by God? Or was it because of the three persons of the Holy Trinity? The Son brings us into righteousness; the Holy Spirit gives us self-control; and the Father, in judgment, offers mercy? Or perhaps Paul was thinking much more of the promise of the Holy Spirit offered in John 16:8–11 where Jesus says: "When he comes, he will convict the world of guilt in regard to sin and righteousness and judgment."

I lean to the last of these explanations. Paul knew what it was that the Holy Spirit had promised to bless. Conviction is the prerogative of the Holy Spirit. The communicator of the gospel finds concepts that the listener will find persuasive, but the transformation from unbelief to belief is only legitimate when God brings about that change, not our eloquence or genius. The apologist clears the bushes so the listener can take a good look at the cross, and it is the Holy Spirit who brings about the change in the heart of the individual.

What happened next in this encounter is fascinating! Felix kept Paul around for some time to see if Paul would offer him a bribe. Do you see what is going on here? What would Felix have inferred if Paul had tried to bribe him? He would have dismissed Paul's message of righteousness as all theory!

He would have uncovered Paul's offer of self-control as duplicitous. He would have mocked Paul's caution of judgment as hypocritical. In short, the cardinal claims that the messenger had laid before the skeptic were now being tested within the messenger himself.

Marie Chapian in her book *Of Whom the World Was Not Worthy* tells of an evangelist named Yakov who was witnessing to an older man by the name of Cimmerman who knew a great deal about the church and politics, and despised the hypocrisy he had seen in the church. When Yakov talked to him about the love of Christ, Cimmerman said, "Don't talk to me about Christ! You see those priests there, with all their vestments, all of their cloaks, all of the big crosses on their chests? I know what they're like. They're violent people. They have abused their power. Don't tell me about Christ! I know what it is like to watch them kill our people, even some of my own relatives."

Yakov paused for a moment and then said, "Cimmerman, can I ask you a question? What if I stole your coat and your boots, put them on, broke into a bank and took the money? I was chased by the police but I outran them. What would you say if the police came knocking on your door and charged you with breaking into a bank?"

Cimmerman said, "I would deny it because I did not."

"Ah! But what if they say that they recognized your coat and your boots from a distance? You had to have broken into the bank!"

Cimmerman said, "Yakov, just leave me alone. I know what you're driving at. I do not want to get into this discussion."

Yakov went away, but he kept coming back only to live the love of Christ before him. Finally one day Cimmerman said, "Yakov, tell me about this Christ that you so love and live for. How can I know him?" Yakov told him how to commit his life to Christ. Cimmerman knelt down on the dust outside his home with Yakov and received Christ into his life. He stood up and embraced Yakov and said, "Thank you for being in my life. You wear his coat very well."

The morning after I finished my open forum at the University of Iowa, one of the organizers told us of a conversation he had with a medical doctor he had brought with him the previous night, who was a very outspoken skeptic. As his wife drove this doctor back home, she looked at her and said, "What did you think of this evening?"

She answered, "Very, very persuasive. I wonder what he is like in his private life?"

What our culture needs is an apologetic that is not merely argued, but also felt. There has to be a passion in the communication. There must be a felt reality beyond the cognitive, engaging the feeling of the listener. Second, it must be an apologetic that is not merely heard, but also seen. We live within a context that listens with its eyes. So much has happened over the last few years to discredit the carriers of the gospel that seeing is indeed going to be a precursor to believing.

Finally, we need an apologetic that will rescue not only the ends but also the means. I bemoan the loss of linguistic strength in our time. Jacques Ellul rightly describes this culture as one that has humiliated the word; we have lost the beauty in language. Alexander Pope described the conversion of water into wine: "The conscious water saw its master and blushed." A thousand pictures could not do better than that word picture for us.

Our postmodern mind-set has not only relegated words to a lesser value but has lost the splendor of possibilities in verbal communication. The apostle Peter in his letter has a worthy reminder to all who tend to get preoccupied with the experiential and lose the propositional. He himself experienced one of the grandest spectacles ever vouchsafed to the human eye. He was witness to the transfiguration of our Lord and had seen Moses and Elijah descend in that momentous event. He was so overcome by this glimpse of the eternal that he wanted to make his home on that mountain and not return to the drabness of ordinary existence any more. Yet it is this very Peter who in his epistle warns us to stay firm in our commitment because "we now have the most sure word of prophecy." The written had a more eternal reality than the momentary exhilaration of a single experience.

In the beginning was not video. In the beginning was the Word. To a generation to whom life and feeling have become inseparable, how wonderful to bring the answer in which life and word become inseparable, even as the Word became flesh and dwelt among us, full of grace and truth.

References

Behe, Michael. 1996. *Darwin's Black Box*. New York: Free Press.

Chapian, Marie. 1978. *Of Whom the World Was Not Worthy*. Minneapolis: Bethany.

Guinness, Os, and John Seel. 1992. *No God but God*. Chicago: Moody Press.

Lewis, C. S. 1955. *Surprised by Joy*. New York: Harcourt, Brace and World.

Macartney, Clarence E. 1974. *Bible Epitaphs*. Grand Rapids: Baker.

Polkinghorne, John. 1989. *The Quantum World*. Princeton: Princeton University Press.

PART TWO

The Challenge

CHAPTER 3

WHY IS RELIGIOUS PLURALISM FUN—AND DANGEROUS?

Harold A. Netland and Keith E. Johnson

Jim and Bill were engaged in a late night conversation about religion in their dorm room. Although he was initially quite interested in Jim's impressive testimony about how his relationship with Christ had changed his life, Bill became increasingly disturbed as the conversation began to focus on verses such as John 14:6 and Acts 4:12. Jim continued to explain in a gentle but insistent tone that Scripture makes it clear that Jesus Christ is the only Savior for all peoples. Suddenly Bill cut him off: "Come on, Jim, be reasonable. I'm glad that Christianity works for you, and I do think Jesus said some good things. But how can anyone today believe that there is only one true religion? Just look at all the good people in other religions. Why do you Christians have to be so narrow-minded and intolerant?"

Underlying Bill's response to Jim is a particular way of thinking about the relationship between Christianity and other religions that is enormously popular today. The set of assumptions and values shaping Bill's response is part of a broader perspective known as "religious pluralism," and there can be little question that this way of thinking about religious matters presents some of the more significant and controversial issues facing the Christian church today. The frequency and intensity with which Bill's objection is expressed today is indicative of the difficulty many people have with the idea that there is only one true religious perspective and one Savior for all people in all cultures. This presents obvious problems for evangelism, but the difficulties are also to be found inside the church as growing numbers of professing Christians struggle with the exclusive teachings of Christianity. High on the agenda for the church in the coming decades must be the development of a theologically sound and culturally sensitive response to the issues of pluralism.

But in order to respond appropriately, we must first understand the nature of the challenges and the factors producing a cultural context in which religious pluralism seems so plausible. For the ideology of religious pluralism has not emerged in a vacuum. The "plausibility structures"[1] supporting pluralism are the product of several centuries of profound intellectual and social transformations. In this essay we will consider briefly the greater openness toward other religions found within the Christian community, examine some of the factors underlying the contemporary appeal of pluralism, and then suggest some ways in which Christians might respond to the challenges raised by religious pluralism. In doing so, we will draw on both theoretical discussions of issues and on our own practical experience in dealing with pluralism.

CHANGING PERSPECTIVES ON OTHER RELIGIONS

In recent years an enormous volume of literature has emerged on the subject of Christianity and other religions, and it has become customary to distinguish three broad paradigms for understanding the relation of Christian faith to other religions: exclusivism, inclusivism, and pluralism.[2] This can be a useful taxonomy for sorting out various perspectives on other religions, but it also tends to be a bit misleading because the increasing complexity of the discussion makes it difficult for some thinkers' positions to fit neatly within any one paradigm. It is probably best not to think of these as three clearly distinct, mutually exclusive categories so much as three identifiable points of reference on a broader continuum of perspectives, with both continuities and discontinuities on various issues across the paradigms, depending on the particular issue under consideration.

In very broad terms we can say that the traditional perspective of Christianity up until the mid–twentieth century, both Roman Catholic and Protestant, has been what is often called "exclusivism." The term itself is a pejorative one with highly negative connotations, initially introduced by those who rejected this position in favor of more accommodating approaches to other religions. Thus, following a number of recent evangelicals, we will use the term "particularism" rather than "exclusivism" to refer to this traditional position (Okholm and Phillips 1996, 15–17). Particularism can be defined theologically in terms of the following principles: (1) the Bible is God's unique revelation written, true and fully authoritative, and thus where the claims of Scripture are incompatible with those of other faiths, the latter are to be rejected; (2) Jesus Christ is the unique Incarnation of God, fully God and fully man; (3) only through the person and work of Jesus is there the possibility

HAROLD A. NETLAND AND KEITH E. JOHNSON

of salvation; (4) God's saving grace is not mediated through the teachings, practices, or institutions of other religions. Obviously different Christian traditions would articulate one or more of these points slightly differently, but generally something like these four principles have shaped Christian perspectives on other religions until recent times.

We should note several things about this position. First, in spite of popular caricatures to the contrary, there is no reason to suppose that particularists cannot be culturally sensitive and appropriately tolerant of people from other religious traditions. Furthermore, particularism does not imply that all the beliefs of the non-Christian religions are false or that there is nothing of value in other religions. Finally, particularism, as defined above, should be distinguished from what Clark Pinnock has recently called *restrictivism*—the view that only those who hear the gospel of Jesus Christ and respond explicitly in faith to Christ in this life can be saved (1992, 14–15). The question of the fate of those who never hear the gospel has always been controversial and troubling to sensitive Christians, and a variety of answers have been proposed by those who fall broadly within the particularist paradigm.[3] Too often in discussions of pluralism, evangelicals focus exclusively on the question of the destiny of the unevangelized, as if this is the only issue that pluralism raises. Significant as it is, however, this is just one of a whole set of issues stemming from pluralism that demand response.

With these caveats, however, we can say that something very much like the particularist paradigm has been dominant in Christianity up until the early twentieth century. More accommodating views on other religions became increasingly accepted among Protestants in the late nineteenth and early twentieth centuries. It was not until after Vatican II (1962–65) that dramatic changes in views on other religions became widely accepted in Roman Catholicism. These recent shifts away from particularism and toward more open perspectives on other religions have been labeled "inclusivism."

Inclusivism can be defined in terms of the following principles: (1) there is a sense in which Jesus Christ is unique, normative, or superior to other religious figures; (2) in some sense it is through Jesus Christ that salvation is made available; (3) God's grace and salvation, which are somehow based upon Jesus Christ, are also available through the other religions; (4) thus, other religions are generally to be regarded positively as part of God's purposes for humankind. These statements are deliberately vague, for there is enormous variety among inclusivists on many issues, including just how it is that Jesus is normative or superior to other religious figures, or precisely what is meant by "salvation" and its relation to the person and work of Jesus. Nevertheless, the distinctive of inclusivism is the desire to maintain, in some sense, the uniqueness of Christ, while also admitting that God's grace and salvation are present and effective in other religions as well.[4] Thus, other religions tend to be regarded positively as part of God's intention for humankind, as somehow preparing the way for God's definitive self-disclosure in Jesus Christ.

By the 1970s and 80s, however, a growing number of leading Western theologians were unhappy with inclusivism and were calling for the rejection of a critical assumption common to particularism and inclusivism—the superiority of Christianity and the notion that salvation is found in Jesus Christ— and thereby embraced pluralism.[5] *Pluralism*, then, rejects the suggestion that there is anything significantly unique, normative, or superior about Jesus Christ and the Christian faith. Salvation (or enlightenment or liberation) is said to be present *in its own way* in each religion. No religion can claim to be normative and thus superior to all others. All religions are in their own way complex historically and culturally conditioned human responses to one divine reality. For pluralists, then, although Christians can hold that Jesus is unique and normative *for them*, they cannot claim that Jesus is unique or normative in an objective or universal sense. In other words, Jesus may be the savior for Christians, but he is not necessarily the one Savior for all peoples.

In the Western academic context no one has done more to champion the cause of pluralism than John Hick. One of the more influential philosophers and theologians of the twentieth century, Hick describes his college years as a time when he experienced a "spiritual conversion" and "became a Christian of a strongly evangelical and indeed fundamentalist kind" (1982, 14). In succeeding decades, however, Hick was to pursue a theological journey away from Christian orthodoxy—beginning with the acceptance of higher critical views of Scripture; acceptance of soteriological universalism as the only solution to the problem of evil; increasing questioning, and finally rejection, of orthodox Christology and the deity of Christ; and growing acceptance of other religions, culminating in a thoroughgoing religious pluralism by the late 1970s.[6]

One factor that led Hick to embrace a pluralist position was his perception that the religious experiences of Muslims, Hindus, Buddhists, and Christians share a common element—a perception that arose from his experiences with these religious traditions. Reflecting on these experiences Hick notes, "And occasionally attending worship in mosque and synagogue, temple and gurdwara, it was evident that essentially the same kind of thing is taking place in them as in a Christian church—namely, human beings opening their minds to a higher divine Reality, known as personal and good and as demanding righteousness and love between man and man" (Hick 1982, 5).

HAROLD A. NETLAND AND KEITH E. JOHNSON

Hick's 1986 Gifford Lectures—a sophisticated and rigorous statement of the pluralist paradigm—were published as *An Interpretation of Religion* (1989) and represent the fullest development of his views.[7] In over four hundred pages of text, he argues for a model that intends to account for the following four phenomena: (1) people the world over seem to be inherently religious; (2) religious beliefs and experiences cannot be ruled out in general as delusory or non-veridical; (3) there is enormous diversity in religious belief and practice; (4) there seems to be a common element in all the major religious traditions— the transformation of people from "self-centredness to Reality-centredness."

Hick intends that his model provide a new way of thinking about religion that allows us to recognize the great diversity among religious traditions, acknowledge the basic validity of the major religions, and enable religious believers to remain fully committed to their own traditions while also accepting other religious traditions as equally legitimate paths for others.

At the heart of Hick's pluralist model is the idea that there is one ultimate divine reality—what Hick calls "the Real"—which, although never the object of direct human experience, can be thought of and responded to in varying ways, shaped by human history and culture. At the heart of Hick's pluralist model is the idea that

> the great world faiths embody different perceptions and conceptions of, and correspondingly different responses to, the Real [the religious ultimate] from within the major variant ways of being human; and that within each of them the transformation of human existence from self-centredness to Reality-centredness is taking place. These traditions are accordingly to be regarded as alternative soteriological "spaces" within which, or "ways" along which, men and women find salvation/liberation/ultimate fulfillment. (1989, 240)

Or as he puts it elsewhere,

> One then sees the great world religions as different human responses to the one divine Reality, embodying different perceptions which have been formed in different historical and cultural circumstances. (1982, 11)

The various religions, then, are the product of both the Real "revealing" itself to humankind, and humankind, in turn, responding in historically and culturally conditioned ways to the Real. Salvation, enlightenment, and liberation are realities that are more or less equally available in all religions.

It is important to see that religious pluralism is not merely the latest fad in certain chic academic circles. Pluralism is certainly well entrenched in the academic world, but it is also widely accepted on a popular level among those never exposed to academic pluralism. What we have in the pluralism of John Hick is a sophisticated treatment of an assumption that is widely accepted on a popular level among many with no formal study of religion. It captures very nicely the spirit of the age.

For example, the ethos of pluralism permeated the speeches and activities of the 1993 Parliament of the World's Religions, an event with widespread and highly favorable media coverage. In his closing address at the parliament, standing before 20,000 people at Grant Park in Chicago, the Dalai Lama, head of the Gelugpa order of Tibetan Buddhism, stated:

> Each religion has its own philosophy and there are similarities as well as differences among the various traditions. What is important is what is suitable for a particular person. We should look at the underlying purpose of religion and not merely at the abstract details of theology or metaphysics. All religions make the betterment of humanity their primary concern. When we view the different religions as essentially instruments to develop a good heart—love and respect for others, a true sense of community—we can appreciate what they have in common. . . . Everyone feels that his or her form of religious practice is the best. I myself feel that Buddhism is best for me. But this does not mean that Buddhism is best for everyone else. (1996, 17–18)

This captures well not only the spirit of the parliament but also that of the broader culture, which hailed the parliament as a new milestone in interreligious relations.

The ethos of pluralism presents a twofold challenge to the Christian faith. First, the idea that one particular religious figure and one religious perspective can be universally valid and normative for all peoples in all cultures is widely rejected today as arrogant and intellectually untenable. Second, even if in principle it is granted that one religious tradition might be superior to the rest and that one religious figure might be universally normative, why should we assume that Christianity and Jesus Christ are in this privileged position? Why Jesus and not the Buddha? This is a profound challenge that strikes at the heart of the Christian faith—the conviction that Jesus Christ is the one Lord and Savior for all peoples in all cultures and that only through Jesus Christ is there salvation and reconciliation with God.

FACTORS UNDERLYING THE CONTEMPORARY APPEAL OF PLURALISM

We cannot understand the contemporary attraction of religious pluralism without grasping the underlying intellectual and social transformations of the past several centuries, for it is the massive cultural shift accompanying these changes that has produced the context in which pluralism appears so plausible. We cannot discuss these in any detail, but several especially significant factors should be noted.[8]

The most obvious factor driving pluralism is the increased awareness that we have in the West of religious diversity. No longer are other religions exotic novelties encountered only by the few; they are part of the social and cultural fabric of American life. Immigration has brought different cultures and religions into our neighborhoods. In Chicago alone, in addition to Jews and Christians, there are over 2,500 Jains, 100,000 Hindus, 155,000 Buddhists, and 250,000 Muslims, as well as the ubiquitous New Agers and neo-pagans (Hirsley 1993, 14–17). Travel abroad has increased exposure to other religious traditions; nevertheless, those who never leave home can explore the iconography of Hindu temples or the rituals of Santeria through the marvels of satellite technology. Globalization—the increasingly complex manner in which institutions and patterns of contemporary life are interconnected worldwide, transcending national and cultural boundaries—is changing how we perceive those who are culturally and religiously different.[9] This is true not only in economics, politics, and pop culture, but also in religion. The portrait of the Dalai Lama is as familiar in the West as it is in the East—a fact put to good advantage by Apple computers in its recent advertising. Globalization and increased awareness of diversity significantly affect religious beliefs and commitments. Bryan Turner observes, "The multiplication of religious faiths in a multicultural society has in this everyday world a profoundly relativizing effect."[10] As the number of religious options multiply, the relative authority of any individual tradition seems to diminish.[11]

Closely related to this is the contemporary tendency to regard religion in highly pragmatic, consumerist terms. One does not expect religion to provide "objectively true" answers to basic questions about the cosmos and human destiny. Rather, religions are assessed pragmatically simply on the basis of how well they meet the desires and felt needs of their adherents. If Christianity meets a person's needs, then it is right for him. The multiplication of options encourages religious consumerism. As Berger observes,

> Modern man finds himself confronted not only by multiple options of possible courses of action but also by multiple options of possible ways of thinking about the world . . . [T]his means that the individual may choose his *Weltanschauung* very much as he chooses most other aspects of his private existence. In other words, there comes to be a smooth continuity between consumer choices in different areas of life—a preference for this brand of

automobile as against another, for this sexual lifestyle as against another, and finally a decision to settle for a particular "religious preference." (1979, 17)

Religious commitments—especially those of a more controversial nature—if not abandoned entirely, are held much more tentatively than before.

These effects on religious commitments are further reinforced by the tendency in the modern world to distinguish between the public world of facts—most clearly demonstrated in the physical sciences—and the private realm of opinions, values, and preferences with religion being relegated to the latter category.[12]

Put in a more positive light, much of contemporary pluralism is driven by the desire to affirm the increasing cultural diversity of our times. Can we indeed learn to live together harmoniously, with all of our cultural and religious differences? Clearly we must do so—hence the heavy emphasis today on the necessity of tolerance in religion. But it is notoriously difficult to separate cultural from religious issues. And thus, for many in today's society, acceptance of cultural diversity becomes largely indistinguishable from endorsement of religious diversity—endorsement not simply in the sense of legally and socially accepting the place of non-Christian religions in American society but also in the sense of affirming the beliefs of such religions.

This tendency is also related to a deep sense of "post-colonialist guilt." We are increasingly aware of the many injustices of colonialism, and it is often assumed that one way to atone for the past sins of colonialism is to uncritically embrace the cultures of the non-Western world. This often means not making any negative judgments about other religious beliefs and practices.

Other significant factors could be mentioned as well, including the intellectual patterns of the past three centuries that have produced a pervasive loss of confidence in the idea that we can know religious truth. Similarly, the legacies of a host of modern thinkers have encouraged *perspectivalism*—a term that includes a whole constellation of views united in their assumption that we have no access to "reality itself" but only to our varying, limited "perspectives" on reality, with no way of determining which (if any) perspective is in fact true.

These factors, together with the social transformations mentioned earlier, work together with and reinforce the "pluralist intuition"—that is, the assumption that large numbers of morally good, sincere, and intelligent people simply cannot be mistaken about their basic religious beliefs. It is the cumulative effect of these factors that makes insistence upon the truth of the Christian faith, with its commitment to salvation through Christ alone, so very problematic for many today in the West. As Peter Berger correctly observes,

We do have a problem of belief, and it not only raises the question of why we should believe in God but why we should believe in *this* God. There are others, after all, and today they are made available in an unprecedented way through the religious supermarket of modern pluralism. (1992, 146–47)

INFORMAL PLURALISM

Having examined some of the factors that contribute to the extensive appeal of contemporary religious pluralism, we will now discuss our response to pluralism in evangelism. It will be helpful at this point to return to the conversation between Bill and Jim to which we referred at the beginning of the chapter. Bill's objection to the gospel—that no sensitive thinking person living in the twentieth century could possibly believe that Christianity alone is true when there are so many other religions—is probably one of the most frequently voiced objections to the gospel, especially on university campuses. This objection to the gospel reflects what we will refer to as *informal pluralism*. Informal pluralists are united in their view that no one religious perspective or figure is normative for all people and that each religion can be valid for its followers. Informal pluralism is a popular expression of the kind of sophisticated pluralism expressed by a scholar like John Hick.[13] In the remainder of this essay, we will identify several components of informal pluralism and then explore possible responses to informal pluralism in evangelism.

Earlier this year one of the authors gave an evangelistic lecture to several hundred students at a university in the Midwest. The lecture was entitled "Comparative Religions: Do All Paths Lead to the Same Destination?" The thesis of the lecture was that, in light of the fact that religious traditions make conflicting truth-claims, it does not make sense to believe that all religions are true. A student present at the lecture wrote the following response in the campus newspaper a week later:

> If there is anything I accept least of all, it is man's susceptibility to judge and condemn. When I first saw Campus Crusade for Christ's advertisement for the lecture on "Comparative Religions" in the ResCo cafeteria, however, my reaction was complete disgust. (With God's help, I think I managed to relax long enough to forgive those ignorant enough to spread such propaganda and write an objective response). . . .
>
> The lecture itself was even more disappointing. Whirlwinding [sic] through five major world religions in 30 minutes (was it even that long?), the speaker took every opportunity to poke fun at "weird" sounding words from other religions, at

which point listeners would spill out a bit of canned laughter. Is this a study of comparative religions, I asked myself, or a study of religions compared to Christianity? I have a dream that one day Christians will realize that we are not the be all to life, and if anything we have on too many occasions been the end all of it. I also dream that one day Christians will realize that we are no longer the persecuted; we are the persecutors. . . .

Every day I share my life with Christians, Muslims and Hindus from the International Unit at ResCo. I tease my Muslim friend and say that she must convert because I worry for her soul. In reality, I would *never* want her to do any such thing. I love her just the way she is—wild, funny, caring, crazy, affectionate. If she and my other non-Christian friends are going to hell, then I will be the first to grab their shirt tails, because I want nothing to do with a heaven or a God what would reject them. Fortunately I do not believe such a God exists and feel sorry for those who do. . . .

What right do any of us have to spit on the face of our neighbors simply because we cannot understand their faith? What right do we have to mock their beliefs when we purport to be an advanced society and most importantly when we purport to be their friends. . . .

Researchers are also finding numerous ways in which religions thousands of miles apart often correspond with one another. The Aztecs envisioned their own demise through prophesy [sic]. Other native cultures have their own Jesus-like figures who came to them around the same time Jesus had appeared in the Middle East. . . .

Now there are some fascinating studies in comparative religions. So many paths can lead to the same destination, even if we think we disagree on the destination itself. What unifies us all is an acceptance of man's excessiveness, at times cruelty, and his need to believe in something higher than himself. Our solution to the problem is discipline and fulfillment through adherence to some spiritual order.

I know Campus Crusade means very well. I only wish its members could pull off the Jesus-tinted glasses and see that people all over the world are managing just fine without believing Jesus Christ is their savior—or is that what Christians are afraid of? Are we ourselves so dubious about the existence of God that we must demean others and negate their way of life to prove to ourselves that 2,000 years of Christianity have not been in vain? . . .

Religion is not the sum of its parts, it is the heart of its followers.[14]

HAROLD A. NETLAND AND KEITH E. JOHNSON

Several elements of informal pluralism that are representative of a set of issues that arise regularly in evangelism can be seen in this students' response.

TOLERANCE

A major theme in this student's response is a concern for religious tolerance. Notice some of the phrases used to describe the intolerance of Christians: "persecutors," "spitting on the face of our neighbors," "mocking their beliefs," and "demean[ing] others." These examples of intolerance stand in stark contrast to the author's treatment of individuals from other religious traditions. "I tease my Muslim friend and say that she must convert because I worry for her soul. In reality I would never want her to do such a thing. I love her just the way she is. . . ."

THE ASSUMPTION THAT ALL PATHS LEAD TO THE SAME DESTINATION

A second issue that arises regularly in evangelism is an assumption that all religions are equally valid. This may take several forms. The informal pluralist may believe (1) that all religions basically teach the same thing, (2) that all religions are somehow connected to, or in touch with, the same ultimate reality, or (3) that all religions produce similar results in their followers. Notice how this assumption arises in this student's response: "Researchers are also finding numerous ways in which religions thousands of miles apart often correspond with one another." The author points out how many cultures have had "Jesus-like figures," and concludes, "So many paths can lead to the same destination."

RELIGION EXISTS TO MEET PSYCHOLOGICAL AND SOCIAL NEEDS

This third issue is a common assumption shared by many informal pluralists that religion exists to meet people's needs.[15] This assumption too is interwoven throughout this student's article. Reference is made to a person's "need to believe in something higher than himself," and finding fulfillment "through adherence to some spiritual order." Furthermore, it is suggested that "people all over the world are managing just fine without believing in Jesus." If the purpose of religion is to meet psychological and social needs, and if all religions meet these needs, then it makes little sense to insist that one religion is true and others are false.

RELIGIOUS TRUTH AS METAPHOR

To most informal pluralists, the truths of religion are not like the truths of science or history. Instead, they are often viewed as powerful symbols or metaphors. A vivid example of this can be seen in the PBS series *The Power of Myth* that Joseph Campbell did with Bill Moyers several years ago. Many informal pluralists would find the following statement by Campbell quite appealing: "Every religion is true one way or another. It is true when understood metaphorically. But when it gets stuck to its own metaphors, interpreting them as facts, then you are in trouble" (1988, 67). This radical reinterpretation of religious truth-claims explains why informal pluralists find it strange when Christians attempt to apply the laws of logic (like the principle of noncontradiction) to religious claims. It is not unusual to encounter people who claim that the law of noncontradiction simply does not apply to religion.

THE ISSUE OF SINCERITY

Many informal pluralists will suggest that the important thing is not *what* people believe but merely that they are sincere in their belief. Notice the last sentence in the article quoted above: "Religion is not the sum of its parts, it is the heart of its followers."

THE INAPPROPRIATENESS (OR IMPOSSIBILITY) OF JUDGING OR EVALUATING OTHER RELIGIONS

This assumption can take several forms: (1) it may be that they think evaluating other religions is simply wrong; (2) it may be that they think religions should be evaluated only by their outward moral fruits; or (3) it may be that, from a postmodern perspective, they simply think there is no objective way to evaluate religions. All judgments are relative.

RESPONDING TO INFORMAL RELIGIOUS PLURALISM IN EVANGELISM

Before considering our response to these specific issues, five preliminary points must be made. First, we need to grow in our understanding of contemporary religious pluralism. We cannot effectively respond to something we do not understand. One who has a basic understanding of Hick's position will be better equipped to respond to almost any form of informal pluralism.[16]

Second, to respond effectively to informal pluralism we need to understand some of the basic differences between religious traditions. There are at least four categories that are helpful in understanding regarding the major reli-gions:[17] (1) what this religion teaches regarding the nature of the ultimate real-ity; (2) what this religion teaches about the fate of individuals at death; (3) what universal problem, according to this religion, faces humanity; and (4) what solution this religion proposes for this problem.

Third, in our response to informal pluralism, we frequently need to adjust our starting point. Rather than beginning with an attempt to prove that Jesus Christ is the only way to God, it is often more fruitful to back up and address the assumption of the informal pluralist that all paths lead to the same desti-nation. When the informal pluralist recognizes that all religions cannot be true at the same time, he or she is generally more open to considering evidence for one particular faith.

Fourth, it is crucial that we present the gospel to informal pluralists within the framework of the Bible's story line. There are at least two reasons for this. First, apart from the Bible's story line, the content of the gospel makes little sense to biblically illiterate pluralists.[18] Second, many informal pluralists assume that the exclusivity of Christianity is merely another manifestation of ethnocentrism. Presenting the gospel within the framework of the Bible's story line helps them recognize that the exclusivity of Christianity is not the result of Christian ethnocentrism but is related integrally to the Bible's diagnosis of the human condition resulting from the Fall and the solution found in Christ.

Finally, it is important that we treat pluralists with kindness, compassion, and respect.

We will now discuss our response to the six expressions of informal plu-ralism that we identified.

TOLERANCE

First, it is crucial that we identify with a legitimate concern that underlies the emphasis on tolerance: Can Buddhists, Hindus, Christians, Muslims, and others all live together without resorting to violence? World history does not offer a very encouraging picture in this regard. Thus, it is critical for Chris-tians to affirm that they are against racism, bigotry, and other forms of intol-erance that deny people the right to believe what they want. This may seem obvious, but many informal pluralists assume that Christian particularism either directly causes these things or inevitably leads to them.[19]

Second, it is helpful to identify the limitations of tolerance. A person watch-ing a gang rape and making no attempt to stop it would hardly be described as tolerant. We all believe there are certain behaviors that should not be tolerated. This illustrates the unavoidable necessity of making judgments.

Furthermore, it is important to point out that although truth is sometimes narrow, this does not make it intolerant. One of the authors has frequently used the following illustration to help clarify this distinction. The University of Michigan won the NCAA championship in basketball in 1989. Imagine a disgruntled Duke fan who, upon hearing Keith claim that Michigan won the championship, retorted, "Well that is an incredibly intolerant thing to say!" This response is at best confusing, and it blurs an important distinction. Does this statement mean that Keith's communication style is unkind or that his assertion is false? Being a zealous Michigan fan, he may have been obnoxious. Nevertheless, the way in which he *communicated* his claim must be carefully distinguished from its truthfulness.

Finally, when dealing with informal pluralists it can be very helpful to point out that all religions—even seemingly accommodating religions like Hinduism—make exclusive claims.[20] Thus, it is unreasonable to dismiss Christianity merely because it makes exclusive claims.

THE NATURE OF RELIGIOUS TRUTH

One of the central issues in the pluralism debate concerns the nature of religious truth. What kind of claims do religions make? Is religious truth different from truth in science or history? One cannot respond to pluralism—informal or academic—without addressing these questions. It is important to note that almost all expressions of informal pluralism identified above are in some way related to the nature of religious truth.

Identifying the nature of religious truth involves a number of complicated epistemological questions.[21] In his book *Truth in Religion*, Mortimer Adler suggests that we must carefully distinguish what he calls "matters of taste" from "matters of truth" (1990, 2). Consider the following statements:

- Carmen's has the best stuffed pizza in the city of Chicago.
- The Cubs are my favorite baseball team.
- Star Trek is my favorite television show.

Adler would describe these statements as matters of taste. They refer to preferences, opinions, and desires. Consider, however, the following statements:

- The University of Michigan is a member of the Big Ten conference.
- The Titanic sank into the icy waters of the Atlantic on April 15, 1912, at about 2:20 a.m.
- Over six million Jewish men, women, and children died in the Holocaust.

Adler would describe these statements as matters of truth. These statements describe realities that exist independent of our perception and must be either true or false.

Next, ask the informal pluralist to consider the following religious claims:

- Jesus Christ was a Jew who lived in Palestine during the early part of the first century.
- Jesus was executed on a cross by Roman soldiers about A.D. 30.
- Jesus rose from the dead after three days and appeared to over five hundred witnesses.

The important question to ask the informal pluralist is, "Into which category do these religious claims fit? Are they merely matters of taste, or are they matters of truth?" It is important to help the pluralist understand that there are many statements regarding the Christian faith that cannot be labeled matters of taste and must therefore be evaluated for their truthfulness.

This discussion of the nature of religious truth enables us to answer three of the common assumptions of pluralists: that religion exists merely to meet psychological needs, that sincerity is more important than truth, and that religious beliefs should be interpreted metaphorically.[22] First, consider the assertion that religion exists to meet psychological and sociological needs.[23] When responding to this belief, it is important to help the pluralist see how this assumption distorts the teaching of almost every religion. The fact is that each religion makes statements about the nature of reality, and the truth or falsity of those statements does matter.

Imagine that you are sick and visit the doctor. Because of the unusual nature of your illness, you see several specialists who all disagree about the nature of the problem. While all of them recognize that something is wrong and that you need treatment, they disagree in their diagnosis. You are unsure which of the doctors to believe. If a friend said to you, "It doesn't matter which doctor or hospital you go to; the purpose of a hospital is to overcome your psychological fear," you would think he is missing the point. Being in a hospital may meet some psychological needs, but the more important question remains: What is wrong with your body and which diagnosis is correct? The claim that religion exists to meet psychological and sociological needs is similar to the claim that the purpose of hospitals is to help overcome fear. It ignores the unique diagnosis of the human plight that each religion offers and the solution it proposes. It is helpful at this point to describe briefly to the pluralist the unique problem each religion identifies along with the solution it prescribes.

Second, the pluralist's insistence that sincerity—not belief—is what really matters blurs the distinction between the sincerity with which one holds a particular belief and its truthfulness. Imagine that you are in a chemistry lab and the professor places a 500ml Pyrex beaker of clear liquid on the lab table and says, "This is sulfuric acid." In response to this explanation Jim—a student in the class—blurts out, "I don't believe that is sulfuric acid. It looks like water to me." Jim is so sincere in his belief that the Pyrex beaker contains water that he decides to drink it. What will happen to Jim? Obviously, he will be lucky if he lives long enough to participate in next week's lab. Despite his sincerity, Jim's belief that the beaker contained water did not change the nature of its contents. The same principle applies to religion. Sincerity is a laudable quality, but by itself it is not an adequate test for the veracity of religious truth-claims.

Third, consider the common tendency of pluralists to reinterpret religious truth-claims as symbols, metaphors, or myths. We have frequently seen informal pluralists make this move when pressed with the fact that religions make contradictory claims. To reinterpret all religious language metaphorically, however, is little more than a thinly veiled denial of the factuality of religious claims.[24] It is helpful to point this out to the pluralist and to ask what justification they can offer for interpreting religious claims in this way.

THE INAPPROPRIATENESS (OR IMPOSSIBILITY) OF JUDGING OR EVALUATING RELIGIONS

If there is any verse from the Bible that the informal pluralist is likely to know, it is probably Matthew 7:1: "Do not judge lest you be judged" (NASB). When responding to this issue, it is important to ask some clarifying questions: Are you saying that it is wrong to make religious judgments? If so, why? If not, what kind of religious judgments are legitimate?

Several important points can be made to the informal pluralist. First, it is helpful to point out that it is impossible to avoid making religious judgments. Even the statement "Don't judge other religions" itself includes a religious judgment. Furthermore, people make religious judgments all the time. Few people find it difficult to condemn Jim Jones or David Koresh, for example. Thus the issue is not Will we evaluate religions? but On what grounds will we do so? Second, because religions make truth-claims, these truth-claims deserve careful evaluation. To pretend that religions do not make truth-claims is demeaning and fails to take religions seriously on their own terms. Third, although this is a complex issue that we cannot pursue here, there are criteria one can use to evaluate religious truth-claims. These include logical consistency, adequate factual support, ability to explain the whole range of human experience, consistency with other fields of knowledge, and morality. This is not to suggest that the evaluation of religious claims is easy, but simply that it is *possible*.[25] These criteria are applied regularly to the evaluation of theories in science, history, and other fields in inquiry.[26]

Finally, for those who suggest that we have no basis on which to evaluate truth-claims, it may be helpful to point out the consequences of this line of thinking. An interesting example is the recent denial of the Holocaust. Although it is one of the best-documented examples of mass genocide in recent history, a very small but vocal group of Holocaust deniers maintain that the Holocaust is a hoax.[27] Emory professor Deborah E. Lipstadt carefully documents their activities in her book *Denying the Holocaust: The Growing Assault on Truth and Memory* (1993). Professor Lipstadt suggests that one reason deniers have gained a hearing on university campuses is because of the relativistic thinking that permeates the academy (1993, 17–18). One cannot have it both ways. One cannot affirm the historicity of an event like the Holocaust and insist, at the same time, that there are *no criteria* by which to make historical judgments.

THE ASSUMPTION THAT ALL PATHS LEAD TO THE SAME DESTINATION

Three blind men were touching an elephant. The first blind man was holding the elephant's leg and said, "I think an elephant is like the trunk of a tree." The second blind man was holding the elephant's trunk and said, "An elephant is like a large snake." The third blind man said, "An elephant is like a great wall," while touching the elephant's side. Each blind man was convinced he was right and others were wrong without ever realizing they were all touching the same elephant.

Many informal pluralists are familiar with this ancient Indian parable and find in it an attractive interpretation of religion. We have found it helpful in evangelism to refer to it because it leaves one important question unanswered: How do we *know* the blind men were all describing the same elephant? Perhaps the first blind man was holding an oak tree and said, "I think an elephant is like the trunk of a great tree." Perhaps the second blind man, while holding a fire hose, exclaimed, "An elephant is like a snake." What if the third blind man, while touching the side of the Sears Tower, asserted, "An elephant is like a great wall." The problem with this parable is that it assumes the very thing it allegedly proves—that all the blind men are touching an elephant. Yet how do we know the blind men are touching an elephant? Only because the story assumes it.

Furthermore, what if each of the blind men made assertions about an alleged elephant that were not merely different but were also contradictory? What if the first blind man said there is only one elephant, and the second blind man said there were two? What if the third blind man said there were no elephants at all? Now would it make sense to suggest they are all describing the same elephant?

Yet this situation is similar to the claims of the world's religions. Each religion makes truth-claims that contradict the truth-claims of other religions. If their claims really contradict each other, then the principle of noncontradiction states they cannot all be correct. One might introduce the principle of noncontradiction to the pluralist by asking him or her to consider two contradictory statements such as the following:

- On June 14, 1998, the Chicago Bulls won the NBA championship.
- On June 14, 1998, the Chicago Bulls did not win the NBA championship.

Obviously both of these statements cannot be true. Similarly, if two religions make mutually contradictory truth-claims, they cannot both be right. When Hindus claim there are many gods and Muslims insist there are not many gods, they cannot both be right. In light of the conflicting truth-claims of various religions, it does not make sense to believe that all religions are equally valid.[28] This was the thesis of the evangelistic lecture we referred to earlier to which the student's article responded.[29]

CONCLUSION

It is clear from the preceding discussion that Christians should not treat Bill's objection to the gospel—that no rational person living in the twentieth century could possibly believe that Christianity alone is true when there are so many other religions—as a smoke screen to be ignored in evangelism. We have observed that a multiplicity of factors in contemporary American culture converge to render this view of religion both plausible and intuitively appealing. Thus, success in evangelism with pluralists will not come merely from insisting that Christianity is objectively true—although that certainly is important—but also from identifying the specific expressions of pluralism underlying objections to the gospel and responding to them in thoughtful ways.

References

Adler, Mortimer J. 1990. *Truth in Religion: The Plurality of Religions and the Unity of Truth*. New York: Macmillan.

Berger, Peter. 1967. *The Sacred Canopy*. New York: Anchor Books.

_____. 1979. *The Heretical Imperative: Contemporary Possibilities of Religious Affirmation*. New York: Doubleday.

_____. 1992. *A Far Glory: The Quest for Faith in an Age of Credulity*. New York: Anchor Books.

Beuscher, John. 1989. "Religion from a Global Perspective." *Humanities* 10 (January-February): 36–38.

Beyer, Peter. 1994. *Religion and Globalization*. Thousand Oaks, Calif.: Sage.

Bruce, Steve. 1996. *Religion in the Modern World: From Cathedrals to Cults*. New York: Oxford University Press.

Campbell, Joseph. 1988. *The Power of Myth*. Ed. Betty Sue Flowers. New York: Anchor Books.

Carson, D. A. 1996. *The Gagging of God: Christianity Confronts Pluralism*. Grand Rapids: Zondervan.

Carter, Stephen L. 1993. *The Culture of Disbelief: How American Law and Politics Trivialize Religious Devotion*. New York: Basic Books.

Clendenin, Daniel B. 1995. *Many Gods, Many Lords: Christianity Encounters World Religions*. Grand Rapids: Baker.

Dalai Lama XIV, The. 1996. "The Importance of Religious Harmony." In *The Community of Religions*, ed. Wayne Teasdale and George Cairns, 17–21. New York: Continuum.

D'Costa, Gavin. 1986. *Theology and Religious Pluralism: The Challenge of Other Religions*. Oxford: Basil Blackwell.

_____, ed. 1990. *Christian Uniqueness Reconsidered: The Myth of a Pluralistic Theology of Religions*. Maryknoll: Orbis.

Dupuis, Jacques. 1997. *Toward a Christian Theology of Religious Pluralism*. Maryknoll: Orbis.

Edwards, David, and John Stott. 1988. *Evangelical Essentials: A Liberal—Evangelical Dialogue*. Downers Grove, Ill.: InterVarsity Press.

Erickson, Millard. 1975. "Hope for Those Who Haven't Heard? Yes, But . . . ." *Evangelical Missions Quarterly* 11 (April): 122–26.

_____. 1996. *How Shall They Be Saved? The Destiny of Those Who Do Not Hear of Jesus*. Grand Rapids: Baker.

Gaede, S. D. 1993. *When Tolerance Is No Virtue: Political Correctness, Multiculturalism and the Future of Truth and Justice*. Downers Grove, Ill.: InterVarsity.

Geivett, R. Douglas, and W. Gary Phillips. 1996. "A Particularist View: An Evidentialist Approach." In *Four Views on Salvation in a Pluralistic World*, ed. Dennis Okholm and Timothy R. Phillips, 211–45. Grand Rapids: Zondervan.

Halverson, Dean C., ed. 1996. *The Compact Guide to World Religions*. Minneapolis: Bethany House.

Hick, John. 1982. *God Has Many Names*. Philadelphia: Westminster.

————. 1989. *An Interpretation of Religion*. New Haven: Yale University Press.

————. 1993. *Disputed Questions in Theology and the Philosophy of Religion*. New Haven: Yale University Press.

————. 1994. *The Metaphor of God Incarnate*. Louisville: Westminster/John Knox.

————. 1995. *A Christian Theology of Religions*. Louisville: Westminster/John Knox.

————. 1996. "A Pluralistic View." In *Four Views on Salvation in a Pluralistic World*, ed. Dennis Okholm and Timothy R. Phillips, 29–42. Grand Rapids: Zondervan.

Hirsley, Michael. 1993. "Common Cause." In *Chicago Tribune Magazine*, 19 August, 14–17.

Holmes, Arthur F. 1983. *Contours of a World View*. Grand Rapids: Eerdmans.

Johnson, Keith. "Do All Paths Lead to the Same Destination?" Available at http://wri.leaderu.com/articles/paths.html.

————. "John Hick's Pluralistic Hypothesis and the Problem of Conflicting Truth-Claims." Available at http://www.leaderu.com/theology/hick.html.

Knitter, Paul. 1985. *No Other Name? A Critical Survey of Christian Attitudes Toward the World Religions*. Maryknoll: Orbis.

Küng, Hans. 1976. "The Challenge of World Religions" In *On Being a Christian*, 89–116. Garden City: Doubleday.

Lipstadt, Deborah E. 1993. *Denying the Holocaust: The Growing Assault on Truth and Memory*. New York: Free Press, 1993.

McGrath, Alister. 1996. "A Particularist View: A Post-Enlightenment Approach." In *Four Views on Salvation in a Pluralistic World*, ed. Dennis Okholm and Timothy R. Phillips, 149–80. Grand Rapids: Zondervan.

Mitchell, Basil. 1973. *The Justification of Religious Belief*. New York: Seabury.

Nash, Ronald. 1992. *World-Views in Conflict: Choosing Christianity in a World of Ideas*. Grand Rapids: Zondervan.

————. 1994. *Is Jesus the Only Saviour?* Grand Rapids: Zondervan.

Netland, Harold. 1991. *Dissonant Voices: Religious Pluralism and the Question of Truth*. Grand Rapids: Eerdmans; reprint: Vancouver: Regent College Publishing, 1997.

————. 1994. "Truth, Authority, and Modernity: Shopping for Truth in the Supermarket of Worldviews." In *Faith and Modernity*, ed. Philip Sampson, Vinay Samuel, and Chris Sugden, 89–115. Oxford: Regnum/Lynx.

Newbigin, Lesslie. 1989. *The Gospel in a Pluralistic Society*. Grand Rapids: Eerdmans.

Okholm, Dennis, and Timothy R. Phillips, eds. 1996. *Four Views on Salvation in a Pluralistic World*. Grand Rapids: Zondervan.

Packer, J. I. 1990. "Evangelicals and the Way of Salvation." In *Evangelical Affirmations*, ed. Kenneth Kantzer and Carl F. H. Henry, 107–36. Grand Rapids: Zondervan.

Pannenberg, Wolfhart. 1993. "The Religions from the Perspective of Christian Theology and the Self-Interpretation of Christianity in Relation to the Non-Christian Religions." *Modern Theology* 9 (July): 285–97.

Pinnock, Clark. 1992. *A Wideness in God's Mercy: The Finality of Jesus Christ in a World of Religions*. Grand Rapids: Zondervan.

_____. 1996. "An Inclusivist View." In *Four Views on Salvation in a Pluralistic World*, ed. Dennis Okholm and Timothy J. Phillips, 93–123. Grand Rapids: Zondervan.

Piper, John. 1993. *Let the Nations Be Glad! The Supremacy of God in Missions*. Grand Rapids: Baker.

Richard, Ramesh. 1994. *The Population of Heaven: A Biblical Response to the Inclusivist Position on Who Will Be Saved*. Chicago: Moody Press.

Robertson, Roland. 1992. *Globalization: Social Theory and Global Culture*. London: Sage.

Smith, Tom W. 1995. "The Polls—A Review: The Holocaust Denial Controversy." *Public Opinion Quarterly* 59 (1995): 269–95.

Stott, John. 1985. *The Authentic Jesus*. London: Marshall, Morgan and Scott.

Turner, Bryan. 1994. *Orientalism, Postmodernism, and Globalism*. London: Routledge.

Waters, Malcolm. 1995. *Globalization*. New York: Routledge.

CHAPTER 4

EPISTEMOLOGY AT THE CORE OF POSTMODERNISM:
RORTY, FOUCAULT, AND THE GOSPEL

Jon Hinkson and Greg Ganssle

The context for the gospel today is shaped by postmodernism. The receptivity of many people to the message we proclaim is a function of a set of assumptions that are themselves strongly influenced by postmodern thought. To one steeped in the culture of postmodernism, the gospel seems irrelevant at best. At worst, it appears appalling.

Postmodernism in general culture is the effect of the trickle down from postmodern theory. Postmodern trickle down, unlike postnasal drip, cannot be cured by simple application of standard remedies. We must engage the thinkers who lead the way in shaping the plausibility structures on the campus, in the media, and throughout the culture. Few in the media or in government, and not as many as you might think in the university, have actually read Richard Rorty or Michel Foucault. Most, however, have been deeply influenced by their work and the work of other postmodern theorists.

If postmodernism has the widespread influence that we believe it has, we must read postmodern theorists. We cannot be content with merely treating symptoms or with a superficial engagement with the ideas that are pushing the gospel to the periphery of the contemporary mind. Shaping the formal and informal discourse in the university and in the general culture has always been and continues to be a central part of bearing witness to Christ. This conference is a step in recognizing that a long-term faithful witness to Christ must take seriously the shape of the contemporary discourse.

In this essay we will introduce the projects of two leading postmodern theorists, Richard Rorty and Michel Foucault, and we will draw out some implications of their work for the evangelist. Again, we want to stress that few people consciously adopt all the views of either Foucault or Rorty or any other thinker. Most people hold a hybrid view that is picked up from various sources along the way without much critical reflection. Exposure to their projects, however, will help us understand how the ideas of so many are shaped.

Richard Rorty

Born in 1931, Richard Rorty completed his Ph.D. in Philosophy at Yale in 1956 and taught at Princeton University until 1982. From 1982 until 1988, he was Kenan Professor of Humanities at the University of Virginia. Now he is emeritus professor of the humanities at UVA and professor of comparative literature at Stanford University. Rorty edited *The Linguistic Turn* (1967) and wrote *Philosophy and the Mirror of Nature* (1979) and *Contingency, Irony and Solidarity* (1989). Some of his major papers published from 1972 to 1981 were published in *The Consequences of Pragmatism* (1982). Two additional volumes of his papers were published in 1991: *Objectivity, Relativism and Truth* and *Essays on Heidegger and Others.* A third volume of Philosophical Papers, *Truth and Progress,* appeared in the spring of 1998 as did *Achieving Our Country: Leftist Thought in Twentieth-Century America.*

Rorty has made a unique contribution to contemporary philosophy and postmodernism not only because of the intrinsic value of his work but also because he is one of the first philosophers trained in analytic philosophy to adopt self-consciously a posture interacting with that of continental postmodern philosophy. Rorty calls his position "pragmatism" and sees himself in continuity with William James and John Dewey in America as well as with Heidegger on the Continent.

The Failure of Epistemology: Rorty's Starting Point

Much of *Philosophy and the Mirror of Nature* is an explication of the failure of epistemology and, consequently, of the entire history of philosophy.[1] Rorty calls for a new mission in philosophy. This mission is not to take a new kind of look at traditional problems but to leave the traditional problems of philosophy behind altogether. Because the traditional problems of philosophy have proven themselves to be no longer fruitful, it is time to explore new problems.

The failure of epistemology is the failure of a metaphor or a picture of the mind's relation to the world. The picture is that of a mirror. The mind has been thought of as a mirror in that it reflects accurately a mirror-independent reality (Rorty 1979, 42–43). This picture has failed, Rorty claims, because accurate reflection of mind-independent objects requires two things that we cannot have. First, it requires privileged access to certain items of knowledge. This privileged access to the "given" is immune from doubt. Second, we need to be able to make a sharp distinction between contingent, synthetic truths that we learn from experience, and necessary, analytic truths that we learn independently from experience.

Since Descartes, many have thought that we have privileged access to the contents of our own minds.[2] If I am thinking, I know I am thinking. If I am experiencing the sensation of brown in a table, while I might not know that the table *is* brown, or even that the table itself is a mind-independent object, I can have certainty of what my experience is like—that it seems as if there is a brown table.

In recent years, the claim to privileged access has been challenged. Rorty thinks this challenge has been decisive. One of the main protagonists in this challenge was Wilfrid Sellars (1963), who claimed that there is no privileged "given" at all. There is nothing to which we have indubitable access. If this claim is true, we have no sure premises from which to infer securely everything else we claim to know. There is no sure foundation for our knowledge claims, and as a result, our entire system of knowledge is on shaky ground. So without privileged access, the epistemological project fails.

The second requirement for a sure epistemology is the distinction between analytic and synthetic truths, that is, between statements that are truths of fact such that they depend for their truth on how the world is, and statements that are truths of reason whose truth is independent of how the world is. The fact that a table is in the room is a truth of fact. Whether or not it is the case depends on things in the world. It is a *synthetic* statement in that it is a synthesis of two concepts, the concept of a table and the concept of being in the room. The fact that a rectangular table top has four corners does not depend on the way the world turns out to be. There is no possible way for the world to go such that the rectangular table top has only three corners. This statement is *analytic* in that an analysis of the concept of rectangularity reveals that any rectangle must have four corners.

If there is no possible way the world could be such that the rectangle had three corners rather than four, then the rectangle's having four corners is a *necessary truth*. The thing about a necessary truth of this kind, it has been held, is that we do not need to look around to learn it. We can deduce from the meaning of the word *rectangle* or from the concept of a rectangle that it has four corners. This kind of knowledge is sure, because nothing can change these facts. So if there are statements that are necessarily true in this way, we can ground our theory of knowledge and have the kind of certainty we want.

Now according to Rorty and many others, this requirement has also been shown to be impossible. The foremost influence on this trend was Willard Van

JON HINKSON AND GREG GANSSLE

Orman Quine (1961, 20–46). Quine holds that statements that we think are analytic (and therefore undoubtable), such as "a rectangle has four corners," turn out to be psychologically undoubtable, but only given our present conditions. There is, however, nothing metaphysical or epistemological about such statements that make them intrinsically undoubtable. As psychologically difficult as it may be to doubt these statements, they are open to revision. Every statement, even those of arithmetic and logic, could be rejected.

Another result of seeing that any belief in our system of beliefs is subject to being revised is that the relationship between beliefs and facts in the world is not a one-to-one correspondence. Rather, it is the entire system of related beliefs that is confirmed or disconfirmed by evidence. For example, let us say that an ornithologist is mapping the distribution of bird species in a given area and that she comes across a bird that she has never seen before. For all her abilities to discern (and they are many), it appears to be an example of a white crow. Let us say (and I do not know if this is the case) that the established theory holds that all crows are black. What will our ornithologist do with a bird that has all of the properties of a crow except that it is white? Given the Quine, Sellars, and Rorty approach, there is no one thing she must do. She can either revise her belief in the established doctrine that all crows are black and take this bird to be a crow, or she can take this bird to be another species. It is like a crow, but it is not a crow. All crows are in fact black, but birds of the species "almost crow" can be white.

In this simplistic example we can see that the one piece of evidence, the white bird, does not prescribe how the ornithologist's theory should go. As long as the theory accommodates the evidence, the theory is adequate. So we can have two theories that conflict but are each evidentially adequate.

This relation between evidence and theories seems relatively benign in an example such as this one. Quine, Sellars, and Rorty, however, take it to pervade all of our theory construction.[3] There are no beliefs that could not be revised in the face of challenges to our system of beliefs. It is a whole system rather than a particular belief that is confirmed or disconfirmed by evidence. Thus these philosophers are advocating a holism in theory of knowledge and philosophy of language. Furthermore, the point of the theory is, for example, to cope with the various birds, not in any way to represent accurately the world. Rorty explains the point of such theories.

On this view, great scientists invent descriptions of the world which are useful for purposes of predicting and controlling what happens, just as poets and political thinkers invent other descriptions of it for other purposes. But there is no sense in which *any* of these descriptions is an accurate representation of the way the world is in itself. These philosophers regard the very idea of such a representation as pointless. (1989, 4)

Combining the rejection of privileged access with the denial of the distinction between analytic and synthetic truths results in the failure of the entire enlightenment epistemological project. There is no certain foundation for knowledge.

PRAGMATISM AND ETHNOCENTRISM: RORTY'S METHOD

Classical epistemology has failed. The idea that the mind represents the world like a mirror has foundered on the twin shoals of the myth of the given and the failure of the analytic-synthetic distinction. Central to the classical picture was the theory of truth as correspondence. Rorty rejects this theory but does not substitute for it another theory of truth at all. Rather, he takes up the mantle of *pragmatism*. The pragmatist has no theory of truth but holds that our knowledge and our beliefs simply help us cope with the world. There is no need for a theory of truth. Rorty writes:

> For the pragmatist, true sentences are not true because they correspond to reality, and so there is no need to worry what sort of reality, if any, a given sentence corresponds to—no need to worry about what "makes" it true. . . .
>
> [The pragmatist] drops the notion of truth as correspondence with reality altogether, and says that modern science does not enable us to cope because it corresponds, it just plain enables us to cope. (1982, xvi–xvii)

Rorty characterizes the pragmatism of James and Dewey that he is following in three ways. First, pragmatism is "simply anti-essentialism applied to notions like 'truth,' 'knowledge,' 'language,' 'morality,' and similar objects of philosophical theorizing" (1982, 162). Rorty refers to James's definition of "the true" is "what is good in the way of belief." There is nothing more to the essence of truth, because truth has no essence. The point behind any theory of truth is to help us decide what it is good for us to believe. What is true is what it is good for us to believe in much the same way that what is good is that which it is right for us to do. What makes something good for us to believe is how the belief will help us negotiate our world or our community or our image of ourselves in the way that we want to negotiate these things. Since no theory of truth actually helps us with these decisions, the theories turn out not to be helpful at all. "Pragmatists," he writes, "think that if something makes no difference to practice, it should make no difference to philosophy. This conviction makes them suspicious of the distinction between justification and truth, for that difference makes no difference to my decisions about what to do" (1998b, 19).

The second characterization of pragmatism is that there is "no epistemological difference between truth about what ought to be and truth about what is, nor any metaphysical difference between facts and values, nor any methodological difference between morality and science." He goes on to say that "for the pragmatist, the pattern of all inquiry—scientific as well as moral—is deliberation concerning the relative attractions of various concrete alternatives" (1982, 163, 164). So at bottom, the methodology of the sciences and the methodology of moral reasoning are of the same kind. Rorty is not asserting that morality ought to be approached the way some take science to be approached, with a universally valid method grounded in human nature or in the way the universe is. The opposite is the case. Rorty is claiming that our scientific reasoning is as much a matter of constructing a vision of how we want to see ourselves as is our moral reasoning. There is no set of rules for rational discourse to which science is bound and which is firmly grounded beyond our historical situation. We choose which picture seems best to us, given the values and concerns of our community.

The third characterization of pragmatism is that the only constraints on inquiry are conversational constraints "provided by our fellow inquirers" (1982, 165). The nature of the mind or of objects in the world does not constrain inquiry. Inquiry is conversation. It is conversation about what picture of the world or of politics or of morals is the one we want. It is the conversation about what sorts of people we want to be and what sorts of behavior we want to encourage. There is no constraint from human nature or moral reality on this conversation. The only constraints are those we find in the community of those in the conversation. Rorty rejects the attempts to make truth out to be anything more than what our peers will let us get away with saying (1979, 176).

So Rorty's pragmatism is such that he is not offering a new theory of truth but that he thinks theories of truth have outlived their usefulness. We ought to direct our attention to more important matters than truth. The most important of these matters is building a liberal society in which the conversation flourishes.

Rorty's pragmatism walks hand in hand with his ethnocentrism. By ethnocentrism, Rorty does not mean racism. Ethnocentrism is the recognition that in our actual practice we appeal to, argue with, and take seriously those who share our general take on the world. We justify our beliefs primarily in and to our own communities:

> To be ethnocentric is to divide the human race into the people to whom one must justify one's beliefs and the others. The first group—one's *ethnos*—comprise those who share enough of one's beliefs to make fruitful conversation possible. In this sense, everybody is ethnocentric when engaged in actual debate, no matter how much realist rhetoric about objectivity he produces in his study. (1991, 30)

In any discussion or disagreement, we have to begin where we are. We have to begin with the things we already believe and the ways we go about believing. Any challenge to our ideas will have to be evaluated, but we evaluate such challenges by our own lights. Rorty explains: "For now to say that we must work by our own lights, that we must be ethnocentric, is merely to say that beliefs suggested by another culture must be tested by trying to weave them together with beliefs we already have" (1991, 26).

When Enlightenment epistemology died, the ideal of neutrality died with it. The fact is that we simply look at the world in a certain way. It is not that we cannot or will not change the way we see the world, but that this change will begin with the things we already hold. We cannot hope to escape from our own starting points into some neutral and objective vantage point. Rorty lays this out:

> One consequence of antirepresentationalism is the recognition that no description of how things are from a God's-eye point of view, no skyhook provided by some contemporary or yet-to-be-developed science, is going to free us from the contingency of having been acculturated as we were. Our acculturation is what makes certain options live, or momentous, or forced, while leaving others dead, or trivial, or optional. (1991, 13)

We start the conversation in our particular contingent historical position. We believe some things and reject others. We think some options are plausible, and we think others are not. Furthermore, we do not take every challenge with equal seriousness. Which challenges deserve serious attention is in a large part influenced by what we already believe and how we go about the process of discussion.

Of all of the features of his project, it is Rorty's pragmatism that seems least compatible with Christian belief and the grounding of Christian practice. The truth-claims of the gospel are not merely pragmatic. They are intended to track the way the universe is, independently of the way we see it. A few weeks ago, I asked Rorty whether the pragmatism he espouses is compatible with orthodox Christian theism. He replied that most orthodox Christians would think that they are not compatible. He added that the incompatibility of pragmatism with orthodox Christianity revealed a problem not with pragmatism but with Christianity. In other words, it is Christianity that ought to be rejected, not pragmatism.

LIBERAL IRONY: RORTY'S END

Rorty advocates the goal of a *liberal society*, that is, one in which there is solidarity among all persons. No one is thought to be on the outside and therefore to be a legitimate subject for mistreatment. This increasing solidarity is not grounded on some purported fact about human nature or objective moral obligation. A liberal society is simply committed to human solidarity. Although this commitment to solidarity requires no philosophical grounding, in an ideal society the majority of the population would no more think to question or defend their commitment to solidarity with all people than a sixteenth-century European would question whether or not to be a Christian (1989, 87).

The liberal society is completely open in the realm of ideas. This openness is borne not out of the conviction that truth will prevail in any encounter but that such openness "should be fostered for its own sake." Rorty claims that "a liberal society is one which is content to call 'true' whatever the upshot of such encounters turns out to be" (1989, 52). There are no philosophical foundations to ground such a society because the presence of philosophical foundations already assumes that the encounters in the realm of ideas will or ought to go in a particular direction. What holds such a society together is not a shared philosophical position, but "a consensus that the point of social organization is to let everybody have a chance at self-creation to the best of his or her abilities, and that that goal requires, besides peace and wealth, the standard 'bourgeois freedoms'" (1989, 84).

Each person has what Rorty calls a "final vocabulary." A final vocabulary consists in the terms by which someone justifies his or her actions and beliefs. Rorty calls it final not because it is not subject to change, but because if it is challenged, the user "has no noncircular argumentative recourse" (1989, 73). In a liberal society, intellectuals would take the posture of an ironist regarding their final vocabularies. An *ironist* is one who recognizes the inevitability of ethnocentrism and realizes that there are no justifications for one's basic commitments, including one's commitment to human solidarity. To be an ironist is to think of one's final vocabulary in ethnocentric and pragmatic terms. Rorty defines an ironist as one who fulfills three conditions concerning her final vocabulary:

(1) She has radical and continuing doubts about the final vocabulary she currently uses, because she has been impressed by other vocabularies, vocabularies taken as final by people or books she has encountered; (2) she realizes that argument phrased in her present vocabulary can neither underwrite nor dissolve these doubts; (3) insofar as she philosophizes about her situation, she does not think that her vocabulary is closer to reality than others, that it is in touch with a power not herself. Ironists who are inclined to philosophize see the choice between vocabularies as made neither within a neutral and universal metavocabulary nor by an attempt to fight one's way past appearances to the real, but simply by playing the new off against the old. (1989, 73)

A liberal ironist is one who does not harbor the idea that his view of the world is right in that it corresponds with some reality that is independent of human minds. Nevertheless, he is committed to fostering a society in which there is solidarity among an ever-expanding circle of people.

These dual commitments may seem at odds with each other. If we are suspicious of any claim that there is an essence to human nature, how can we be thoroughly committed to solidarity with all people? What link is there between people that makes us realize that we want to include them in our circle of understanding? The link is the ability of all people to feel the pain of humiliation. Rorty describes the liberal ironist:

She thinks that what unites her with the rest of the species is not a common language but just susceptibility to pain and in particular that special sort of pain which the brutes do not share with humans—humiliation. On her conception, human solidarity is not a matter of sharing a common truth or a common goal but of sharing a common selfish hope, the hope that one's world—the little things around which one has woven into one's final vocabulary—will not be destroyed. (1989, 92)

So there is motivation to work for a liberal society even if there are no philosophical justifications for such a society in terms of some real moral order or human nature. In this way we can be ironists in our doubts about our own way of looking at the world while we are committed liberals in our insistence that the sense of solidarity felt in our society be expanded to include all people, simply because all people are possible subjects of humiliation. In his most recent book, Rorty claims that "for purposes of thinking about how to achieve our country, we do not need to worry about the correspondence theory of truth, the grounds for normativity, the impossibility of justice, or the infinite distance which separates us from the other. For those purposes, we can give both religion and philosophy a pass. We can just get on with trying to solve what Dewey called 'the problems of men'" (1998a, 97).

THE QUESTION OF RELATIVISM

One nagging doubt about Rorty's project is that it looks as if he undermines with one hand what he relies on with the other. Once we abandon the notion that there is a human nature and a reality that is independent of our thinking about it and a moral order that we did not invent, how can we speak of humiliation as bad? Hasn't Rorty painted himself into the relativist corner? Rorty addresses this concern quite explicitly, and he denies being a relativist:

> "Relativism" is the view that every belief on a certain topic, or perhaps about *any* topic, is as good as every other. No one holds this view. Except for the occasional cooperative freshman, one cannot find anybody who says that two incompatible opinions on an important topic are equally good. The philosophers who get *called* "relativists" are those who say that the grounds for choosing between such opinions are less algorithmic than had been thought. (1982, 166)

Rorty thinks that some views are better than others. What he denies is that what makes these views better is some truth about the way the world is, apart from our views about the world or some facts about human nature. The denial of these grounds for holding one view over another does not amount to the claim that anything goes in the area of beliefs. Many of our beliefs about morals or society can be well justified even if we do not claim that they accurately reflect mind-independent reality. Rorty insists that he cannot be considered a relativist because he does not hold a relativistic theory of truth or knowledge. In fact, he does not hold any theory about these things:

> For the pragmatist is not holding a positive theory which says that something is relative to something else. He is, instead, making the purely *negative* point that we should drop the traditional distinction between knowledge and opinion, construed as the distinction between truth as correspondence to reality and truth as a commendatory term for well-justified beliefs. The reason that the realist calls this negative claim "relativistic" is that he cannot believe that anybody would seriously deny that truth has an intrinsic nature. So when the pragmatist says that there is nothing to be said about truth save that each of us will commend as true those beliefs which he or she finds good to believe, the realist is inclined to interpret this as one more positive theory about the nature of truth: a theory according to which truth is simply the contemporary opinion of a chosen individual or group. Such a theory would, of course, be self-refuting. But the pragmatist does

not have a theory of truth, much less a relativistic one. As a partisan of solidarity, his account of the value of cooperative human inquiry has only an ethical base, not an epistemological or metaphysical one. Not having *any* epistemology, *a fortiori* he does not have a relativistic one. (1991, 23, 24)

Rorty thinks that his pragmatism is a sound guard against the dangers of relativism. It is only when we think that there *is* some mind-independent reality that our theories are supposed to represent accurately that we are in danger of falling into relativism. On such a nonpragmatic view, if the evidence equally supports two incompatible theories (and Rorty thinks this will always be the case), one has to say that as far as evidence is concerned, they are both equally good theories. How does one choose which theory to hold? All that is left are "less rational" means of choosing. So one's choice of theory will be relative to some consideration other than evidential adequacy. If the goal of theorizing is accurate representation, neither of the theories accomplishes the purpose better than the other.

The pragmatist avoids the danger of relativism by denying that accurate representation is the purpose of theory making. Rather, we choose theories based on what is best to believe where what is best is cashed out in terms of the needs and purposes we find in life. Once we give up the impossible ideal of accurate representation, we can see that we do have criteria by which to choose theories, and we do not fall into relativism.

"So the real issue is not between people who think one view as good as another and people who do not. It is between those who think our culture, or purpose, or intuitions cannot be supported except conversationally, and people who still hope for other sorts of support" (1982, 167).

SUMMARY

Richard Rorty's project is to commend pragmatic approaches to philosophy with the end in mind of fostering a liberal society in which human solidarity is the supreme value. While he rejects the correspondence theory of truth, he denies being a relativist about truth or knowledge or goodness. He thinks it is meaningless, and therefore fruitless, to worry about the way the world might be independently of how we think about it. Rorty's work has been very influential at providing some of the theoretical support for postmodernism.

MICHEL FOUCAULT

Foucault was born in Poitiers, France, in 1926. He attended the Ecole Normale Superieure in Paris, a school reserved for the best and the brightest (and, judging from the student body, the most eccentric). He took degrees in philosophy and psychology, and with his *Madness and Civilization* (1961), was awarded a doctorate. From 1969 on, he held the chair of "History of Thinking Systems" at France's most prestigious institution, the College de France. In addition to numerous articles and published interviews, Foucault wrote *The Birth of the Clinic* (1963), *The Order of Things*(1966), *The Archaeology of Knowledge* (1969), *Discipline and Punish* (1975), *Power/Knowledge* (1980), and the three-volume *History of Sexuality* (1976; 1984; 1984). After a sojourn at Berkeley, Foucault died of AIDS in 1984.

"WHAT IS ENLIGHTENMENT?": FOUCAULT'S STARTING POINT

Any attempt to distill the essence of Foucault's thought is rendered difficult by its seeming intractability to ready synthesis. In Isaiah Berlin's deployment of Archilochus's metaphor—"The fox knows many things, but the hedgehog knows one big thing"—Foucault is definitely a fox.[4] He is the artisan of many and various intellectual artifacts and manifestly relishes his own elusiveness: "Do you think that writing would be that much fun for me if I didn't prepare with a feverish hand a labyrinth in which I wandered about?"[5]

Perhaps the best place to pick up the thread that winds through Foucault's labyrinth is an essay he wrote in his final year (1984) that affords the most succinct statement of his critical project. The title "What Is Enlightenment?" recapitulates that of Kant's essay of 1784, which Foucault takes to be pivotal for modern philosophy and in certain ways in continuity with his own project.

One point of affinity for Foucault is that Kant's critical reflections arise out of, and attempt to respond to, his "specific moment" in history (1984a, 38). Foucault likewise takes his agenda from his own present. He scans the contemporary scene for what he perceives to be intolerable features and deploys his critique to combat these ills. He sees his project as "curative."[6]

Foucault finds himself in continuity with Kant at another point. Kant defined enlightenment as a coming of age, an exit from a position of tutelage to authority: *Aude sapere* rang the watchword—dare to know—which meant dare to deploy your own reason, for it is only the immature who take matters on authority. Foucault finds this metaphor of exit or way out aptly descriptive of his own project, which is also concerned with "exiting"—exiting from the modes of being, doing, and thinking in which we find ourselves and which are given to us. For both Kant and Foucault, the exit is fostered through critical reflection upon limits. Kant analyses the bounds that limit true knowledge. By his prescriptions, we exit from immaturity by renouncing any transgression of those limits. Scrupulously abiding by good epistemological methodology is the key for Kant.

But for Foucault it is precisely from limits that he seeks an exit. The very limits that he analyses are all those notions that present themselves as absolute, universal, obligatory, or necessary. These limits attempt to define, confine, govern, and restrict how we are, think, and act. He analyses limits not as things needful and things to be adhered to, but as things fanciful and things to be transgressed. Thus, despite a few points of contact with Kant, Foucault seeks to escape the very thing Kant sought to erect: a governing structure of universal truths and values. The very tool Kant forged for man's rescue, Foucault identified as a chain that binds.

Predictably, Foucault condemns as misguided and positively dangerous any Kant-like "search for formal structures with universal value" (1984a, 46). While Kant moved toward "maturity" in dispensing with religious authority as affording grounds for truth, he did not dispense altogether with the absolute. Instead he simply sought to reground it in epistemology—in a rational and universal method for knowing. But for Foucault this falls short of maturity, which requires that we face up to the utter absence of any absolute. We "must turn away from all projects that claim to be global or radical" (46)—to state for us how things are in some sort of universally valid and profoundly real sense. We "have to give up hope of ever acceding a point of view that could give us access to any complete and definitive knowledge" (47).[7]

For Foucault, truth is not something discovered but something that is fashioned. It never stands in blinding white light, pristine and pure, but bears the birthmarks of its earthly origin and the alloy of a thousand grubby hands, each with its own agonistic agenda. No one simply knows something. We know something *for* something, and as such, knowledge is inextricably tied up with power—or, as Foucault puts it, "[T]ruth isn't outside power. . . . Truth is a thing of this world: it is produced only by virtue of multiple forms of constraint" (1984c, 72–73). Thus knowledge exists only in complex with power, and Foucault refers to this complex as "Power/Knowledge" (the title of one of his writings).

Much of the philosophical enterprise since Kant has sedulously striven to distill truth in its unalloyed form, obsessing over "the question of the conditions in which true knowledge is possible." Foucault dubs this tradition "the analytics of truth" and distances himself from its concerns, opting instead for what he calls "an ontology of the present, an ontology of ourselves" (1988, 95). By this he means a critical inquiry into what it is that constitutes us as subjects. What are the things that define us and delimit us, that tell us what we are or are supposed to be? Since Foucault believes we have no essence, any such conception can only be an imposition, arbitrary and enslaving. I vividly recall encountering this Foucauldian repudiation of being constituted in any way, by the incensed clamor raised by some students when part of one of our surveys asked the student to check "male" or "female." This "arbitrary and tyrannizing imposition" many declared unconscionable. How dare we delimit and circumscribe them by such a classification?

Foucault's work, it may be hazarded, is basically an elaborate pun on the word *subject* (1982, 212). All that renders us a *subject* sub*jects* us. The observation is remarkably satisfying despite its simplicity, for it is being given what we are that Foucault perceives as the intolerable condition we are subjected to and from which we must free ourselves. We must engage in "a permanent creation of ourselves in our autonomy" (1984a, 44). Only we ourselves may determine what we are. We promote "new forms of subjectivity" through refusal of what has been imposed on us. Stating it succinctly, Foucault writes: "Maybe the target nowadays is not to discover what we are, but to refuse what we are" (1982, 216).

Thus Foucault's project focuses on an ontology of ourselves that involves "the historical analysis of the limits that are imposed on us and an experiment with the possibility of going beyond them" (1984a, 50). This work is "carried out by ourselves upon ourselves as free beings" (47). "A patient labor giving form to our impatience for liberty" (50). This articulation of Foucault's project in terms of two aspects—the historical analysis of limits imposed, and the experiment with going beyond those limits—affords a helpful path to follow for exposition.

ARCHAEOLOGY AND GENEALOGY: FOUCAULT'S METHOD

Foucault's aim is to break the hold of the shackles that subject us in order to liberate us fully for the ongoing enterprise of autonomous self-creation. These shackles are the dominating conceptions about what is human, healthy, right, rational, normative, and normal that we are given to realize and reflect. But these governing assertions, which purport to be sound or scientific, are discovered by Foucault to be far from definite and unalterable. What are such truths more than simply a "discursive regime"?

Each society has its regime of truth, its "general politics" of truth: that is, the types of discourse which it accepts and makes function as true; the mechanisms and instances which enable one to distinguish true and false statements; the means by which each is sanctioned; the techniques and procedures accorded value in the acquisition of truth; the status of those who are charged with saying what counts as true (1980, 131).

Foucault's analysis of these systems of ordered procedures for the production and regulation of what a given culture counts as true, he calls the "Archaeology of Knowledge." It is a method that digs up and exposes the conceptual substructure beneath any particular pronouncement, the system of rules and assumptions more fundamental than any assertion. It is at this more fundamental level that Foucault is convinced the battle must be fought. It is not a matter of changing minds about some specific truth-claim. Rather, it is the struggle to change the rules of the game. The battle is for what determines what could even count as true. It is for the status of assertions (1980, 132). As Foucault writes: "The problem is not changing people's consciousness—or what is in their heads," but changing the "régime of the production of truth" (133). The task of the intellectual is not to criticize contents but that of "ascertaining the possibility of constituting a new politics of truth" (133).

Some may recall the not-too-distant controversy over the claim by a Native American tribe that some discovered bones were those of their ancestors, rendering the site a sacred burial ground. The identification was ascertained by them through the performance of a magic ritual. Opposing their claim was the Smithsonian, basing their pronouncements on DNA tests. The Foucauldian will grasp that the real battle is not over the identity of the bones but over the politics of truth—the rules that will dictate whether the pronouncements of the smocked Smithsonian scientist will trump the shamanistic tribal ritual or vice versa. Whose method of truth production will be given status and whose marginalized? Which regime of rules will prevail? "The successes of history," writes Foucault, echoing Nietzsche, "belong to those who are capable of seizing these rules . . . controlling this complex mechanism . . . so as to overcome" (1984c, 86).[8]

The method Foucault deploys to unsettle and dislodge current regimes of truth, his means of neutralizing their power to oppress, is by neutralizing their power to mesmerize. Regimes mesmerize by the impression evoked through the robed priest, celebrated professor, smocked scientist, or number-spouting statistician that their pronouncements are unalterable or that they reveal the divine will, a deciphered essence, the dictate of reason, the data of nature, or the facts of the matter and as such demand our obeisance and conformity.

But Foucault seeks to expose that the origin of what purports to be revealed or rational or scientific or statistical is murky indeed, marvelously motley—and rooted in relationships of subjugation and power. This exposure of the murky, compromising origins Foucault dubs "genealogy." Genealogy sets out to disturb what is considered stable and to fragment what is thought unified. It unearths a play of accident and contingency and the sordid sources of pettiness and passion, malice and fanaticism, which are the sources of everything we call truth. "[H]istorical beginnings are lowly," writes Foucault, "capable of undoing every infatuation" (1984c, 79). Thus the dark ambiguities spawn a disturbing ill-ease and create space for something quite different to be imagined—a counterdiscourse. I remember the subversive effect the observation had on me that in every U.S. presidential race, the taller of the two candidates had been elected. It opened up space for a counterdiscourse to the presumed rationality of the electoral process. Foucault is the master of such subversive historical analysis. But to what end does he deploy his talent?

POLITICAL AND ETHICAL HORIZON: FOUCAULT'S END

As his "What Is Enlightenment?" indicates, Foucault's "historical analysis of the limits that are imposed on us" is in the interest of "an experiment with the possibility of going beyond them" (1984a, 50). Once genealogy has liquefied the seemingly solid structures that operate to limit and confine what we are, do, and think, a new horizon opens for our own autonomous self-creation. Everything is surpassable. Our only compass is the self-styled vision of a life that is pleasurable and satisfying. Foucault's is really an aesthetic vision of existence. We "create ourselves as a work of art" (1984b, 351), deciding wholly ourselves what will be the colors and contours. Though Foucault uses the term *ethic*, it has, as he deploys it, nothing to do with a moral law. Indeed, he thinks any such submission to a moral standard would be "catastrophic" (1985, 12). Putative rules provide only the permanent provocation to transgression, the occasions for resistance and refusal, which is the very lifeblood of the self-shaping subject. "It is through revolt," writes Foucault, "that subjectivity . . . introduces itself into history and gives it the breath of life" (1981, 8).

This experiment in going beyond, of resistance and reshaping, of refusing what we are and inventing what we are, Foucault particularly applies to sexuality. There is no one way sexuality has been understood or practiced. Thus there is no one thing sexuality must always or most naturally be. It is not biologically or eternally fixed, but is socially induced and thus is an arena of power. We must free ourselves from this power by refusing its control and invent ourselves sexually. "I dream," he once said, "of a new age of curiosity."[9] With such an unbounded horizon for self-shaping freedom, it is little wonder that Foucault reaches high for analogies: "[T]he subject of his own freedom, conscious of his own freedom, is at bottom a sort of image correlative to God."[10] Thus Foucault's horizon beckons the subject to assume the place of the absent Absolute.

THE QUESTION OF COHERENCE

Questions as to the coherence of Foucault's project have been raised in several quarters. A critique, it is said, surely presupposes some standard, some basis for judging. Yet by denying all standards, Foucault seems to undermine his own critical efforts. If indeed all discourses are inextricably linked to power and subjugation, so too is Foucault's own discourse about emancipation. What is sauce for the goose is sauce for the gander.

Yet Foucault claims no grand cognitive status for his critiques. He seeks to challenge universal totalizing discourses without himself claiming any privileged standpoint or universality. He makes reference to no neutral or overarching grounding. "For the moment," Foucault writes, "and as far ahead as I can see, my discourse . . . is avoiding the ground on which it could find support" (1972, 205). But this is no concern for him, because he is not trying to establish his own grand theory; rather, he aims simply to subvert those theories presently in place. In this regard his task is far easier. He must simply disrupt conventional convictions, excite a sense of discord and discrepancy within the received orthodoxy. Like the burden of a defense advocate, he must simply raise lingering doubts as to the clarity and finality of the scenario of the prosecution. He need supply no superior definition; he simply subversively throws a plucked chicken over the academy wall.[11]

And as to the charge that his own discourse is also implicated in power, this too he readily concedes. Foucault does not pretend to offer truth apart from power, neither is this his aim. His aim, rather, is to break up concentrations of power, to dismantle hegemonic power. As Foucault puts it, "It's not a matter of emancipating truth from every system of power (which would be a chimera, for truth is already power) but of detaching the power of truth from the forms of hegemony" (1980, 133). And such counterhegemony insurgencies are only engaged at the local, concrete level. They do not strive to achieve sovereignty, only to fragment it. And yet questions persist. While Foucault disavows standards that could be applied across the board, he certainly deploys standards parochially. Even if his insurrections are merely local, they still espouse some value. Something is demonized and something valorized. Foucault does not avoid the question of guiding values altogether; he simply relocates it. What struggle ought I engage in? And why this particular struggle and not another? Could I equally elect to take the opposite side? Why even prefer emancipation to subjugation, freedom to bondage? Foucault's project begins with discerning current dangers. But danger is a value-laden notion. Dangerous for whom? According to whose top-ten-dangers list? Foucault's or Falwell's? Derrida's or Dobson's?[12]

So whence come these values that will guide us in the fray? What dictates what we valorize and what we despise? No word from above, transcendent and high, no revelation from within, an essence deciphered from the deep, may serve us here. For Foucault, our values emerge only in our concrete experience of subjection. This is the engine that drives Foucault's project. Philosophy is the handmaid of experience. Foucault incites us to a voyage in search of freedom with neither compass nor star to navigate by and only bruised experience at the helm. An ill-fated voyage? Surely an illusory hope that "even without the Truth, we may still be made free."[13]

IMPLICATIONS FOR EVANGELISTS

While our universities may not be teeming with doctrinaire devotees of Rorty or Foucault, their ways of thinking are increasingly seeping into the structures of student thought, and their vocabularies noticeably pervade campus discourse. This fact has bearing for those attempting to press the claims of the gospel. Let me mention four attendant challenges and four opportunities.

CHALLENGES

Central to the postmodern structures of thought is the inadmissibility of any universal claim that is applicable and binding on all everywhere. While one is welcome to tell one's own story, it may only be personal or parochial, never complete or cosmic in its sweep. Any such totalizing account is dismissed as totalitarian and taboo or, for those who follow Rorty, naive. But the gospel is a story that is universal in its claims. It calls "all people everywhere to repent" (Acts 17:30). It is the ultimate metanarrative declared to a culture incredulous of metanarratives. Thus the universal claims of Christianity typically register as irritating atavisms of enlightenment hubris. And so the gospel is often rejected simply because it claims to be true, not because it has been examined and found to be false.

A second challenge encountered where a postmodern mind-set reigns is the increasing acclimatization to a lack of grounding. There is less and less nostalgia for absent absolutes. A generation ago, there were many who came to the conclusion that there are no transcendent truths or values. Yet this culminating conviction was for them traumatic. But yesterday's conclusions are today's starting points. The once terror-stricken tones have become calm and even carefree: "There are no absolutes, and I'll have my eggs over easy." In consequence, apologists and preachers who are looking for restlessness as a ready beachhead for the gospel will find such shores steadily eroding. Postmoderns seem to have a striking capacity to endure groundlessness and incoherence quite calmly—to live as ironists with equanimity.

A further challenge for the evangelist is that where postmodern assumptions predominate, it cannot be taken for granted that life is conceived of in moral categories. The ironist may have deep moral commitments, but these are self-chosen, and she answers to no one for them but herself. The self is the only creator recognized. There is no thought of a transcendent Creator to whom one must give an account. Thus the project of life is not as much a moral as it is an aesthetic enterprise. It is, as Rorty says, "self creation" (1989, 84). And where it is believed that we "create ourselves as a work of art" (Foucault 1984b, 351), any challenge to a person's worldview or lifestyle in the name of the gospel will be heard as akin to expressing disdain for the artist's creative work and will be dismissed as evincing a narrow, cramped sensibility. Preaching the law is simply propounding prejudice. It is not, of course, that resistance to the gospel is unique to a postmodern sensibility. Rather, Foucauldian and Rortian rhetoric helps to reinforce and rationalize our instinctive resistance to the gospel's challenge to our pretended autonomy. It is rhetoric convenient to rebellion.

The fourth challenge encountered, especially where Foucault is read and absorbed, relates to the central thesis that truth-claims are always implicated in power. Accordingly, any effort to persuade anyone to embrace the view you espouse is viewed as a sort of intellectual colonization, a pernicious imperialism of the mind that attempts to bring someone under the thrall of your way of seeing. Of course, gospel-bearing evangelicals or proselytizing Christians (as they are dubbed) are inveterate offenders to this sensibility, and all new arrivals on campus are duly warned of their presence and agenda.

These are some of the challenges to the progress of the gospel as a result of the influence of thinkers such as Rorty and Foucault. But the increasing pervasiveness of postmodern structures of thought also affords the evangelist new opportunities.

OPPORTUNITIES

Under the regime of modernism, with its typically strident secularism, Christianity was badly bullied. The postmodern critique, however, has cut the modernist bully down to size, leaving him a lot less menacing. The breathing space is noticeable. Furthermore, the postmodern ambition to break the modernist hegemony by including marginalized and excluded voices has even at times resulted in a measured sponsorship of a Christian voice. We have found

Jon Hinkson and Greg Ganssle

ourselves occasionally (if only reluctantly) invited to the table and allowed to articulate our story or final vocabulary. While this is by no means a home-coming, it is still, in a limited sense, a return from exile and to be acknowledged as a beneficial turn of providence.

A second opportunity is that some of the postmodern analysis accords well with the biblical doctrine that the effects of our rebellion touch even our reasoning processes. While the modernist imagines herself a perfectly fit arbiter and neutral judge of any gospel claim put forward, it is a truism for postmodernism that we know or judge nothing neutrally. A postmodern thinker will not be surprised at the biblical teaching that her determination to preserve her rebellious autonomy skews her spiritual judgment and incites her to deploy her rationality evasively in the face of God's sovereign claim. I have often said to students, "Let me tell you why, if the biblical story is true, you will hear it threateningly, and why you ought to apply a hermeneutic of suspicion to that very reaction." In this way a key biblical truth is related to their familiar grid, and this point of contact helps the gospel be heard more fruitfully.

Another feature of a Foucauldian frame of reference that can afford the evangelist opportunity is the fact that its central theme is the emancipation of the subject. This dovetails nicely with a major axis of the gospel: being set free. When a Foucauldian is holding forth on (what is for her) the heart of the matter, a Christian need not change the subject to bring up the heart of the gospel.[14] There is agreement on the need to be set free. The disagreement is about the nature of the bondage and what it takes to be set free.

A final opportunity stems from the fundamental desire for coherence and community. For all of the postmodern celebration of fragmentation, there will inevitably remain in any such worldview a deep dissonance with what is surely a basic human drive for coherence. The biblical account that the gospel sets forth is a summons that, among other things, bids rebels to come into coherence. We should keep playing this card.

Also, for all of the postmodern talk about community, postmodernism supplies none of the resources to attain it. The aesthetic self-fashioning life it champions is a self-centered enterprise and is ultimately isolating. Perpetual experimentation through the transgression of limits will never forge community. Only a willing selflessness that embraces the moral life—the walking by a common rule—can suffice. And this truth the church must render, not only audibly but visibly. So let us hold out a compelling vision of coherence and community, and demonstrate in the very reality of our experience that it is only in knowing the truth that you are, in fact, set free.

References

Berlin, Isaiah. 1978. *Russian Thinkers*. New York: Viking Press.

Bernstein, Richard. 1994. "Foucault's Critique as Philosophical Ethos." In *Critique and Power: Recasting the Foucault/Habermas Debate*. Ed. Michael Kelly. Cambridge: MIT Press.

Fink-Eitel, Hinrich. 1992. *Foucault: An Introduction*. Philadelphia: Penbridge.

Foucault, Michel. 1972. *Archaeology of Knowledge*. Trans. A. M. Sheridan Smith. New York: Pantheon.

————. 1980. "Truth and Power." In *Power/Knowledge: Selected Interviews and Other Writings 1972–1977*. Ed. C. Gordon, 109–33. New York: Pantheon.

————. 1981. "Is it Useless to Revolt?" *Philosophy and Social Criticism* 8 (Spring): 1–9.

————. 1982. "The Subject and Power." In *Michel Foucault: Beyond Structuralism and Hermeneutics*. Ed. Hubert L. Dreyfus, 208–26. Chicago: University of Chicago Press.

————. 1984a. "What Is Enlightenment?" In *The Foucault Reader*. Ed. Paul Rabinow, 32–50. New York: Pantheon.

————. 1984b. "On the Genealogy of Ethics: An Overview of Work in Progress." In *The Foucault Reader*, 340–72.

————. 1984c. "Nietzsche, Genealogy, History." In *The Foucault Reader*, 76–100.

————. 1985. "Final Interview: Michel Foucault." In *Raritan* 5 (Summer): 1–13.

————. 1988. *Politics, Philosophy, Culture: Interviews and Other Writings of Michel Foucault 1977–1984*. Ed. Lawrence D. Kritzman. New York: Routledge.

Gutting, Gary. 1989. *Michel Foucault's Archeology of Scientific Reason*. Cambridge: Cambridge University Press.

————, ed. 1994. *Cambridge Companion to Foucault*. Cambridge: Cambridge University Press.

Quine, Willard Van Orman. 1961 [1953]. "Two Dogmas of Empiricism." In *From a Logical Point of View*, 2d ed., 20–46. Cambridge: Harvard University Press.

Rorty, Richard. 1979. *Philosophy and the Mirror of Nature*. Princeton: Princeton University Press.

————. 1982. *Consequences of Pragmatism*. Minneapolis: University of Minnesota Press.

————. 1989. *Contingency, Irony, and Solidarity*. Cambridge: Cambridge University Press.

————. 1991. *Objectivity, Relativism, and Truth*. Cambridge: Cambridge University Press.

JON HINKSON AND GREG GANSSLE

_____. 1998a. *Achieving Our Country: Leftist Thought in Twentieth-Century America*. Cambridge: Harvard University Press.

_____. 1998b. *Truth and Progress*. New York: Cambridge University Press.

Sellars, Wilfrid. 1963. "Empiricism and the Philosophy of Mind." In *Science, Perception and Reality*, 127–96. London: Routledge and Kegan Paul.

PART THREE

Critical Topics

CHAPTER 5

WHY SHOULD ANYONE BELIEVE ANYTHING AT ALL?

James W. Sire

L et's begin with the title of this essay: "Why Should Anyone Believe Anything at All?" I have given a talk under this title over two hundred times, after first giving it three times under a different title. Reflecting on the title will set the stage for a major point of the present essay: that traditional apologetics still has a role in the postmodern university, but that often one can't begin where traditional apologetics begins.

THE TITLE

Over the past twenty years as I have lectured on campuses in North America and Europe, I have discovered that before my talks are given, there is an important prepresentation preface—the selection of the title. This is especially important where the speaker is not well known by the intended audience. Since this is very much the case with me, titles have loomed large in my lecture preparation. It's vital that the title be attractive.

Of course, the topic is important. Engineering students—even if they come to the lecture—will not stay long if the topic is, say, the mating habits of the tsetse fly, the sprung-rhythm prosody of Hopkins's lesser-known poems, or even—to put the matter religiously—the architectonic structure of Augustine's *Confessions* or the concept of the Logos in the Gospel of John. Topic and title are both important.

Among the titles I have found effective in attracting student interest are "Will the Real God—If Any—Please Stand Up?" (on religious pluralism), "Tolerance, Relativism and a Just Society" (relevant in an era of multiculturalism), "Evolution and Ethics" (developed for Eastern Europe interest, where in both evolution and ethics has been high), and "The University in Two Minds: A Postmodern Condition" (for faculty and graduate students). I have used these titles over and over with some success in acquiring an audience. I have had, for example, the privilege of giving "The University in Two Minds: A Postmodern Condition" to the entire faculty of Oglethorpe University in Atlanta, with good response afterward.

One topic close to the heart of postmodernism and immediately relevant to university students is religious relativism. Here I have given the same talk under two different titles. Normally I recommend to the Christian students sponsoring the lecture the title "I'm Okay. You're Okay. And That's Okay. Okay?" Its tone is therapeutic and postmodern and effective. But students at the University of Michigan think of themselves as somewhat above and beyond ordinary students, and, by the way, not fully postmodern. So they chose instead the title I use with graduate students and faculty: "Religion and Absolute Truth." Same talk, same basic structure, different tone to the title.

But there is a special reason for focusing on the title "Why Should Anyone Believe Anything at All?" The title itself is peculiarly relevant in a postmodern world. I did not realize this until years after the title was first used. Here's the story.

In 1982 David Suryk, InterVarsity Christian Fellowship campus staff member at Illinois State University, asked me to make an evangelistic presentation. I chose the title "Is Christianity Rational?" Attendance was good, questions lively, and afterward we sat for over an hour continuing the dialog.

Six months later I was asked to give a similar lecture at the University of Rochester (New York), so I used the same title. This time after the formal presentation, a student asked if he could read something. He had come prepared with five written reasons why Christianity is not rational. His brief paper provided a marvelous counterpoint to the lecture, and the question and answer period extended for almost two hours.

Three months later still, I gave the same lecture, same title, at Harvard University. Again, good response. But more important to my own campus lecture ministry was what the Harvard Christians did to promote the lecture. They plastered the campus with posters listing five or six questions that I would address. One of them leapt from the poster. I knew it was especially apt: "Why should anyone believe anything at all?" The Harvard students had seen what I had not: the real issue is not whether Christianity is rational, but whether it is worthy of belief—more poignantly, whether anything is worthy of belief.

What is more amazing still is that the lecture was already structured to answer this fundamental question. I had, from the first presentation over a year earlier, started with that basic issue. Now I had been given a title, one that I have used for a book deriving from the lecture, and that has proven itself apt, if not in every one of the two hundred plus presentations, at least in enough for me to be deeply thankful to those Harvard Christians of 1983.

What did the Harvard students see that I had not? Simply this: the rationality or irrationality of Christianity is not important if rationality itself is not a useful test for belief. And that is the postmodern problem. Traditional Christian apologetics has assumed that rationality is, if not the most important aspect making Christianity worthy of belief, at least vital to its defense. "Always be prepared to give an answer to everyone who asks you to give the reason for the hope that you have," the apostle Peter wrote (1 Peter 3:15). Does this not imply that Christian faith is rational and rationality is important? I think so. And so has much of our culture until the past decade or so. If Christianity is not rational, then it is not worthy of belief. So ran the premise. But no longer.

If culture has shifted, if so-called proofs—for the existence of God, the deity of Christ, the resurrection of Jesus—are no longer relevant, if belief is to be justified on other than the grounds of truth, what can an apologist/evangelist do? One response is, of course, to capitulate. Ignore rational arguments; go for emotional music, drama, clever rhetoric, psychological or sociological manipulation. Some Christians have done this, not just those from Christian subcultures where this has long been the norm, but from those that were previously traditional in their apologetic approach. There is value in nonrational (not irrational; that's a different matter) presentations of the gospel.

It is, however, dangerous to ignore the mind. I am reminded of a comment by my colleague, Tom Trevethan, who once told students, "The heart will not long rejoice in what the mind knows is not true." So a second approach is to free the postmodern student from his or her captivity to the culture, to show them that truth does matter, and that rationality is relevant. The approach taken in "Why Should Anyone Believe Anything at All?" seems to do exactly that.

The question itself burrows beneath the barriers set up by postmodern assumptions. When students see this question posted all over campus, when they meet Christians who hand them a blank sheet and ask them to answer the question, they are surprised into thinking. The fact is that postmodern students can think—and do, even if unwittingly. Think about it! Of course, some ignore the question, others find it funny or odd. But many are not just puzzled but intrigued. The question strikes deep in their psyches.

One student at a university in Tennessee, for example, approached the table where Christians were taking a survey using this lone question. He saw the question in huge letters above the table. "Oh, no," he said, "There's that question again. I've seen it all over campus. It makes my head hurt." And he walked away. A few minutes later he returned. A student handed him a sheet and asked him to write what he thought about the question. He puzzled a while, then handed back the sheet. "I can't do it," he said. "I can't do it." Surprised by thought, he couldn't think. But his emotional reaction shows how profoundly his thought had been stimulated.

Most students do not show such obvious frustration. They do show their interest. At this university and at most others, when students use this question on posters and do surveys, the audience for the lecture is usually at least twice the size of the sponsoring organization. Sometimes the attendance is even higher.

My first point, therefore, is this: Students in this postmodern world at all the postmodern universities can still think. We only need to find how to get them started. Then, of course, we need to keep them with us as the gospel message is proclaimed.

THE LECTURE

I have been calling the presentation I am describing a lecture. It is really a lecture/discussion, not quite a happening, as they used to call spontaneous events in the 1960s, but not a formal lecture either.

I start by briefly discussing the nature and necessity of belief. In the back of my mind is the idea—unstated in the lecture—that *to believe is to trust that one knows the truth.* The presentation is designed to demonstrate this without stating it.

I do, however, state that *everyone's knowledge rests on belief.* This is true in every human area: in ordinary life (how can you be sure you are awake and not dreaming?); in science (how can you be sure that the universe is orderly, that your vision when you read the instruments is accurate, that your mind is functioning properly?); in philosophy (how can you be sure that the law of noncontradiction actually applies to reality?); in religion (how do you know whether there is a God?). Strictly speaking, everyone's knowledge rests on pretheoretical commitments that cannot be proven, though it can be shown that some are more likely than others. The question is, therefore, what justifies those beliefs we do have? Should we have them?

JAMES W. SIRE

Then to illustrate the panoramic sweep of the issues that underlie an answer to the question why should we have them, I put a diagram on a chalkboard or overhead (see diagram).

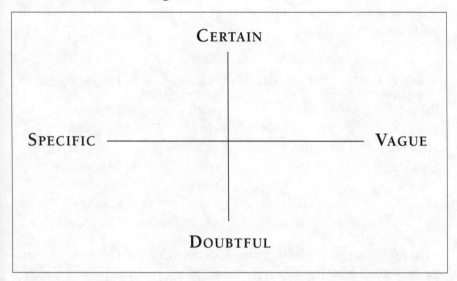

Some of our beliefs are psychologically quite certain; some are less so; some are doubtful indeed. Some of our beliefs (religious ones in particular) are specific and detailed: witness the lists of beliefs that are taught in the various catechisms and the strict religious traditions. Some are very vague (say, the notion that God is some sort of force). I explain what it is like to be in each of the quadrants: specific and certain; specific and doubtful; vague and certain; vague and doubtful. Then I further explain that we often move from one to the other. We begin, for example, believing what we are taught about God (or not God), and then after a few months at the university, we wonder about these beliefs and eventually abandon them for doubt or substitute other beliefs in their place.

Then I ask three questions. The first two are thought questions:

1. Where are you on the chart?
2. Why are you where you are?

After a short pause for them to reflect (think!), I ask:

3. Why *do* people believe?

Their answers are then placed on the chalkboard (in four columns) as they are given. The columns are not labeled until students are asked where these "reasons" are studied in the university. What emerges quite easily from the students, then, are the categories: sociological, psychological, religious, philosophical.

(These categories show how basic belief is, how many facets need to be explored before even its origins are understood.) Each column will have several entries, others will be added in the discussion to follow.

The table shows the essential nature of what will have been received from student answers.

SOCIOLOGICAL	PSYCHOLOGICAL	RELIGIOUS	PHILOSOPHICAL
PARENTS	COMFORT	SCRIPTURE	CONSISTENCY
FRIENDS	PEACE OF MIND	PASTOR	COHERENCE
SOCIETY	MEANING	PRIEST	COMPLETENESS
CULTURE	PURPOSE	GURU	(BEST EXPLANATION
	HOPE	CHANNELER	OF ALL THE
	IDENTITY	CHURCH	EVIDENCE)

The next step is dialogic. Beginning with the sociological column, I ask students how good or strong these reasons are: "If, say, your parents were the only reason you had for believing what you do, would that be a good, strong reason or a weak one or no reason at all?" No student—well, almost none—will say parents are a good reason. So I ask why. The answers fall into two types: one ("It's not *my* belief") is psychological, so I add that to the psychology column. The other reason is more profound and helpful ("My parents might be wrong"), so I add right or true to the philosophy column. Neither of these is often suggested by students on their own, so imbued they are with a therapeutic or postmodern mind-set.

As the discussion proceeds through the other sociological reasons, it becomes clear to the students that none of the reasons is strong. Friends, society, even whole cultures could be significantly wrong about basic beliefs. So I point out that sociological factors—though they inevitably produce our original beliefs—are actually causes, a cause being something that makes you what you are, something that has had nothing to do with your own choice or consideration. In an era of I'm okay/you're okay, this realization does not go down well. Students want to be their own arbiters of belief.

As we proceed to examine each item in each column—sociological, psychological, religious—it becomes clear to the students that they themselves are using the category of truth to evaluate the strength of the reasons that are on the chalkboard. If a reason—say, "comfort"—is indeed a reason (which it is), is it a strong one? Only if giving comfort points to truth, and it does not always do that. Some things give comfort in the short run (like the drug thalidomide) and tragedy in the long run. A belief could give comfort until you died, but what then?

Scripture is a reason, but which Scripture—the Bible, the Koran, the Upanishads? They contradict each other. Contradictions can't be true. Eventually, the discussion is designed to produce in students themselves the recognition that they actually operate their lives based on whether they think something is true or not. A holy book, a pastor or guru, a religious tradition is only worth trusting if it points to the truth. So we end by briefly investigating tests for truth: consistency (logic), coherence, completeness (best explanation of all the evidence—public and private). The dialog is now on the ground trod by traditional apologetics.

Often only a very few philosophic reasons will have been suggested by students. The list of psychological and social reasons for belief will be long; the philosophical list will usually be quite short (though here it depends on who is attending—philosophy students, engineers, psychology or arts majors).

In any case, at this point I hand out a bibliography (given at the end of this chapter) and offer five types of reasons why Christianity should be considered true. The lecture and this list are not so much an apologetic as a prologue to apologetics. I do not develop the reasons but open the session for questions after I have briefly explained each one:

1. Jesus himself is the best reason for believing in the truth of the Christian religion (a rationally strong, personally compelling reason).
2. The Gospels give a reliable account of what Jesus did and, especially, said about us and himself (rationally compelling).
3. The Christian worldview is consistent and coherent. It explains better than any alternative the vast array of phenomena presented to human beings (rationally strong, personally compelling).
4. Christians testify to their changed lives (philosophically weak but personally compelling).
5. The history of the church points to the attractiveness of Jesus' agenda, the kingdom of God; witness the St. Luke hospitals around the world (an ambiguous but ultimately positive reason).

I close the presentation with an encouragement to seek the truth: to read the Gospels, to meet with their Christian friends to study the Gospels with them, and generally to stick around those who know Jesus personally.

In the question and answer period I am open to questions of any kind, hoping that more specifics of the gospel will be able to be presented. This often happens.

THE POSTMODERN CONNECTION

The appeal of this lecture/discussion to today's students is due in part, perhaps, to the connections it makes with postmodern students in a postmodern culture. First, it does not assume that the best reason to believe is rationality. Rather it allows students to discover the value of rationality for themselves. Second, it stimulates self-reflection that leads to the recognition that it is, after all, the truth that one should believe. Third, it suggests how truth about spiritual matters can be acquired. Fourth, it provides a bridge from the personal and individual to the objective and communal. Fifth, it opens the door for the Bible to be heard as a legitimate source of truth. Sixth, it focuses attention on the reason above all other reasons for believing in the Christian faith: a personal encounter with Jesus Christ.

As time slips by and our university culture shifts and continues to lose its center, the approach of this lecture may no longer be effective. No matter. Even Harvard students can't be right forever. But Jesus can. He addresses every culture. May he direct us to those ways that help us make his presence known however and wherever our cultures—all of them—move!

Bibliography

There are five basic reasons—or families of reasons—why anyone should believe Christianity is true. This bibliography provides a guide for anyone wishing to investigate these reasons. All five reasons are presented in James W. Sire, *Why Should Anyone Believe Anything at All?* (Downers Grove: InterVarsity Press, 1994).

The Character of Jesus Christ as Presented in the Gospels

The Gospels of Matthew, Mark, Luke, and John in the Bible. See especially a modern translation.

Kreeft, Peter. 1982. *Between Heaven and Hell.* Downers Grove, Ill.: InterVarsity Press.

Stott, John. 1971. *Basic Christianity,* 2d ed. Downers Grove, Ill.: InterVarsity Press.

JAMES W. SIRE

The Historical Reliability of the Gospels

Barnett, Paul. 1986. *Is the New Testament Reliable?* Downers Grove, Ill.: Inter-
    Varsity Press.
Blomberg, Craig. 1987. *The Historical Reliability of the Gospels.* Downers Grove,
    Ill.: InterVarsity Press.
Dunn, James D. G. 1986. *The Evidence for Jesus.* Philadelphia: Westminster.
Wenham, John. 1984. *Christ and the Bible,* 2d ed. Grand Rapids: Baker.
Wilkins, Michael J., and J. P. Moreland, eds. 1995. *Jesus Under Fire.* Grand
    Rapids: Zondervan.

The Internal Consistency and Coherence of the Christian Worldview

*(And Its Power to Explain What We Perceive as Human Beings in Our
Surrounding Environment, the Wonders of the Cosmos, the Greatness
and Wretchedness of Human Beings, the Pervasive Quality of Love,
the Notion of Good and Evil, the Possibility of Knowledge)*

Chesterton, G. K. 1959. *Orthodoxy.* Garden City: Image.
Lewis, C. S. 1958. *Mere Christianity.* New York: Macmillan.
Moreland, J. P. 1987. *Scaling the Secular City.* Grand Rapids: Baker.
Neill, Stephen. 1984. *Christian Faith and Other Faiths.* Downers Grove, Ill.:
    InterVarsity Press.
Sire, James W. 1997. *The Universe Next Door,* 3d ed. Downers Grove, Ill.: Inter-
    Varsity Press.
Wenham, John. 1985. *The Enigma of Evil.* Grand Rapids: Zondervan.

The Testimony of Its Adherents

Clark, Kelly James, ed. 1993. *Philosophers Who Believe.* Downers Grove, Ill.:
    InterVarsity Press.
Colson, Charles. 1976. *Born Again.* Old Tappan, N.J.: Chosen Books.
Lewis, C. S. 1966. *Surprised by Joy.* New York: Harcourt-Brace.
Goricheva, Tatiana. 1987. *Talking about God Is Dangerous.* New York: Cross-
    road.
Morris, Thomas V., ed. 1994. *God and the Philosophers.* New York: Oxford
    University Press.

The Witness of the Church through the Ages

Latourette, Kenneth Scott. 1970. *A History of the Expansion of Christianity.*
    Grand Rapids: Zondervan.
Shelley, Bruce. 1982. *Church History in Plain Language.* Waco: Word.

CHAPTER 6

TWO WAYS TO LIVE—AND BIBLICAL THEOLOGY

Phillip D. Jensen and Tony Payne

It is held to be true in our beloved land of Oz that any trend, movement, fashion, or gadget that grips the public imagination in the United States will turn up in Australia within the following five or ten years. Thanks to the great cultural and economic current that seems to flow mostly in one direction across the Pacific, we dutifully collect the flotsam and jetsam of American culture as it washes up on our shore, in the process gaining much that is good and much that is not.

Elsewhere in this collection, it has been argued that America is increasingly in the grip of what is termed postmodernism. This is seen in a growing lack of shared theistic assumptions in society, a decline in biblical literacy, an erosion of common cultural memories, an absence of common concepts of morality, and an increasing pessimism about whether truth and knowledge are ever attainable, even in principle.

Will Australia soon pick up and mirror this latest American fashion? For once, the answer is no. For here is one of the areas (apart from cricket and rugby) in which Australia is already well in advance of America. We have been living with this kind of godlessness and paganism for decades. To some extent we have always been a more pagan nation than the United States. America's founding mythology involves the fight for Christian religious freedom and a principled revolution against a nation that we Australians still haven't gotten rid of. American currency is stamped with "In God We Trust." Australia's founding mythology involves convicts in a penal colony. Our historical heroes are gold-diggers and outlaws. Our national song ("Waltzing Matilda") is about a hobo who steels a sheep, is cornered by the law, and commits suicide. Our official national anthem ("Advance Australia Fair") is a

PHILLIP D. JENSEN AND TONY PAYNE

Tower-of-Babel-style humanist hymn to making a name for ourselves in the name of progress.

ADVANCED AUSTRALIA

When it comes to paganism, Australia is a world leader. In the part of Sydney where we minister, only 1.7 percent of the population of 300,000 go to a Protestant church of any description (and that includes every Protestant church from the most liberal to the most Pentecostal). The particular suburb in which our church is located is the homosexual center of Sydney, and Sydney is one of the homosexual capitals of the world. The annual Gay and Lesbian Mardi Gras parade is promoted and endorsed as the leading cultural event of the year, with hundreds of thousands of people coming to witness it.

In Sydney, we are seeking to evangelize a biblically illiterate people. We generally have to explain to university students what the big numbers and the little numbers mean in the Bible. We are an unchurched, multicultural, apathetic, spiritually indifferent, relativist, and fundamentally hedonistic society. In comparison to this, many of our American brethren don't know what paganism (or postmodernism) is.

As we have sought to preach the gospel in this environment, two particular challenges have confronted us. The first is the challenge to Christians themselves, who swim every day in this postmodern sea and who inevitably come to church a little waterlogged. Many facets of postmodernity are seeping into Christianity, leaving us with a trend toward emptiness, relativism, and confusion. And when Christians become confused about the gospel itself, they become prey for alternative gospels and alternative Christs. The first challenge, then, is to articulate the gospel with absolute clarity and simplicity for our own people, so that they can understand and embrace it in a hostile environment. The second challenge, of course, is to take that same message to the world. How do we explain the gospel of Jesus Christ to a biblically illiterate community?

Before we describe how we met these challenges in one particular way, there is something else distinctive about Sydney to which we should draw attention—and that is its biblical theology.

By biblical theology we do not mean "theology that is biblical" (which of course all theology should be), but a particular approach to theology that is different from systematic theology. If we wanted to analyze and summarize the message of, say, *War and Peace*, there are (at least) two ways we could proceed. At one level, we could construct a kind of index, cataloguing Tolstoy's attitude to a range of important subjects by going through the book, picking out passages relevant to war or peace or monarchy, and synthesizing the material into a logical and coherent summary of Tolstoy's views. Alternatively, we could analyze the novel in terms of its story line—how the main themes are introduced and gradually developed, how Tolstoy shapes the material, and how the whole story unfolds to yield a total effect. Systematic theology is the "index" method of Bible study; biblical theology is a method that traces the story through, showing how God's plans and promises find their fulfillment in Christ. For example, it shows how the whole idea of God's rule and kingdom is introduced right from the beginning of the Bible and develops through Israel and her kings to the Messiah figure, and how it finds its fulfillment in Jesus.

Both branches of theology—the systematic and the biblical—are important and complementary. What is distinctive about Sydney is that we have always been strong in biblical theology, for various historical reasons.[1] We aren't unique in it, of course. You can find biblical theology in some North American writings (such as Edmund Clowney's fine book *Preaching in Biblical Theology*). All the same, it is fair to say that in most parts of the world (including the United States), biblical theology is very lightly done. It is simply not part of the program of theological study or enquiry. The seminary system, with its often rigid demarcation between the Old Testament department and the New Testament department, doesn't encourage it. As a result, not much time is spent tracing the important themes all the way through the Scriptures and seeing how the Bible is a unity leading to, and culminating in, Christ and the gospel.

And so, in an environment marked by rampant paganism and biblical illiteracy, and with a love for biblical theology, we came up with *Two Ways to Live*.

TWO WAYS TO LIVE

Two Ways to Live is a simple summary or outline of the gospel. It has six basic points, which can be presented in various levels of detail, in different styles, and with drawings if that is appropriate. The basic "skeleton" of *Two Ways to Live* is as follows:

1.   God is the loving ruler of the world [draw crown]. He made the world [draw world]. He made us rulers of the world under him [draw man].

You are worthy, our Lord and God, to receive glory and honor and power, for you created all things, and by your will they were created and have their being. (Revelation 4:11)

But is that the way it is now?

2. We all reject the ruler—God— [draw crown and cross it out] by trying to run life our own way without him [draw rebel with own crown]. But we fail to rule ourselves or society or the world [draw world under God].

There is no one righteous, not even one; there is no one who understands, no one who seeks God. All have turned away. (Romans 3:10–12)

What will God do about this rebellion?

3. God won't let us rebel forever [draw crown]. God's punishment for rebellion is death and judgment [draw judged rebel].

Man is destined to die once, and after that to face judgment. (Hebrews 9:27)

God's justice sounds hard. But . . .

4. Because of his love, God sent his son into the world: the man Jesus Christ [draw crown, world, and letter J]. Jesus always lived under God's rule [begin to draw Jesus under God]. Yet by dying in our place, he took our punishment and brought forgiveness [draw Jesus' outstretched arms].

Christ died for sins once for all, the righteous for the unrighteous, to bring you to God. (1 Peter 3:18)

But that's not all . . .

5. God raised Jesus to life again as the ruler of the world [draw crown, world, J]. Jesus has conquered death, now gives new life, and will return to judge.

In his great mercy he has given us new birth into a living hope through the resurrection of Jesus Christ from the dead. (1 Peter 1:3)

Well, where does that leave us?

6. The two ways to live:

OUR WAY: [draw rebel]

Reject the ruler—God
Try to run life our own way

GOD'S NEW WAY: [draw Christian]

Submit to Jesus as our ruler
Rely on Jesus' death and resurrection

RESULT:

Condemned by God
Facing death and judgment

RESULT:

Forgiven by God
Given eternal life

Whoever believes in the Son has eternal life, but whoever rejects the Son will not see life, for God's wrath remains on him. (John 3:36)

Which of these represents the way you want to live?

What Must I Do?

Pray   for God to change me so that I may:
Submit   to Jesus as my ruler
Rely   on Jesus for forgiveness for eternal life

When the whole presentation has been drawn out it looks like this:

1.	2.	3.
Revelation 4:11	Romans 3:10-12	Hebrews 9:27
4.	5.	6.
1 Peter 3:18	1 Peter 1:3	John 3:36

These six basic points are in one sense six key doctrines logically linked together: creation, sin, judgment, atonement, resurrection, and the response of repentance and faith. In this sense, *Two Ways to Live* has something of systematic theology about it.

However, in the way that the outline fits together it is also a simple summary of the whole story of the Bible. It traces the history of our planet in the purposes of God, with the focus being on the death of Jesus for sins and his resurrection and ascension as ruling Messiah, which is the consistent focus of what the New Testament calls gospel. The presentation starts with the creation of the world, moves on to humanity's rebellion and the judgment that follows, then skips forward to the historical events of Jesus: his being sent into the world by the Father, his atoning death, powerful resurrection, current rule, and future return to judge. The response called for by the gospel (repentance and faith) comes in the context of this cosmic narrative—that Jesus now rules and will return, and that the choice before us is to turn back and submit to him or else to continue in rebellion and face eternal judgment.

As part of this biblical theology approach, the rule or kingship theme is the thread that runs through the outline. God is the ruler who creates man to rule the world under his authority. Man rebels and is judged, and it is only when the Last Adam, who does perfectly submit to God's rule, comes, that human rule is restored and fulfilled (in the person of the God-man, Jesus Christ).

As an outline of the gospel, *Two Ways to Live* has two basic functions: it allows Christians to know the gospel and to share the gospel. Let's deal with these in reverse order.

SHARING THE GOSPEL

We should point out first of all that in using *Two Ways to Live* to share the gospel, we would never encourage people simply to recite the outline as it appears above in its skeletal form. The outline is a framework that Christians learn carefully by rote and then flesh out and adapt—both to their own style of speech and to the situation they find themselves in. The six points are six pegs on which to hang a gospel conversation; they might not even be dealt with in order. A conversation might begin with some problem in the world, at which point the Christian says, "Well I still think the underlying cause of all our problems is humanity's basic rejection of God" (point two in the outline). When this provokes some discussion or debate, the Christian can go back, and starting with point one, explain what he or she means, and proceed to what God has done in Christ about this problem.

This flexibility also extends to the drawings. You can scribble them on the back of an envelope as you talk to someone, or present them on a blackboard to a Scripture class, or not use them at all if you judge it inappropriate. Whether you use them or not, we have found that the drawings are a tremendous aid to the Christian in learning and remembering the basic material.

As a tool for sharing the gospel in our pagan, postmodern world, *Two Ways to Live* has some obvious advantages. Very little is assumed, even about such a basic concept as God. When we use the word *God* in Australia, it could mean anything (and usually does). We need to define just which "God" we're talking about—that is, the God of the Bible who created all things. Likewise with "sin." When we use the word *sin*, most Australians think that we are speaking about sex. We have used a word like *rebellion*, which captures the heart of what sin is in a clear way.

The outline fills in the whole story to an audience who now increasingly have no knowledge of that story. It explains why Christ died by explaining that we are under rightful judgment for rebelling against our loving Creator.

Moreover, telling the story in this way naturally leads to a challenge to respond. If evangelism is regarded as a slightly frightening task by many Christians, the actual challenge to someone to become a Christian is the most scary part of all. With *Two Ways to Live*, the story only has one ending, and it is the only ending that it can possibly have—namely, that if all this is true, a choice is required from each of us as to how we are going to live (in unbelief, rebellion, and death or in faith, submission, and life).

KNOWING THE GOSPEL

Perhaps an even more basic function of *Two Ways to Live* is its role as a catechism for Christians. As we have already suggested, modern Christians are under great pressure from our relativistic, postmodern society. It is a pressure not simply to cease believing in Christ, but to cease believing that it matters. "Be a Christian. That's nice," says society. "Don't be doctrinaire about it or get all dogmatic on me. But if your faith helps you to deal with life, then I'm really glad for you."

In the face of this, modern Christians are under great pressure to adopt a watered-down Christianity, empty of content; to focus on personal experience and "telling my own story." In this context, it is crucial that we teach Christian people the basics with renewed clarity and vigor. In one sense, of course, this is not a new problem. The New Testament is replete with examples of apostolic warnings to stick with the gospel "tradition" as it was handed down, to learn

PHILLIP D. JENSEN AND TONY PAYNE

it and defend and contend for it and continue in it in the face of false alternatives (see 1 Cor. 15:1–8; Col. 2:6–8; 2 Tim. 3:14–4:5, to name just three).

Two Ways to Live is a simple and effective way to teach Christians the fundamentals of the gospel. It is invaluable in giving a congregation or fellowship an agreed upon theological framework for life and ministry together. We all have these six fundamental gospel categories in our heads; there is no confusion about what the gospel is or about how it relates to our lives. Nor is there any doubt as to the message we are bringing to the world around us.

THE TRAINING METHODOLOGY

In order to teach Christians the *Two Ways to Live* outline and how to use it in evangelism, we have a developed a seven-week training course.[2] During the course, trainees learn the statements, drawings, and verses by rote before working out how to express the material in their own words and style. However, there is much more to the training course than this, because we are imparting not simply a block of information, but a skill and a lifestyle. As well as learning the actual content of the outline, trainees also:

learn the importance of prayer in evangelism (by doing it)
look at the biblical principles of sharing the gospel
learn how to answer common questions
gain some practical experience in sharing the gospel

This last aspect is particularly important. Learning how to share the gospel with someone is a skill that cannot really be learned in a classroom or from textbooks. It has to be practiced, preferably with the help and guidance of someone more experienced. This practice is built into the fabric of the course as the leader takes each trainee with him/her to share the gospel with someone in a context-appropriate way.

In connection with this emphasis on personal, prayerful, practical training, we have found that it is much better to start the training program with just one or two very small groups and to build it up over time as experienced leaders become available (through having been trained themselves).

We began by claiming that Australia was in advance of the United States at least in the arena of public godlessness and paganism. Whether this has led to Australian evangelical Christians being more adept at articulating the gospel in the context of this postmodern confusion is much harder to say. We are certainly aware of having a very long way to go in bringing the gospel to our society, which is so resolute in its spiritual apathy.

If we have learned anything in devising and using *Two Ways to Live* in our ministry, it is that faithful Christ-centered witness in a postmodern world does not involve diluting, changing, or sidelining the biblical gospel. It requires a renewed clarity in understanding and articulating it, and a renewed confidence in proclaiming it. For all its sophisticated ennui, our rebellious generation still stands under the judgment of the loving Creator and Ruler of the world and still needs to hear gospel of the crucified and resurrected Messiah.

CHAPTER 7

KEEPING CHRIST CENTRAL IN PREACHING

Colin S. Smith

Some years ago I came to know a missionary serving with New Tribes Mission in northern Thailand. His task was to bring the gospel to a tribal group that had not been penetrated by Western culture or by any kind of biblical teaching. These people were not postmoderns! They had a clearly formed worldview that was shaped by stories about evil spirits, but they had no knowledge whatever of the Christian revelation.

The question is, Where do you begin in the task of communicating the gospel to a group of people who do not know who God is, what sin is, who Christ is, or what a Bible is for? I will never forget my friend's answer: "We tell them the big story." Beginning with the creation of angels, he explained the rebellion of Lucifer, the creation of the heavens and the earth and of the first man and woman. He explained the first act of disobedience toward God and the curse that came as a result. He continued with the story of Cain and Abel and on through the Old Testament. Step by step, he built a worldview in order to introduce them to Jesus.

A few years ago I had the opportunity of visiting Uttar Pradesh, the vast Hindu heartland of North India with a population of 140 million people. It is described by Patrick Johnstone in his book *Operation World* as "one of the darkest and most needy parts of the world." There is one church for every thousand villages, one church for every million people. Uttar Pradesh is a stronghold of Hinduism, and among these people it is commonly believed that there is one god for every person in India. How do you proclaim the gospel to a population that has, for centuries, selected its objects of worship from a catalogue of over 900 million items?

Village pastors in Uttar Pradesh are being trained to teach fifty Bible stories that will communicate who God is and what he has to say to us. The approach is fascinating. It is not fifty texts, but fifty stories. "We tell them the big story."

In the past, a great deal of effective evangelism has been done by teaching key Scripture verses about sin, grace, and salvation. Christian preachers have been able to assume the basic building blocks of a Christian worldview. Even when people chose not to believe in God, it was the Christian God they chose not to believe in! Evangelism was rather like hanging washing on a clothesline that was already in place. You could take texts like John 3:16 or Romans 5:8 or Isaiah 53:4–6 and hang them on the line of a Judeo-Christian worldview. The problem in trying to reach postmodern people is that there is no clothesline. So when we try to hang our texts, they fall to the ground in a messy heap.

The great challenge before the preacher is to put up the clothesline. Our task is to present the big story and to persuade postmodern people that it is true. In pursuing this, we have much to learn from our friends in northern Thailand and India. They know that it is not enough to present disconnected truths about peace or fulfillment or family life. We will certainly speak about all of these things, but we must find ways of connecting them clearly to the person and work of Jesus Christ.

Putting up the clothesline is not a new challenge. Judges 2:10 tells us that after the death of Joshua, "another generation grew up who knew neither the Lord nor what he had done for Israel." They did not know the big story! It is alarming how quickly the knowledge of God can be eclipsed in a culture. In Israel it took only one generation.

The book of Judges narrates the sad tale of how, in the absence of the knowledge of God, people developed their own religion and their own morality. The Word of God was scarce in the land in those days until God raised up Samuel and his word came to the whole people (1 Sam. 3). Within one generation, the knowledge of God was restored to the nation. That is the challenge that we face again today. We desperately need to rediscover the power of Christ-centered biblical preaching.

There are three convictions that will help to sustain us in this task: that Jesus Christ is central to the Scriptures, that he is central to Christian preaching, and that he is central to the gospel.

JESUS CHRIST IS CENTRAL TO THE SCRIPTURES

The Bible has a story line, and the story has a point. Evangelical Christians believe that the Bible is one book with one author, with a coherent message

COLIN S. SMITH

that has its center in Jesus Christ. It is liberal theology that has torn the Bible into a collection of fragmented insights on various subjects related to God and to life. We believe that Scripture is God's story, and it is the task of the Christian preacher to tell that story.

The point of the story is found in Jesus Christ, especially in his death and resurrection. Everything else leads to this or flows from it. In Galatians 4:4 we are told that God sent his Son into the world "when the time had fully come." God did not consider it appropriate that Christ should be born of the virgin Sarah in the year 2000 BC. The Old Testament story is given to us so that we may understand who Jesus Christ is and why we need him. When John said, "Look, the Lamb of God, who takes away the sin of the world" (John 1:29), there was a whole framework of understanding and meaning that was communicated to those who heard him say it.

Whether we are preaching from the law, the prophets, the historical books, the wisdom literature, the Gospels, or the New Testament epistles, they all relate directly to Jesus Christ. The whole Scripture speaks of him. The Old Testament prepares the way for his coming, the Gospels record the events of his coming, and the New Testament letters explain the significance of his coming. It follows that if we attempt to preach any part of the Bible without properly relating it to Christ, we have not communicated its meaning.

The following four examples illustrate the centrality of Christ in all the Scriptures:

In Luke 24:27, we are told of how Jesus explained the meaning of the Old Testament to two disciples on the road to Emmaus: "And beginning with Moses and all the Prophets, he explained to them what was said in all the Scriptures concerning himself." Christ himself worked through the Old Testament Scriptures and explained the significance of his own death and resurrection.

In John 5:39, Jesus makes the same point to the Pharisees: "You diligently study the Scriptures because you think that by them you possess eternal life. These are the Scriptures that testify about me."

In Genesis 12:2–3, God gives a promise to Abraham: "I will make you into a great nation and I will bless you ... and all peoples on earth will be blessed through you." There is a fascinating commentary on this in Galatians 3:8, where Paul tells us that in this promise, the gospel was announced to Abraham in advance. This insight ties in with the astonishing statement of Jesus about Abraham recorded in John 8:56: "Your father Abraham rejoiced at the thought of seeing my day; *he saw it* and was glad" (italics added). If Abraham received an announcement of the gospel and rejoiced in the day of Christ, then it is right that we should do the same when we preach from the book of Genesis.

In John 12:40, Jesus quotes from Isaiah 6, where the prophet Isaiah sees the glory of the Lord. John's commentary on this is absolutely fascinating. He tells us that Isaiah saw *Jesus' glory* and spoke about him (John 12:41). So if we speak about the glory of Yahweh and do not see in that the glory of Jesus, then we have missed what is there. Augustine makes the point well when he asks what could be more tasteless and insipid than to read the prophetic books without reference to Christ. Find Christ in them, and what you read will prove not only agreeable but intoxicating.

It is important that we do not think of these connections to Christ as some kind of evangelistic add-on at the end of a sermon. We are not looking to impose some artificial connection to the cross. We are looking to draw out the connection with the cross that is already there. The Scriptures themselves make it clear that Christ is intrinsic to the Old Testament narrative, and if we preach the story without showing its connection to Christ, we have simply missed its point.

Christ is the focus of the whole of the Bible. He is the center point of the big story. He is there at the creation. All things were made by him. The Fall shows us our need of him. The Flood points to the judgment of God and our need for a safe passage into the new world. God's blessing to Abraham was the inauguration of the line from which Christ came. The Exodus was a redemption of God's people pointing forward to our deliverance by Christ. The Law reveals sin and, properly understood, brings us to see our need of Christ. The sacrifices, properly understood, will train the minds of God's people to understand that putting away sin always costs a life. The offices of prophet, priest, and king are all categories that help us to understand who Jesus is. The prophet speaks the very word of God to the people. The priest presents people to God and intercedes on their behalf. The king has the right and responsibility of sovereign rule.

The Old Testament gives us the categories for understanding the gospel. Without the Old Testament, the New Testament is like coming into a play after the intermission and trying to understand the plot. We have missed most of the clues and do not have the benefit of knowing the trails already pursued that lead nowhere. If we do manage to connect with the story, we will only do so by inferring from the content of act 2 what must have happened in act 1.

When we come to the Old Testament, we do not need to think up some way of making a connection with the person of Christ. The connection is already there. The Scriptures speak about Christ. Our task is to explain what they say and how they relate to Christ.

COLIN S. SMITH

JESUS CHRIST IS CENTRAL TO CHRISTIAN PREACHING

There are two questions that I have found especially helpful in the process of shaping material for preaching. First, it is always worth asking whether what has been prepared could be described as a sermon. And second, is it a Christian sermon?

A sermon is very different from a lecture. The lecturer can speak in the third person, impart general information drawn from another time and place, and rest content that he has done an acceptable job. The calling of the preacher is very different. He must connect his biblical material with the immediate life situation of the hearers. He must speak in such a way that they sense God is speaking to them directly through the Word. A sermon is much more than a collage of biblical information. It is a message, and a message must have a coherent theme. In the words of Haddon Robinson, "No matter how brilliant a sermon is, without a definite purpose it is not worth preaching!" (1980, 107).

Warren Wiersbe has a delightful story in his book *Preaching and Teaching with Imagination* (1994, 57). He describes a fictional character, Grandma Thatcher, coming to church on Sunday morning. She is in pain, and her unbelieving husband has sent her off to church with curses ringing in her ears. She has prayed that fuel prices will not go up in winter, and if it were not for the Lord and her Bible, she would have given up long ago.

Pastor Bowers steps into the pulpit, and as he does, Grandma Thatcher prays silently, "Lord, give him something special for me. I need it!" The text is Genesis 9, and the title, "God speaks to Noah." His headings are:

* Creation presented (vv. 1–3)
* Capital punishment (vv. 4–7)
* Covenant promised (vv. 8–17)
* Carnality practiced (vv. 18–23)
* Consequences prophesied (vv. 24–29)

Nobody can deny that his material was biblical. All these themes are there. His address may have imparted biblical information, but it was not preaching. A sermon is a message from God. It must be drawn from the Scriptures, but it must also be applied to life. The sermon should form a bridge from the world of the Bible into the life of the hearer.

If the preacher is to be successful in building that bridge, he must be familiar with both sides of the chasm over which the bridge is to be built. He must be at home in the Word of God, but he must also be in touch with the pressures and heartaches faced by ordinary people in everyday life. This is one reason why the pastor needs to protect both his time in the Word and his time with people. It is, in my experience, direct involvement in pastoral work that helps to develop sensitivity in the heart of the preacher.

I find myself challenged by the words of James Daane, who reminds preachers that "God only knows the sorrow and pain, the shame and hurt, the intolerable burdens, shattered experiences, crushed hopes and terrors of the spirit which lie in the hearts of those to whom we minister on Sunday morning. Such human wounds are not to be healed lightly, laughed off with the help of injections of humor from a pulpit personality whose model is Bob Hope or Woody Allen" (Daane 1980, 76). As you think through your material for preaching, ask yourself: Is it a sermon? Is there a message from God to the people who will gather? What is that message? Have you formed a bridge from the world of the Bible into the lives of the people?

Once we have established that our material does qualify as a sermon, it is important to ask whether it is distinctively Christian! Jay Adams has given a helpful definition of a Christian sermon as one that would cause you to be thrown out of a synagogue or a mosque. His point is well founded, for this is exactly what happened in the book of Acts.

When I first came across this litmus test, I went back over a number of old sermon notes and was convicted that some of my sermons did not pass the test of being authentically Christian! I have lived with this litmus test ever since. Our calling is not to present general truths about God, or about fulfillment in life, or even about standards and values. Our calling is to present Jesus Christ, and preaching that does not bring us to Christ is sub-Christian.

The apostle Paul establishes this priority in 1 Corinthians 2:2, when he says that he resolved to know nothing among the Corinthians except Jesus Christ and him crucified. Clearly he does not mean that this was the only subject he would speak on, but what he is saying is that he is not interested in any subject that is disconnected from the person and work of Christ.

If Christ is the theme of all the Scriptures, then those who are called to preach and teach the Bible must work hard to make sure that Christ is the focus of their teaching and preaching. There are two questions that I have found helpful in pursuing this goal: (1) What does this tell me about the human condition? and (2) What does this tell me about God and his provision for the human condition in Jesus Christ? The first question will show the need of the cross; the second will show the relevance of the cross. The first will humble me before God; the second will give me hope in God.

I came to these questions by reflecting on the opening sentence of Calvin's *Institutes*: "Nearly all the wisdom we possess, that is to say, true and sound wis-

COLIN S. SMITH

dom, consists in two parts: the knowledge of God and the knowledge of our-selves" (1.1.1). If this is true, then in any part of the Scripture we should find these things.

PREACHING OUR NEED OF CHRIST

I recently talked with a man who told me that he was on a spiritual jour-ney and wondered if I could give him any help. He spoke about God and about Jesus Christ, but it seemed clear that he did not know the Lord. I told him about the occasion when Jesus asked a man, "What do you want me to do for you?" and I asked him what he would have said if he had been given that opportunity. He said, "I would like to know a kind of serenity." I then asked him to think back in his life and to tell me the greatest thing that Christ had done for him already. He said the greatest thing was that Christ had got him to the age of fifty-five. It was a joy to be able to tell him that Jesus Christ could do more for him than he had ever begun to imagine.

I mention this man because he represents many of our contemporaries. This man had a spiritual hunger, but he had no real knowledge of God or of the human condition, and therefore he had no conception of the scale of what Jesus Christ could do in his life. It is difficult to see how a Christ who came to save his people from their sins can ever be of more than marginal interest to someone without a clear grasp of the dark clouds of the judgment of God and the human predicament of helplessness in sin.

We will never bring people to an appreciation of the cross until we can per-suade them of the Bible's analysis of the human condition. James Denney reminds us that "the atonement is addressed to the sense of sin. It presupposes the bad conscience. Where there is no such thing, it is like a lever without a fulcrum" (1951, 168).

The preacher is faced with the problem of presenting people with a Christ to whom they do not wish to come. People have various felt needs, but a sav-ior from sin is not one of them. Sin causes a blindness to our own condition and makes us reluctant to hear about it. Postmodern people are rather like the hospital patient whose mind is closed to an unwelcome diagnosis. Discussion of possible surgery will be fruitless until the bad news has sunk in. In the same way, it will be of little value to speak about Christ unless we have managed to open minds to the need for a redeemer. Without true self-knowledge, the gospel will make no sense at all.

Two things are working for us: the Word of God is light in a dark place, and the Holy Spirit has come to convince of sin and righteousness and judgment.

Armed with these convictions, we must preach in a way that convinces men and women of their need of Christ.

PREACHING GOD'S PROVISION IN CHRIST

We must never leave people with only the knowledge of themselves. Self-knowledge without the knowledge of God is always crushing. We are never to leave people with the contemplation of their own sins. The reason for establishing the human condition is to awaken an appreciation of Jesus Christ. The preacher is to disturb the comfortable but also to comfort the disturbed.

We must present the mercy of God. The knowledge of sin will not be enough to incline a person to repentance. Two things must happen in the mind of the prodigal son before he will get up and begin the long journey home to his father. First, he must come to his senses. Second, he must believe that if he returns, there will be a welcome. In the words of Calvin, "The beginning of repentance is a sense of God's mercy; that is, when men are persuaded that God is ready to give pardon, they begin to gather courage to repent" (cited in Leith 1989, 97).

The knowledge of sin without the anticipation of mercy will only cause a person to keep on running from God. The prodigal needs the knowledge of his misery to give him the *desire* to return. He needs the assurance of a welcome to give him the *confidence* to return. Put these two together and you have the dynamic of the movement the Bible calls repentance.

One great advantage of expository preaching over a topical approach is that the text of the Bible, properly understood, will always lead you to Christ. As I write, we have just passed Mother's Day, a wonderful opportunity, but a preacher's graveyard! How do you get from Mother's Day to saying something significant about Christ?

I decided to explore the story of Hannah, the wonderful story of how God used one mother's prayers and influence. When Hannah brought Samuel to the temple, they brought a bull with them. Imagine the scene, and picture it through the eyes of a small boy.

"Mom, why are we taking a bull to the temple?"

As they get there the small boy's eyes widen, as he realizes what is going to happen next.

"Mom, why are they killing the bull?"

No small boy could ever forget seeing his first sacrifice.

Samuel was learning that you don't simply walk into the presence of a holy God. You cannot come as you are. You can only be accepted by this God on

COLIN S. SMITH

the basis of a sacrifice. All of this is to prepare the minds of the people so that they can understand a greater slaughter, when this God sends his Son into the world, and he becomes the sacrifice for the sins of the world.

Jay Adams says, "Preach Christ in all the Scriptures: He is the subject matter of the whole Bible. He is there. Until you have found him in your preaching portion you are not ready to preach" (1982, 152).

We have considered the centrality of Christ in the Scriptures and in preaching. We must now consider the centrality of Christ in the gospel.

JESUS CHRIST IS CENTRAL TO THE GOSPEL

Have you ever felt that the task of presenting the gospel was overwhelming? I have always found it one of the most difficult things to preach the gospel in such a way that people feel that it is wonderfully free, and yet at the same time that it demands everything. Sometimes I have felt that when I was really strong on the free gift, I was rather weak on the call to radical discipleship. At other times, when I presented the challenge to repentance, I wondered if I was not in danger of obscuring grace.

This connection between faith and repentance is critical for our preaching of the gospel. Catholic theologians have long questioned Protestant teaching at this point. Right back to the time of the Reformation, evangelicals have been accused of preaching a gospel that is simply a lifting of condemnation without accompanying transformation.

We have to hear this criticism carefully. How does repentance (the change God commands in our lives) relate to faith through which God forgives us freely? Compromise either, and we have lost the biblical gospel.

Paul deals with this problem in Romans 5 and 6. Romans 5 is all about free justification by grace alone, through faith alone, because of Christ alone. It is not because of our works and not on account of our performance in the Christian life. This raises the obvious question that Paul articulates in Romans 6:1: "What shall we say, then? Shall we go on sinning so that grace may increase?" Shall we say that sin in the believer does not matter and that sanctification is a kind of upgrade in the Christian life for enthusiasts who want to apply for it?

Paul's answer is clear: "God forbid!" His reason for this is the doctrine of union with Christ. We were baptized into Christ, we died and were buried with Christ, and we are now raised with him to a new kind of life. If we are united with Christ in his death, then we are also united with Christ in his life. The connection between the forgiveness we receive and the change we are called to lies in the Lord Jesus Christ himself. He personally is the link between the two. We cannot have forgiveness without being joined to him, and we cannot be in him without being changed.

There is a big difference between a grocery store and a marriage. The grocery store is arranged for choice. You go around with your cart, and make your selections. The whole thing is set up to help you take what you want and leave what you don't. You are under no obligation whatsoever.

A marriage is different! Suppose a young couple were to come to you for premarital counseling. He says that he likes her eyes but not her hair. He appreciates her interest in sports but not in music. He wants to spend time with her on Tuesdays and Thursdays but not on Mondays and Fridays. It is soon apparent that there is a problem!

The marriage vow expresses a union that involves both privilege and responsibility. *I take you as you are, for better, for worse; for richer, for poorer; in sickness and in health. I am going to live with you whatever happens. I will stick with you however hard, and I will be devoted to you however long.*

Some people think that the Christian life is like a visit to the grocery store. They open the Bible, and they go through the aisles. They see something they would like. Forgiveness! Peace! Joy! Heaven! But there are other aisles that display less attractive items: forgiving others as God forgave you, denying yourself and taking up the cross to follow Christ.

The Bible never describes the Christian life as a visit to the grocery store, but it does describe the Christian life as a marriage to Christ. It is a marriage in which two parties commit to each other unconditionally. The only way Christ can receive us is just as we are, and the only way we can receive Christ is just as he is, and that is as Savior and Lord. If I embrace the Christ who says, "Father forgive them," then at the same time and in the same act I embrace the One who said, "Follow me." I cannot divide who he is. He is the Lord Jesus Christ.

The New Testament only offers us one wonderful gift, Jesus Christ. He is the gift of gifts and contains all of God's gifts in himself. We are blessed with every spiritual blessing in Christ! When we start talking about forgiveness or holiness and separate it from being in Christ, then we quickly fall into imbalance and error.

Calvin asks the question, "Why are we justified by faith?" and then gives this answer:

> By faith we grasp Christ's righteousness, by which alone we are reconciled to God. Yet you could not grasp this without at the same time grasping sanctification also. For he "is given unto us for righteousness wisdom, sanctification and redemption." Therefore Christ justifies no one whom he does not at the

COLIN S. SMITH

same time sanctify. These benefits are joined together by an everlasting and indissoluble bond, so that those whom he illumines by his wisdom, he redeems; those whom he redeems, he justifies; those whom he justifies, he sanctifies. Although we may distinguish them, Christ contains them both inseparably in himself. Do you wish, then, to attain righteousness in Christ? You must first possess Christ; but you cannot posses him without being made partaker in his sanctification, because he cannot be divided into pieces. (*Inst.* 3.16.1)

The New Testament never offers the blessings of the gospel as separate items on a shopping list. If they are not offered in this way, then we should not preach them this way. The gospel does not invite us to take forgiveness, but to take Christ. All God's blessings are in him; none of them are found apart from him. The whole gospel finds its coherent center in him. We either take him as he is with all his gifts and all his demands, or we stand apart from him. We cannot divide him in pieces.

The most searching question to be asked of our preaching is not "Are we preaching forgiveness or repentance or holiness or faith?" but "Are we preaching Christ?"

In the Church of England liturgy, there is a form of worship that goes back to the sixteenth century. The reading of the Word is followed by the sermon, and then the Eucharist or Communion. The connections have profound theological significance. By placing the sermon between the reading of Scripture and the Lord's Table, the Reformers were reminding us that *the preaching must arise out of the Word and should lead us to the Table.*

I try to think about that every time I prepare to preach. Am I forming a bridge between the Word and the Table? In some of our traditions we do not observe the Lord's Supper in every service, but I have found it helpful to ask myself: How would I conclude this message in such a way that it would lead naturally into the Lord's Table?

Whether or not we observe the Lord's Supper at the end of a service, the aim of the preacher should be to come to the place where, feeling our need of Christ and seeing God's provision in Christ, we are able to look up in faith to the crucified and risen Redeemer who pours grace and mercy into our lives.

References

Adams, Jay. 1982. *Preaching with Purpose*. Grand Rapids: Baker.
Calvin, John. 1960. *Institutes of the Christian Religion*. 2 vols. Ed. J. T. McNeill. Trans. Ford Lewis Battles. Philadelphia and London: Westminster Press.

Daane, James. 1980. *Preaching with Confidence*. Grand Rapids: Eerdmans.

Denney, James. 1951. *The Death of Christ*. London: Tyndale.

Leith, J. H. 1989. *John Calvin's Doctrine of the Christian Life*. Louisville: Westminster/ John Knox.

Robinson, Haddon. 1980. *Biblical Preaching*. Grand Rapids: Baker.

Wiersbe, Warren. 1994. *Preaching and Teaching with Imagination*. Wheaton: Victor.

CHAPTER 8

THE UNIQUENESS OF JESUS CHRIST

Ajith Fernando

As we seek to evangelize postmoderns today, one of the key issues that calls for discussion is the Christian affirmation of the uniqueness of Christ. This affirmation seems to be out of step with the way that many people are thinking. There are three challenges to this affirmation: first, the tendency to devalue objective truth; second, the charge that those who hold to this affirmation are intolerant and arrogant; and third, the new interest in non-Christian spirituality. The first of these challenges has been tackled in other chapters of this book. We will look at the other two here.

THE CHARGE OF INTOLERANCE AND ARROGANCE

There is a new mood in the approach to interreligious activity among postmoderns, which has been influenced by today's dominant philosophy of pluralism. A key element is pluralism's understanding of tolerance and humility. Tolerance has become one of the most sacred values to the postmodern mind, and according to the new understanding of tolerance, any claim to possess unique truth is considered arrogant and intolerant. Years ago G. K. Chesterton observed that humility was becoming misplaced. He said that humility no longer pertained to self-opinion, where it ought to be. Rather, it now pertained to truth, where it ought not to be.[1] Whereas humility was earlier judged on the basis of one's opinion of oneself, now it is being judged on the basis of one's understanding of truth. Those who claim to have the truth are regarded as arrogant.

According to the pluralist understanding, no religion can make a claim to absolute uniqueness; therefore, sharing one's faith with conversion as a goal is considered wrong and unethical. A direct result of such thinking is that *apologetics*—defending the truthfulness of one's beliefs against opposing views—is considered undesirable and in need of replacement by *dialogue*. But dialogue here has the aim of mutual enrichment, not conversion. Sri Lankan ecumenical leader Wesley Ariarajah has written, "Anyone who approaches another with the *a priori* assumption that his story is 'the only true story,' kills the dialogue before it begins" (1977, 5).[2]

The church today faces the key challenge of proclaiming the gospel appropriately to a generation that is hostile to the idea of the uniqueness of Christ. Let us look at some features of evangelism in such an environment.

OUR ATTITUDE

It is important to befriend non-Christians in the way that Jesus did with people who were religiously very different from him. He was criticized for this and labeled "a glutton and a drunkard, a friend of tax collectors and 'sinners'" (Luke 7:34). In order to reach these people, he needed to befriend them. Non-Christians are not our enemies or people to be afraid of. They are people we have been called to love into God's kingdom.

As we befriend non-Christians, we use dialogue simply as a means of friendship and encounter with them. That is, we will converse as friends with them on various topics quite naturally. And in that conversation, we will also include discussion about our different religious beliefs. If we can affirm common commitments to issues like family values and ethnic harmony, we will do so. If we can affirm common opposition to such evils as abortion on demand and pornography, we will do so.

We will also use dialogue as we seek to witness to the gospel among non-Christians. This time dialogue is being used as a means of evangelism. As we do this, if we find good things in their lives and beliefs, we will affirm and appreciate them. In addition, we may refer to some beliefs of theirs that we agree with and use them as stepping-stones to presenting Christ. Paul did this with some quotations with which the Athenians were familiar (Acts 17:28). We are not out to win a debate with them whereby we seek to score points and defeat them. If we see some good thing in them that we can affirm and compliment them for, we do not need to be afraid to do so.

Yet we must remember that the very point on which we agree may blind some non-Christians to the truth of the gospel. For example, following the noble ethic of Buddhism may give Buddhists the satisfaction of saving themselves—which is the basic sin of the human race. In this way the ethic of Buddhism can entrench people in their lostness and can be used by Satan to blind them from recognizing their need for a Savior. This is why we cannot agree when people say that all religions teach essentially the same thing: how to be good. Christians and Buddhists answer that question in two completely opposite ways.

OUR LIFESTYLE

If our attitude to non-Christians is one of friendship, our lifestyle among them is one of servanthood. I believe that such a lifestyle is one of the most powerful answers to the charge of arrogance and intolerance. This is not something that we put on simply because it is relevant and effective in evangelism. It is the model Jesus gave us to follow always. As a servant, he often allowed his plans to be frustrated by the needs of people. In his resurrected state, we find him cooking breakfast for his tired disciples who were returning from a night at sea (John 21:9–13). After he donned a servant's towel and washed the feet of his disciples, he asked them to follow his example and do the same (John 13:14–15). Yet he presented himself as an absolute Lord who required the total allegiance of his followers. He made claims for himself that no other religious leader made (Fernando 1995, chap. 3). So he was a Servant Lord, a Servant King, a humble Absolute Monarch.

The Jews found it difficult to put this combination together. The messiah they expected was to be like a king, not like a servant. They were suffering under the yoke of Roman rule, and they had had enough of servanthood. They wanted a messiah who would liberate them. In fact, some Jews wanted to make Jesus king (John 6:15). So in those days lordship was in and servanthood was out when it came to their expectations of the messiah. To them the authority of lordship was incompatible with the humility of servanthood. But Jesus showed that it is possible for the absolute Lord to be a radical servant.

Today people have exactly the opposite problem. In this postcolonial era, many sensitive people in the West are ashamed of the imperialism of supposedly Christian powers (and they should be!). Therefore, lordship is out and servanthood is in. So for the opposite reason from that of the first century, people cannot understand how servants could proclaim a message of lordship.

Just as Jesus showed by his life and ministry that lordship and servanthood are compatible, we must by our lives and ministries show that it is possible for those who have the humility of a servant to believe in and to proclaim the message of Christ's absolute lordship. Paul modeled the fact that it is possible for one who is a servant to preach a message of lordship. In fact, describing his ministry, he said, "For we do not preach ourselves, but Jesus Christ as Lord, and ourselves as your servants for Jesus' sake" (2 Cor. 4:5).

The Dutch missiologist Hendrik Kraemer said that in our evangelism we have "a remarkable combination of downright intrepidity [boldness] and of radical humility" (1938, 128).

The worldwide response to Mother Teresa is instructive here. She was very vocal about her opposition to abortion in the West and to the proposed anti-conversion bill in India. These stands were very unpopular with many people. But her lifestyle made it difficult for them to dismiss her and consequently to dismiss what she stood for. She was a major influence in the dropping of the anti-conversion bill in India.

Nepal is the only Hindu kingdom in the world. Recently there was a big furor about an AIDS patient who had been admitted to a hospital in Nepal but who was thrown out the moment they found out that he had AIDS. This was reported in the front page of the newspapers there. One report said that all the hospitals threw out AIDS patients except one hospital run by Christian missionaries. Though expatriate Christian social workers in Nepal are not permitted to evangelize, they have a good record of compassionate service to the people. Is it any wonder that where Nepali Christians are evangelizing their fellow people, large numbers of people are turning to Christ? It is estimated that although there were only about two hundred Protestant Christians in Nepal about thirty-five years ago, now there are about three hundred thousand.

In the postmodern era in particular, a high value is placed on subjective evidences for the validity of a religion. People are not so interested in whether a religion is true. They want to know whether it works. In such an environment, the servant lifestyle of Christians may be a key to opening the doors for presenting the gospel of a unique Savior.

OUR PROCLAMATION

Of course it is easy to get so carried away with our witness through service that we neglect our witness through proclamation, as the histories of movements that are active in service often show. I have found that one way to avoid this trap is to keep emphasizing the fact that without Christ people are lost and headed for judgment and that their only hope is salvation through Jesus Christ. If this is true, we will never be satisfied with service alone. We will want to do all we can to bring the people we serve within the sound of the gospel. This is not because we are arrogant and think that we are better than they, but because of a conviction that their only hope for salvation is Jesus.

As we proclaim the message, we seek to persuade people to accept the message. The word *peitho* (persuade) is used at least eight times in Acts to refer to the evangelism of the early Christians. They reasoned with people until their minds were changed and they left their old ways to follow Christ. However, when persuasion is used in connection with religious proclamation today, it is often associated with arrogance and intolerance. This is strange, because persuasion is used daily in many spheres of life. Advertisers seek to persuade us to patronize certain products, and politicians seek to persuade us to accept their policies and vote for them. Yet when it comes to religion, this approach to communication is considered inappropriate.

Mahatma Gandhi once told his friend, the missionary E. Stanley Jones, "Don't attempt to propagate your faith; just live it. Be like the rose, which, without a word, silently exudes its perfume and attracts the attention of the people." Jones responded by reminding Mr. Gandhi that he was the greatest propagandist of all, seeking to propagate his views on independence and freedom to the British Empire and to the whole world.[3]

Persuasion becomes intolerant and arrogant when we use imposition and manipulation. John Stott defines *imposition* as "the crusading attempt to coerce people by legislation to accept the Christian way" (1990, 46). This took place often in the past, and we need to be ashamed of it. As an example of imposition, Stott presents the Inquisition, which was set up by the Roman Catholic Church in the thirteenth century to combat heresy. Imposition also takes place when employers or parents use their authority to force people to become Christians. It took place in colonial times when the missionaries came along with the European (especially Spanish and Portuguese) conquerors and, by making Christianity the official religion of the colonies, compelled many to accept it for the sake of survival and progress in society.

Manipulation takes place when we use things alien to the heart of the gospel to induce others to accept Christianity: when material inducements like the promise of a job or aid are used as bribes to induce people to become Christians, or when people's emotions are manipulated so that they accept Christianity in a way that doesn't involve the proper use of the mind. For example, an emotionally charged evangelistic message may be concluded with a highly emotional story and immediately followed by an invitation to discipleship. Some may respond because of their emotional state rather than because they have thought through the implications of the message. Manipulation also takes place in cults where "mind bending" or brainwashing takes place through the use of mental pressure so that the subjects are unable to make intelligent and free choices about what is being thrust upon them.

Biblical persuasion is an expression of our respect for people. The supreme Lord of creation, God himself, invites people to reason together with him (Isa.

1:18). Similarly we, as his servants, respect people's freedom of choice and give them an opportunity to make informed responses to the message of Jesus.

Today the claim to uniqueness and the practice of persuasion in evangelism are often associated with the imperialist mentality of the colonial era. The pluralist scholar John Hick has said, "The . . . doctrine of a unique divine incarnation has long poisoned relationships between Christians and Jews and between Christians and Muslims, as well as affecting the history of Christian imperialism in the Far East, India, Africa, and elsewhere."[4] In Sri Lanka opponents of evangelism are saying that the current evangelistic impetus of Christians is a "new colonialism" or "new imperialism" in which the West is trying to dominate and control people through religion. They say that earlier the Western imperialists came with the Bible in one hand and a gun in the other. Now they come with the Bible in one hand and material aid in the other.

The doctrine of the uniqueness of Christ is said to have thrived in the monolithic Western culture dominated by Christianity. But, we are told, we can no longer hold such views in this pluralistic society. Let us not forget that the doctrine of Christian exclusivism developed in a strongly pluralistic society in the first-century Roman Empire (Carson 1996, 270–72). There the Christians did not belong to the side of the colonial masters, but were oppressed by them. Yet they believed in a unique Savior and proclaimed this message. Many had to sacrifice their lives because they did so. The gospel, then, did not need imperialism to thrive.

In Sri Lanka the Protestant church made minimal progress under the British. Many joined the church for economic gain. Naturally the membership dropped after we received independence, with many reverting to Buddhism. Many thinkers in the established churches took on a pluralistic attitude to the uniqueness of Christ that was more in keeping with the mood of embarrassment over the past imperialistic connections of the church. But about fifteen years ago, more than three decades after independence, after Buddhism had been firmly established as the national religion, the church started a remarkable period of growth. Those doing evangelism, as well as converts from Buddhism, have to face much persecution. But the proclamation of the unique Savior goes on unabated. The same thing is happening in the church in India. Perhaps the three countries where the church has grown fastest in Asia in recent years are Nepal, China, and South Korea. There the church has received no help at all from colonial rulers, but the

AJITH FERNANDO

belief in a unique Savior has motivated Christians to be active in bold and costly evangelism.

RELIGIOUS FREEDOM FOR NON-CHRISTIANS

The assertion of the uniqueness of Christ, however, does not mean that we should deny people of other faiths the freedom to worship and share their faith. The New Testament Christians, especially Paul and Luke throughout the book of Acts, tried hard to show that Christians have a right to practice their faith in the multifaith context of the Roman Empire. Luke tried to show that the Roman Empire generally gave them the right to do so. We are grateful for this. Would it not be right for us to do to others this thing that we wish for them to do to us?

Sri Lanka is a Buddhist nation, and according to the constitution Buddhism is the national religion. But we are grateful for the freedom we have to practice and propagate our faith. Some Buddhist, Hindu, and Muslim fundamentalists are trying to restrict this freedom in several countries in Asia. They have succeeded in doing this in many Muslim countries. Sometimes when I hear some Christians in America speak, I must confess that they sound very much like these Buddhist, Hindu, and Muslim fundamentalists. We don't need to be so afraid of other faiths that we restrict the freedom of devotees to practice their faith. It was in a multifaith context that the early church grew. This can happen today too.

Take the churches in countries where Christians are a very small minority but are proclaiming the gospel boldly at great personal cost to themselves. In those churches the uniqueness of Christ is not a big issue as it is in many Western countries. Some churches in Western countries are not doing evangelism, and spiritual rot has set in. We find that in these churches some of the hard truths of the gospel, such as the uniqueness of Christ, are being jettisoned. But when you believe the Bible and put Christianity into practice, you create an environment that is not hostile to the belief in uniqueness. The way to protect the doctrine of uniqueness, then, is not to restrict the freedom of others, but to live out Christianity by proclaiming the message of Christ boldly and sacrificially.

THE NEW INTEREST IN NON-CHRISTIAN SPIRITUALITY

While objective truth may be out among postmoderns, spirituality is in. All over the world we are seeing a resurgence of interest in spirituality. But the spirituality toward which people are attracted is often New Age spirituality.

THE DISCOVERY OF RICHES IN OTHER FAITHS

For many years Christians in the West referred to those of other religions as heathens. While this word may not have originally had a derogatory meaning, it has developed such a meaning today. To many in the West, non-Christians were considered culturally unrefined people. Since the last century there has been a fresh discovery of the religious heritage of other nations, and people are surprised by the richness they have seen. They now see that the religious heritages of these nations were not as backward as they thought, and that they were wrong in viewing these cultures as inferior to their own.

POSTMODERN INTEREST IN SPIRITUALITY

A parallel trend has been the interest in spirituality by postmoderns revolting against the tyranny of the rationalism of the modern era. They claim that owing to the preoccupation with objective facts, the individual with his or her feelings and drives has been neglected. One of the things neglected is the spiritual side of the human being.

Twenty years ago there was a lot of talk about secular humanism, which generally ignored or denied the spiritual aspect of the human being. Now this has given way to an attitude toward life that gives a higher place to the spiritual. But the spirituality that the postmodern is attracted to is generally more New Age than Christian. So we see people taking interest in astrology, in magic and the occult, in psychic and spiritual "counselors," and in Eastern religions. Meditation and belief in reincarnation have become commonplace even in the West. Many new versions of old films and television serials, like *Star Trek, Robin Hood,* and *Sinbad the Sailor,* give evidence of such spirituality. I found it quite amusing to see the Muslim Sinbad, who calls God "Allah," involved in many magical activities that are generally scorned by Muslims.

DEFECTIVE EVANGELICAL SPIRITUALITY

Unfortunately, many expressions of evangelical Christianity in the West have been defective in the area of spirituality. In many evangelical traditions conversion was defined as intellectual assent to the message of the cross. After conversion the emphasis was on obedience to Christ, so sanctification was equated with obedience. There was little emphasis on the work of the Spirit in sanctification. The teaching on the assurance of salvation was almost entirely an appeal to the rational—the Bible says those who believe are saved; therefore, if you have believed, you are saved. There is little mention of the experience of Christ through the Holy Spirit, the transformed life, or the witness of the Spirit as means of assurance. Any display of emotion in religion, or what Jonathan Edwards called the religious affections, was viewed with suspicion. So to many postmoderns, Christianity was an expression of the dry rationalism of modernism that they were revolting against. Happily, this situation has changed in the charismatic and other wings of the evangelical church where there is a resurgence of interest in spirituality. But when some reject Christianity and look for spirituality elsewhere, they find non-Christian spirituality very attractive. As they look at certain forms of non-Christian spirituality, they wonder whether those forms are superior to Christian spirituality. Therefore, the postmodern interest in spirituality has posed a challenge to our belief in the uniqueness of Christ.

THE DANGERS OF IDENTIFYING CHRISTIANITY WITH ONE CULTURE

The first point to make in response to the above situation is that the discovery of riches in other faiths is coming alongside a discovery of riches in other cultures. Some cultures may have preserved good features in God's original revelation that got obliterated in the West owing to its pragmatism or to some other cultural features. I remember one summer in the mid–1970s when I was a student in the United States. I was struggling with what women wore (or maybe I should say, didn't wear!). I met in an airport an American Hare Krishna follower gracefully dressed in a sari. I found it so refreshing! As far as wholesome appearance was concerned, she was so much more attractive than many of the Christian women I met at that time. Then there are the strong family ties, the close community life, and the commitment to the contemplative life that is found, for example, in Asia.

People made in the image of God are made with the capacity for spiritual experience. And living in a world fashioned by God, they can achieve significant heights of moral and spiritual understanding and experience without a Christian influence. Of course, many of these emphases are found in the Bible, but they may have been neglected in some forms of Western Christianity. Therefore, our claim for the uniqueness of Christ is not a claim for the uniqueness of Western culture. In earlier times some confused the two. They saw mission as Christianizing the heathen, but Christianizing actually meant Westernizing. The new appreciation of riches in non-Western cultures forces us to stop identifying the gospel with Western culture. It also forces us to ask where the church in the West has been deficient in her understanding of the whole counsel of God.

THE "HOLISTIC" SPIRITUALITY OF THE BIBLE

The Bible has a fully developed and deeply meaningful understanding of spirituality. Much of it is given in the Old Testament, which was the Bible of the early church and therefore did not need to be reemphasized in the New Testament. Because many Christians do not assign sufficient significance to the Old Testament, they may not have fully grasped this emphasis. Essentially, biblical spirituality is founded on a personal relationship with God, who is both loving and holy. Deepening this relationship gives life's most fulfilling experience. David said, "You have made known to me the path of life; you will fill me with joy in your presence, with eternal pleasures at your right hand" (Ps. 16:11). We believe that our relationship with God is most fulfilling because God is the creator of human spirituality and Jesus is God's answer to human need. Jesus himself said, "I have come that they may have life, and have it to the full" (John 10:10).

GOD IS LOVING

The heart of Christian spirituality is a love relationship with a personal God. This is very different from New Age spirituality, which is the prominent expression of spirituality in the postmodern era. The God of the Bible is separate from humanity but has reached down to establish an interpersonal relationship with us—a relationship of love. New Age spirituality has a pantheistic understanding of God that understands everything as being God: God is not personal; you are God, and I am God; our task is to become one with the divine. The official Hare Krishna magazine is entitled *Back to Godhead*. New Age analyst Theodore Roszak says that our goal is "to awaken the God who sleeps at the root of the human being."[5] Therefore, these spiritualities have to do with experiences of the divine through spiritual disciplines. To many they are satisfying because they give some fulfillment to the spiritual nature of humans. But they fall short of complete satisfaction. Humans are made to find their fullest satisfaction through personal relationships of love. This is why love songs are so popular in music, which is the language of joy. The heart of Christian spirituality is just this—a love relationship with God.

Yet like the marriage relationship, which is often used to describe our relationship with God, a personal relationship with God takes time to cultivate through the practice of spiritual disciplines. Many Christians are not doing this, and they are missing out on the beauty of Christian spirituality. The "one-minute devotionals" that are available today in abundance are not helpful here, unless they become means by which an appetite for the spiritual life is kindled. One must soon graduate from them to lingering with God through the spiritual disciplines of prayer, praise, adoration, Bible reading, meditation, and corporate worship. Christians who do not know the joys of lingering in the presence of God will be at a loss to know how to respond when people speak of serenity through New Age disciplines like transcendental meditation.

When those who have practiced non-Christian spiritual disciplines come to Christ, they take to Christian spirituality with relish! Their skills in the art of the spiritual disciplines help them to cultivate a deeply satisfying spiritual life. A young man who was a devout Hindu was sent by the accountancy firm where he was employed to work on the Youth for Christ annual audit. Someone in our office spoke to him about Christ, and that led him to become a Christian. I had the privilege of meeting him weekly to help him in his spiritual growth. I found that he had cultivated a deep prayer life. Later, when he joined our staff, this prayer life became a key to his phenomenal success in leadership development. He prayed people through into leadership. If we were to ask him whether he would go back to Hinduism, he would decisively say, "Never!" The rewards of practicing the Hindu spiritual disciplines could not be compared with the glory of a relationship with a loving God. But this background in the disciplines would have given him a head start in his spiritual pilgrimage as a Christian.

Sadhu Sundar Singh was a young man in India who was skilled in Hindu and Sikh disciplines. But he was engaged in a quest for peace that was yet to be satisfied. He "attained a mastery of the Yoga technique and became oblivious of the external world for short spells." Sundar Singh said that during these moments he experienced in some measure the peace and joy for which his soul craved. "But when he returned to consciousness, he was again plunged into the turmoil of unrest and discontent" (Appasamy 1966, 77). When Sundar Singh finally met Christ, he became a "master" of the spiritual life. He also found that God established a relationship with him that did not end at the mountaintop, for God came down to the valley with him. Sundar Singh once said, "Without Christ I was like a fish out of water. With Christ, I am in an ocean of love!"

GOD IS HOLY

Because God is holy, if we have a relationship with him we must become holy like him (1 Peter 1:16). So Christian spirituality requires moral and ethical purity. The beauty of it is that just as justification is by grace through faith, so is sanctification by which we are made holy. On our own we do not have the strength to become holy, but as we repent of our sin and trust in him and obey him, he makes us holy. Therefore to many in the Protestant tradition, the words *spiritual* and *holy* and *saint* are almost synonymous with moral and ethical purity. When we use the word *saint,* we generally refer to a righteous and loving person, even though that is not its essential meaning. This is perhaps the great strength of evangelical spirituality. Catholic and Orthodox spirituality emphasized the sacramental and mystic aspects of spirituality. Charismatic spirituality emphasized the power aspect of spirituality. But evangelical spirituality emphasized the ethical and moral aspects of spirituality. There is truth in all three emphases.

There is no developed concept of a supreme God who is holy in pantheistic cultures. Therefore, in pantheistic spirituality a concerted push for morality is often lacking. This is why, despite the strong tradition of spirituality in Asia, our countries are plagued by corruption today. The gods of Hinduism were morally neutral, and they are often seen to be doing things that we consider quite unholy. The emphasis in those spiritualities is not so much on holiness in the sense of moral purity as on holiness in the sense of spiritual power—of power over the mind, over the body, over anxiety and circumstances. We have seen that even in Christian circles when there is an emphasis on spiritual power, sometimes there is a tendency to neglect teaching on moral issues.

People from the West go to places like the Himalayan mountains in search of exotic spiritual experiences. They often have such experiences. But many of them are seen to behave in ways that are morally very impure, such as dabbling in drugs and promiscuous sex. Though there are exceptions, generally pantheistic spiritualities have not succeeded in producing just, morally upright, and fair societies. Presently the societies in many countries in the West are fashioned according to a system of trust based on transcendent absolutes and of submission to a supreme God. Values and structures such as freedom of expression, democracy, and even the supermarket operate on these assumptions. I shudder to think what will happen as one by one these presuppositions are being jettisoned in the West and replaced by values derived from a pantheistic worldview.

In Christian spirituality we enter into the experience of a personal relationship with the holy God through humble recognition of our sinfulness and inability to help ourselves. We first bow down before the supreme God in repentance. Once we enter into a relationship with God, we submit to his lordship and become subject to his will for our personal lives.

The pantheistic approach is quite opposite to this. We can see how this approach fits in with the postmodern mood with its quest for self-actualization. You don't need to bow down before a supreme God who is an objective

AJITH FERNANDO

reality outside of yourself. You *are* God! An influential spiritual teacher in America, Swami Mukthananda, has said, "Kneel to your own self. Honor and worship your own being. God dwells within you as You!"[6] That sounds much better to postmodern ears than the words, "Kneel in humble submission and repent for your sin before the almighty God."

So we shouldn't be surprised by the growth of pantheistic spirituality today. It fits in with the aspirations of the postmodern soul. People want something spiritual to answer the heart-cry that secular humanism could not meet. Pantheism provides an answer without violating the quest for a life without submission to objective realities like a supreme God, a strict moral code, and an infallible Bible.

Yet no one can find full satisfaction without solving the sin question in his or her life. An American Methodist preacher of an earlier generation, Henry Clay Morrison, is reported to have said, "God did not fix me up so that I couldn't sin. He fixed me up so that I couldn't sin and enjoy it." According to the psalmists, the law of the Lord is not a burden that enslaves us, it is a delight that gives life.[7] The objective truth of the Word is not an obstacle to freedom. Jesus said that the truth will make us free (John 8:32–36). The context of that affirmation shows that the freedom Jesus spoke about had much to do with living a life freed from enslavement to sin.

And what can we say about liberation from our own past actions? The law of karma, with its belief in repeated incarnations, seems to have replaced the Christian emphasis on sin and judgment, grace and justification in the minds of many postmoderns. But can people completely negate all their bad karma by their own efforts accumulated through several lives? Many honest people who are committed to this scheme would admit that this is a long and dreary climb along a path that does not carry much hope of liberation at the end. Although the adherents of this path have the satisfaction of doing something to save themselves, they will not experience the freedom of knowing that their wrong actions are behind them eternally and forgotten. The Christian gospel, on the other hand, speaks of "having our hearts sprinkled to cleanse us from a guilty conscience" (Heb. 10:22) through the perfect and sufficient sacrifice of Christ Jesus. Without such freedom from a guilty conscience, there can be no permanently fulfilling experience of spirituality.

AN OPPORTUNITY FOR THE CHURCH

So while the new interest in spirituality is a challenge to the church, it is also a great opportunity. Christian spirituality is one of the key aspects of the uniqueness of Christ. Therefore it may figure prominently in our evangelism. Sooner or later people will realize that the serenity that New Age spiritualities provide does not fully satisfy. Though New Age spirituality has been described as holistic, only the Creator of human life can give humans a truly holistic spirituality. It is he who created every aspect of the human makeup, and therefore only he can satisfy the yearnings of the whole human soul. This is why Jesus, who was God's answer to the human dilemma, said, "I have come that they may have life and have it to the full" (John 10:10). Christ is unique because he alone offers the only life that can be called life to the full.

This discussion has shown that the current interest in spirituality can be a stepping-stone in the evangelization of postmoderns. Worship, the supreme expression of Christian spirituality, can therefore be an important means to evangelism in the postmodern era. We have found this to be so in our evangelism among youth. Vibrant Christian worship demonstrates to people that what they are yearning for is found in the Christian gospel.

So the current interest in spirituality is a challenge to the church to get its act together. We have the answer that the world is looking for. But have we ourselves experienced it? Do we know the glory of intimacy with the loving and holy God who is supreme above creation? Has this relationship transformed us into morally pure people? If we can answer these questions in the affirmative, we will truly be light to the darkness of the world in this postmodern era.

References

Appasamy, A. J. 1966. *Sundar Singh: A Biography*. Madras: Christian Literature Society.

Ariarajah, Wesley. 1977. "Toward a Theology of Dialogue." *Ecumenical Review* 29 (1): 3–11.

Carson, D. A. 1996. *The Gagging of God: Christianity Confronts Pluralism*. Grand Rapids: Zondervan.

Fernando, Ajith. 1995. *The Supremacy of Christ*. Wheaton: Crossway.

Griffiths, Paul J. 1991. *An Apology for Apologetics: A Study of the Logic of Interreligious Dialogue*. Maryknoll: Orbis.

Groothuis, Douglas. 1986. *Unmasking the New Age*. Downers Grove, Ill.: InterVarsity Press.

Hick, John. 1980. *God Has Many Names*. Philadelphia: Westminster.

Kraemer, Hendrik. 1938 (reprint 1969). *The Christian Message in a Non-Christian World*. Grand Rapids: Kregel.

Phillips, Gary. 1997. "Religious Pluralism in a Postmodern World." In *The Challenge of Postmodernism: An Evangelical Engagement*, ed. David S. Dockery, 254–56. Grand Rapids: Baker.

Roszak, Theodore. 1977. *Unfinished Animal*. New York: Harper and Row.
Seamands, J. T. 1964. *The Supreme Task of the Church*. Grand Rapids: Eerdmans.
Stott, John. 1990. *Decisive Issues Facing Christians Today*. Old Tappan, N.J.:
    Revell.

CHAPTER 9

COMMUNICATING SIN IN A POSTMODERN WORLD

Mark E. Dever

Today is a wonderful time of opportunity for sharing the good news of Jesus Christ. We need not be scared by postmodernism, feeling that it is too complex to understand, and therefore concluding that only scholars can be evangelists today.

The church that I serve in Washington, D.C., looks old. The congregation was gathered over a hundred and twenty years ago. The building is old, and some of the members are even older! Sometimes friends of mine have asked me, "What are you doing here? It looks like you're serving a church of the past." My response is, "No. This is the church of the future."

We don't have the kind of homogenized community around us that so often characterizes suburban communities. We have high transience, high crime, high education, and great diversity of lifestyles. These attributes of our community also seem likely to be attributes of most of our communities in the future and even of our culture as a whole. If we can see an evangelical witness grow in that kind of place, then by God's grace, what we're seeing is a church, not of the past, but of the future.

THE POSTMODERN PROBLEM

There's no doubt that old modern skepticism is on the wane. Beliefs seem to be filling the air again. But simply abandoning the old skepticism is not the same as embracing faith. We need to be aware of that as we note the encouraging things that we as evangelicals might find in postmodernism.

A good biblical illustration of how this happens can be found in Mark 6, where Jesus performed a nature miracle. He walked on the water to the boat,

MARK E. DEVER

and the seas calmed down. The disciples were terrified. They clearly had no modernist skepticism about Jesus' authority over nature. But neither did they possess Christian faith. They certainly had shed any antisupernaturalism that may have been lurking in them, and yet that doesn't mean that they had embraced a full understanding of Jesus of Nazareth. So even as we are encouraged by the falling walls of skepticism in our culture, we shouldn't mistake that as possession of Christian faith. This new faith-friendly world seems particularly presented again and again without mentioning sin. That lack is the topic of this chapter.

Recently, an occasional attender at our church told me that one of his hesitancies in getting involved in a Christian church was that his therapist told him that he had enough shame and guilt. He therefore didn't want to go down that route again.

I met another person, John, on the airplane a few days before that. His intelligence was evidenced by the fact that he was amusing himself by calculating actuarial statistics! Soon we struck up a conversation, and it became clear that he considered himself both a Christian and sinless. When I asked him to explain that, he said, "The way I like to think of it is that every day my life is created anew; it begins again. So who I am as a person is defined again and again every day with a freshness and a newness that I think the Bible says is very much the way God continually loves us."

During our hour-long conversation, I asked, "Well, what about the cross? And Jesus' words about the atonement, the wrath of God, and his teaching that he was a ransom?" He responded, "Oh well, I don't like that stuff very much."

This conversation continued until the end of the flight. As we were standing up and walking off the plane, I said, "John, excuse me. One last question. I'm just curious. Have you ever heard of postmodernism?" "No, I haven't," he answered, and he commented that he had never even heard the word.

The Fonz, it seems, was the John the Baptist of postmodernism in our popular culture. Remember the one word he could not pronounce? He could not say the word *wrong*. And so he seems to have heralded what's common in our culture now.

This evasion of responsibility is not new, but it is dangerous. And the more pervasive it becomes and the more accepted it is, the more dangerous it is, from the reports of brutal infanticides to the fears of totalitarianism. Hannah Arendt said that "nobody's rule" is the most tyrannical of all forms of power because under such circumstances nobody can be held responsible (Beck 1997, 6).

What is behind all this? A quick sketch will have to suffice. Relativism is not a new idea. The Enlightenment brought to the fore the importance of the observer and of the process of interpreting the reality that we sense. Bias has long been known and admitted. John Locke, in the beginning of his *Letter Concerning Toleration*, written over three hundred years ago, said that "everyone is orthodox to himself."

In John Milton's *Paradise Lost* is an amazing picture of Satan being cast down from heaven into the nether regions of hell. And do you recall what Satan says when he lands there and begins to look around?

> "Is this the region, this the soil, the clime"
> Said then the lost Archangel, "this the seat
> That we must change for heav'n, this mournful gloom
> For that celestial light? Be it so. Since he
> Who now is sovereign can dispose and bid
> What shall be right: farthest from him is best,
> Whom reason hath equaled, force hath made supreme
> Above his equals. Farewell, happy fields,
> Where joy forever dwells! Hail, horrors, hail,
> Infernal world, and thou profoundest hell
> Receive thy new possessor: one who brings
> A mind not to be changed by place or time.
> The mind is its own place, and in itself
> Can make a heav'n of hell, a hell of heav'n."[1]

Those last two lines have to be one of the best expressions of a part of postmodernism. The mind is a place in its own self. And in itself it can make a heaven of hell and a hell of heaven. But today there is a refined relativism. There is a hardening coolness to the idea of truth. And this is happening not just in elite academic circles where Richard Rorty and Stanley Fish are quoted, but in popular culture. So the British actor Hugh Grant said not too long ago, "I don't believe in truth, I believe in style."[2] He may have said that with confidence, but I don't believe the Los Angeles police were quite as skeptical of unargued objective reality.

Such offhand affirmations of self-expression over and against a standard outside of ourselves are not so benign and winning as they may initially seem. At first such affirmations may appear wonderfully nonjudgmental, leading us into an era of tolerance and pluralism and therefore certainly of peace. After all, isn't beauty in the eye of the beholder? But such resigned perspectivalism takes on a new sting as we consider the economic systems of some Marxists, totalitarian states, marketers who would sell by careless sexual arousal, and

MARK E. DEVER

the Nazi looking at the finely designed and efficiently built ovens of Auschwitz or Bergen-Belsen. With so much at stake, we must care about this newly prominent cultural mood. And we must try to understand it as best we can.

Today there is a widespread denial of a metanarrative. The metanarrative is, of course, the narrative that is above all the others. It is that by which we interpret all the others. It is the plot. And it is this that intellectuals for a hundred years have been concerned to deny (Carey 1992).

An unusually candid admission of this denial was made by Aldous Huxley in midlife, when he was in the process of moving from agnosticism to various forms of Eastern mysticism. He mentions that he, like so many of his contemporaries, took it for granted that there was no meaning. "This is partly due to the fact," writes Huxley, "that I shared the common belief that the scientific picture of an abstraction from reality was a true picture of reality as a whole; partly also to other nonintellectual reason, I had motives for not wanting the world to have a meaning; consequently assumed that it had none, and was able without any difficulty to find satisfying reasons for this assumption." Then, after he uses the Marquis de Sade as a particularly graphic example of life following thought, Huxley continues, "The philosopher who finds no meaning in the world is not concerned exclusively with a problem in pure metaphysics. He is also concerned to prove that there is no valid reason why he personally should not do as he wants to do. Or why his friends should not seize political power and govern in the way they find most advantageous to themselves." Then Huxley changes to an even more personal note:

> For myself, as no doubt for most of my contemporaries, the philosophy of meaninglessness was essentially an instrument for liberation. The liberation we desired was simultaneously liberation from a certain political and economic system and liberation from a certain system of morality. We objected to the morality because it interfered with our sexual freedom. We objected to the political and economic systems because it was unjust. The supporters of these systems claimed that in some way they embodied the meaning of the world. There was one admirably simple method of confuting these people, and at the same time justifying ourselves and our political and erotic revolt: we could deny that the world had any meaning whatsoever. (1937, 269–73)

The denial that there is a meaning, a metanarrative, is not new. What is new is the extent to which this denial has pervaded our society and our culture. It is not just Aldous Huxley or people who teach Nietzsche at the local college who think this way now. It is the people who watch our television sets and who write what is broadcast on them. Yet without standards of good and truth, how can sin be said to exist? And without sin, what need is there of a Savior?

The situation we face can be summarized by the simple observation that people today are hiding. They are doing exactly what Adam did when he first ran to hide himself from God.

Modernism is a revolt against revealed religion. It is a revolt against the truth. Postmodernism is a further revolt, fundamentally against modernism and secondarily against Christianity and the truth as well.

In modernism, or the modernist revolt, there was thought to be a meta-narrative, an overall plot and meaning to life, but without a metanarrator. The one speaking it was not needed. Reality was seen as all material. Nothing super-natural was necessary. Any moral sense in this narrative was only that which could be established by objective reason; no God was needed. It was essentially an atheistic system. One could have a God, but he would be only a "God of the gaps." He was posited simply to fill in what science had not yet told us.

In revolting against this, postmodernism has gone further, saying that, in fact, there is not only no metanarrator, but there is no metanarrative either. There is only my narrative. Furthermore, as overall meaning recedes from view and the metanarrative vanishes, the self becomes fragmented and tends to take its definition from the community around it. The self in postmodernism is unable finally to be judged by any other, except in terms of power. The self becomes the ultimate; the self is divinized.

Christianity responds to both modernism and postmodernism. Without digressing about Christianity's response to modernism, we can clearly say that Christianity's response to postmodernism must include a reassertion of the real-ity of sin. Of course, the beginning of any solution is clarity about the problem. If this is the problem with which postmodernism presents us, what are we to do?

SOLUTIONS

From my vantage point in the trenches of ministry, I want to make sug-gestions about solving the difficult problem of the vanishing of the idea of sin in postmodern minds. The offered solutions are clustered around four basic ideas: (1) communicating, (2) community, (3) conscience, and (4) con-version.

COMMUNICATING

First, communicate God's truth. Teach the truth. In order to do that, you have to know the truth, and you have to understand somewhat the vocabulary of the people you're talking to. You must not carelessly assume that everyone means the same thing by the word *God* and certainly not the same thing by the word *sin*. In that sense, this time that we are in can be a time of special opportunity for Christians to learn more about being careful with the gospel, to weed out some of the cultural assumptions that have wedded themselves in our minds to the gospel, and to learn to listen more carefully to those who talk with us.

Specifically, of course, postmodern people need to grasp hold of the category of evil and wrong. The simple existence of a widespread difficulty in understanding what sin is, is hardly unprecedented. In the Old Testament when God called out the Israelite nation, one of the reasons he gave all the rules there in Exodus, Leviticus, Numbers, and Deuteronomy about almost everything conceivable was in order to begin to teach people that there is nothing finally that is neutral to a holy God in a fallen world. He began to teach this people categories of right and wrong. We need to be involved in a similar exercise.

As Christians we are not about merely setting up impersonal standards. Our postmodern friends may take us at first to be like modernists because we too talk about an objective, external standard. The difference, though, is that with Christianity, the truth is finally personal. We are not simply saying that there is an eternal law by which we are all to be judged. Rather, we are speaking of sin, as James does in chapter 2 of his letter, where he argues that if you have broken one commandment you have broken them all, specifically because you have offended the one Lawgiver.

Christians understand sin fundamentally to be a breaking with God's character and with his will for us to reflect that character. This is where the theologians among us must avoid the error made by Karl Barth (and repeated by some self-consciously evangelical believers) in pitting the propositional against the personal. Such a posited opposition is unhelpful and unfruitful. Propositions do not exhaust God's revelation, and yet propositions are essential for God's revelation as he has revealed himself to us. You will not increase the relational or personal nature of Christian revelation by trying to extract the propositions from it. In fact, you will do precisely the opposite.

If you have any doubt that cognitive, propositional communication is at the very heart of relationship, let me ask this to those of you who have dogs at home: Would you say you had a good relationship with them? Probably most of you dog-owning readers of this chapter would say that, yes, you do have a good relationship with your dog. Yet even so, I predict that the quality, indeed the very nature of that relationship would change if you were to go home this evening and be greeted verbally by your dog. If your dog introduced speech into the relationship, it would change the nature of that relationship. That dog could both more fully know you and be more fully known by you.

Our God is not a mute God. Not only is he active in history, but he has spoken. And so we must care about cognitive truth. God has revealed himself as a personal God, and part of that personhood is his communication to us of truth.

So we should communicate truth in all kinds of ways: by telling illustrative stories, by helping people to see the truth about their own worldview, by helping non-Christian friends to reflect on the inadequacies of their own understanding of the world.

Some years ago, I was meeting weekly with a group of atheists at my college in Cambridge. No other Christians were allowed. One particularly irritating fellow (whom I'll call Richard) repeatedly attacked any kind of belief in God and even me as such a belief's chief proponent (within reach). He was absolutely intransigent. Others were at least somewhat moved. Most were kindly deferential and respectful. But Richard was simply and continually abusive. At one point he was going on and on about how intolerant this idea of exclusive truth is. Exasperated with his repeated verbal jabs and insinuations, I said, "Richard, let me just break in here and make one thing perfectly clear. If anyone in this room were ever going to kill anyone else for their views, it would not be that I would kill you, but that you would kill me. It doesn't matter how much you disagree with me, I believe that you were made in the image of God. I believe that you have a life that is of more value than I know how to calculate. And that I have absolutely no right, before my Creator (who I believe will judge me regardless of what you do), I have no right to coerce you physically or any other way whatsoever. However, to you, Richard, I am but a collection of electrons and atoms. I am accidental. If the popular opinion would allow it, you might snuff me out if I became too troublesome. And you have no reason in your own worldview why you shouldn't do it, ultimately. If there is a threat of intolerance and danger, Richard, it doesn't come from me and what I am saying; it comes from you and what you are saying." Rather uncomfortably, Richard agreed. We can at least thank God for the honesty that postmodernism encourages.

Certainly in claiming to communicate the truth, Christians are not claiming that we possess all knowledge; yet the mere fact that we do not know everything does not mean we do not know anything. We need to teach the truth we know about God, particularly about his holiness, his transcendence.

A couple of years ago at a dinner party, I met a person who had a completely secular upbringing. Holding a typical Washington job, she had never

MARK E. DEVER

really had any exposure to evangelical Christianity. She was fascinated by the Christian gospel. In God's providence, after we had begun to study through Mark's gospel, she was confronted with a truly heinous situation. She struggled with the realization that she was revolted by what a particular person had done, and she found difficulty writing about it with the objectivity that her secular upbringing told her that she should have. She wanted to be indignant, but she found no vocabulary of indignation within herself.

And then one day she told me, "But do you know what I just realized last night? Through talking to you in these Bible studies, I realized that what this man did is wrong." When she said that word *wrong,* she experienced almost incredible relief. There seemed to be a correctness to the world that came all of a sudden when she began to recognize the category of wrong.

Let me give you some bibliographical resources for thinking about telling the truth. Look at Romans 1:18, and meditate on what Paul meant: "The wrath of God is being revealed from heaven against all the godlessness and wickedness of men who suppress the truth by their wickedness." Notice how Paul is certain of the truth of the resurrection in 1 Corinthians 15, particularly of its facticity in verse 19. In Romans 10:17, Paul writes about faith coming by hearing, which is not merely, but is not less than, a cognitive activity.

There are many works written about this problem: Aldous Huxley's *Ends and Means,* which I quoted from above; Stanley Fish's *There's No Such Thing As Free Speech and It's a Good Thing Too;* Karl Popper's *The Open Society and Its Enemies,* especially the final chapter where he explains why there must be no meaning to history. Though Popper wrote during the end and in the aftermath of World War II, his argument is parallel to the arguments that are made by postmodernists.

For help in beginning to construct some answers, read the book by John Carey, professor of English at Oxford, *The Intellectuals and the Masses.* In this book, Carey criticizes postmodernism. Although he is not writing from a Christian perspective, he gives devastating criticism nonetheless. Look too at E. D. Hirsch's *Validity in Interpretation.* Don't miss Frederick Crews's little book, *The Pooh Perplex.* In this book, Crews examines the literary sources for the Winnie the Pooh tales. The whole thing is a sarcastic send-up of literary criticism, in which Crews shows what utter nonsense can be made out of simple ideas in simple minds.

Ernest Gellner's *Postmodernism, Reason and Religion* is a good modernist critique of postmodernism. D. A. Carson's book *The Gagging of God* provides a good assessment and critique of postmodernism from an evangelical perspective. You might want to give a postmodern friend a copy of Francis

Schaeffer's *Escape from Reason* or even J. I. Packer's *Fundamentalism and the Word of God*. Another approach to begin communicating an understanding of sin to a postmodern friend is to watch a video together. For example, watch *It's a Wonderful Life* or *The Truman Show* and then talk about meaning in life and about metanarrative.

An important thing to note is that the loss of the metanarrative above means the loss of the continuing person below. The postmodern loss of meaning results in a loss of the responsible self. So we understand Calvin in the very first sentence of his *Institutes*: "Nearly all the wisdom we possess, that is to say, true and sound wisdom, consists of two parts: the knowledge of God and of ourselves. But, while joined by many bonds, which one precedes and brings forth the other is not easy to discern" (1.1.1).

We must recognize the relationship between the perception of God and the perception of self. We have to know God to truly know ourselves. Therefore, you won't be surprised at my second piece of practical advice: emphasize the community.

COMMUNITY

I recently began a talk to one university group with the line, "If you are not a member of the church you are attending, you may well be going to hell." It immediately got their attention, and I was able to explain.

As I've preached through various portions of the Bible, particularly John's gospel and letters and the letter of James, I've been struck again and again by the way the church functions in Jesus' thoughts and in the New Testament, and how that contrasts with the way that we as modern American evangelicals tend to think of the congregation. If you will, think of your involvement in a covenanted community of believers as the indicator lights of your car's dashboard—they won't make it go, and they won't stop it, but they might at least give you an honest reflection of what's going on.

The Christian life is to be lived, in part, by folding yourself into a series of committed relationships, not just with your friends (with whom you may have all kinds of other things in common) but with a local church, open to all, united around faith in the Lord Jesus Christ. If you try to live your Christian life without such relationships in such a community, then you must beware, because there are many places in the New Testament that warn you that you could be fooling yourself.

One woman who came to know the Lord in our church recently had been a Unitarian for many years. She had no previous experience in an evangelical church. For some reason she began attending our church, and within a year

MARK E. DEVER

she became a Christian. Her adult son saw her life and was struck by the difference Christ had made in her life. So he began coming to church with her. He noticed the way people treated each other in the church, and after studying Scripture, he too became a Christian. Months later her other son too came to Christ, in no small part because of the witness of Christians committed in love to God and each other. In the local church and the nexus of committed relationships there, the boundaries of our identity are set by our interactions with others. Even if the postmodernist denies that the self exists, that self cannot escape interaction with others. And if that person—even while in spiritual rebellion—is consistently treated as someone made in the image of God, this powerfully communicates truth.

Many biblical passages describe attempts at the rejection of responsibility. Of course, there is Genesis 3, the story of the first couple in the Garden. And 2 Samuel 12 is the incredible story of Nathan confronting David, who comes to see his own fault, though before that time he had completely justified his own actions in his mind. Again, in James 1 Christians are warned not to look at the Word of God and then turn away from it and so deceive ourselves. See too 1 John 4:19–20 and 1 Corinthians 5.

There are a number of interesting and useful works related to these topics. Look at Paul Vitz's *Psychology as Religion*; a couple of Christopher Lasch's books, *The Culture of Narcissism* and *The Minimal Self*; David Wells's *No Place for Truth*; or Peter Berger's *A Far Glory*. A vivid portrait of an individual is presented in Augustine's *Confessions*. In his book *The Reformed Pastor*, Richard Baxter encourages the careful cultivation of relationships in the church. Read Jonathan Edwards's tremendous series of sermons from 1 Corinthians 13 that he was preaching when the Great Awakening broke out—*Charity and Its Fruits*. These are wonderful sermons on how to treat others in such a way as to reflect the image of God. Read C. S. Lewis's *The Screwtape Letters*, Robert Bellah's *Habits of the Heart*, Ray Stedman's *Body Life*, or Gene Getz's books on the church. Chuck Colson's *The Body* is a good popular presentation of the life that is supposed to make the gospel visible. In the final chapter of his book *Losing Our Virtue*, David Wells spends ten pages calling for a renewed congregational life for the reasons outlined above.

One caution here: some evangelicals are taking on board the critique that postmodernism makes of evangelical Christianity, and in response are adopting communitarian language. For example, though there is much that I as a Baptist and congregational Christian appreciate in his writings, some of Stanley Grenz's materials have a troubling lack of reference to a vertical dimension to sin—that is, to the truth that sin is fundamentally against God (e.g., Ps. 51).

Again and again, it is described only in a horizontal dimension (Grenz 1993). Miroslav Volf's provocatively titled book *After Our Likeness: The Church as the Image of the Trinity* (1998) seems to fall into much the same error. In recovering the importance of community, don't ever think that it replaces the vertical—the relationship with God. The role of the community is to supplement and reflect this relationship.

There is much that you could give postmodern friends to read in order to show how people are worthy of respect, love, and concern. Give them a copy of Charles Dickens' classic *A Christmas Carol* to read, or watch a dramatic presentation of it with them around Christmas. Then discuss with them the values represented in it and why they are or are not true. Or read H. G. Wells' short story "The Land of the Blind" with them and discuss it. Of course, to communicate something of sin by the community, you don't so much give them a book to read as build a relationship with them, and you invite them to church.

CONSCIENCE

We can think of community as providing the external boundaries of the self, as that which helps to make ourselves obvious to ourselves. The community is the circumference of the self, but we Christians must also address the very center of the self. We need to know that postmodern unbelievers have consciences even if they don't think they do. Because they're made in God's image, they do, and Christians should be confident of this fact.

Sometimes we share the gospel with people while secretly only half-believing it's true, wondering what they will concede to us, and not wanting to say much more than that lest we look ridiculous. But we must resolve to look ridiculous. Paul called it "the foolishness of the cross." Don't be put off by the current fad of the times. People need to grasp not only the theoretical concept of evil and wrong, but also the fact that *they* are evil and wrong. They need to experience their own consciences. This is difficult in postmodernism, because the self tends to dissolve away, to disappear. In many ways, that may be the biggest problem we have when we try to communicate the idea of sin today. Postmodernism encourages the evacuation of the responsible self.

But the real reason people don't acknowledge the legitimate moral claims of God is not because of any philosophy; it is simply because it is not in their self-interest to do so. Not too long ago, I was in a conversation that turned to the media's coverage of reputed indecent goings-on in Washington. Particular mention was made of the fact that the media were being very careful and even seemed reluctant to speak about adultery in any judgmental tones. For about

MARK E. DEVER

fifteen minutes, this was a very highbrow discussion as my media friends delicately parried back and forth, considering why the coverage needed to be like this. Finally one of them said, "Now let's be honest. You know the real reason that people don't like to write about this is because they're all committing adultery themselves."

We cannot get rid of the bias that people have in not wanting to hear that they are accountable for their actions. The good news is that postmodernism at least lets us say that! Postmoderns may happily own their biases, but they own them in a very tentative way because they think that a Christian critique of their activity originates merely in our own biases. So beware—what postmodernism seems to give with one hand it takes away with the other.

Nevertheless, we should be confident of the conscience. There are many parts of Scripture that show the reality of sin and guilt. The story of Ananias and Sapphira in Acts 5 clearly shows the seriousness of it. We see it in Jesus' teaching in Luke 18 of the parable of the Pharisee and the publican. And there is much about the conscience in Paul's letter to the Romans, especially in Romans 1–3.

Something that might be helpful and encouraging to read in this regard is John Bunyan's book *The Holy War*. It is the story of the town of Man's Soul. The town is taken over by the upstart Diabolos, who is a false prince. He takes control of the city entirely—except, that is, for the town crier, Old Man Conscience. Though he is usually subservient to Diabolos, every once in a while Old Man Conscience seems to lose his senses. At such times, he grabs his bell and runs up and down the streets of Man's Soul, ringing his bell and yelling out at the top of his lungs, "Diabolos is a liar and a cheat! Prince Emmanuel is the true prince of Man's Soul!" Yet he is regularly captured, and after his outbreak, he is again calmed and brought under control. This is a powerful picture of the conscience.

Have your friends read parts of the Bible. Get them to read the Ten Commandments with you, or the Sermon on the Mount, or the parables of Jesus. Get your friends to read the book of James. Get them to read the medieval morality play *Everyman*. It is a short, dramatic presentation of our own personal responsibility.

CONVERSION

Finally, all of this should serve to highlight the truth that conversion is only by God's Spirit. When I meet those for whom it seems that the metanarrative is gone and the circumference of the self is gone and even the center of the self is evacuated, I confess that I get discouraged. We can go to conferences and read books, argue and try to persuade—yet we cannot bring our friends to spiritual life. When we have learned that, then we have learned one of the most important lessons we could ever learn in Christian ministry.

We cannot bring anyone to life. So our heavenly Father invites us to come to him and entreat him that his Holy Spirit would take that which is eviscerated and gone, that which is spiritually evacuated, and that he would give life again—new life—as he did to the dry bones in the vision he gave to Ezekiel, recorded in chapter 37. This is an amazing passage for those of us who think that words have no meaning any more. If you and I were planning that vision, surely we would put flesh on those bones first, then we would set them in a nice conference center, and then we would have Ezekiel stand up and prophesy. But in this vision God gives to Ezekiel, Ezekiel was to prophesy to a valley of desiccated bones. And by that Spirit, that word that comes out of Ezekiel, God gives life. That is the confidence that you and I need to have—that it is God himself who will do it, regardless of how little we understand postmodernism.

One person who first heard the gospel and began to understand was particularly struck by the phrase "newness of life" in our church literature. This person thought the idea had "such a ring to it" that we must have had a very good writer at our church. After finding a therapist somewhat helpful, this same friend said that, as helpful as the therapist may have been, it was Christianity that had the vocabulary to explain life in all its problems and fullnesses. Christians have the vocabulary to explain, not because we are clever, but because God really is our Creator.

For help in understanding this idea of conversion in the Bible, read John 3–4, Romans 5, and Ephesians 2. John Owen's treatise, *The Dominion of Sin and Grace* and J. C. Ryle's *Holiness* could both be helpful. Will Metzger has written an excellent book that shows how the truth should affect our evangelism—*Tell the Truth*. And J. I. Packer has sorted out many a young student through his little volume, *Evangelism and the Sovereignty of God*. Wilde's *The Portrait of Dorian Gray* and C. S. Lewis's *The Voyage of the Dawn Treader* both present dramatic personal changes that could provide the impetus for serious conversation.

CONCLUSION

We should have hope and good courage in the reality of the truth of God's Word. What a privilege we have, to be able to give people the good news of the gospel. And the gospel is more than up to the challenge of postmodernism. We simply need to be faithful messengers. We don't have to understand everything about postmodernism. We do need to know the gospel. If we do, and we are faithful heralds of it, then regardless of what anyone says or we may fear, we are not members of the church of the past but members of the church of the future.

References

Baxter, Richard. 1974. *The Reformed Pastor*. Carlisle: Banner of Truth Trust.

Beck, Ulrich. 1997. "A Risky Business." *London School of Economics Magazine* 9 (winter): 4–6.

Bellah, Robert. 1985. *Habits of the Heart: Individualism and Commitment in American Life*. New York: Harper and Row.

Berger, Peter. 1992. *A Far Glory: The Quest for Faith in an Age of Credulity*. New York: Free Press.

Carey, John. 1992. *The Intellectuals and the Masses: Pride and Prejudice Among the Literary Intelligentsia, 1880–1939*. London: Faber and Faber.

Carson, D. A. 1996. *The Gagging of God: Christianity Confronts Pluralism*. Grand Rapids: Zondervan.

Colson, Charles. 1992. *The Body*. Waco, Tex.: Word.

Crews, Frederick. 1963. *The Pooh Perplex: A Freshman Casebook*. New York: Dutton.

Fish, Stanley. 1994. *There's No Such Thing as Free Speech and It's a Good Thing Too*. New York: Oxford University Press.

Gellner, Ernest. 1992. *Postmodernism, Reason and Religion*. London/New York: Routledge.

Getz, Gene. 1974. *Sharpening the Focus of the Church*. Chicago: Moody Press.

————. 1975. *The Measure of a Church*. Glendale: Regal.

Grenz, Stanley. 1993. *Revisioning Evangelical Theology*. Downers Grove, Ill.: InterVarsity Press.

Hirsch Jr., E. D. 1967. *Validity in Interpretation*. New Haven: Yale University Press.

Huxley, Aldous. 1937. *Ends and Means*. London: Chatto and Windus.

Lasch, Christopher. 1979. *The Culture of Narcissism: American Life in an Age of Diminishing Expectations*. New York: Warner.

————. 1984. *The Minimal Self: Psychic Survival in Troubled Times*. New York: W. W. Norton.

Lewis, C. S. 1942. *The Screwtape Letters*. London: G. Bles.

Packer, J. I. 1958. *"Fundamentalism" and the Word of God*. London: Inter-Varsity Fellowship.

Popper, Karl. 1966. *The Open Society and Its Enemies*, 5th ed. Princeton: Princeton University Press.

Schaeffer, Francis. 1968. *Escape from Reason*. London/Chicago: InterVarsity Press.

Stedman, Ray. 1972. *Body Life*, 2d ed. Glendale: Regal.

Vitz, Paul. 1994. *Psychology as Religion: The Cult of Self-Worship*, 2d ed. Grand Rapids: Eerdmans.

Volf, Miroslav. 1998. *After Our Likeness: The Church as the Image of the Trinity*. Grand Rapids: Eerdmans.

Wells, David. 1993. *No Place for Truth, or Whatever Happened to Evangelical Theology?* Grand Rapids: Eerdmans.

_____. 1998. *Losing Our Virtue: Why the Church Must Recover Its Moral Vision*. Grand Rapids: Eerdmans.

CHAPTER 10

TURNING TO GOD

Conversion beyond Mere Religious Preference

Michael P. Andrus

I am a pastor, not a seminary professor, conference speaker, or author. In some ways I feel out of my element here, considering some of the distinguished scholars who have been invited to speak at this conference. But in another sense, as a pastor I may be uniquely able to address the topic I have been given. For the past quarter of a century, I have watched two churches grow significantly, and much of that growth has occurred through evangelism.

As a pastor I have the advantage of watching converts over a number of years. The campus minister can count professions of faith, and while he may keep in touch with a handful of those students, he generally will have no idea where the vast majority of them are spiritually two or three years out of college. But as a pastor, I have the opportunity to watch people from their initial contact with Christianity, through a sort of preevangelism stage, until they actually profess faith in Christ. But then I also have the privilege of baptizing them, providing discipleship and mentoring, equipping them for ministry, and finally mobilizing them into service.

One of the lessons I have learned from this experience is to give less attention to "decisions for Christ" and greater attention to "disciples of Christ." We are doing less crusade-type or "cold turkey" evangelism, and more friendship evangelism and evangelistic Bible studies. One tool that has become enormously fruitful for us is our own Discovery Series (Christianity 101, 201, 301, 401, 501, 601), which has resulted in professions of faith *and* effective discipleship of scores of individuals. Virtually every one of these converts is still active in our church and growing in their relationship with Christ.

My topic today is conversion and what it means in a postmodern era. If asked to give a one-word synonym for the verb *convert,* most people would probably offer "to turn" or "to change." In the general field of religion, the term is often used to signify a change of faiths or denominations, whether voluntary or forced. At the beginning of the fourth century, the Emperor Constantine engineered the "conversion" of his entire empire to Christianity. Islam has forced the conversion of entire countries under threat of the sword. Nominal Protestants have often converted to Catholicism in order to have a marriage approved and blessed. Nominal Catholics have sometimes gone the other way in order to get divorced and remarried.

. Such conversions, of course, do not necessarily entail any fundamental heart change. They may, and probably usually do, simply place a person under the influence of a different religious culture. They are little more than an expression of religious preference (either the preference of the individual or of the group that influenced the conversion).

A more meaningful definition of *conversion* is "to turn from one set of beliefs to another." A person may convert from paganism to Christianity, from Protestantism to Mormonism, from Arminianism to Calvinism, or from pedobaptism to believer's baptism. Once again these "conversions" do not necessarily entail a fundamental heart change; they may only signify a change in intellectual or theological perspective. Again, such conversions are often merely an expression of religious preference.

A more evangelical perspective on conversion is that it involves a "turning to God or a turning to Christ." Historically, evangelicals have called upon unbelievers to renounce their self-reliance and to enter into a personal relationship with God or with Christ. The phrases that have often been used to describe this conversion process include: "put your faith in God," "believe in Jesus," "invite Christ into your life," "be born again," "receive the free gift of salvation," or simply "become a Christian." If the invitee acquiesces, and especially if he "prays to receive Christ," he is considered a convert, not so much to a religion or a denomination as to a relationship with God.

Some of these evangelistic terms so commonly used in evangelical circles in the last half of the twentieth century convey the notion that conversion is the automatic result of an action one takes or a decision one makes. The assumption is that if one prays a certain prayer (in good faith, of course) he or she *ipso facto* receives Christ. This whole approach is what might be called "conversion by decision."

The fact that many who have become "converts" in this manner have proved over time to be genuine disciples has lent a certain amount of credence to this approach to the evangelistic enterprise. There are, unfortunately, very few statistics to indicate how many such professions have proved to be false, or at least ineffective in producing a genuine disciple. One wonders how many people who repeat a prayer after a ten-minute, cold-turkey gospel presentation remain not only unconverted but perhaps even gospel-hardened because of a false sense of security.

I believe there is a major danger in our contemporary evangelical culture in viewing conversion as a decision rather than as a change of life and perspective. And that danger is growing steadily in our postmodern culture as more and more people have less and less understanding of a biblical worldview.

Thirty years ago the average evangelistic target might reasonably have been expected to know and accept that the term *God* refers to an infinite, eternal personal being who created the world and who, though invisible, has left his fingerprints on human history; that Jesus was a literal man (but probably more than a man), who lived in the first century of the Christian era, lived a very good life, and was crucified unjustly by his enemies; and that *sin* is any action that violates God's law, especially the Ten Commandments, as well as one's conscience.

But such assumptions can no longer be made. To an unchurched, biblically illiterate individual today, *God* may very well be a term that means no more than ultimate reality. Jesus may be as mysterious and mystical a religious figure as is Gautama Buddha or Confucius.[1] And *sin* probably has no anchor in either God's law or conscience, especially if the person has a conscience seared by constant abuse and never reinforced by any significant moral teaching. To tell such a person that God loves him and Jesus died for his sins may be interpreted in any number of ways; or it may simply sound like nonsense.

Of course, if the person being evangelized happens to be unhappy and searching for some deeper meaning in life, he may respond to such a simple message ("God loves you and Jesus died for your sins") by saying, "Yes, I accept that," hoping to find the fulfillment he is looking for, in much the same way that a tired person might search for a new vitamin combination to give him more energy. But is he converted, in any biblical sense of the term? Or is he simply expressing a religious preference that he will follow until life takes a wrong turn or something better comes along?

I would like to suggest that in order for evangelism to result in true conversion in our present culture (this has probably always been true, but especially today) it must include at least the following three factors: (1) it must be content-specific; (2) it must include the notion that Christ is the exclusive way of salvation; and (3) it must result in a radical change of belief and conduct in the convert.

-156-

TELLING THE TRUTH

CONVERSION MUST BE CONTENT-SPECIFIC

We must define our terms, define our beliefs, and perhaps even define our presuppositions (such as the law of noncontradiction, the law of the excluded middle, the reality of objective truth). In other words, unless there is content to our gospel, we run the risk that any decision we elicit is little more than a psychologically convenient, perhaps even cathartic expression of religious preference.[2]

In his excellent book *Tell the Truth*, Will Metzger presents a compelling apologetic for making sure that the person being evangelized understands the maximum amount of truth possible, not the minimum. He states, "Man-centered evangelism [as opposed to God-centered evangelism, which he claims to espouse] shortens the message. It so focuses on man that it reduces God. It so fears further doctrinal division among true Christians that it allows the most imprecise gospel messages to become common currency" (1984, 31).

Among the most important content issues that need to be presented, explained, and developed as we evangelize the lost are these: who God is, who we are, what sin is, who Jesus is, what Jesus has done about sin, and what we must do about what Jesus has done. Let's examine these one at a time.

God must be known as the Creator of the universe and the owner of each of us; therefore, he has an absolute claim on our lives. We are neither impersonal machines nor animals. Our significance is derived from our unique creation in the image of God. God is love (little argument about that), but he is also holy and righteous (little agreement about that). It is our duty to be obedient to him and to love him with all our heart, soul, mind, and strength.

What about man? A sinful creature by nature, despite his noble status as a special creation of God, he sins by willfully refusing to do what God commands and willfully doing what God forbids. He pretends to be self-sufficient, ignoring God and deciding for himself what is right and wrong. The consequence is that he is plagued by physical and spiritual death (separation from God). If he continues to reject God's authority over him, he will spend eternity in hell.

Jesus Christ, the eternal Son of God, became a man through the incarnation, a miracle that is both incredible and essential at the same time. It is incredible in the same sense that any miracle is, especially one that happened only once and had no eye witnesses. But it is also essential, in contrast to many other miracles, in that it was the only conceivable means by which God could make himself fully known to humankind. Think about the incarnation this way: If there were an infinite God, and he desired to make himself known to

MICHAEL P. ANDRUS

finite creatures, what more effective means could he employ to reveal himself to those creatures than by becoming one of them?

Edwin A. Abbott, in his science fiction classic *Flatland* (1952), combines humor, satire, and logic to describe the difficulty of communication between vastly different universes. The rejection Abbott's "line" experienced when he tried to explain to his two-dimensional colleagues what he had seen when he visited the world of three dimensions, parallels exactly the rejection Jesus experienced when he took on himself the form of a servant and sought to explain (exegete, John 1:18) the nature, character, and demands of God to people who had never seen God.

What has Jesus done about human sin? His rejection, of course, culminated in his execution. But Jesus' death was uniquely chosen. The Gospel accounts make it abundantly clear that he willingly laid down his life, choosing the time and the place as he offered himself as the innocent, substitutionary sacrifice on behalf of all who are willing to acknowledge their sin and turn to him for forgiveness. He endured God's judgment for sin in his death on the cross and rose from the dead three days later.

Finally, it is essential that we present and explain coherently what we must do about what Jesus has done. We must believe. God invites us, even commands us, to turn from our rebellion and turn to Christ with our minds, our emotions, and our wills. We are to trust in nothing we can do, but only in the finished work of Christ as Savior. When we do, he is willing to save us not only from the penalty of sin but also from the power of sin. Since other religions do not have as radical a view of human sinfulness, the salvation they offer is also not as radical. But in biblical Christianity there is no excuse offered for continuing in sin. The Holy Spirit is given to us to bring about the changes God desires.

Of course, all of these truths can and should be conveyed to seekers by use of Scripture texts. Of particular use are the Ten Commandments; the Sermon on the Mount; the story of the woman at the well; the parables of the lost coin, the lost sheep, and the two lost sons; and the story of the conversion of Paul. Conversion must never be treated as a mere intellectual decision or as simply allegiance to a new group. It must be seen as a total life commitment to the truth of the Christian worldview.

CONVERSION MUST INCLUDE THE NOTION THAT SALVATION IS THROUGH CHRIST ALONE

Even if a convert is willing to accept that Jesus is the Son of God, that he died for his or her sins, rose from the dead, and provides the gift of eternal life, can he or she be truly converted while entertaining the opinion that there may be other ways of salvation? Many of those professing faith in Christ say exactly that.

In a recent poll, 74 percent of Americans strongly agreed that "there is only one true God, who is holy and perfect and who created the world and rules it today"; yet in the same poll, fully 64 percent strongly agree or agree somewhat with the assertion that "there is no such thing as absolute truth."[3] In such an irrational atmosphere, it should not be surprising that many claim to be Christians while at the same time entertaining the wider hope of salvation by other means than active faith in Christ.

There have always been those, of course, who have added Jesus to their previous set of beliefs as a sort of spiritual security blanket, a potential fire escape from hell. "What can it hurt?" is the silent question they ask themselves as they profess to believe in Jesus. The fact that a few of those may eventually become genuine believers does not argue against the notion that such professions are essentially meaningless—meaningless because the very essence of faith in Christ is the fact that through him and him alone can one have eternal life.

It is not necessary to debate here the question of whether those who die in infancy or are severely retarded are saved, or even whether there is a wider hope for those who, though unevangelized, are possibly sincere seekers after truth. I am inclined to affirm the former on theological grounds and reject the latter on biblical grounds, but my opinions on these topics are not really germane to the aspect of exclusivity that I am addressing here. What I am saying is that at the very least the one who is being evangelized (being, by definition, neither an infant nor one who has never heard the gospel) must see Jesus as his or her only hope for salvation. If John 14:6 and Acts 4:12 mean anything at all, they must mean that the one being confronted with the gospel cannot "believe in Jesus" in any saving sense and at the same time entertain the notion that there is another way of salvation.

Other faiths may be inclusive in regard to multiple means of salvation without great harm to their integrity, but Jesus has not left that option open to his followers. John 14:6 states the exclusive nature of his salvation positively, in the words of Jesus himself: "I am the way and the truth and the life. No one comes to the Father except through me." And Acts 4:12 states the same truth negatively: "Salvation is found in *no one else*, for there is *no other name* under heaven given to men by which we must be saved" (emphasis added).

Of course, we must face with courage the fact that exclusivity is anathema to the postmodern mind. To much of our culture, all beliefs are merely personal

MICHAEL P. ANDRUS

or at best culturally conditioned options. Therefore, no views can be dismissed except the view that some views can be dismissed. The notion that a particular ideological or religious claim is true and therefore intrinsically superior to another is necessarily wrong. Intolerance of someone else's position is the only thing that is intolerable.

The inimitable George Will wrote a column entitled "Intolerable Tolerance" in *Newsweek*. I quote the first paragraph:

> Too much of a good thing, said Mae West, is wonderful. But that is not true if the good thing is tolerance. Too much of that is both a cause and a consequence of a culture in which "judgmental" has become an epithet. Tolerance is a virtue only when it is difficult—when it involves keeping strong beliefs on a short leash. Tolerance that reflects the absence of strong beliefs is a symptom of a distinctively contemporary form of decadence—the comfortable disbelief in the propriety or importance of ever making emphatic judgments about behavior. (11 May 1998, 94)

Will's concern is with tolerance toward intolerable behavior, but the point applies as well to the modern penchant for tolerance toward intolerable (i.e., clearly unbiblical) beliefs. If we fail to address this issue of the exclusivity of Christ with today's intellectuals (and these views are quickly filtering down to the common man), then we may well find that our converts have simply added Jesus to an intellectual pantheon that includes Eastern philosophies, New Age goddesses, self-help psychology, or even black magic.

CONVERSION MUST RESULT IN A RADICAL CHANGE OF BELIEF AND CONDUCT

The issue here is that when one turns *to* something, he must at the same time turn *from* something else. That something may be idols, self, sin, alien beliefs, agnosticism, atheism, or even spiritual apathy. The New Testament term for this turning away is *repentance*. It means not just remorse, but a turning around so that one goes in an entirely different direction.

One of the issues working against us today is the fact that some very high profile converts to Christianity have exhibited a lifestyle that, far from demonstrating repentance, belies much that the gospel stands for. Jimmy Bakker, Jimmy Swaggart, Henry Lyons, President Clinton, and Mel White are names that come to mind. It is not uncommon for evangelicals to criticize these individuals for their hypocrisy, for they appear to us as people who have more-or-less sound theology but immoral lifestyles.

But have we considered the impact these individuals may have on the unchurched, who may be clueless about the potential gap between theology and practice? Many people may be coming to the conclusion, not that these guys are hypocrites, but that lifestyle doesn't really matter. In other words, they may conclude that one can claim to be a Christian and be an adulterer or a practicing homosexual or an embezzler at the same time.

We must make it clear through our teaching, as well as through our own personal examples, that an attitude of flippancy toward sin is absolutely incompatible with biblical conversion.

In an article in *World* magazine entitled "A Postmodern Scandal," Gene Edward Veith writes, "President Clinton, according to psychologist Robert Jay Lifton, is the nation's first postmodern president. Not bound by objective standards of truth, Mr. Clinton is able to continually reinvent himself, flexibly adapting his ideology, his behavior, and his very personality to the needs of the moment" (21 February 1998, 24). Lifton intends this evaluation as a compliment, but if he is correct, biblical Christians should be scandalized by it, especially since Clinton identifies himself openly as a Bible-believing Southern Baptist.

In this kind of atmosphere, the notion of true repentance from sin must be presented, explained, encouraged, and even demanded of those who claim membership in our churches or leadership in our ministries. Since we cannot read other people's hearts and discern their true status (saved or lost) before God, we need to help them measure themselves by God's standard to see if they are in the faith.

Wade Bradshaw writes perceptively, "The first Reformation was the re-discovery of the theology of Paul—of God's grace given freely to wholly undeserving sinners. A second, postmodern reformation will require the complementary re-discovery of the theology of James—that faith is always manifested" (1998, 116). Not only is such a faith needed today; postmoderns want to see the fruit of a message before they get serious about its doctrines.

Metzger (1984, 70) offers six tests of genuine faith from 1 John:

1. Test of consciousness of sin (1 John 1:8, 10)
2. Test of obedience (1 John 2:3–5, 29)
3. Test of freedom from habitual sin (1 John 3:9; 5:18)
4. Test of love for other Christians (1 John 3:14; 4:7–8)
5. Test of belief (1 John 5:1)
6. Test of overcoming the world and Satan (1 John 2:13–14)

In other words, what we should be looking for in our evangelism efforts is changed persons—*possessors,* not just professors of faith in Christ. By the

MICHAEL P. ANDRUS

way, this may provide an argument against immediate baptism of those who profess faith. No one would dispute the view that immediate baptism was the norm in the New Testament. The examples of the new believers on the day of Pentecost (Acts 2:41), the Ethiopian eunuch (Acts 8:36–38), and the Philippian jailer (Acts 16:33) are sufficient to demonstrate this practice. However, the cultural meaning of baptism was so strong in those days (and in many Middle Eastern cultures even today) that the mere willingness of a person to endure the persecutions associated with identification with Christianity was a sufficient guarantee that the candidate for baptism was sincere.

In our day, however, when baptism has almost no cultural significance (indeed, one could get baptized every week, and in most cases one's family and friends couldn't care less), we may need some other means of determining whether a candidate for baptism has been genuinely converted. I suggest that six months of turning from sin and fruit-bearing for Christ may be appropriate evidence of genuineness.

PRACTICAL SUGGESTIONS

What are some of the practical things we can do in our evangelistic efforts that will result in conversions that are real, rather than just an expression of religious preference? Consider the following:

1. Counsel seekers in a way that focuses on deeds, not words; change of life, not just change of beliefs. The last thing we should communicate is that by merely saying yes to a proposition, they can be assured of eternal life.
2. Focus on a biblical view of sin. Wade Bradshaw writes that postmoderns "suffer beneath a sense of meaninglessness rather than guilt. They are guilty, but they do not realize they need salvation from anything. The word sin is only used ironically" (1998, 17). But God uses it far more seriously. The apostle James exhorts his believing audience: "Come near to God and he will come near to you. Wash your hands, you sinners, and purify your hearts, you double-minded. Grieve, mourn and wail. Change your laughter to mourning and your joy to gloom" (James 4:8–9). We don't hear much preaching like that. A casual attitude toward sin has invaded the church. To those who presume too much on God's forgiving and merciful nature, this passage offers a plea for a radical, thoroughgoing repentance. We must take sin seriously.
3. Teach the Bible and Christian doctrine so that potential converts grasp that the plan of salvation is God's counsel, not human wisdom.
4. Abandon the facile language of decisionism ("just believe," "pray to receive," "invite Jesus into your heart") in favor of the more rigorous language of

conversion ("surrender to the Lordship of Jesus Christ," or "turn from sin, accept the forgiveness purchased by Jesus through his death, and live a life of obedience to him").

There is little doubt that when our evangelistic efforts take seriously the fact that turning to God means conversion beyond mere religious preference, we are going to experience a temporary statistical setback. The number of converts resulting from an evangelistic sermon or a series of evangelistic meetings will not even be countable until months or years later. Even the number of nominal Christians willing to take up space in our services may decline as they find themselves resisting the heightened attention given to the demands of the true gospel.

But in the long run, the results will be very positive for the church. The focus will return to disciple making, where it belongs. The church will become leaner and meaner (by which I mean more effective). The world will sit up and notice—and perhaps even fear—a company of followers of Jesus who mean business. And we may find that seekers are actually more attracted to a cause worth giving their lives to.

References

Abbot, Edwin A. 1952. *Flatland*. New York: Dover Publications.

Barna, George. 1991. *What Americans Believe: An Annual Survey of Values and Religious Views in the United States*. Ventura: Regal Books.

Bradshaw, Wade. 1998. "Reaching the Postmodern Generation." *Covenant Magazine* (February/March 1998): 16.

Carson, D. A. 1996. *The Gagging of God: Christianity Confronts Pluralism*. Grand Rapids: Zondervan.

Metzger, Will. 1984. *Tell the Truth: The Whole Gospel to the Whole Person by Whole People*. Downers Grove, Ill.: InterVarsity Press.

PART FOUR

Crucial Passages

CHAPTER 11

THE GOSPEL PARADOX

Declaring Sinners Righteous (Rom. 3:21–26)

John W. Nyquist

There is a paradox at work here: our world is increasingly skeptical of texts in general, and of the biblical text in particular. The paradox is simply that in such a world, evangelicals are being challenged as never before because of their foundational belief in the integrity and truthfulness of that text. Biblical Christians believe that the Bible contains a wonderful story of God's creative and redemptive activity, a story that begins in the first book of the Old Testament and continues throughout the entire New Testament. This overarching narrative demonstrates God's infinite love and concern for his people, who continue in their rebellion and sin. Again, this explanation is not welcomed in general, and those who attempt to tell this story are repeatedly told that it is somehow out of sync with the virtual reality of today's society, that what we need is not global or universal explanations, but community—locally generated stories that emerge from diverse cultural situations and contexts.

The confusion that has resulted from the intersection of gospel proclamation and skeptical ideologies is the impetus that has propelled us to address some of the issues that emerge from this confusion. Let us be clear about the confusion: evangelical theology does not need to be defensive in the presence of the critique of the cynics. Indeed, part of the strategy must be a commitment to listening to those critics. And having listened intently and carefully, today's evangelists must then formulate their proclamation with grace, truth, and boldness, being careful not to entertain the hint of compromise at any point in the presentation of the gospel message.

The confusion seems to present itself when Christian evangelists are found to be on the defensive and are put into reactive postures rather than ones that are proactive and confident. Whether it is a pastor in a Sunday morning sermon, a missionary in a cross-cultural context, or a campus missionary among high school or university students, the challenge is basically the same. Using the biblical text, is it possible to communicate the message of God's love and forgiveness to sinful people in a context of confusion, hopelessness, and indifference to the clear call of God on the lives of men and women today? And more to the point of this chapter, is it possible to maintain the integrity of Holy Scripture while contextualizing the essence of the gospel: God's activity in justifying sinful creatures through the substitutionary death of Christ? It is to this precise challenge that we now turn.

A friend was invited to speak in a large Australian church in the context of evangelism. A New Age Expo had recently visited the city, and thousands had visited the various exhibits. The media coverage had been extensive. The speaker rightly concluded that he would be addressing a postmodern audience. That night a woman gave her testimony of how she had moved from being a New Age devotee to being a Christian. How did she sum it up? She had been looking for relationship with a person, whom she found in Christ. But the New Age was about power to enhance the self. "But how do you have a personal relationship with a power station?" she asked (Cole 1998). Relationships are the key to life, so the ultimate question in nontheological terms is: How does one gain a relationship with God? How does one hook up with the Source of power, the uncreated Creator of the universe?

The Bible explains that there is an infinite distance between the Creator God and the creatures he created. The separation has been caused by disobedience and rebellion against that Creator God, and the biblical story line chronicles the ups and downs of the many ways that God has pursued his creatures in spite of their stubbornness. The gospel announces that this distance between the Creator and his creatures has been negotiated in the person of Jesus Christ. The door has been opened for reestablishing that original relationship. In fact, that door is a representation of the one who made the journey for our sins. What is this good news that the Bible claims is for all people (Luke 2:10)? And why wouldn't this gospel be received readily and wholeheartedly? What is the exact nature of the paradox that evokes considerable explanation and illustration in our postmodern culture?

The exclusivity of the gospel centered in Jesus Christ and the focus of the message on his death and resurrection will challenge the church to reflect much more carefully on the ways we explain it and invite people to assimilate it. What appears to be narrow and unrealistic is the paradox of the whole idea: the good news is that these very parameters eliminate any hope of human success in attaining favor in God's eyes. The great temptation will certainly be to

John W. Nyquist

avoid the demands of the cross and to offer something that postmodern people can embrace without too much trouble or effort. The energy we spend on devising strategies for reaching people for Christ must reflect the clear demands of Jesus to follow him in humble and obedient discipleship; we compromise at this stage to our peril.

Doubtless the personal arena is the area where we have the greatest opportunity to demonstrate truth: the evangelist is called to live a life of holiness and consistency. Integrity and faithfulness will go a long way in providing unbelievers with a "new revised plausibility structure," to echo Peter Berger (1967) and Os Guinness (1983). I believe that although the Bible teaches that all Christians are to be held to the same standards of conduct, there is a sense in which Christian leaders must take their calling more seriously than ever before. The great apostle's words to the Thessalonians still apply to us today, perhaps even more so:

> We loved you so much that we were delighted to share with you not only the gospel of God but our lives as well, because you had become so dear to us. Surely you remember, brothers, our toil and hardship; we worked night and day in order not to be a burden to anyone while we preached the gospel of God to you. You are witnesses, and so is God, of how holy, righteous and blameless we were among you who believed. For you know that we dealt with each of you as a father deals with his own children, encouraging, comforting and urging you to live lives worthy of God, who calls you into his kingdom and glory. (1 Thess. 2:8–12)

THE ESSENCE AND THE CENTER OF GRAVITY OF THE GOSPEL

Martin Luther called Romans "the chief part of the New Testament and the very purest gospel"; he believed that "every Christian should know it word for word, by heart, [and] occupy himself with it every day, as the daily bread of his soul" (1546, xxiii). In the margin of Luther's Bible (at Rom. 3:23), he referred to this passage, where Paul speaks of justification by faith, as "the chief point, and the very central place of the Epistle, and of the whole Bible."[1] Leon Morris, in his commentary, suggests that this passage may be "possibly the most important single paragraph ever written" (1988, 173). Murray Harris, retired professor of New Testament exegesis at Trinity Evangelical Divinity School and former Warden of Tyndale House in Cambridge, offered this simple logic about this passage on the occasion of his last faculty devotional before retirement in 1997: "Where is the center of historic Christianity in terms of theology and significance? When you add up all the doctrines, statements, creedal pronouncements, and attempts at systematization, what do we have? Take the Bible, go to the New Testament, turn to Romans, find chapter 3, locate verses 21–26, and focus in on verse 24. There you have the central teaching of the Bible on the Christian faith."

THE TEXT AND ITS CONTEXT

The apostle Paul has presented his readers with the opportunity to follow him—and his line of argument—in his engagement with some dialogue partners. His carefully prepared responses to real and concrete questions form the bulk of the letter through the first part of the epistle. Paul's reasoning demonstrates a theological perspective in which the sovereign God of creation has provided a solution to the human dilemma. The history of the race is characterized by sinful disobedience and a deliberate rejection of the gospel. Paul shows that all of us are culpable and stand guilty before a holy and righteous God. Furthermore, because God's provision has been evident throughout human history, we are responsible agents: "[A]lthough they knew God [from the evidence of his creative hand in nature], they neither glorified him as God nor gave thanks to him, but their thinking became futile and their foolish hearts were darkened" (Rom. 1:21).

It is this thankless disobedience that brings Paul to his presentation of the gravity and the universality of sin in the first section of chapter 3. Paul has convincingly shown that Jews under the system of law, or Gentiles with the law written in their hearts (2:15), are both judged impartially in God's holy presence. This is certainly a picture of hopelessness and despair, especially when we read that "no one will be declared righteous in his sight by observing the law; rather, through the law we become conscious of sin" (Rom. 3:20). The paradox that we are seeking to illuminate, then, is summarized in this last verse. Such a system of works righteousness puts humans on the thin edge of a sword: it is unable to provide salvation, while at the same time it provides exactly what we need to know in preparation for receiving the gospel.

Paul's logic is that unless a person is convinced of the totality of his sin and the depth of that sinfulness in relation to God, God's provision will not produce any kind of enthusiasm for applying it. Indeed, we will often encounter apathy and indifference. Increasingly, we meet people who comment on the arrogance of the Christian position, which not only implies a universal problem (sin), but even worse, insists that there is but one solution to the dilemma.

To such people this seems to represent the height of intolerance; it is impertinent. They maintain that what we believe is okay if we just keep it private. "That's fine for you," they say, "but don't try to foist your beliefs on me."

Now it is time to engage our biblical passage more closely. Romans 3:21–26 provides a sharp contrast to the gloom and hopelessness of the previous chapters. It begins with a novelty: the strong adversative clause is introduced by the two words "but now." They signal the heartening and encouraging news that in Christ—and apart from law keeping—God has made provision for a rescue mission. And it is a relief as well, because it doesn't finally depend on the efforts that we humans could muster; it depends only on God and his grace. Furthermore, this solution is not a stopgap affair, covering over something that will surface again at some later time. No! This is God's own righteousness, which is provided as a substitute for our unsuccessful efforts to redeem (justify) ourselves. Homiletically, this righteousness is a divine attribute, a divine activity (salvation), and a divine achievement.

The great apostle is "straining at the leash of language" to indicate this wondrous breakthrough on behalf of all those who have faith in Jesus Christ, "all who believe" (3:22). This plan of salvation has been initiated by none other than God himself and deals with the most perplexing problem in history: How does a sinful human being gain a right standing before a holy and righteous God? When we look at the Bible's story line from beginning to end, we discern that God created human beings to worship him. But man chose to gain independence from God, resulting in alienation and estrangement from his Creator. There was, however, a deep longing within humankind that constantly expressed that alienation by attempting to recover the original setting without relying on God's available presence and provision. This passage describes what God has done in Christ in overcoming the barrier of sin as well as man's disposition to self-reliance.

Initially, we must note that the subject of these six verses is the righteousness of God (referred to no fewer than four times). A closer look reveals that the thematic development of God's righteousness is continued in the proposed solution to the problem. In verses 24 and 26 the lemma (viz. *dik-*) common to the words translated "justified," "just," and "justifier," is employed three more times in embellishing the whole development. Furthermore, the idea of faith is used four times, underscoring the means by which God's righteousness is made available.

These words describing God's activity on our behalf must be understood in the context of believing faith. Paul puts it this way, "This righteousness from God comes through faith in Jesus Christ to all who believe" (3:22). But this righteousness is beyond the reach of any and all human effort, requiring that God do something for sinful humans that was humanly impossible. The whole story of the Bible pictures the futility of attempting to please God "in the energy of the flesh." From the beginning, the guidelines are clear: "Without faith it is impossible to please God" (Heb. 11:6) and "everything that does not come from faith is sin" (Rom. 14:23). So how *do* sinful human beings come into right relationship with God?

Three "gospel words" allow Paul to paint colorful pictures for his readers—words with familiar histories, words that carried significant meaning in this crucial context. The words are *justified, redemption,* and *propitiation.* Each of these words carries with it a kind of cultural and legal history, conjuring up specific scenarios, aiding the members of Paul's audience to identify with him and his line of argument.

Justification is a legal term, transporting the reader into the law court, where the judge is required to hear a case and pass some sort of judgment. The judge has the responsibility of bringing the appropriate law or laws to bear in the case and, at the same time, of pronouncing the penalty in the case of guilt. In the event that the defendant is found not guilty, the judge is required to set the accused person free. Paul brings this courtroom scene to bear in referring to the purpose of Christ's death on the cross. If man is the defendant, the law merely functions in an advisory capacity to secure a judgment in the case. In the biblical context, man is disobedient and legally guilty for transgressing the law, and some sort of penalty has to be paid. The Bible repeatedly reports that the penalty for sin against a holy God is death. But Paul maintains here that it is precisely those who have transgressed the law's demands who are "justified freely by his grace" (3:23–24). This remarkable statement needs some embellishment, and Paul obliges by enlarging the picture.

The second word, *redemption,* draws the reader into the marketplace of business and commerce. Paul states that the guilty are justified freely by God's grace "through the redemption that came by Christ Jesus" (3:24). If we can allow Paul the license to mix his metaphors, we can discern his line of thinking. The sinner has been pronounced guilty by virtue of disobeying the law of God. The judge then paradoxically declares the sinner not guilty in view—not of man's repentance or good intentions—but of God's pure and unmerited grace. But, we may ask, by what means can even God do this? Is it not unjust to see a guilty person get off the hook without having to assume the responsibility for what he has done?

By introducing the concept of redemption, Paul shows that the sinner is a slave and belongs to a wicked slave master. Later, in chapter 6, Paul enlarges

JOHN W. NYQUIST

on this concept of slavery and refers to the unbeliever's enslavement to sin (vv. 16–18). "When you were slaves to sin, you were free from the control of righteousness. What benefit did you reap at that time from the things you are now ashamed of? Those things result in death! But now that you have been set free from sin and have become slaves to God, the benefit you reap leads to holiness, and the result is eternal life" (vv. 20–22). God is both the righteous judge and the redeeming master who hears the sinner's guilty plea and proceeds to pardon the sinner on the basis of offering the purchase price sufficient to liberate the now-justified, now-redeemed sinner! Christ's death on the cross accomplished these two divine objectives proclaimed with such clarity by Paul.

But a third concept—*substitution*—is visualized by the apostle-theologian, and by using this idea, Paul can conclude his case. One could argue up to this point that justice has not been done; in fact, perhaps a case could be made for flouting the law, sweeping the law aside, and introducing a foreign element that is hidden for convenience. Can the law be skirted in such a way without having to answer to the charge of malicious intent?

At this point, Paul takes us to the temple, where worship is the appropriate activity. Sacrifices are brought to offer oneself in submission to God. But how does one produce an adequate and satisfactory sacrifice that pleases a holy and righteous God? Again, man is helpless because no human sacrifice is adequate compared to our imperfections and blemishes. Flawed offerings are unacceptable; only clean and perfect ones will do. In fact, in God's eyes, only one sacrifice will bring delight to his heart. There can be only one sufficient substitute for us against whom the sentence of death has been pronounced: the perfect Son of God, Jesus Christ, must die in our place. Paul teaches elsewhere that "Christ died for the ungodly" and that "while we were still sinners, Christ died for us" (Rom. 5:6, 8). In 1 Corinthians 15, Paul explains, "For what I received I passed on to you as of first importance: that Christ died for our sins according to the Scriptures" (v. 3). This "sacrifice of atonement" (NIV) or "propitiatory sacrifice" (NASB margin) simply means that Christ's death on the cross was to act in our place, and thus the holiness of God was "propitiated" in this perfect sacrifice.

In the contemporary world of proliferating legal maneuvering and endless litigation, the picture Paul uses of the legal (forensic) aspect of Christ's death is very appropriate. Lawyers, district attorneys, plaintiffs, defendants, juries, and other legal terms are common currency today. So when we want to explain the gospel to our postmodern friends, this picture will serve us well.

When we encounter people in the business world who monitor the stock market ticker on CNN or engage their broker in negotiations relating to mutual funds and T-bills, Paul's marketplace reference affords the evangelist the platform to enter the world of economics as well as to confront the more sinister complex of conspicuous consumption and the accumulation of wealth. Christ's death on the cross performed a rescue mission, freeing those enslaved by whatever guilt or burden or anxiety. Paul thus preached a genuine theology of liberation.

Finally, we often meet people who are very religious and are attempting to attain a right standing with God by their own efforts. The analogy of the temple suggests a place where sacrifices are made, and it is only the God of the Bible who is qualified to determine the acceptability of those offerings. In Hebrews 9 we read: "Then Christ would have had to suffer many times since the creation of the world. But now he has appeared once for all at the end of the ages to do away with sin by the sacrifice of himself. Just as man is destined to die once, and after that to face judgment, so Christ was sacrificed once to take away the sins of many people" (vv. 26–28).

In all of this, God demonstrated his righteousness by acting fairly as a just judge in passing over the sins committed in the past, not ignoring them. He could do this because of the time when he would accept the sacrifice of his only son, Jesus Christ, the redeemer and perfect sacrifice for our sins. Paul says that in so doing, God demonstrated his justice, "so as to be just and the one who justifies those who have faith in Jesus" (Rom. 3:26). This is certainly good news for those who struggle with their own guilt, confusion, and despair. God in Christ has provided the perfect solution to the hopelessness and disappointment that characterizes many people in today's world.

The challenges of postmodernity are formidable for the Christian evangelist. But these same challenges provide open doors for new and creative gospel conversations. And the biblical material in Romans 3 addresses the fundamental question of the human spirit. Blaise Pascal expressed it this way: there is a God-shaped vacuum in the heart of every man, and it cannot be filled by any human thing, but only by God the Creator, through his son, Jesus Christ. The death and resurrection of Christ closed the gap between a holy God and sinful humans. Here the apostle Paul effectively demonstrates that when God's powerful grace is linked with believing faith, the dynamic of the gospel comes to bear on the repentant sinner. We "are *justified* freely by his grace through the *redemption* that came by Christ Jesus. God presented him as *a sacrifice of atonement*, through faith in his blood" (Rom. 3:24–25, emphasis added).

One of the slogans of postmodernity puts it bluntly: Truth is relative, history is being rewritten, and experience is the judge of all things. F. Lyotard (1984) defines postmodernity as: "incredulity towards metanarratives," which

JOHN W. NYQUIST

Kevin Vanhoozer translates, "Distrust any voice that purports to tell you that 'that's the way it is'" (1995, 7). Properly understood, the Bible is indeed a metanarrative in that its history, theology, poetry, prophecy, and eschatology are brought together in one big all-encompassing story. The God of the Bible has supervised the entire project, demonstrating continuity, meaning, and significance within each biblical book as well as among them. The Christian evangelist is enlisted to tell this story and to work at living consistently with that same story. And this big story is encapsulated in Romans 3:21–26 in a remarkable way. Since the Bible has God as its author, its contents are true. This brief overview by Paul the apostle insists that the human dilemma is so serious as to call forth God's highest and best effort: the gift of Jesus Christ as a perfect and God-satisfying sacrifice. This sinless Son of God died for our sins and thereby procured our redemption and salvation, pronouncing believing sinners forgiven and justified. The war is over, and all these justified sinners (see again Rom. 5:6–8) have been liberated, reconciled to God, and given God's clothes of righteousness to wear (Rom. 13:14; 2 Cor. 5:21; Gal. 3:27).

In our present cultural context, then, the Christian evangelist must be committed to the proclamation of the gospel, using the words of God in the Bible and focusing on Jesus Christ. This proclamation will inevitably center on Christ's substitutionary and sacrificial death on the cross for our sins. And it will emphasize that God provided this salvation in his own free grace so that none of us can ever boast about what we have done to earn or deserve it. In the end, the good news is that God has exchanged our sinfulness for his righteousness: "God made him [Christ] who had no sin to be sin for us, so that in him we might become the righteousness of God" (2 Cor. 5:21). All of this contributes to the powerful answer to the ultimate question: How can a sinner come into a right relationship with the holy triune God? The answer is that the solution has already been worked out: Christ died for our sins and rose again the third day according to the Scriptures.

The Christian gospel is based on the truth contained in God's Word, the Bible. The evangelist who bases his message on this revealed truth will be on solid ground. Furthermore, the biblical story is an overarching record of God's faithfulness to his people in spite of their rebellion and disobedience. This salvation-history has a great ending for those who respond to the call to repent and believe the gospel (Mark 1:15). As evangelical evangelists, we stand in a long line of those whose experience has given credibility to the truth of the Bible story. At the end of the second millennium, we are called to live out the gospel, to be consistent with its wholeness and its truth.

Kevin Vanhoozer warns of a "cheap inerrancy," by which he means "the profession of inerrancy without discipleship" (1995, 19). This combination of speaking and doing the truth is certainly the best and most convincing way of sharing our faith in a postmodern culture. Evangelicals can learn from the New Testament evangelists whose passion for truth took the form of "evangelism, with a goal to conversion." But in our passion for truth, we must avoid linking God's truth with coercion. Many of our contemporaries have experienced such encounters with some of us and have become hardened to the truth of the gospel as a result. With all the talk of tolerance in the postmodern/pluralist environment, Christian evangelists must learn to "combine a passion for the truth with a tolerance for others. . . . A passion for truth need not make us intolerant of others, though it will make us intolerant of falsehood and deceit" (Vanhoozer 1995, 24).

References

Berger, Peter. 1967. *The Sacred Canopy: Elements of a Sociological Theory of Religion*. Garden City: Anchor Books.

Cole, Graham A. 1998. "Proclaiming Christ in Postmodern Times." Unpublished paper given at Oak Hill Theological College, 29 April.

Guinness, Os. 1983. *The Gravedigger File: Paper on the Subversion of the Modern Church*. London: Hodder and Stoughton.

Luther, Martin. 1546 [1967]. *Commentary on the Epistle to the Romans*. Trans. J. Theodore Mueller. Grand Rapids: Kregel.

Lyotard, Jean-Francois. 1984. *The Postmodern Condition: A Report on Knowledge*. Minneapolis: University of Minnesota Press.

Moo, Douglas J. 1996. *The Epistle to the Romans*. Grand Rapids: Eerdmans.

Morris, Leon. 1988. *The Epistle to the Romans*. Grand Rapids: Eerdmans.

Vanhoozer, Kevin J. 1995. "Exploring the World; Following the Word: The Credibility of Evangelical Theology in an Incredulous Age." *Trinity Journal* 11 (1995): 3–27.

CHAPTER 12

THE AMBASSADOR'S JOB DESCRIPTION

2 Corinthians 5:11–21

Colin S. Smith

It has been a long flight to the capital, and you are anxious because you do not know the agenda for the meeting. All you know is that he wants to see you—personally. Although you are in regular communication, he has not made this kind of invitation before, so you sense that something is afoot.

The journey has given you the opportunity to reflect on all that has happened since you were given the position in Materialistia. For many years it was thought to be one of the best jobs—offering a warm climate and delightful people with a respect for teachers, doctors, the police, and even attorneys, not to mention folks like you who have been given important assignments. Materialistia is a prosperous place, and your mission there has been quite successful.

You arrive early and wait nervously until, on time, you are ushered into the magnificent office. You have seen it in pictures many times, but being there is different. "It is good to see you, my friend," he says. "You have been doing a fine job for us in Materialistia."

"It is a delightful place to serve, sir," you reply. "The people hold you in high regard, and I have been well received. There is a great deal of good will toward us."

"Yes, yes," he says. "Of course you must never confuse good will with compliance."

"Of course, sir, and there are many who dislike our policy. But at least they know what it is, and when their boats sail onto the rocks, they know where to turn."

"Well, I've called you in because we have a new assignment for you," he says. "As you know, the population of Materialistia is dwindling. The birth rate has fallen, and a lot of people have emigrated. We need to have a strong presence where the people are, and so I want you to go and lead our enterprise among the booming population in Postmodernia."

"Postmodernia, sir?"

"Yes, Postmodernia. Millions of people have found it an attractive place to live, though I can't think why. None of these people have ever visited our country, and most are completely ignorant of what we are doing. Where you have been working in the past, people recognized our government even if they ignored us, but in Postmodernia, the people do not even know who we are!

"You will find the people very charming. They will receive you well. In fact they receive everybody well, irrespective of their assignment. When you explain our policies, you will find that they think these fine for you because you come from this country, but have nothing whatever to do with them, because they live in Postmodernia."

"But surely, sir, these people must know the high level of commitment we have to them, and how much they depend on our aid. Without our exports their food supply would be exhausted. Without our protection their defenses would easily be overrun. Without our support their entire economy would collapse!"

"Very few are aware of these things," he says. "The people of Postmodernia live with the illusion that they are self-sufficient."

His eyes narrow as he leans forward. "This is a tough assignment. It has ended the careers of some of our best people. The last man we sent proved quite unreliable. We sent him out fully briefed on our policy, and he did a marvelous job of engaging the people. He seemed very drawn to them. But over time we heard less and less from him, and now he has broken off contact altogether. Whatever he is doing now, he is certainly not working for us. So now I am trusting this operation to you. I want you to do the same job you have been doing in Materialistia. Represent us. Raise awareness of what we are saying, and do everything you can to persuade the people of our cause."

In 2 Corinthians 5:20, the apostle Paul gives us a marvelous illustration of the nature of Christian ministry: we are Christ's ambassadors. We are sent by the risen Christ and commissioned to operate on his behalf in a particular cultural setting.

Many of us have been used to serving Christ in a culture where the basic categories of the gospel have been known, even if they were not believed. In this new century, the Lord is giving us a new assignment. We are ambassadors for Christ, called to bring the word of Christ to a postmodern culture.

We may define an ambassador as a government representative, commissioned to serve in a foreign country for the purpose of accurately communicating the position and policies of the government he represents so that the people to whom he speaks will be brought into, and kept in a good relationship with, the government of the country he serves.

It is not easy to serve as an ambassador for Christ in the postmodern world. The people we speak to have not visited the country we represent. Some do

COLIN S. SMITH

not accept the authority or the existence of the government for which we speak. Others find it difficult to see how our country's policies have anything to do with them. Increasing numbers question whether there can be any such thing as government policy, and even if there is, most doubt our ability to describe it accurately! But the embassy is open, and our task is to serve as ambassadors for Christ in Postmodernia.

THE AMBASSADOR'S PROFILE

Put yourself in the shoes of the secretary of state considering the appointment of a new ambassador. What qualities will you look for in the person you choose to send?

LOYALTY

In selecting a candidate, loyalty will be the foundational qualification. The greatest pressure on any diplomat sent on a mission overseas will be to become so immersed in the alien culture around him that he forgets he has been placed in that culture to represent a different voice.

If the ambassador is to be effective, he must remember that he is accountable. His work may be praised or criticized by the people to whom he is sent, but it is his own government's evaluation that matters. Paul kept this in the forefront of his mind. "We make it our goal to please him . . . For we must all appear before the judgment seat of Christ" (2 Cor. 5:9–10).

Here is a first principle of ministry. One day I will stand alone before Jesus Christ who has sent me, and I will give an account for my ministry. This is not something that any of us should take lightly. Paul says, "We know what it is to fear the Lord" (v. 11). While no Christian will endure the wrath of God, our work will be tested with God's fire, so we must be careful how we build.

An ambassador who forgets this accountability is a disaster waiting to happen. The effective ambassador for Christ lives in the daily awareness that he is sent by and accountable to God, and this knowledge guides his priorities and activities.

INTEGRITY

An ambassador's integrity is important for two reasons. First, if an ambassador lacks integrity, his presence will lower the reputation of his government in the eyes of the people to whom he is sent. Second, the whole point of sending an ambassador is that through the establishing of personal relationships of trust, there should be a bridge to understanding and communication.

It would be much cheaper for countries to communicate via e-mail than to establish embassies and send ambassadors throughout the world. But the most effective communication is personal. When we listen to any communication, we use our perception of the speaker as a filter through which we sift his words. Where we trust the integrity of the speaker, we will be more open to considering what he has to say.

Paul picks up on this in 2 Corinthians 5:11: "What we are is plain to God, and I hope it is also plain to your conscience." That is a statement of integrity. Of course, Paul had many detractors. People tried to impugn his motives and his effectiveness, but they had no basis for doing so.

HUMILITY

The job of an ambassador is in its nature self-effacing. His task is to commend not himself, but the government he represents. His calling is to use his personal influence, not in his own interests, but in the interests of his government. His success is not that he is well accepted by the people but that the people accept the policy of his government. An ambassador whose main interest is in advancing his own position is unlikely to be an effective advocate for his government.

This is of great importance in speaking to a culture that is sensitive to the use of truth-claims as a means of exercising power. There have been not a few Christian pastors whose ministries have had more than a smack of tyranny about them.

Notice how Paul puts it here: "We are not trying to commend ourselves to you" (2 Cor. 5:12). In other words, "We are not building a personal power base." There is great humility here. This was Paul's key to handling criticism. "I care very little if I am judged by you or by any human court. . . . It is the Lord who judges me" (1 Cor. 4:3–4). Paul was never short on criticism from the surrounding culture. You get a flavor of it here. "If we are out of our mind, it is for the sake of God" (2 Cor. 5:13). Why would Paul have said this if it were not that some people in Corinth were alleging his insanity?

We are not without the same criticism today. According to psychologist Robert Jay Lifton, "Those who are consistent in their beliefs, who try to live according to a specific set of principles, and who imagine that they have a single core identity are . . . mentally ill."[1]

Christ has told us that the price of ministry would include men saying all kinds of evil against us. It will take humility to represent Christ in an alien culture.

SPIRITUALITY

There would be something rather strange about an Italian ambassador who showed no appreciation for art, or an American ambassador who showed no initiative or enterprise! We naturally expect that an ambassador will personally express the core values of the culture he represents. So what qualities would we most expect to find in the life of an ambassador of Jesus Christ?

It is very interesting that Paul contrasts two kinds of people who were involved in Christian ministry. On the one hand there are "those who take pride in what is seen," and on the other there are those who are concerned with "what is in the heart" (2 Cor. 5:12).

When the world asks us, "What have you got?" it is very easy to point to our programs or our numbers. These things are good, but they are the things that are seen. What about the things of the heart? Effective ambassadors of Jesus Christ in this alien culture need to cultivate spirituality in their own lives. An effective ambassador must be a good personal expression of what he or she commends.

LOVE

The effective ambassador combines patriotic loyalty to his own government with a passionate love for the people to whom he is sent. Any trace of racism or prejudice against the people who are the object of his mission will render him unsuitable.

Notice how Paul puts it: "Christ's love compels us" (2 Cor 5:14). He is not saying that the driving force of his ministry is his love for Christ. Our love for Christ rises and falls and at times is less than it should be. He is saying that the driving force of his ministry is the compelling love that *Christ* has for the people to whom he has been sent. When he thinks about how much Christ loves these people, it drives him forward.

Putting these qualities of loyalty, integrity, humility, spirituality, and love together, it is very clear that the first thing that is needed to reach any culture is character. Robert Murray McCheyne was right in his conviction that his people's greatest need was his personal holiness. It is not so much great gifts that God uses as it is great likeness to Jesus. The biblical qualifications for spiritual leadership (e.g., Acts 6 and 1 Tim. 3) make it clear that God's first interest is character. A postmodern world will not hear our words until its attention has been engaged by the quality of our lives.

THE AMBASSADOR'S RESPONSIBILITY

The importance of an ambassador's role will depend almost entirely on the level of interest his government has in the people to whom he is sent. In a delightful book about the life of an ambassador, British diplomat Humphrey Trevelyan describes embassy life in a remote outpost. The ambassador, he says, "can sit in his study at ease reading the latest newspapers from home, happily conscious that he can be interrupted by only two clerks and one stenographer . . . and that no one at home is likely to make him move to his desk by the inopportune use of the telephone!" (1973, 29).

Such a life may be very pleasant, but it is hardly significant. Visit the American embassy in London or in Peking, however, and you will find a very different scene. Every day there is fresh communication and constant activity. If the government never speaks, the ambassador has nothing to say. But where the government has vital interests in a country, the ambassador will carry a great responsibility.

As ambassadors of Christ we are assigned to a "country" in which our Lord has vital interests. If God had no word for the people around us, we would have nothing to say. But the people among whom we live have the daily focused attention of the Sovereign. God has a word for the people to whom we are sent, and he trusts its communication to us.

Our definition of the role of an ambassador makes this clear. An ambassador is a government representative commissioned to serve in a foreign country *for the purpose of accurately communicating the position of the policies of the government he represents* so that the people to whom he speaks will be brought into, and kept in a good relationship with, the government of the country he serves. Two things will be required of us if we are to fulfill this responsibility: to listen as one who is under authority, and to speak as one given authority.

THE AMBASSADOR MUST LISTEN AS ONE WHO IS UNDER AUTHORITY

"[God] has committed to us the message of reconciliation" (2 Cor. 5:19). The effective ambassador is one who faithfully communicates what he is given to say. His agenda is written for him. His primary concerns are the primary concerns of his government. He is not at liberty to put his own spin on the government line. In fact, it would be extremely dangerous if he did.

The church is an embassy. It must be sensitive to the culture in which it is set but responsive to the authority of the government it serves. The will of its government determines its program, priorities, and policies. We must certainly speak to the questions that people are asking, but that does not give us the right to be silent on the issues that the government has told us to raise.

This means that the first priority for the ambassador must be to maintain good communication with the government that sent him, to hear the word from home and be responsive to it. An ambassador does this by giving careful attention to statements, briefing papers, and policy documents that are given to him. His task is to study them and communicate their content in such a way that the people around him grasp the meaning intended by the government when the policy was first written.

God has given us a statement of his policy. He has given us his Word. Our task is to study it, to understand how it impinges on our own actions and the culture around us, and to express its message in terms that the people around us can understand.

It is crucial that we recognize the primacy of the written Word that God has given to us. Imagine an American ambassador to China trying to discern American policy through quiet times of silence and meditation! Imagine him sitting in a reflective posture, listening to his feelings, and then telling the Chinese government the thoughts that have come to him. Imagine him equating these thoughts with American foreign policy!

Subjective impressions are the native language of non-Christian religions. Their gods do not speak, so the only voice that can be heard is the echo of one's own. But our God speaks! There is a Word outside of ourselves that has been trusted to us. Just as the ambassador absorbs government policy through reading documents that are sent to him and reflecting on their meaning, so we listen to what God is saying to our culture with an open Bible.

When we come to the Bible, we are to listen to what it actually says. The ambassador who reads policy documents looking for themes that will scratch where his audience itches has simply not understood the nature of his task or of the documents that have been given to him. This is the approach of the entertainer. The ambassador has a higher calling. He reads the text with two questions in mind: first, What is the government saying? and second, How can I express this in a way that these people will understand?

The moment the ambassador ceases to operate under the authority of the government that sent him, he ceases to have any useful contribution to the culture in which he lives. He may be popular, but he is irrelevant at best and dangerous at worst.

THE AMBASSADOR MUST SPEAK AS ONE WHO IS GIVEN AUTHORITY

All authority is given. None of us has authority in ourselves. We receive it when we come under it. There is a wonderful example of this in the words of the centurion whose servant was sick. Jesus offered to come to this man's home, but the centurion declined. It would be enough for Jesus just to speak the word, and the servant would be healed. The centurion explains his confidence to Jesus in this way: "I myself am a man under authority, with soldiers under me. I tell this one, 'Go,' and he goes; and that one, 'Come,' and he comes" (Matt. 8:9). This man did not speak as a private individual but as a centurion, and in this official capacity he spoke with all the authority of Rome. He recognized that when Jesus spoke, he spoke with all the authority of God.

In 1965 the American government established the Henry Jackson subcommittee to review the diplomatic service. Its report states, "When an ambassador overseas negotiates or speaks in private or in public, his audience needs to feel that he . . . speaks with the authority of the President of the United States."[2] The same principle applies to ambassadors of Christ. When we speak the word faithfully, it is "as though God were making his appeal through us" (2 Cor. 5:20).

In the Old Testament, it was the distinctive mark of the false prophets that they aired their private opinions rather than the Word of God (see Jeremiah 23). They evaded uncomfortable truths about the judgment of God and spoke about peace where there was no peace. Imagine the confusion and anger of people on finding that an ambassador who lived among them has been recalled home because hostilities from his government were about to be unleashed against them. Imagine their consternation as bombs rain down and they wonder why the ambassador did not warn them that this was coming!

What use is an ambassador to the people around him if he does not tell them what his government actually says? There will be times when the well-being and safety of many people depend on his faithfulness to his task. The ambassador who fails to speak the Word he is given is a dangerous distraction and an expensive irrelevance.

THE AMBASSADOR'S MESSAGE

Having established that the ambassador must be an attentive listener and a faithful speaker, we now come to consider the issues that Christ's ambassadors are specifically commissioned to raise. In the Scriptures, God clearly defines the message that he has given us to communicate.

COLIN S. SMITH

WE ARE TO SPEAK ABOUT GOD

Paul clearly establishes the centrality of God in our message. We are to speak about him.

> "All this is from *God*."
> "*God* was reconciling the world to himself."
> "*God* committed to us the ministry of reconciliation."
> "It is *God* who is making his appeal through us."
> "Be reconciled to *God*."
> "*God* made Christ to be sin for us."
> "We are to become the righteousness of *God*."

In Stuart Briscoe's words, our ministry must be God-centered and people-related (1994, 125). It should not be the other way around.

In Postmodernia, we will need to explain who this God is. We are speaking to a culture that is not familiar with his identity. We will need to tell his story. We must explain that in our country he has absolute authority, and that Postmodernia rightly belongs to him too. This will not go down well, but whatever the difficulties, our message is about God.

This gives us a wonderful opportunity. There is something stifling about a culture in which there is nothing beyond self. Postmodernia is an incredibly lonely place. A Christian student on a secular campus told me of her experience in witnessing to a New Age colleague. The Christian girl had gone through her arsenal of Christian apologetics without sensing any breakthrough. They were about to part when the Christian said, "Before you go can I pray for you?" She began to pray and was surprised to find the New Age girl breaking down into tears. "I just can't believe you're speaking to him!" she said.

We have a wonderful opportunity to share the God who is there! We must tell postmodern people that they are not trapped in the claustrophobia of a lonely universe where there is no voice but the echo of their own. There is someone out there, and to know him is eternal life. When Augustine said to God, "You have made us for yourself, and our hearts are restless until they find their rest in you," he was saying something that is true, even in Postmodernia.

WE ARE TO SPEAK ABOUT JESUS CHRIST

It is not enough for us to speak about God in general terms. We are sent specifically to speak about what God has done through Jesus Christ. The God we speak of is known supremely as the God and Father of our Lord Jesus Christ. Notice the centrality of Christ here:

> "If anyone is in *Christ* he is a new creation."
> "God has reconciled us to himself through *Christ*."
> "We are *Christ's* ambassadors."
> "We implore you on *Christ's* behalf, be reconciled to God."
> "*Christ* was made sin on our behalf so that in him we might become the righteousness of God."

This is important when we think of our ministry in Postmodernia. The primary aim of our preaching is not that people will understand Christian doctrines, but rather that they will know and appreciate Jesus Christ. When I preach a sermon on justification by faith, I will be pleased if someone says, "Thank you, pastor, I never understood justification so clearly before"; but I will be much more pleased if someone says, "I never realized Jesus Christ is so wonderful."

Paul gives us a fascinating insight into his preaching ministry when he reminds the Galatian Christians, "Before your very eyes Jesus Christ was clearly portrayed as crucified" (Gal. 3:1). The word he uses for portrayed literally means "placarded." This image gives us a marvelous insight into the heart of Christian ministry. Paul depicted Christ. We are to present this compelling Savior to our hearers. And when Christ is lifted up, he will draw men and women to himself, even in Postmodernia.

When we exalt him, people will grow in faith, because they will see how trustworthy he is. The Puritans used to speak about "getting a view of Christ," by which they meant that there are times when the soul apprehends a glimpse of the glory of Christ, so that from deep within there is a profound expression of worship. Paul said, "May I never boast except in the cross of our Lord Jesus Christ" (Gal. 6:14).

It is a challenging exercise for any preacher to review his sermons, asking: "Am I presenting Christ?" "Does my material give people a clear view of the Savior?" "Is there some way in which people are lifted out of the stifling 'me-world' and given a glimpse of the glory of the Lord?"

WE ARE TO SPEAK ABOUT SIN

God reconciled the world to himself by "not counting men's sins against them" (2 Cor. 5:19). The way in which God did this was by counting our sins against Christ: "God made him who had no sin to be sin for us, so that in him we might become the righteousness of God" (2 Cor. 5:21).

This is a core issue on which we have been commissioned to speak. The ambassador has briefing papers that tell him to raise this issue in the culture

COLIN S. SMITH

to which he has been sent. The ambassador is not at liberty to replace this with some other issue that he judges more appropriate. We cannot have a gospel without sin any more than we can have a gospel without Jesus. If we replace the message of sin and atonement with a message of fulfillment and satisfaction in Jesus, we are preaching a different gospel.

When the ambassador speaks about sin in Postmodernia, he is again faced with the problem of Bible words and perceived meanings. During a recent trip to the grocery store, I was interested to notice some attractively packaged chocolate chip cookies called "Sinful Selections." They were displayed alongside the equally enticing "Raspberry Temptations." On the side of the packet, I was informed that "our Sinful Selection chocolate chip cookies are a truly sinful 40 percent pure chocolate chip by weight. Old-fashioned goodness never tasted this good."

A great deal of thought goes into marketing a product like this, and it seems clear that the manufacturers regarded *sinful* as a word that would be attractive to the majority of people. Instead of being a degrading thing that leads to the judgment of God, sin is perceived as an enjoyable thing that only the stuffiest people would avoid.

So if we say that God takes sin seriously and that we need to repent of it, many people in Postmodernia will conclude that we are getting uptight about petty matters that grown-up people ought to be able to take in their stride. The gospel says, "Christ died for our sins" (1 Cor. 15:3), but if our sins are not perceived to be a problem, the gospel will sound like an antidote to a remote disease from which few postmodern people suffer. That is one of the great challenges that we face. For most people in our society, the word *sin* has been emptied of its true meaning and filled with another meaning that renders it harmless.

The biblical understanding of sin revolves around the idea of offending God, and it is this that makes it serious. We make judgments about the seriousness of an offense in relation to the thing or person offended. For example, if a man is digging in his yard and in the course of swinging his spade he injures a worm, he will probably not give the incident much further thought. If, however, he swings his spade and accidentally injures a passing bird, he may have it on his mind as he goes to sleep that night. Suppose, however, that in swinging his spade he injures a dog. The man would feel an obligation to stop working and take the dog to the vet. But if in a wild swing of his spade he injured a passing pedestrian, he may find himself in court.

The measure of the seriousness of sin is that it is an offense against Almighty God. Dr. Jim Packer comments helpfully that "to preach sin is not to make capital out of people's felt frailties, but to measure their lives by the holy law of God. To be convicted of sin is not just to feel that one is an all-around flop, but to realize that one has offended God, and has flouted his authority and defied him and gone against him and put oneself in the wrong with him" (1961, 61).

The loss of a sense of sin in Postmodernia is in no small measure related to the loss of the knowledge of God. The Christian preacher is called to speak of God in such a way that the weight of God's glory is communicated. When it is, the people of Postmodernia will see themselves in a new light.

WE ARE TO SPEAK ABOUT RECONCILIATION

"God . . . reconciled us to himself through Christ and gave us the ministry of reconciliation: that God was reconciling the world to himself in Christ, not counting men's sins against them" (2 Cor. 5:18–19).

We are never to leave people with the contemplation of themselves. We are to awaken them to their own sins in order to help them appreciate the significance of Jesus Christ and receive the reconciliation that God offers in him.

We are to tell the people of Postmodernia that God is reconciling the world to himself in Christ, not counting men's sins against them, but counting them against Christ. "God made him who had no sin to be sin for us, so that in him we might become the righteousness of God" (2 Cor. 5:21).

Luther expresses this profound truth powerfully in these words:

> Our most merciful Father, seeing us to be oppressed and overwhelmed with the curse of the law, and so to be holden under the same that we could never be delivered from it by our own power, sent his only Son into the world, and laid upon him all the sins of men saying: Be thou Peter that denier; Paul that persecutor, blasphemer and cruel oppressor; David that adulterer; that sinner which did eat the apple in Paradise; that thief which hanged upon the cross; and briefly, be thou the person which hath committed the sins of all men; see therefore that thou pay and satisfy for them.[3]

God has made reconciliation in Jesus Christ, and it is the task of Christ's ambassadors to persuade men and women to receive it. Luther uses a helpful picture of how this happens when he speaks of faith uniting the soul with Christ as a bride is united with her bridegroom:

> By this mystery, as the Apostle teaches, Christ and the soul become one flesh. And if they are one flesh and there is between them a true marriage . . .

Colin S. Smith

it follows that everything they have they hold in common, the good as well as the evil. Accordingly the believing soul can boast of and glory in whatever Christ has as though it were its own, and whatever the soul has Christ claims as his own.[4]

We Are to Speak about Hope

"If anyone is in Christ, he is a new creation; the old has gone, the new has come!" (2 Cor. 5:17).

Postmodernia is populated by some pretty pessimistic people. In a culture where people do not believe in a God outside of themselves, they quickly become prisoners to themselves. As I look back over nearly twenty years in pastoral work, I am struck by the number of people who are locked into despair because of a popular psychological determinism. They have believed that they are products of their heredity and environment and that their lives are shaped by their parents and early experiences.

Many of the people of Postmodernia have had unhappy early experiences. Some have been deeply wounded. Most are conscious of some area of their lives that has been spoiled because of past experiences. If there is no source of help outside of a broken self, where can one look to find hope?

Ambassadors for Christ in Postmodernia have a wonderful opportunity to speak about the God who has power to straighten out twisted people and to heal bruised and broken lives. This is the hope of the gospel. There is a way to break out of the small horizons and the limited possibilities of the prison that is called "me."

The Bible is full of stories that illuminate this hope. Jacob was fighting from the day he was born. It was in his nature. His early experience was of a fractured family where deception was the norm. By early adult life he appears to have become comfortable in habitual deception himself. His history of conflict led to him becoming alienated from his family. But then he met the God who straightens out twisted people. He began to struggle with God too, but this God made him a new person.

The gospel offers something that is much more than any self-development program. It is the life of God invading the human soul and giving a new identity and new capacities. It is the arm of God reaching into the troubled waters of human experience and lifting a person up. This is the message that has been trusted to Christ's ambassadors. We are specifically commissioned to raise these themes in Postmodernia.

THE AMBASSADOR'S GOAL

What is the ambassador actually trying to achieve, and how might we go about measuring the effectiveness of his work?

We have defined an ambassador as "a government representative commissioned to serve in a foreign country for the purpose of accurately communicating the position and policies of the government he represents, *so that the people to whom he speaks will be brought into, and kept in a good relationship with, the government of the country he serves.*"

That is the goal! We want to see a good relationship established between the Savior we love and the people he has set around us. But how do we measure effectiveness in this work?

Measuring spiritual effectiveness is often elusive, but the image of an ambassador is helpful to us. The difficulty of the task assigned to an ambassador will depend in large measure on the disposition of the culture around him toward the government he serves. There is all the difference in the world between the task of an American ambassador in London and in Tehran. Eric Clark describes the task of the American ambassador in London as "mostly nonexistent" (1973, 134). What he means, of course, is that there is such a warm relationship between these two countries that in most international issues America can count on the support of Britain. That makes life a lot easier for the ambassador. There would be no such luxury for an American ambassador in Iran or China or Cuba.

But how do we respond to this? Do we say that the ambassador in London is of greater value than the ambassador in Peking because he delivers more consistent agreement with American government policy? Ambassadors do not play on a level field. It is in the nature of their work that some have considerably harder tasks than others. It would be quite ludicrous for any government to say, "We need to put our money where we can get results, so let's send ambassadors only to the places that are well disposed toward us." In fact, it is more likely that a government will send its very best ambassadors to the toughest places.

So when we say the ambassador's goal is that "the people to whom he speaks should be brought into, and kept in a good relationship with, the government he serves," that is a goal to aim at, not a goal to be judged by. This is so important for our understanding of ministry. As we send out ambassadors for Christ to the nations of the world, we have to recognize that they operate in different spiritual climates.

Two men move into neighboring homes in spring of the same year. They are both gardeners and they both decide to grow vegetables in their yard. The first one begins to dig and finds that the earth is baked like clay, and every time he puts the fork in, he is pulling up stones. It is backbreaking work, and at the end of the summer the vegetables are pretty small. Next door, his neighbor has a different experience. He finds that the soil is fertile. It is free of stones, and as he puts in his fork, it crumbles beautifully. He sows the same seed, and at the end of the summer his vegetables are magnificent. Which one is the better gardener?

The difference is not in the gardener but in the garden. One garden has been neglected. The previous owner never used a spade. The other garden has been worked and watered and fertilized year after year, and the new owner has the joy of reaping the benefit of another man's work.

Where the soil is hard someone has to start digging, and God sends some of his best ambassadors to the hardest places. But even in the hardest places, the goal is the same. Ambassadors are always sent in hope, and Paul makes it clear that we are to pursue our goal by means of persuasion and invitation, with a view of transformation.

PERSUASION

"Since, then, we know what it is to fear the Lord, we try to *persuade men*" (2 Cor. 5:11, emphasis added). The word *persuade* is very significant. Conversion is not a set of religious feelings. A person becomes a Christian when he or she is persuaded of the truth of the gospel and on that basis confesses Jesus Christ as Lord (Rom. 10:9). The book of Acts is full of this kind of vocabulary:

> "He talked and *debated* with the Grecian Jews." (Acts 9:29)
> "As his custom was, Paul went into the synagogue, and on three Sabbath days he *reasoned* with them from the Scriptures." (Acts 17:2)
> "Every Sabbath he *reasoned* in the synagogue, trying to *persuade* Jews and Greeks." (Acts 18:4)
> "Paul entered the synagogue and spoke boldly there for three months, *arguing persuasively* about the kingdom of God." (Acts 19:8)
> "So Paul stayed for a year and a half, *teaching* them the word of God." (Acts 18:11)
> "Boldly and without hindrance he *preached* the kingdom of God and *taught* about the Lord Jesus Christ." (Acts 28:31)
> "From morning till evening he *explained and declared* to them the kingdom of God and *tried to convince* them about Jesus from the Law of Moses and from the Prophets." (Acts 28:23)

Paul is not suggesting that we can argue people into the kingdom, but he is quite clear that nobody comes into the kingdom without being convinced of the truth about Jesus Christ.

This is why a faithful ambassador must be committed to teaching the Bible. There are many ways in which we can draw a crowd, but if we are to evangelize, we must put the truth of the gospel into words so that people will understand what God is saying to them. If that does not happen, evangelism has not taken place.

INVITATION

"We are therefore Christ's ambassadors, as though God were making his appeal through us. We implore you on Christ's behalf: Be reconciled to God" (2 Cor. 5:20).

There is a passion behind the word *implore*. Paul is deeply concerned about the response of the people around him to the message of Christ. He is not a philosopher who finds fulfillment in giving well-crafted lectures. He is a pastor with a burden for people's souls.

An ambassador of Christ cannot pursue his work in a detached way. The issues are of eternal significance. His mind must be filled with the truth of God. His heart must be filled with the passion of God.

When Paul implores people to be reconciled to God, he tells us that it is "as though God were making his appeal through us" (2 Cor. 5:20). The idea of God appealing is quite astonishing. Normally, the weak appeal to the strong. The poor appeal to the rich. It would not be surprising to read about sinners appealing to God, but here we have God appealing to sinners! At the creation, God speaks and it is done: the stars are suspended in space by a single word of his command. Yet in Christ, God appeals to us to be reconciled to himself.

The way in which God makes this appeal is through the words of his ambassadors. When we speak, it is *"as though God himself were making his appeal through us."* This is the mystery of preaching. A man gets up and speaks from the Bible, and something more happens. God speaks. As his Word is opened up, he reaches out through the words of the speaker into the hearts of those who listen.

The ambassador seeks to elicit a verdict and to broker a relationship. He is passionately committed to his own government, and he cares deeply about the people to whom he is sent. He sees the incredible benefits for them in reconciliation and the dire consequences of continued alienation. He will have no greater joy than to see reconciliation between the people to whom he is sent and the Lord he serves.

TRANSFORMATION

As ambassadors for Christ, our aim for the people around us is that they "should no longer live for themselves but for him who died for them and was raised again" (2 Cor. 5:15). This would be a truly radical transformation in Postmodernia!

The incredible thing is that God has given us the dignity of being his fellow workers. As his ambassadors seek to persuade and invite, God himself will be at work to transform. Our God can take postmodern people who are bent in on themselves and release them into lives that are redirected for his glory.

It is difficult to think of a higher privilege than the calling to be an ambassador for Christ in Postmodernia. God sends us to communicate his word of reconciliation to our contemporaries who do not know who he is or what he has done. Christ will speak through the mouths of his ambassadors, and through their work he will reconcile many postmodern people to God.

References

Bailey, T. A. 1968. *The Art of Diplomacy: The American Experience*. New York: Appleton-Century-Crofts.

Briscoe, Stuart. 1994. *Fresh Air in the Pulpit*. Grand Rapids: Baker.

Clark, Eric. 1973. *Diplomat: The World of International Diplomacy*. New York: Taplinger Publishing Company.

Dillenberger, J., ed. 1961. *Martin Luther: Selections from His Writings*. London: Lutterworth.

Packer, J. I. 1961. *Evangelism and the Sovereignty of God*. London: InterVarsity Press.

Stott, John R. W. 1986. *The Cross of Christ*. Leicester: InterVarsity Press.

Trevelyan, Humphrey. 1973. *Diplomatic Channels*. Boston: Gambit, Inc.

PART FIVE

Church, Campus, Ethnicity

CHAPTER 13

CHURCH/CAMPUS CONNECTIONS

Model 1

Phillip D. Jensen and Tony Payne

In the pages that follow, we will attempt to do the following:

- Sketch in the context of Australian university life, in which our own particular model of ministry has been built.
- Draw some salient lessons from the history of evangelical university ministry.
- Outline a theology of church.
- Explore the relation between church and parachurch.
- Explore the relation between church and worship.
- Explain the strategy for training that we have developed at the University of New South Wales.

With a program like that, this paper (like the address it was based on) is no doubt as strong on sweeping generalizations as it is weak on footnotes and detail. We hope the reader will forgive the flaws that come from working with a broad brush. In trying to explain how our church has gone about ministering to a campus—in other words, to distill twenty-five years of biblical reflection and practice—it is hard to leave out any of the above subjects. We trust that the result will be in some way stimulating and encouraging.

ABOUT OUR CAMPUS CONTEXT

The heart of this paper will (in due course) be theological, and it must be so, because unprincipled pragmatism is in the end not only unfaithful, but also unpragmatic. We must be driven by what God calls us to do, not simply by what we think works, because God alone ultimately knows what works. We must trust him and follow his instructions.

Before we get to that, let us begin by sketching a picture of the campus side of our church/campus connection. For a start, we don't call it school; we call it university. In Australia, school is where you send young children. University is where you go to begin your tertiary education at around age eighteen. And when we say "go to university," we don't literally mean go, because that is another profound difference between the Australian and American scene. Whereas American teenagers commonly leave home to undertake tertiary studies at a residential college in another city or state, Australian eighteen-year-olds almost always stay within their state and within their capital city. Nearly every subject offered at, say, the University of New South Wales (UNSW) in Sydney is also offered at the University of Melbourne, Adelaide University, and so on. So we stay put and live at home until we are twenty-one or twenty-two.

This creates the commuter university—such as our own UNSW, which has 20,000 students, of which approximately 12,000 are there at any one time. It is a prestigious university in the Australian context, indeed in the Southeast Asian context, being one of the top destinations for overseas students from our near Asian neighbors.

Being a commuter campus means that a majority of students will travel to and from home each day up to a maximum of around two hours of travel each way. The average would be around half that. This means that the only free or disposable time students have on campus is lunchtime. They arrive as late as possible before lectures and leave as early as possible because of how much of their day is already wiped out by travel. Their commitment to the life of the university is minimal. They are commuters.

However, the commuters are not the only groups on our campus. There are two other important groups. The first is those students who have traveled from the country areas of New South Wales to university in the city and who live in residential colleges for a year or two before moving into apartments close to the university. The second is a group who have also left home and traveled, not just from country to city, but from overseas—mainly from Malaysia, Indonesia, Hong Kong, and mainland China. They have entered a whole new culture.

Both of these residential groups have an experience of university life that is almost totally different from the experience of commuter students from the suburbs. They sit in the same classes and take the same exams but have almost nothing else in common.

So we run different kinds of ministries—a lunchtime ministry to the commuters, and more broad-ranging work that ministers in different ways to our overseas students and residential students. The ministry with residential students

PHILLIP D. JENSEN AND TONY PAYNE

is vastly more effective than the commuter work. What we would not give for a campus environment like that of many American colleges, in which the majority of the students are residential! A residential student is fully committed to university life. You can get them at breakfast, at supper, on weekends, even at 2:00 A.M.!

Much of our effort, then, is put into the numerically smaller groups on the campus—the students from the country and from overseas. In fact, the overseas student work is perhaps our most significant, and we devote considerable resources to it. By law, our overseas students must return to their Asian homelands after they have completed their degree. So by evangelizing, teaching, and training them during their stay at UNSW, we are evangelizing Southeast Asia more effectively than any missionary organization could. We are sending back the cream of a country's young people, soundly converted, trained, and ready to minister the gospel to their countrymen. It is an exciting and strategic work.

LESSONS FROM HISTORY

The history of university ministry is one of the most significant chapters in the history of Protestantism, and those who would undertake campus ministry need to learn it. They need to learn about the Student Volunteer Movement, and the incredible impact it had on Christian and missionary history. They need to learn of the Student Christian Movement (SCM) that stemmed from it. And let us issue a plea that no evangelical contemplate entering student ministry until he or she has studied the Great Crisis of 1910. It was the defining moment of student ministry in our century; indeed it was one of the defining moments for all evangelicalism in our century.[1]

In 1910 a small group of men in Cambridge (England, that is, not Massachusetts), took issue with SCM, which was the worldwide Christian student movement at the time. SCM was large and influential. Yet these few men at Cambridge University argued that the steady theological broadening that had been taking place in SCM had gone too far. And the issue on which the storm broke was the centrality of the atonement.

It is important to note that both sides of the controversy agreed on the atoning work of Jesus Christ on the cross, and both sides subscribed to the doctrine of penal substitution. The difference was this: SCM said that you could preach the gospel without preaching the atonement, whereas the small group of Cambridge students argued that it was central to Christian doctrine and to Christian gospel preaching. They argued that without the atonement, you no longer have the gospel. They insisted that Christian proclamation must have at its heart Christ crucified.

Over this dispute, the Cambridge students split from SCM and formed the Cambridge Intercollegiate Christian Union, or CICCU as it is known. It was the moment at which the Intervarsity Fellowship came into being.

If we can be somewhat rude for a moment, it seems to us that many current evangelical student ministries have lost touch with their history on this matter. Many today have more in common with SCM than with CICCU. They have not ceased believing in the cross and the atonement. They have simply moved it off-center, and spend their time speaking about other things—things that are no doubt worthwhile and important in themselves but that are not the death of Christ for our sins. Their preaching could no longer be simply summarized as Christ crucified. If you lose that at the center of your ministry, then like SCM you cease being an evangelical ministry, and you are headed for disaster. It may only be a slight difference at first, but it is a watershed. The subsequent flow is in the wrong direction. The SCM, of course, became the World Council of Churches, which itself started out as an evangelical organization before degenerating into liberalism. SCM as a student movement went the same way and has largely disappeared.

The other important feature of the history of student ministry has been the prominent role played in it by parachurch organizations, starting with Dawson Troppman and the Navigators, and Bill Bright and Campus Crusade. The growth of these sorts of movements and their widespread success during the last fifty years or so has been the result of a number of factors, not least of which has been the failure of churches to do their job properly. Churches have not (on the whole) seen the strategic importance of university ministry and have not plowed resources into it.

In one sense, it was a harvest waiting to be reaped, and the visionaries who started the various Christian student movements saw this. At another level, however, Christian student movements have usually established themselves quite deliberately as nonchurches. They have kept their distance from the established denominations and have avoided at all cost referring to themselves as churches—either to avoid conflict (over establishing a "rival church") or to avoid the negative influence of ungodly church structures.

In Cambridge, for example, when CICCU was founded, all the residential colleges had their own chaplains, but hardly any of these were evangelical. CICCU, therefore, quite deliberately established a constitution that required anyone who would speak at a CICCU meeting to sign their doctrinal basis. The effect was to exclude the heretics who were running the chapels—which

PHILLIP D. JENSEN AND TONY PAYNE

was the right thing to do—but it also bred a certain anticlericalism into the nature of the Intervarsity movement, perhaps a certain anti-ecclesiasticism.

CICCU, and most student ministries since, have called themselves para-church organizations, which means that you go to your student parachurch meeting on Saturday night or Wednesday night (or both), but still go to your local church on Sunday morning. While this situation may have come about as a solution to various problems, the solution itself has now become a problem. What we have done is to create a whole generation of Christians who have learned to minister and evangelize without reference to church, and therefore don't know what to do with church when they leave university. This is especially true of those students converted by that university ministry. They end up requiring a conversion to church, a step that some never successfully make.

A further problem stems from how successfully the parachurch movements have been at student ministry. In view of this success, the churches have said, "Well, we'll leave student evangelism to you guys; and we'll leave women's evangelism to Know Your Bible and CWCI, and we'll leave men's evangelism to Promise Keepers—in fact, we don't need to do any evangelism in our church at all." Taking different segments of ministry out of the context of church creates problems for the healthy functioning of the church. In fact, it only reinforces the general confusion that reigns as to what church is and what it is for.

WHAT IS CHURCH?

To understand how the model of ministry we have developed at UNSW is quite different from most campus ministries, we need to dig back into the Bible's theology of church. This must be the starting point, and it can be a painful starting point, mainly because of our entrenched denominationalism. Denominations are essentially historical hangovers or relics of a bygone age. It may be quite possible to construct justifications for every jot and tittle in our canons and creeds and constitutions, but too often the traditions of our denominations prevent us from thinking theologically out of the Bible. We need to open our minds to a fresh reading of how churches were being planted in the first century, rather than seeing everything in terms of the struggles our forefathers went through merely four hundred years ago.

When we commenced the ministry at UNSW, it was quite explicitly through the Anglican chaplaincy. However, the church we planted on the campus was nondenominational. When we arrived, we inherited 120 people from the previous chaplain. Of these 118 left in the first twelve months. When we took over at the parish church of St. Matthias (which is some ten minutes from the UNSW campus), there were 35 members, of which 18 resigned in protest at our arrival.

However, we still had a church. And what we decided to do from the outset was to have the University of North South Wales as our church's mission field. It wasn't that we were running a church and running a university ministry. We were a church that was reaching out to a particular university. It wasn't exclusive—anybody who wanted to come along could. In fact, the first person converted in one of the student congregations we planted was the grandfather of one of the students. That congregation ran on a Friday night, which was a superb time to reach students. But a church on Friday night? In a lecture theater? With orange plastic chairs and no organ? Could that still be *church*?

In thinking about what church actually is, the most sensible place to start is with the meaning of the word itself—which is, of course, an assembly. In both secular and Christian contexts in the New Testament, we find that the word *ekklesia* simply connotes a gathering, a group of people, even a mob. It can be a Christian gathering that meets in the name of the Lord Jesus Christ for his purposes; or it can be an angry, riotous non-Christian *ekklesia* (as in Acts 19:32). It is not a religious word. It just means an assembly.

What then is special or significant about the Christian assembly? In biblical theology, there is a particular gathering that essentially defines what is distinctive about the Christian gathering. It is the gathering of God's people at Mount Sinai, the definitive time in the Old Testament when all God's people gathered to hear God's word. It is called the "day of the *ekklesia*" in Deuteronomy 9:10 and 10:4 (LXX), and Stephen reflects this usage in Acts 7:38 when he refers to it as the "*ekklesia* in the wilderness." That crucial day of the church is also referred to in Hebrews 12—in Christ we have come, not to Mount Sinai, but to the heavenly Jerusalem, where all God's people are gathered around his throne in joyful assembly, for which reason we must not refuse him who speaks and who warns us from heaven (Heb. 12:18–25). This is the church that belongs to Jesus Christ and that he has decreed he will build (Matt. 16:18).

That essentially is what a Christian church is—a gathering of Christ's people to hear the Word of God, to meet in obedience to that Word. Our particular local earthly gatherings are expressions of the great heavenly gathering of Hebrews 12. Thus, when Christians meet in the name of Jesus Christ in a lecture hall to hear his Word, then that particular gathering (or church) is a Christian one. You don't need a fancy building, stained-glass windows, organs, or any of the normal paraphernalia that we associate with church. You only need a place in which to proclaim God's Word to his people as Paul did daily in the lecture hall of Tyrannus and as we do on the campus of UNSW. We book a lecture theater, expound a chapter of the Bible, and invite anybody and everybody to come and hear the Word of God. And as Christian people gathered to hear the Word of Christ, that is by definition a Christian "church."

While we are thus churching, outsiders and unbelievers also come. Those charming people of 1 Corinthians 14:24—the *idiotes*—often wander in, and as they hear the Word of God, the secrets of their hearts are laid bare and they say, "God is really among you." It is the same gospel for both believers and unbelievers.

CHURCH AND PARACHURCH

These may be radical ideas to many readers, but it is where the New Testament pushes us—that the preaching of God's Word to the assembly of God's people is the central and defining activity of a Christian church. In fact, any gathering in which that takes place is a Christian gathering (or church). When you have an Intervarsity cell group that meets together weekly, reads the Bible, prays, evangelizes their friends, cares for each other, and encourages each other, in what sense is it not a Christian church? Because it doesn't have the sacraments? Well, why doesn't it? Because if it did, we'd have to call it a church. And if it became a church, we'd lose our nondenominational status and arouse conflict in the Christian community.

We find ourselves in the unfortunate position of denying what we essentially are for the sake of ecclesiastical politics. It is time we came clean—the parachurch has very little that is para about it. It is a church movement. It participates in the heavenly gathering of Jesus Christ, and it gathers locally in expression of that to hear and respond to Christ's Word. It is a church.

That this is true is demonstrated by the loyalty that, say, Navigators or Campus Crusade members give to their organizations above the "church" they go to on Sundays. In terms of involvement, commitment, learning, real Christian growth, and ministry, it is during the week on campus that the action is. And there is nothing wrong with this! What is slightly crazy is our ongoing insistence that this midweek activity is somehow not church, and hence our dutiful occupation of pews on Sunday in order to fulfill all righteousness. (Let me hasten to add that we are not singling out Navigators and Campus Crusade— they are fine organizations. They are simply examples of what is true of a great many, if not most, parachurch movements, whether student or otherwise.)

We would like to see the Navigators run a meeting on Sunday to reach more people. Let your people be undivided in their loyalties and involvement.

Call it church and be done with it. Stop trying to pretend that you aren't a church, when you transparently are. If the Navigators were to do so, we might lose some people from our Sunday gathering—but that would be all right. They are essentially passengers in our gathering and would no doubt be more effective in their witness and ministry if they concentrated on "Navigator church."

The fact that you have a particular focus or target group for your ministry is no barrier to being a church. What we have found is that in planting a church aimed squarely and specifically at students, we have also seen all sorts of other ministries spring up through the people God has brought to us. We have a Korean congregation and a Greek congregation; we have planted two churches for Italians and one for Vietnamese; we now have two family congregations, a ministry to the elderly, and a congregation of young professionals. And these congregations are not homogenous and sealed off from each other. Each of them has a mix of people.

CHURCH AND "WORSHIP"

At this point, many readers may be thinking: "But don't we basically go to church to worship God, and isn't this what Sunday supplies that the midweek parachurch activity cannot?"

That this view is so common among evangelicals today is testimony both to our lack of serious engagement with what the Bible actually says about church and to our short historical memories. We write as Anglican evangelicals, whose denomination has basically been destroyed by this view of church and worship over the past 150 years. When we hear evangelicals talking about church being worship, and our buildings being sanctuaries, with the Lord's table as an altar, it is greatly disturbing, not least of all because it is so biblically wrong. All the language of temple, altar, sanctuary, service, priests, and offerings is taken up and fulfilled in the death of the Lord Jesus Christ, our great High Priest. He is our temple, our tabernacle, our offering, our sacrifice. In him God's presence is continually with us (through the indwelling Spirit), and thus our whole lives are our spiritual worship as we obey him and do his will. We do still worship in church—but only in the sense that we breathe in church. We don't go to church to worship any more than we go to church to breathe.

The purpose of church is fellowship with God's people around God's Word. We worship in every aspect of our lives day by day as we offer our bodies as living sacrifices to God. To confuse the two, as most evangelicals seem to today, is a drastic error. You certainly won't find the two confused in the New Testament. In fact, it is an interesting exercise to try to find even one reference in the New Testament where worship language is used in association with Christian gatherings.[2]

These ideas no doubt go somewhat against the grain. We have sat, Sunday after Sunday for years on end, hearing our pastor say, "We welcome you today to our hour of worship." Yet study the Scriptures and see.

OUR STRATEGY OF TRAINING

Our chief strategy as a university church is to get rid of our members. We want to export them, not hold onto them. In other words, we don't believe in church growth. The modern penchant for church growth, it seems to us, is largely self-centered. For which church is it that you want to see grow? My church, of course.

We should be far more interested in gospel growth, as Colossians 1:3–6 puts it, in men and women all over the world acknowledging the Lord Jesus Christ. You could say that this was church growth, so long as you recognize that the church involved is the church of Jesus Christ, the great gathering in heaven of all his people that he is building.

The church of Jesus Christ grows through the preaching of the gospel, so our chief strategy is to recruit and train more gospel preachers. We won't reach the world and see the assembly of Jesus Christ grow simply by trying to make our own church bigger. We need to plant many more churches, and for this we need many more gospel preachers.

Our approach to campus ministry, then, is conditioned by our belief that the university is a key place for recruiting and training gospel preachers. At university you have people for around four years at that crucial stage of their lives when they are beginning to make decisions as adults and to launch themselves into life. We want them to launch into gospel ministry, whether as a full-time minister or as mission-minded, evangelistically active laypersons. We want them to be so shaped and changed by the gospel at university that when they leave us, they do so as motivated, well-taught, well-trained gospel people. Some of them will continue on in their chosen profession. We try to persuade as many as possible to give up their small ambitions for professional success and become full-time gospel preachers instead.

Many of the training programs that are now available through Matthias Media were first developed and field-tested in this campus context as we sought to train people in the basics of Christian ministry—the "Two Ways to

Live Training Course" for personal evangelism; "Just for Starters" and the "Personal Follow-up Training Course" for teaching people how to disciple a new believer; "Growth Groups" for training small group leaders; and so on. Through regular weekly Bible teaching, these training courses, and personal discipling, we aim to get each of our undergraduates to the point of being what we call a self-starter—that is, someone who will leave university, go to a church somewhere, and begin to minister, whether they are asked to or not. We want them to be the sort of people who look for opportunities to minister the gospel wherever they happen to be. (Here again, it is important to remember the difference between the commuters and the residents at our campus. In this whole program of training, we have far more success with the residential and overseas students than with the commuters, simply because we see more of them each week, and they typically stay with us for longer.)

Throughout this ministry to the students, we are always on the lookout for people whom we call blokes worth watching (BWWs). These blokes (and blokesses) are those who seem to have real gifts for ministry. At university this can be as many as a third of the students who are with us, because they have already been preselected by our educational system to be the clever people, the able people, the leaders. Our aim with the BWWs is to direct them, over time, into full-time gospel ministry. It usually takes around ten years from the time that we first spot a likely looking BWW to when he or she ends up on the mission field or in pastoral work. We believe in training them properly for the long haul. And to do so we have evolved two important structures.

The first is called "Club 5." This is an informal organization that aims to inform, encourage, and generally help people through the process of thinking about full-time ministry. Each member of Club 5 is assigned a coach—someone who sticks by them over the years, who is on their side, and who talks with them personally about all the decisions and hurdles to actually making it into full-time Christian work. We called the organization Club 5 because we wanted to recruit five hundred full-time evangelists in five years. Our first five years have now passed, and we have more than reached our target. We're now aiming at five thousand in the next five years. We don't know if we'll make it, but we're going for it!

The second important structure is called the "Ministry Training Strategy." This is essentially a two-year apprenticeship course in which our preachers-to-be test their gifts and gain practical experience in gospel work before they head off to Moore Theological College (which is a further four years of full-time study). We currently have around thirty trainees in this program at UNSW. We pay them enough to stay alive (just) while they learn by doing

PHILLIP D. JENSEN AND TONY PAYNE

gospel work on the campus. It's a model that has now spread to other churches in Australia, with thirty-five different training centers and more than a hundred trainees currently involved in the program.

This is our church/campus connection: we run churches on and around a campus with the aim of bringing biblical revival to the world. We seek to so evangelize and train students while they are with us that when we export them to other churches as members or evangelists or pastor-teachers, they will not only preach the gospel, but they will train other people to do so as well.

References

Barclay, Oliver. 1977. *Whatever Happened to the Jesus Lane Lot?* Leicester: Inter-Varsity Press.

Horn, R. M. 1971. *Student Witness and Christian Truth.* London: InterVarsity Press.

Peterson, David. 1992. *Engaging with God.* Leicester: Apollos.

CHAPTER 14

CHURCH/CAMPUS CONNECTIONS

Model 2

Mark Gauthier

Some time ago I was having lunch with a very influential leader in a particular denomination. We were discussing the growing movement of churches and Christian organizations joining together in formal partnerships toward a common mission. At the end of our conversation he commented to me, "This isn't only right; it's smart too."

I want to talk about partnering in the body of Christ. More specifically, I want to focus on the smartness of partnership in the light of our postmodern context. Partnerships of this kind are first and foremost right. But for the purposes of our discussion, we will limit ourselves to the examination of the pragmatic side of this issue. Why is it smart to work in partnership? What is it about postmodernism that leads to this outworking of ministry?

In Campus Ministry of Campus Crusade for Christ we are pursuing our mission of helping to reach the 60 million students around the world. We have a growing confidence that God is able and willing to reach this generation. We believe this generation marked by postmodernity will be the generation God uses to help fulfill the Great Commission in the next millennium. While the forces of evil work to thwart the expansion of his kingdom, God still reigns and will not be hindered by the current cultural context. Yet on the other hand, we, like Paul, do all things that we might "win as many as possible" (1 Cor. 9:19). So our discussion today rests in the context of a strong, mighty, and ruling God.

POSTMODERNISM: A UNIQUE OPPORTUNITY REQUIRING A NEW VISION

Over the past several decades the church and Christian student organizations have coexisted in a variety of ways. At our worst, we have competed. We

MARK GAUTHIER

have competed for territory, for people, and for the numbers that communicate our "success." We have desired growth at the expense of another group. We have fought over that sharp student contact. We may even have competed for leaders. In the end, we might all agree that our efforts have not been maximized. And more important, God was neither honored nor pleased.

In other situations we did better. We recognized that we each brought certain strengths to the mission in an informal and distant partnership. While we have not joined our activities, we could honestly cheer one another on. Yet many times we have concluded that our efforts weren't as synergistic as possible. They were more complementary than collaborative.

The third form of this relationship has been one of cooperation. Perhaps we joined with other groups for prayer or an occasional outreach. Maybe the leaders met to update and encourage one another. While this is commendable, I wonder if there is potential yet to be realized.

Who is most effective at reaching this postmodern generation? Is it the church or the Christian organization? Certainly both will have a role and are making inroads with the gospel. Perhaps the best answer will be *neither alone, but both together*. Maybe our particular cultural context provides a great opportunity to work more closely together as we enter the new millennium. This is the vision we want to craft today, a vision of the local church working with the local Christian organization—reaching out hand in hand, coordinating efforts for the sake of the glory of God, the advancement of the gospel, and for those who do not know Christ.

Let's examine four characteristics of the postmodern context. First is the focus on *subjective experience versus objective reasoning*. I remember my early years of ministry at Harvard. Many conversations with students would go like this: "If I could prove to you that this was true would you believe?" "Yes" would be the response more often than not. Over the years this yes drifted to the "No, not really" category as students weren't as interested in the intellectual viability of a belief system. In fact, what I heard them say was, "Show me how this can change my life; let me see someone else who has found that it works for them."

A second mark is *the preeminence of the community rather than the individual*. It isn't so important what pilgrimage I am on, but rather what pilgrimage *we* are on. The autonomy that was the lead foot of the previous generation has been replaced with an authentic desire to be known. Yet even with this value, many still aren't experiencing it. For example, it is interesting to note that despite this characteristic and the strong emphasis on reconciliation, university officials are still looking for answers and solutions to the growing fragmentation on many campuses. Diversity and reconciliation are two dominant issues on every campus, yet there are few manifestations of community in the midst of a diverse university.

Third is an emphasis on *the transcendent rather than the objective*. This is a very "spiritual" culture, and many desire an experience of something that is beyond them. At the same time, there isn't a transcendent whole that is overarching their experiences or thoughts. Pluralism and relativism have dominated the cultural landscape, leaving people to make sense of the pieces of their personal experience. Our society doesn't have a metanarrative, and therefore one has a very difficult time reconciling the past with the present and the present with the future. Today there aren't the objective roadways to understand the transcendent. The result is a generation of fragmented people. This fragmentation leaves a life numb and without meaning. Life and our experiences become somewhat shallow.

Finally, far from being triumphalistic, *our culture is hungry and needy* and knows it is looking for answers. Our world is very complex, and the pain is real. There are deep needs that a fragmented, relativistic worldview cannot meet. This generation is skeptical and disillusioned with the promise of former generations that theirs would be a better world. To most, the world isn't a better place to live, and statistics prove it.

In the midst of these cultural characteristics, there is strong reason to be hopeful and confident in the power of the gospel. Our landscape is fertile with great opportunities for the kingdom of God to take root. In light of the cultural landscape described, why should a church and a Christian organization form a partnership? Consider the numerous resources available for effective ministry in this postmodern world when the church and Christian organization come together for effective ministry.

We have communities that experience real things, like life change, relationships with people, and relationships with God. At our best, we have an authentic community, experiencing both grace and truth—something the postmodern person is screaming for. We can provide meaning flowing from the ultimate connection with the Transcendent One, who became incarnate in Christ. We have diversity and can model reconciliation within the body of Christ. We can make the connection with the past and use it to help understand the present and to enable us to move ahead into the future. We have the gospel, and therefore we can provide hopeful and authentic help.

The local church brings diverse communities and real family. The church provides strong biblical teaching, counseling, manpower, and finances. The church can provide multiple opportunities for people changed by Christ to make a difference in their communities. Yet many times the local church is hampered in a particular mission field because of denominational bias on the part of those they are trying to reach. Often leadership resources are so limited that there isn't the critical mass to break into a new field of ministry. Or perhaps there is a lack of expertise with a specific group of people. For example, I have had numerous conversations with pastors of churches who genuinely want to reach the college students in their communities, but who do not have the time or the manpower to do it.

Consider the contribution of the Christian organization. They have trained and experienced laborers and leaders. They have specific resources and tools developed over the years of targeted attention. They can provide resourcing in the form of leadership development, training, and opportunities for ministry. They can provide a platform for ministry that is seen by the audience as interdenominational and unbiased. Yet so often the Christian organization takes on a church life of its own. The people involved in the organization never make the transition to the local church. People are often left to choose between a church and a Christian organization. Such organizations lack the diversity of a church and the multitude of resources a church offers.

When these two parties join forces, they have a plethora of resources and relationships that position a ministry to have a chance at actually accomplishing their mission—at going after the scope of their calling. Why not work together? Why not create a partnership where the interests of the church and the Christian organization are honored and fulfilled? And why not bring all resources to bear to enable us to be as effective as possible in giving people multiple opportunities to know Jesus Christ?

Imagine the resources available for our evangelistic efforts. First, there is the witness of the body of believers in the local church. The Christian organization can be the bridge to lead those without Christ into this dynamic testimony and expose them to the witness of Christ's people. Imagine the advantage of having numerous people in the church equipped and developed in evangelism by those in a Christian organization with years of evangelistic experience. Finally, there are the broad sowing activities that enable the church and the Christian organization to proclaim the gospel to each and every person in a target area, a task often impossible without adequate financial resources. The church providing the money and the Christian organization providing the tools makes this a reality. A partnership brings all possible resources together to provide a comprehensive evangelistic strategy to a mission field.

THE MINISTRY PARADIGM EXPLORED: BOSTON CASE STUDY

Let me share one story with you. It is my story. I realize there are many expressions of partnership and this is just one of those expressions. In 1992 I approached the senior minister of Park Street Church in Boston with this question: "What can we do together to reach the 300,000 college students in the Boston area?" While both Campus Crusade for Christ and Park Street Church had effective college ministries on a few campuses, we both knew we were falling short of the entire scope of our calling—every student in the city.

This question led to a dialogue on what it would look like to lower our organizational flags and unite in a true partnership. What transpired was an embracing of a common mission and vision that became the foundation for all the strategies we talked about. We examined our resources. What did Campus Crusade for Christ have to offer, and what did Park Street Church bring to this partnership? We then defined what it was we were looking to accomplish. What would it look like if our partnership experienced success?

There were many strategies and plans implemented through this relationship. We developed an internship program called the Campus Ministry Internship that was designed to give graduating students an experience of ministry in the local church and a Christian organization. We helped the church with a contemporary evening worship service and outreach service designed to reach and minister to students and young professionals. Once each month the church would host an evangelistic outreach that we used to bring lost students into an experience of the body of Christ. We used a home owned by the church and turned it into the nerve center of the entire student ministry in Boston.

Students began to see their involvement in Campus Crusade for Christ as involvement with Park Street Church. This became synonymous for them. Going to a Bible study on their campus was involvement with PSC, and going to church on Sunday at PSC was involvement with CCC. Many of the graduating students decided to make their home in Boston to work and continue with their involvement in the church.

And finally there was the international impact of the partnership. PSC has a rich history of world missions and remains very involved around the globe. CCC too has a desire to proclaim the gospel to students around the world. So in conjunction with a partnership in Central Asia, we started a ministry to students in Tashkent, Uzbekistan. We dreamed of planting a church or resourcing an existing church through the PSC connection. The final outcome included involvement by some lay members and the senior minister of PSC in Tashkent, as well as a visit by the pastor of another church in Boston. It was that particular pastor that God led to uproot his family and move to Tashkent to help a newly formed church comprised primarily of new university student converts. The power of partnership was felt around the globe.

The evangelistic implications of the partnership were numerous as well. First, the church had resources to program a relevant and effective evangelistic service. CCC helped provide leadership, but they had a facility, equipment, money, and lots of creativity in the church to create an effective experience. We had students connected with hundreds of friends without Christ who could use this service to lead their peers to Christ. We saw much more evangelistic activity because of this outreach.

Second, in an age of spiritual skepticism a person with a credible platform professionally can use that platform to gain a listening audience. In the congregation at PSC there were numerous people with professional expertise and experience that captured the interest of students. We simply identified these people and created opportunities for them to share their story in small and large groups. This always led to evangelistic fruit.

Then there was the witness of the church service and the variety of church activities. While not every student was interested in these, many were. We viewed the church as a legitimate venue for witness. The life of the body at the church was a form of evangelism that complemented the initiative of the students on campus.

Park Street Church also had a strategy to minister in the economically challenged environments of the city. Social service has been and continues to be of interest to students. We simply combined this interest with the existing opportunities in the church and had students invite their non-Christians friends with them to minister to the poor. This provided a meaningful opportunity for those without Christ to have exposure to the body of Christ and the incarnational apologetic this form of witness takes.

All of these forms of outreach are extremely effective and are not that difficult. They are effective because they tap into all the resources God has given us to reach the world with the gospel. In Boston we began to see the reality of this.

The partnership wasn't without its challenges. The need for regular communication was heightened with the partnership. Because there were many interests involved, the pace was slower than expected. As the relationship progressed, we learned how to work together effectively. We also discovered that partnering was very messy and required much intellectual flexibility. The tensions created by loss of control raised issues both for the partnership and for me personally. These were great challenges, but they weren't insurmountable.

GUIDING PRINCIPLES: MAXIMIZING THE PARTNERSHIP

In the light of this story here are some principles to help provide some framework for partnerships:

First, remember that it is a partnership. It is not a hostile takeover where one group loses its interests, objectives, and purpose or is subsumed by another. It is not a compromise with those involved moving to the lowest common denominator. A partnership is a mutually beneficial relationship where the interests and goals of all involved are realized. This is a relationship where all involved win.

Second, a partnership is rooted in common mission, vision, and values. While a partnership can be powerful, not all situations call for a partnership. Both must be called to the same objective, thereby enabling a wholehearted embracing of the mission. The Boston example began with the question "What can we do together to give every student an opportunity to know Christ and grow in that relationship?" Implied in the question is a mission and a vision we both held.

Third is a mutual recognition of the resources involved. Consider drawing a line down a blank piece of paper and discussing what each participant brings to the partnership: staff resources, tools and ministry resources, finances, and so forth.

Fourth is a clearly defined result. What are the expected outcomes or "success criteria"? This helps establish expectations and ensure that resources are being invested wisely. In Boston we looked at the number of new campus ministries opened, numbers of students coming to Christ and getting involved in Park Street Church and Campus Crusade for Christ, and the number of students hearing the gospel.

Fifth is a commitment to evaluation in light of effectiveness. This principle relates to the stewardship of the partnership and the resources invested. This involves regular reports and updates to all concerned constituents along with timely reviews and evaluation of the partnership and the ministry in general.

These principles can be very helpful and effective as one navigates through the negotiating process.

CONCLUDING REFLECTIONS

Imagine activating more people in the church to share their faith with friends or in a nonintimidating environment. Just last week I received a letter commending the work of one of our staff members. It came from a judge who had an opportunity to speak to one hundred students in the Greek system about his faith and his life. Through this one man several students placed their faith in Christ. He was a layman activated and given an opportunity to share with a very receptive audience. One benefit of a powerful partnership is that it provides clear bridges of opportunity to a particular mission context.

Imagine having multiple leaders focused on a target area throughout the week, all of them seeking ways to make Christ an issue in a specific context, whether it is a high school or a university. Because truth travels on the pathway of relationship in this culture, why not employ more individuals with multifaceted opportunities to reach out to students?

The postmodern context provides the church with an incredible opportunity. Why not look at the area you are seeking to reach and examine all the resources that God may have provided to enable effective witness? For those of you with a Christian organization, why not seek to identify others who share with you a passion for lost students and determine how you can work together for a result that is greater than the sum of the parts?

What the church needs is an arm connected to the mission field. What the arm needs is a body to provide context and power to its activity. Why not ask: What can we do together to reach every student on a campus?

CHAPTER 15

PENETRATING ETHNIC PLURALISM

African-Americans

Charles Gilmer

I don't really think about postmodernism very much because postmodernism is not really where ethnic minorities live and think and operate in many respects. Ethnic minorities were not true participants in the transition from modernity to postmodernity. We were objects of the change, or subjects whose presence helped to inform the thinking of what we now call postmodernism. Or we were one of the problematic elements to the formulations of the modernist worldview and, to some extent, to the evangelical Christian response to modernism.

AMERICAN ETHNIC MINORITIES: ICONS OF POSTMODERNISM

When I look at American ethnic minorities, I think of us as icons of postmodernism, as sort of visual representations of the issue. In many respects the presence, influence, and visibility of American ethnic minorities in our society has helped to create the backdrop of postmodernism. We have provided the cases that those who are seeking to influence others use in order to prove their theses.

The clash of worldviews and values, and the divergent interpretations of history that the various ethnic groups bring to the table of public life have helped to create the need for a reevaluation of the assumptions of modernism. How we as evangelical believers respond to, or interact with, the ethnic pluralism that is our world today may be one of the leading indicators of whether we will be effective in making the transitions required to be able to relate to this generation—not least the rising number of our audience who are not of

European descent. Among college students, excluding international students, fully one in four now springs from an American ethnic minority.

THE DESTABILIZATION OF MODERNITY

THE REALITY OF RELATIVISM

Imperialism and its attendant problems undermined the positivistic assumptions attached to modernity. Western Christianity was not quite prepared to handle the responsibility that it had as a partner or beneficiary of the imperialistic era. Political and economic imperialism gave way at the same time that cultural and religious imperialism began to be acknowledged. The cultural biases implicit in the early modern missionary movement became undeniable.

Ethnic minorities have often questioned the views of the dominant society, as evidenced by the spiritual, "Everybody talkin' 'bout heaven ain't goin' there." The myth systems that have been popular in our history, such as Manifest Destiny, have claimed to be a part of (or have attached themselves to) the ultimate metanarrative that we talk about postmoderns rejecting. The ethnocentrism of many of these myth systems has been made manifest, and the metanarrative of the Christian church in this country has consequently come into question. When people hark back to the founding of this country as a Christian nation, as an African-American that's normally offensive to me, because that heritage was not so spotless.

So there is a vacuum of a credible metanarrative, because many of those myth systems (derived from a Christian metanarrative) assigned to non-Europeans an inferior status or viewed their cultures as deficient. There is a wholesale rejection of that idea and an embracing of relativism, particularly cultural relativism.

WHY THE REJECTION OF METANARRATIVE?

I believe the rejection of metanarrative is really a Western or European issue. One of my suppositions is that the failure of modernity to ensure appropriate and effective means of relating to the peoples of the world fuels the postmodern impulse. Among Western intellectuals, the abuses that took place in Europe and the oppression that was inherent in the practice of imperialism caused many to question the validity of the metanarratives that were consciously or unconsciously adhered to. You see different manifestations of this. Sometimes you read writers who are fascinated with these new cultures in a detached, intellectual way; others manifest empathy for, and shame over how Europe has related to, the people groups from which American ethnic minorities derived; and then there are those who dabble in seeing the real alternatives these various systems of thought and life provide. You can see this in the interest in Eastern religions and other practices. All these have helped to draw this generation into the pattern of thought and behavior that is in some ways defined as postmodern.

In its claim to provide a means to respect difference, postmodernism is an understandably attractive alternative to the arrogantly ethnocentric or Eurocentric views of the past—those that said, "There is objective truth, and I possess it—you don't."

THE INTERSECTION OF POSTMODERNISM WITH ETHNIC STUDENT AUDIENCES

The aforementioned realities are the context for the existence of ethnic minority groups in the United States. In many respects, ethnic minority students are not postmodern in the strict sense of the word, for it is hard to support the contention that they ever went through a period of modernity. However, they are contributors to, and they interact with, the postmodern milieu. How do they intersect with the themes of postmodernism? The following is an admittedly limited analysis.

SIGNIFICANCE OF METANARRATIVE TO ETHNIC MINORITY COMMUNITIES

In the African-American community there is an active groping for a compelling metanarrative. (Other American ethnic minority groups also seem to need metanarratives to give meaning to their struggle to effectively engage American society without falsifying their own ethnic experience.) Carl Ellis has cited the work of others in concluding that one of the essential struggles of oppressed people is the search for dignity, meaning, and purpose. To survive oppression requires a transcendent dignity. Meaning and purpose require an objective position from which to evaluate meaning and purpose. So the rejection of metanarrative is not a broad-based phenomenon in the African-American community.

In fact, we grope for a satisfying metanarrative. That groping is demonstrated by the popularity of the myth systems of various Afrocentric cults, from the ubiquitous Nation of Islam to ones you have probably never heard of, like the Black Hebrews or the Higher Knowledge Movement. They provide an alternative metanarrative that addresses the unanswered questions of the African-American psyche. Even groups that have adopted nihilistic values, like the gangster culture, often adhere to some sort of mythology that has sweeping themes. We see a similar groping and awareness among Hispanic and Latino students, but my knowledge is more limited in those arenas.

We need a contemporary, application-oriented metanarrative that addresses the concerns of this generation. The Scriptures actually do contain that metanarrative. I contend that the church has never fully articulated it to our audience. Nor have we wrestled with what it will mean to live in the light of that metanarrative. In the next section, I will give some suggestions as to what is missing in our metanarrative.

On the Affirmation of Ethnic Cultures

Obviously the acknowledgment of the value of cultures other than those of Europe and its derivatives is a very appealing aspect of postmodern thought and values to American ethnic minorities. The debate is being lost by the apologists of the Eurocentric view. As evidence, we may note that, when it comes to identifying regions that have contributed heavily to Western advancement, even an ultraconservative columnist, a committed opponent of multiculturalism in any and all forms, has had to broaden his circle from Western Europe to include Asia and the Mediterranean basin.

As Christians, we need to adopt and bathe in the following formulation as it relates to culture:

- All cultures are at once a reflection both of God's image and of the fall of humankind. God's Word is the only means by which we can effectively evaluate any culture.
- Jesus died for people of every culture.
- Every culture needs to see an incarnational representation within their culture of the person (body) of Christ.

We need to wrestle with what it means to know that cultures really are an expression of the duality of our existence in this life—the fact that we are created in the image of God but that we are fallen and that the cultures that we create reflect that. So every culture has good points and bad points, looking at it from a biblical grid, and every culture then has the opportunity to see the life of Christ manifested among those who come to know Christ from that culture and who operate within that culture in order to express the gospel.

A Proposed Amendment to Our Metanarrative

So I would like to propose an amendment to our metanarrative as inheritors of the Reformation tradition. Our metanarrative as evangelicals focuses on the individual and how he or she receives salvation. It is very individualistic in most of its formulations. What is missing is a collective and corporate under-standing. In other words, the Reformation focused on what an individual must do to be saved: *sola fide*. And it focused on the source of authority: *sola scrip-tura*. Denominations are institutionalizations of various reform movements. We really have come to a fair amount of consensus on the doctrinal issues. We know where the limits are. We agree to disagree on some finer points of the-ology, while adhering to an evangelical orthodoxy on the major issues of man, Christ, and salvation.

What we have not discussed thoroughly, nor lived out consistently, are the incarnational dimensions of the Reformation. How do we relate to others in the body of Christ—as individuals, as assemblies, as cultural incarnations of the body of Christ? Each of those cultural incarnations forms a part of a larger incarnation. We must be committed to living out that larger connectedness that Jesus prayed for in John 17:20–23 and that Paul taught us in 1 Corinthians 12.

Ephesians 4 describes the relationship between various individuals in the body as being necessary for maturity. Ephesians 5:25–27 describes Jesus return-ing for a bride without spot or wrinkle. When I apply these principles to the cultural diversity that comprises the body of Christ in this country and around the world, I begin to get a vision of how these various cultural expressions of the body of Christ will interact with one another to help us all weed out our cul-tural biases, embrace more fully our biblical identity and obligations, and be a beautiful, compelling representation of the person and work of Christ to a world that is dying for relationship, for meaning, and for purpose.

Christ does indeed transcend culture, but in the incarnation he enters into culture in order to draw us ultimately out of those cultures into a new king-dom. But that will be perfectly known only around his throne.

I believe we are in the process of seeing, not a doctrinal or propositional reformation, but an incarnational, relational reformation. Postmodernism drives us in that direction because of its emphases on relativism and tolerance and the desire for community. And that is where we should have been all along. It is thoroughly biblical. Jesus prayed for our unity in his High Priestly Prayer. And so, as God often does in his sovereignty, he allows the forces around us to push us in the direction that he has always intended us to go.

Look at what God has done in Promise Keepers in sort of a prophetic way, raising the issue of racism in the body of Christ and really dealing with that. This is something that had never happened in the evangelical church. We went through the whole Civil Rights Movement, and the evangelical church was by and large silent. Or look at the globalization of the church and the interaction between the maturing Christian communities around the world and the churches that came out of the Western tradition. When I look at all the discussion of missiology and the theological formation, I really believe that this is something God is going to do—that there will be another stage in the evolution of the Reformation as we wrestle through these issues.

What I am suggesting is that we need as Christians to add the facts that I just described to our metanarratives. We have undersold these issues, in many cases, because it does have implications on how we live our lives, how we conduct ourselves in the body of Christ. How are we going to live out what it means to be Christian? Is it appropriate to build a multimillion-dollar church and not be involved with other ethnic churches that may be struggling?

We need to add to our metanarrative this fact: Not only is Christ coming again, but he is coming for a multiethnic, multicultural, multinational, multilingual body of Christ. We are the only ones . . . no, Jesus is the only one who can really make unity in diversity work.

So what do we do?

A CONCEPTUAL FRAMEWORK FOR PENETRATING ETHNIC PLURALISM

What I have observed as I have wrestled with this is that two biblical principles—missiology and ecclesiology—have to be held in tension.

THE MISSIOLOGICAL CHALLENGE: 1 CORINTHIANS 9:22

The missiological challenge is summarized in 1 Corinthians 9:22 when the apostle Paul talks about becoming "all things to all men." It really is a mandate to effectively communicate with the audience we're trying to reach. The problem is some people try to relate to a number of cultures at once. We do need to be committed to inclusiveness and not be demeaning to other cultures, but to think that you can create one ministry strategy that will relate equivalently to all cultures is a bit short-sighted.

One of the passages that has informed my thinking on this is Acts 15:19, where James is giving his answer in the Jerusalem Council. He says this: "It is my judgment, therefore, that we should not make it difficult for the Gentiles who are turning to God." He is talking about a much bigger issue than ethnic pluralism, of course. He is talking about the relationship between Judaism and Christianity. But I think the principle still applies. Unwittingly we have developed ministry that puts invisible stumbling blocks to ethnic minorities when it comes to either receiving the gospel or becoming disciples because our ministry has built into it our own cultural grid, whether we realize it or not. In some respects, for ethnic minority Christians it feels like not just embracing the gospel but leaving African-American culture to involve themselves in white culture.

In order to penetrate ethnic pluralism, we must take seriously Paul's approach of adapting to his audience. Contextualization—critical contextualization—of the ministry is a concept that we need to apply to mission endeavors within this country as well as overseas. We must allow for ministries to develop that speak in the idioms of the minority cultures and define expressions of the body of Christ that operate within the cultures. This may affect resources and materials, music—even theology.

THE ECCLESIOLOGICAL MANDATE: 1 CORINTHIANS 12

While pursuing the missiological mandate, we must also hold in tension the need to honor the principle of unity and interconnectedness in the body of Christ that we see in 1 Corinthians 12 and that Jesus prayed for in John 17:20–23.

A CASE STUDY: EVOLUTION OF CAMPUS CRUSADE FOR CHRIST'S EVANGELISM OF ETHNIC MINORITIES

If you look at the evolution in Campus Crusade for Christ's evangelism of ethnic minorities on the college campuses, you will see that we have gone through three identifiable phases.

The first is the *color-blindness* phase. If you look back at the origins of our organization back in 1951 on the UCLA campus, you will see that the inner circle of leadership in that year included a prominent African-American athlete, which in 1951 was a pretty radical thing to do. In that way of approaching it everybody was equal, everybody was welcome, the doors were open. The problem is that we were really not dealing with a level playing field, because the African-Americans that were encountered in that way were not coming out of the same cultural grid. Issues like raising your own support, going to conferences—even where the conferences were located—became stumbling blocks. As far as I know there was no African-American on the CCC staff until well into the 1960s. So the outcome was very little in terms of ongoing ministry, because we were calling people out of one culture into another.

In the 1960s there was a realization that that couldn't continue, so the second phase began—a period of *targeting, representation, and integration*. Some minority staff were recruited, and some aggressive things were done to help them make it financially and to send them around the country. The goal was "an integrated ministry at every level and in every facet of organization." The outcome, though, was limited effectiveness. It did engender some response, and we were able to recruit and retain some leadership, but in retrospect we were not able to develop sustainable growth. If you trace the history, during the 1970s when universities began to integrate aggressively, there was a sort of a willingness on the part of African-Americans to give it a try. But as we got into the later 1970s and the 1980s, a disillusionment began to set in. It was during that period that this whole question of ethnic identity began to be much more important. People were wearing Kente cloth, and there was a lot of outward expression of identification with their culture. The idea of leaving their culture to become part of a white organization became more and more problematic. This has hardened in the 1990s into a sort of skepticism, a sort of a priori assumption that they are not going to leave their culture for anything or anybody—because they *can* encounter the gospel in their culture in the context of the black church.

So we have had to develop our thinking to embrace the principles I mentioned earlier, and this is the third phase: *contextualization and reconciliation*. What this means is taking both the missiological mandate and the ecclesiological mandate seriously. *Contextualizing* means targeting; establishing a distinct identity; providing conferences, materials, projects, and so forth that speak in the context of the students' culture, not asking them to step outside of that culture in order to engage the message or even to become a disciple. When bringing ethnic student movements together with the mainstream, we must be very intentional and frontal about the reconciliation dynamics. This is an area of intense spiritual battle—the enemy does not yield ground easily. This is part of the strategic plan and the local organizational mandate for our ethnic student ministries.

To give you a brief idea of what has happened: At the beginning of the 1980s, we had a national conference for African-American students, Chicago 1981, and then for ten years we never did anything like that again. But in 1991 we had an African-American conference called Impact, and 550 students came—far more than we expected. In 1994 we actually contextualized the conference even more, and we had eleven hundred students come. In 1996 we did the conference again and had 1,850 students. For Impact 1998 we expected 2500 or so people.

We are seeing similar responses to our strategies for reaching Hispanic students and Asian-American students. We recently had our third year of Hispanic student leadership conferences. We first called together a Hispanic ministry task force from among the campus ministries, and I think we were able to identify six Hispanic-American staff out of the 1,800 CCC staff nationwide. This past year at our third conferences in San Diego, California, and El Paso, Texas, called Destino, we had over two hundred students. So it is growing and developing.

CONTEXTUALIZATION APPLIED		
THE IMPACT MOVEMENT	*DESTINO (HISPANIC-AMERICAN STUDENT MOVEMENT)*	*ASIAN-AMERICAN STUDENT MOVEMENT*
1991–550		Zebulun conference in
1994–1100	Over 200 at the third	California—120
1996–1850	installment of Hispanic	attending
1998–2500+	student conferences in San Diego and El Paso	

WHAT ARE THE KEY ISSUES TO ADDRESS?

The issue of identity is very crucial to ethnic minorities in this country. We often feel like strangers in a strange land. I would like to propose a formulation of how to integrate ethnicity into identity as Christians in this country.

For ethnic minority Christians this means embracing their ethnicity as being from God. We teach our students that they need not abandon or abdicate their ethnic identity in order to be a Christian. God made us the way we are, and we should embrace our identity as a gift from him. Biblically, it is appropriate to view ourselves as African-American Christians. The apostle Paul provides a pattern for us to follow in integrating an ethnic and nationalistic identity into his view of himself as a Christian.

Paul belonged to an oppressed people. He was a citizen of the oppressing Roman Empire. He had to deal with pressures from nationalists who thought it was something special just to be a part of the nation of Israel. There were the revolutionaries who wanted to burn it all down. And there were the secularists who thought that all of his talk about the supernatural was emotionalistic, superstitious nonsense.

Paul saw himself as a Hebrew Roman Christian. He identified with his background as a Hebrew (2 Cor. 11:22; Rom. 9:1ff.). He also embraced his identity as a Roman citizen (Acts 16:37–38). Yet he found his most important point of reference was his Christianity (Phil. 3:1–11).

In the same way, we should embrace and celebrate our African-ness. We should appreciate and make the most of our American-ness. But our highest allegiance must be to Jesus Christ.

For African-American students, it is important to be able to integrate these aspects of who they are into a coherent whole and be able to feel good about it. As you may know, the question of whether Christianity is a white man's religion is still a live issue. It is still being asked on campuses across the country on a daily basis.

IMPLICATIONS

What are the implications of all this? First, we have to remember to keep Christ central as we embrace and celebrate our cultural heritage. One's ethnic heritage is to be valued, celebrated, and understood. God doesn't make mistakes, and he made us who we are. God will use who you are (an African-American Christian) to help win others to himself (Acts 1:8).

Second, America is our home. We need to appreciate the opportunities that our presence here affords us. Our welfare is related to the welfare of this nation. We should obey the biblical admonition to pray for the political leaders of the United States.

Finally, our Christian brothers and sisters are more our spiritual family than those of our own race who don't know Jesus. We must not act as if we don't need them (John 17:20–23). While we need not wink at racism or deny its existence, we must not sink into bitterness or excuse our sin of partiality (racism) against white people because of their actions. This would be falling prey to a new bondage. For Jesus said, "I tell you the truth, everyone who sins is a slave to sin" (John 8:34).

For those who are from the dominant culture and yet are committed to seeing ethnic communities reached with the gospel, it means grappling with the implications of the incarnational reformation that is in process and considering the incarnational elements of your eschatology. It means being committed to empowering discipleship—your goal must be to raise up leadership to become your peer or equal, perhaps even that which you will one day follow. Christian discipleship is not some pyramid strategy like Amway or Mary Kay.

Understand the need for focus. While it is good to engage in periodic acts to express your commitment to the unity of the body and to seeing the gospel proclaimed to all, effectiveness will not be achieved by those means. One needs to consider a long-term commitment to cross-cultural ministry if there is to be hope of reproducing indigenous leadership. Of course, then you must prepared to release that ministry.

CHAPTER 16

REACHING OUT TO POSTMODERN ASIAN-AMERICANS

Peter Cha and Greg Jao

For bicultural Asian-Americans, an important aspect of our daily life has always been learning to negotiate between two contesting cultural forces, that of the East and that of the West. During the past decade, however, another competing worldview and value system has emerged in our midst, adding a new dimension to our culture wars. Postmodern ways of looking at reality, at one's self, and at life in general were beginning to influence the younger generation of Asian-Americans. Given this changing context, interpreting our Asian-American experiences simply as a struggle between Asian and American might be inadequate if not outdated. We would like to propose that a more holistic and perhaps more accurate way of looking at our experiences might be through the grids of the traditional, the modern, and the postmodern.

What happens when these three competing worldviews come together in an Asian-American immigrant family, church, and community? Can the traditional, the modern, and the postmodern peacefully coexist under the same roof? These are some of the questions with which Asian-American families and churches will struggle for years to come. However, we will limit our focus here to the following questions: Who are postmodern Asian-Americans? What are some of the critical challenges they face today? And how can we effectively reach out to these Asian-Americans with the good news of Jesus Christ?[1]

THE EXTENT OF POSTMODERN INFLUENCES IN THE ASIAN-AMERICAN CONTEXT

A well-known fable tells the story of six blind Indian men who, after touching different parts of an elephant, walk away with six different mental pictures

PETER CHA AND GREG JAO

of what an elephant is. Similarly, it seems that people who come from different cultural backgrounds and social locations experience and perceive postmodernism somewhat differently. Given its antifoundational nature, postmodernism is a phenomenon that eludes a neatly packaged definition. However, as Stanley Grenz suggests, most of us can agree that postmodernism is our society's strong reaction against modernism: "Whatever else it might be, as the name suggests, postmodernism signifies the quest to move beyond modernism. Specifically, it involves a rejection of the modern mind-set, but launched under the conditions of modernity" (1996, 2).

It would seem, then, that the extent to which a given people group might be affected by postmodernity would be determined partly by the extent to which that group has participated and invested in modernity. An African-American colleague recently told me that the African-American community, on the whole, is not affected by the emergence of postmodernism because the community—largely owing to racism—did not fully participate in America's modernity, which is characterized by the notion of progress and the spirit of optimism. Not having invested themselves in modernity, most African-Americans are neither threatened by nor attracted to postmodern conditions.[2] (Of course, this valuable insight presupposes particular definitions of modern and postmodern.)

How about Asian-Americans? Unlike African-Americans, most Asian-Americans have intentionally embraced modernity and what it promises. Certainly we Asian-Americans experienced our share of racism and discrimination. However, most Asian-Americans, particularly those who immigrated after 1965 and their children, have struggled to achieve "the American dream" and have embraced the optimism of modernity. Some scholars, in fact, argue that most of the post–1965 Asian immigrants, a significant number of whom were well-educated professionals, chose to come to the United States in their quest for modernity (Abelmann and Lie 1995, 49–84). Given this sociohistorical context, we want to propose that postmodernism—as a form of reaction against modernism—can potentially affect Asian-Americans and their communities in significant ways.

Another reason why Asian-Americans might be very susceptible to various postmodern influences has to do with the phenomenon that some sociologists call institutional carriers. Peter Berger, a prominent sociologist, identified technological productions—that is, manufacturing industries—and bureaucracy as two primary carriers of modernization, functioning as the twin engines of the modernization process (1973, 23–62). What, then, are the carriers of postmodernism? What particular sociocultural institutions function to propagate and legitimize postmodernism in our society?

There seem to be two main institutions that promote this new worldview. The first embraces the cultural media—movies, TV programs, the music industry (Harvey 1989, 308–49). The media do a subtle but effective job. *Titanic*, the recent box-office hit and the winner of numerous Oscars, illustrates the point. In the movie, an attractive young lady, Rose, is surrounded by three significant individuals who are vying for her love and loyalty. Each of these three individuals, in turn, represents a particular worldview and value system. Her fiancé, a rich, prideful industrialist, is an appropriate icon for modernity; he represents both the achievements and failures of modernity. Her new lover, a poor artist (not incidentally an image maker), who rejects the goods of modernity such as wealth and social status, and approaches his life with a very playful attitude, makes a perfect postmodern Gen X icon. And then there is Rose's mother, who persistently reminds her daughter that she must marry the industrialist because their family's financial situation demands it. By insisting that family responsibilities and obligations come before an individual member's personal happiness, she defends traditional values and life views. After vacillating and agonizing over these choices, the young woman chooses the young artist and the worldview he embodies, and the rest of the movie is the celebration of this choice.

It's no wonder millions of teens and young adults, including many Asian-Americans we know, went to see this movie—not only once but several times. Those who produced the film may not have used the terms traditional, modern, and postmodern, but they clearly favored one worldview over the others; and they spent more than two hundred million dollars to construct a potent medium that would promote it to the global community.

The second institution that validates and promulgates postmodernism is higher education.[3] While cultural media affect everyone in our society—and in our global village—America's higher education system affects Asian-American young people particularly. Demographically, a far higher percentage of Asian-Americans attend our universities. According to the 1990 census, 21 percent of the U.S. population over the age of twenty-five graduated from college. The percentage jumps to 40 percent for Asian-Americans; that is, almost twice the percentage of the national population. Therefore, a proportionally higher number of Asian-Americans are exposed to the influences of postmodernism in the university setting.

Furthermore, for Asian-Americans the whole university experience can be seen as a very postmodern experience. These young people enter into a contextless environment in which the text they study does not really relate to their own family or cultural context. They are exposed to a multitude of different ethnic, cultural, and socioeconomic classifications without any coherent organizing structure provided by the university. For many Asian-Americans—particularly those who are children of recent immigrants who do not yet have much of a history in this country—this contextless environment can create an even deeper sense of being homeless.

At the same time, many Asian-American college students are attracted to postmodernism because postmodernism and multiculturalism go together in the United States.[4] Encouraged and stimulated by multiculturalism, many Asian-Americans begin to explore their ethnic identity during their college years and begin to participate in various ethnic/cultural programs that validate who they are as Asian-Americans. As ethnic minorities, many Asian-American college students embrace multiculturalism to a varying degree, and in doing so, they knowingly or unknowingly also appropriate some underlying assumptions of postmodernism.

Reaching Out to Asian-American Postmoderns

According to Iwa, an Asian-American Christian research and consultant group, up to 97 percent of Asian-Americans are currently unchurched, making Asian-Americans one of the most unreached people groups in the United States. It seems that the situation is even more challenging in our campus world. According to Paul Tokunaga, the director of Asian-American ministry in InterVarsity Christian Fellowship, a generous estimate indicates that fewer than one percent of the 797,000 Asian-American college students are currently involved in various campus ministry groups. In Luke 15, our Lord told the parable of the lost sheep in which a good shepherd leaves ninety-nine sheep in the open country to go after the one lost sheep until he finds it. If we were to situate this parable in today's Asian-American context, we would find one sheep in safety and ninety-nine sheep lost, wandering in confusion.

Many who closely observe Gen Xers, today's twenty-something crowd who are identified as the first postmodern generation, note that a pervading sense of confusion and hopelessness characterize this generation.[5] And Asian-American Gen Xers are not an exception. Given some of the unique and peculiar aspects of the Asian-American context, however, what exactly are the source and nature of the confusion and hopelessness found among Asian-American postmoderns?

The Project of Self-Identity: A Critical Challenge for Asian-American Postmoderns

Among many possible factors, we would like to focus particularly on the project of self-identity in our postmodern world, a project over which most

Asian-American young adults greatly struggle.[6] In Asian-American families, young adults' quest for self-identity has always been a focal point of conflict and tension between immigrant parents and their American-born children.[7] On the one hand, coming from a traditional perspective, many parents see that identity is not a project one works on; rather it is something that is given, something that is passed down from one generation to another. This is especially true for those of us who come from a Confucian-based culture in which a child, no matter what his or her age might be, is identified as an extension of the parent. On the other hand, Asian-American young adults, deeply influenced by contemporary American culture, commonly assume that the making of self-identity is their own personal project and perceive their parents' involvement as unnecessary if not intrusive.[8] Into this picture enters the postmodern perspective of self-identity, radically redefining and reinterpreting what self is.

From postmodern perspectives, the self is seen as an ever-changing phenomenon that is constantly constructed and reconstructed in and through multiple role performances and constant dialogue with others.[9] The postmodern self is a fragmented self that is often expressed in a manner that lacks coherence, continuity, and inherent meanings. Furthermore, if the modern self was an optimistic and active agent that confidently wrote its own biographical text, the postmodern self is a passive, decentered entity residing amidst various perspectives and voices that define and redefine him or her. Such a perspective would make the project of self-identity a very anxiety-provoking task for any young adult who is trying to make sense of life and find his or her place in the vast world. But for Asian-American young adults, for whom understanding one's identity has always been a confusing and even a painful negotiating process, the emergence of the postmodern view of self only brings a deeper sense of meaninglessness, powerlessness, and hopelessness.

According to an Asian-American counselor, up to 80 percent of the crisis counseling services of a university in the Chicago area is taken up by Asian-American students even though Asian-Americans make up only 20 percent of that student body. Indeed, some studies indicate that a significant number of Asian-American young people—though commonly portrayed as whiz kids who are successful and well-adjusted—are struggling with deep depression (Rue 1993; Uba 1994). Asian-American researchers have also noted a sharp rise in the suicide rate among Asian-American young adults. According to one study, it has risen as much as threefold over the past two decades (Yu et al. 1989). One of the leading causes of their depression and suicide, these studies found, is the inability of these young people to deal with their parents' expectations, coupled with societal pressures for these young adults to become

PETER CHA AND GREG JAO

someone they are not (Rigdon 1991). For some Asian-American postmoderns, the project of self-identity literally becomes a matter of life and death.

TELLING THE TRUTH THROUGH THE GRAND NARRATIVE OF THE GOOD NEWS

Recently some theologians, such as Stanley Grenz and Anthony Thiselton, have noted that the postmodern understanding of self opens new opportunities of ministry for the church. "Postmodernism ... tells part of the story about the human self, but not the whole story," Thiselton writes. "An adequate account of the self and of personhood cannot stop with its situatedness in some instantaneous moment within processes of shifting flux. Selfhood discovers its identity and personhood within a larger purposive narrative which allows room for agency, responsibility and hope" (1995, ix).

How can the church assist Asian-American postmoderns with their critical task of understanding who and what they are? Indeed, one important way is to provide "a larger purposive narrative" that serves as a context in which our individual narratives can find their rightful place. In contextless postmodernity, providing a firm and meaningful context in which Asian-American young people can situate their own stories is no small service.

But the grand narrative of Christianity offers more than simply a suitable background, because our living God is not a God who is hidden in a historical or cosmic backdrop, but is a God who speaks and relates to each of us today. To put it differently, the grand narrative of the gospel invites Asian-American postmoderns to come to know our Creator, our heavenly Father, who desires to teach and remind us who we really are and to fellowship with us as we continue to write our own life narratives. Postmodern scholarship asserts that one's identity is never fully achieved during adolescence and young adulthood as modern social psychologists once assumed. Rather, it is continuously and reflexively changing and evolving as we engage and interact with those who are significant to us. If this is the case, our need—or perhaps desire—to have a continuing dialogue with God or someone like God becomes stronger than ever before.

What, then, is the grand narrative that can effectively draw Asian-American postmoderns into such a relationship with our living God? The Bible explains the story of the gospel using various images. Using a legal image, the Bible teaches that we were once condemned before a righteous and holy God, but Christ's death on the cross turned aside God's righteous anger against us and declares us righteous (Rom. 3:21–26; 5:18–19). Another biblical image, drawing upon the ancient practice of slavery, shows God redeeming or providing ransom for formerly enslaved people through the sacrificial death of his Son (Eph. 1:7; 1 Tim. 2:6; Heb. 9:12). Yet another rich biblical image is that of the relational reconciliation between the heavenly Father and his alienated image-bearers. Jesus came to become our reconciliation (Rom. 5:6–11; 2 Cor. 5:18—though Paul's emphasis in these passages transcends restrictively familial reconciliation).

All of these biblical images of Christ's work of salvation, taken together, illustrate how Jesus is God's complete provision for human sin. They enable us to gain a deeper and richer understanding of the nature of human sin as well as of the full sufficiency of Christ's salvific work. In reaching out to Asian-American postmoderns, however, we find one of these images particularly effectual—the theme of reconciliation between God and his children.

Given our particular cultural context and immigrant experiences, the theme of estrangement and reconciliation between parent and child speaks to Asian-American young people with much pathos and poignancy because so many have been and are experiencing intensely ambivalent relationships with their parents. Therefore, in many Asian-American evangelistic contexts, one of the biblical passages that we and others have frequently used is the parable of the prodigal son (Luke 15:11–32). In this familiar passage we find the story of the gospel—the story of being lost and found—framed in the parent-child relationship. For many Asian-American postmoderns, however, the tremendous appeal of this parable is not so much that we can readily identify with the prodigal son—although to a certain extent all of us can—or the amazing ending of the story. Rather, the most striking and appealing aspect of this parable is the picture of the long-suffering, loving father.

In the parable we find the father faithfully searching the horizon for a trace of his lost child, until one day his straining eyes catch sight of the prodigal in the distance. The father doesn't hesitate. He doesn't wait for the child to come closer. The father does something amazing. He runs. He runs to the prodigal, embraces and kisses this child who sinfully squandered everything. The lost has been found. Almost before the prodigal begins to mumble an apology, he knows he is welcomed. Cherished. Embraced.

In his commentary on Luke 15, Kenneth Bailey states that such a picture of a father must have shocked the Palestinian audience of Jesus, for it challenged their cultural image of a respectable father (1992, 142–61). For the very same reason, this parable has a haunting grip on Asian-American audiences. Many Asian parents, fathers especially, model emotional and verbal restraint, characteristics that are identified as virtues in a Confucian-based culture. Furthermore, many of our parents push us hard to succeed, affirming us sparingly while criticizing or punishing us unduly—at least it appears that way to us as their children. In short, many Asian-American young people perceive their parents as demanding taskmasters who are never quite satisfied with their children's performances and whose love for them is at best conditional.

In *Sometimes It's Hard to Love God* (1989), Dennis Guernsey points out how our past unhealthy relationships with our parents can distort our image of the heavenly Father. We believe this challenge is particularly real and formidable for those of us who are reaching out to Asian-American postmoderns. Given their personal experiences and their postmodern attitudes that hold any authority figure suspect, the notion of submitting oneself to another father figure may seem unattractive or even irrational—until they get a clearer picture of this Father whose dealing with his prodigal son is characterized by grace, not shaming, by unconditional love, not conditional acceptance. This is a picture of our heavenly Father that has consistently touched the hearts of Asian-American young people in our campus and local church ministries.

This loving Father not only provides comfort and a sense of acceptance to these young people but also offers them a lasting identity that can provide a sense of purpose, continuity, and hope in this postmodern world. In his devotional work based on the parable of the prodigal son, Henri Nouwen notes the significance of the theme of Christian identity in the parable. In his view, whenever we seek our identity outside of our loving Father, we are wandering like the prodigal son. Our act of coming home occurs when we come to him and hear his voice that calls us his beloved and find our identity in that truth (1994, 37–58). Reflecting on his own life journey, Nouwen writes:

> There are many . . . voices that are loud, full of promises and very seductive. These voices say, "Go out and prove that you are worth something." . . . Almost from the moment I had ears to hear, I heard those voices, and they have stayed with me ever since. They have come to me through my parents, my friends, my teachers, and my colleagues . . . [But] as long as I remain in touch with the voice that calls me the Beloved, these [voices] are quite harmless. (1994, 41)

Prompted by the Confucian understanding of the relational self and the postmodern notion of the dialogical self, Asian-American postmoderns are searching for and yearning to hear the voice that would call them the Beloved and deliver them from the sea of competing and conflicting voices. Our task is to invite them to hear his truth-telling voice that reminds all of us that before we are Asians or Americans, before we are students or career workers, before we are men or women, we are his beloved, redeemed through the blood of his Son shed on the cross. The grand narrative of the gospel provides Asian-American postmoderns with a core identity that does not change over time, that does not fragment in the multiple, shifting contexts we live in today, and that does not get reduced to a mere collage that lacks coherence. This is indeed great news for many Asian-American young people who are "being tossed back and forth by the waves, and blown here and there by every wind" of postmodern perspectives and moods and of culture wars being waged in Asian-American families.

TELLING THE TRUTH THROUGH THE COMMUNITY OF GOD'S PEOPLE

As they are engaged in the critical task of understanding who and what they are in contextless postmodernity, the other critical element that Asian-American young people are looking for is a community. To begin with, as it shifts from modernity to postmodernity, our society in general is gradually moving from being individual-centered to being community-centered. Tribalism or balkanization is one of the consequences of this sociocultural shift. Those who are examining the Gen X phenomenon have noted that most young postmoderns strongly desire to be part of a community and derive much of their self-understanding from their community life.

For Asian-American postmoderns, this notion of forming self-identity within a community is reinforced by our Confucian-based culture that teaches that our identities are shaped largely by our families and community. One scholar notes that while Western culture says, "I think therefore I am," the Asian culture declares, "I belong, therefore I am." No matter how Americanized they are, many Asian-American students seem to desire to be part of an Asian-American community on their campus, prompting various Asian-American cultural, political, and religious groups to mushroom on our campuses.

During the past decade, responding to this development, InterVarsity Christian Fellowship has sponsored Asian-American chapters on a number of large university campuses. In doing so, the intention has not been to promote ethnocentrism or to participate in the balkanization generated by postmodernity. Rather, the aim is to provide a community setting in which students can explore their identities, including their ethnic and spiritual identities, and to reach out to non-Christian Asian-American students with more effectiveness.[10] We find that many unchurched or previously churched Asian-American young people are willing to visit and participate in these chapters' ministries and encounter our living God in a significant way. During the past decade, the number of Asian-Americans participating in the overall InterVarsity ministry increased by 167 percent.

PETER CHA AND GREG JAO

But not all Asian-American Christian communities are effectively reaching out to Asian-American young people. In fact, when we survey the current Asian immigrant church situation, we find the tragic picture of a massive exodus of young people from these churches. A few years ago in the *Los Angeles Times*, a front-page article titled "Trying to Halt the 'Silent Exodus'" reported that the vast majority of second-generation Korean-American young adults have left or are in the process of leaving their immigrant churches (Carvajal 1994, A1). One study shows that well over 75 percent of American-born Chinese in Chinese immigrant churches end up leaving their churches (Wong 1990, 1–2). These reports remind those of us who are in the Asian-American ministry that it takes more than simply offering an Asian-American community experience to win unchurched and previously churched Asian-American postmoderns.

So what kind of a Christian community effectively reaches out and ministers to them? What kind of a community provides a safe and nurturing setting in which they will encounter our loving Father, be enfolded into his family, and understand their identity in Jesus Christ? We believe these are very critical and urgent questions with which Asian-American ministries must grapple. Given the text—what Scripture teaches about the community of God's people—and the context—what Asian-American postmoderns are looking for and need in community—we want to focus on three aspects of community: grace, the practice of power and authority, and the Word.

A Community of Grace

We must first learn what it means to be a community of grace, a community that particularly brings healing to those Asian-Americans who are weighed down with toxic shame. Many Asian-American scholars and Christian leaders have observed that while Western culture is guilt-based, generally speaking, Asian culture is shame-based.[11] Tom Lin, an Asian-American InterVarsity staff worker observes:

> Shame is interwoven into the fabric of the Asian family. Because our actions affect not only ourselves but entire generations of relatives and family, Asian-Americans have a tough task ahead when they make mistakes and try to "fix" it. . . . Instead of feeling guilty that we have made a mistake, suddenly shame makes us feel like we are the mistake. As a result, trying to "fix" the problem becomes a daunting task because we are the problem. We feel isolated and alienated from others. (1996, 43)

Lin's statement identifies two aspects of Asian shame that deserve our attention. The first is that shame occurs in a relational or communal context.

Because the Confucian-based culture places a high emphasis on the collective identity, any shame brought to one family member is often felt by the entire family. For example, when an Asian-American young person fails to gain admission to a reputable university, the individual not only has failed to attain an important personal goal but has brought shame to the family. And as the family responds by expressing its disappointment—"You have failed us" or "How could you shame us like that?"—the person sinks deeper into shame.

Second, while guilt focuses on our violation of specific moral laws or standards—thus affecting our conscience—shame focuses on who we are as a person, thus affecting the core of our identity. To put it differently, guilt tells us that we made a mistake, but shame tells us that we *are* a mistake. Shame thus affects our sense of identity deeply and directly by teaching us to be ashamed of who we are.

But precisely because of these deep struggles, the promise of the gospel is wonderfully attractive to shame-bound Asian-Americans. The gospel does not promise forgiveness of sins here and there, but it promises that when we place our faith in Jesus Christ, our Father will forgive, love, and heal us in our very core self. At a critical point in the parable of the prodigal son, the wayward son confesses both his guilt—"Father, I have sinned against heaven and against you"— and his shame—"I am no longer worthy to be called your son." The father, in response, does not simply forgive his returning son for his past wrongdoings. Instead he embraces, restores, and loves his undeserving son. The Scriptures teach us that our heavenly Father delivers his children from their guilt and shame. This is great news for unchurched and previously churched Asian-Americans.

Unfortunately, many Asian-American churches and campus fellowship groups fail to demonstrate this good news in our community life. Instead, intentionally or unintentionally, these communities typically reflect many aspects of shame-based Asian families (Fong 1990, 93). One of these aspects is that our churches often use legalistic behavioral standards to promote people's spirituality and to define their spiritual identity. Using a long list of do's and don'ts, our churches often shame our people, constantly rebuking them for their spiritual failures and shortcomings. At a recent Asian-American pastors' conference, one Korean-American lay leader lamented that there were too many Korean-American pastors who are richly endowed with a gift not found in the biblical list of spiritual gifts—the gift of rebuking. Many Asian-American Christian leaders remind our young people of their demanding Asian parents, not of their gracious heavenly Father.

Another factor that causes our churches to function as shame-producing places is that they often resemble art museums. Many Asian-American young people grow up in immigrant churches where people talk incessantly about achievements of their own or of their children. So for them, the church is gradually identified as a place where people come together to show off, even if it is done in a very self-effacing Asian way. It is not a mere coincidence that Asian-American ministries in general have a particularly difficult time ministering to those who experience difficult challenges in life or who do not fit neatly into the constructed category of the model minority. We have great news to share with the confused and hurting Asian-American postmoderns, but the church's shame-producing practices keep getting in the way.

How will Asian-American young people experience the gracious embracing of our Father that would deliver them from shame and sin? We believe that will happen most effectively in and through the Christian community that understands and practices the grace that comes from our Father. If shame occurs in a relational context (through what others have told us and how they have treated us), it seems that healing from it can be best experienced also in a relational context, specifically in a context where we can clearly and regularly hear the voice of our gracious Father, and where the communal life is strongly shaped and guided by a life in grace. There is a deep yearning for this in the many Asian-American young adults we know and work with.

A Community with the Biblical Practice of Power and Authority

One of the conspicuous characteristics of a Confucian-based culture is that it is deeply hierarchical. Our culture sanctions and teaches men's exercise of power over women, parents over children, older over younger, ruler over ruled, and the educated over the less-educated. The "superior" partners of these vertical relationships are given control over their "inferior" partners, often leading to abusive practices. Some of these teachings and practices are found not only in our Asian-American families but in our churches as well, thus alienating many Americanized young adults, who view them not only as outdated but also as oppressive.

This is particularly true for today's postmoderns. Educated in postmodern academia, many of our young people are not only familiar with the concept of the hermeneutics of suspicion but are quite apt to use such tools to analyze their social surroundings. Postmoderns constantly seek to identify and disclose certain hegemonic ideologies that protect and sustain the power and privilege of certain interest groups. Furthermore, seeing themselves as the victims of various deceptions and manipulations of various power groups, many postmodern young people believe that their project of identity calls for the continuing and vigilant exercise of such an analysis. For many Asian-American postmoderns, their family and church are the first set of institutions to which they direct their hermeneutics of suspicion.

Not too long ago, I (Peter) was talking to an Asian-American woman who is a recent graduate of a master's program in education. Although she grew up in a strong Christian family and maintained a deeply committed spiritual life up until her undergraduate years, today she is far from God mainly because she sees Christianity as a form of oppression and manipulation. She feels that her Christian family and her immigrant church have victimized her in the past because she is a woman, because she is American-born and not too familiar with her ethnic culture and language, and because she is an independent-thinking person who is willing to raise critical questions. Her perception of Christianity, unfortunately, is shared by many Asian-American postmoderns.

So how can we help our unchurched or previously churched postmodern friends to go beyond their distorted images of Christianity? One important way is to demonstrate that the biblical notion of power and authority is neither abusive nor self-seeking. The Scriptures teach clearly that the leadership that our Savior modeled for his church is that of servanthood (Matt. 20:25–28) and of sacrificial love (Eph. 5:25–28). Such an expression of leadership was critical for the health of the church throughout church history; however, in postmodernity, where all forms of power and authority become immediately suspect, an authentic demonstration of selfless and humble leadership becomes even more critical, especially in the Asian-American setting.

Second, our churches need to grow in the practice of team ministry in the spirit of the priesthood of all believers. Too often our Asian immigrant churches are led by one person, usually an autocratic pastor, or by a team of leaders who are very homogeneous in terms of their age, education, socioeconomic, and gender backgrounds. Recently I overheard Korean-American seminarians joking that an important qualification for being an elder in their immigrant churches is that the person own a black suit and drive a black Mercedes Benz. Such an expression of leadership only contributes to a perception that the power and authority in the church are monopolized by a single person or by a single interest group. We believe that the Bible exhorts the church to become a corporate body in which a much wider circle of believers participate in the life of the body, using those gifts God's Spirit has entrusted to them.

PETER CHA AND GREG JAO

Within the boundary of scriptural teachings regarding leadership, our churches must grow in the ability to exercise plurality of leaders and in the accountability of leaders to one another, to the larger body, and to the head of the church, Jesus our Lord.

Our Asian traditional culture, on the one hand, tells us that power and authority are given to certain individuals and only to those individuals—they cannot be taken or given away. On the other hand, postmodernism challenges these assumptions and asserts that one's loss of power and loss of privilege are due to the oppressive actions of hostile others. It exhorts all victims to reclaim their power and privilege. The ongoing drama of identity politics in our campus world and in our larger society clearly demonstrates the deep level of distrust and hostility among different people groups and individuals. Asian-American postmoderns, surrounded by these cacophonous voices of power struggle and anger, cannot clearly hear or trust the voice of our heavenly Father calling them to yield their lives to him. Until they are exposed to a community that operates by countercultural values of leadership and authority, a community in which its members fully trust and selflessly serve God and one another, they cannot easily understand the paradoxical truth of Christianity that only when we die to ourselves will we find our true selves.

A Community of the Word

In postmodernity, where any kind of truth-claim is seen as an act of violence that oppresses, excludes, and manipulates people, the critical task of *Telling the Truth* calls us to pay attention not only to what our message is, but also to who we are as messengers. In the Asian-American context, given our communal and relational orientation and emphasis, this challenge particularly falls on the Christian church as a witnessing community to grow in its ability to proclaim and demonstrate the good news. In our ministry with Asian-American college students, we observe that fruitful evangelistic ministries often take place in Bible study groups that meet in dormitories, a context in which non-Christians have an opportunity to hear what their Christian friends believe as well as to see how they are living it out.

So how can an Asian-American church, as a witnessing body, reach out effectively to postmoderns? Simply put, our church must grow as a community of the Word—as a community that interprets the Word faithfully and that "performs" the Word authentically. Yet our current experiences in, and practices of, church life point out that there is much work to be done by the Holy Spirit and by our church leaders.

To begin with, one of the requirements of being a faithful interpretive community is that its members possess an adequate knowledge of the Word. Sadly, along with the rest of the postmodern, or post-Christian, society, Asian-Americans are increasingly becoming biblically illiterate. Partly in response to this challenge, Parkwood Community Church is currently in the process of forming a three-year plan that seeks to open the Word to our young congregation in a comprehensive manner. Carefully coordinating our preaching, Sunday school curriculum, small group Bible studies, and special workshops and retreats, we want to present the entirety of the grand narrative of the Bible, inviting our members and seekers to examine the Story. Our hope is that such a study of the Word will dispel many distorted or erroneous views people have about God, about us, and about the church and will lay a sound biblical foundation and framework for the church community and members.

Another step that our interpretive community needs to take is to learn to balance the universal and the particular in interpreting the Word. One of the explicit aims of postmodernism is to decenter any claims of universality while celebrating particularities and discontinuities. Evangelicalism, on the other hand, influenced largely by modernism and its assumptions, tends to overly emphasize the significance of the universal at the expense of recognizing certain transient values and the legitimacy of particularities and diversity.

The Asian-American Christian community needs to avoid the danger of both extremes. If we isolate ourselves from the larger body of Christ in searching for our particularities, we face the possible dangers of misinterpreting the Word owing to our own cultural biases or sins, or of downsizing the Word to fit our narrower context. Therefore an Asian-American church, as an interpretive community, must constantly engage with other Christian communities of the present as well as of the past, thereby constantly checking and testing its interpretation of the Word. Particularly in postmodernity, where individual interpretive communities are given an exclusive and privileged status of interpreting truth for their members, the Asian-American church must resist this current and must proactively dialogue with other evangelical communities of faith.

At the same time, as a community that reaches out to a specific people group, the church must also grow in its ability to address the particular issues and challenges of our context. For instance, one of the critical steps in evangelism is to name those idols and sins that are particularly pervasive and yet subtle in our culture—our deep desire for professional and material success; our deep concern for "face"; our ethnocentrism, perfectionism, conformism, and materialism, to name some of them. Unless Asian-Americans are able to break away from these cultural trappings, from these voices that have certain claims on our identity, we will not be able to experience God's grace fully.

Finally, being a faithful community of the Word, particularly in our post-modern context, also calls our church to be a community that performs the text authentically and passionately. The sin of hypocrisy has plagued churches of all periods. In postmodernity, however, this particular sin becomes one of the biggest obstacles to our evangelism, for it greatly reduces the credibility of the messenger and of the message.

For Asian-American Christian communities, the challenge of becoming a credible witnessing body calls for transparency and authenticity in our community life. When visitors see the community's genuine commitment and submission to the Word of God, delighting in the Word and obeying its teachings, they will come to realize that we are not merely engaged in a playful dialogue with another socially constructed text. As they see how the Word is shaping our attitudes, thoughts, and actions, as they see how God's voice is sculpting our identity, they will be carefully watching and observing.

As we apply the Word to our individual and corporate lives, it is also important that we be transparent, a quality that goes directly against the strong Asian cultural current of saving face. As we struggle to obey the Word, failing as well as succeeding along the way, the temptation for us will be to present the best picture of ourselves. But as long as we are preoccupied with our public face, wearing masks in our community gatherings, we will fail to be effective in our outreach to Asian-American postmoderns because there are then no discernible differences between those who belong to God and those who do not. But if redeemed children of God are willing to lose face because our core identity is firmly anchored in Christ, willing to show the cracks in our earthen vessels so that others can have a glimpse of the precious treasure in them, we will then not only declare but also demonstrate the power of the good news and of his grace.

CONCLUSION

Asian-American ministry is at a critical crossroads. On the one hand, the silent exodus of Asian-American postmoderns from their immigrant churches is continuing today, causing many to wonder about the future of these ethnic churches. On the other hand, particularly on many of our campuses and in large cities, a growing number of Asian-American fellowship groups and local churches are effectively reaching out to this rapidly growing population. Experiencing both great disappointments and optimism, the Asian-American

Christian community is busily working on various models and strategies of ministry to meet the challenges it faces.

At this critical juncture, we have sought to bring attention to two points. The first is that Asian-American ministries must begin to take more seriously the present and future impact of postmodernism on the Asian-American experience and ministry. Rather than continuing to interpret our experiences and challenges only in terms of bicultural polarities, we must seek to understand our experiences within a broader perspective that includes the new complexities postmodernism brings. Second, as we face our old and new challenges, our hope is that the Asian-American church will dig deeper into the Word in order to communicate the good news more clearly to our postmodern seekers and to demonstrate the good news more authentically in our corporate and individual lives. This presentation, we hope, will serve as a step in that direction.

References

Abelmann, Nancy, and John Lie. 1995. *Blue Dreams: Korean Americans and the Los Angeles Riots*. Cambridge: Harvard University Press.

Bailey, Kenneth E. 1992. *Finding the Lost: Cultural Keys to Luke 15*. St. Louis: Concordia.

Berger, Peter, Brigitte Berger, and Hansfried Kellner. 1973. *The Homeless Mind: Modernization and Consciousness*. New York: Vintage Books.

Carvajal, Doreen. 1994. "Trying to Halt the 'Silent Exodus.'" *Los Angeles Times*, 9 May, A1.

Celek, Tim, and Dieter Zander. 1996. *Inside the Soul of a New Generation: Insights and Strategies for Reaching Busters*. Grand Rapids: Zondervan.

Denzin, Norman. 1989. *Interpretive Biography*. Newbury Park, Calif.: Sage.

Fong, Kenneth. 1990. *Insights for Growing Asian-American Ministries*. Rosemead, Calif.: EverGrowing Publications.

Gergen, Kenneth. 1992. *The Saturated Self: Dilemmas of Identity in Contemporary Life*. New York: Basic Books.

Giddens, Anthony. 1991. *Modernity and Self-Identity*. Stanford: Stanford University Press.

Grenz, Stanley J. 1996. *A Primer on Postmodernism*. Grand Rapids: Eerdmans.

Guernsey, Dennis. 1989. *Sometimes It's Hard to Love God: Overcoming Your Inner Barriers to Intimacy with God*. Downers Grove, Ill.: InterVarsity Press.

Harvey, David. 1989. *The Condition of Postmodernity*. Cambridge: Blackwell Publishers.

Inouye, Stanley. 1984. *The Kaki Seed*. Monrovia: Iwa, Inc.

PETER CHA AND GREG JAO

Lidz, T. 1968. *The Person.* New York: Basic Books.

Lin, Tony. 1996. *Losing Face and Finding Grace: Twelve Bible Studies for Asian Americans.* Downers Grove, Ill.: InterVarsity Press.

Long, Jimmy. 1997. *Generating Hope: A Strategy for Reaching the Postmodern Generation.* Downers Grove, Ill.: InterVarsity Press.

Nouwen, Henri J. M. 1994. *The Return of the Prodigal Son: A Story of Homecoming.* New York: Doubleday.

Offer, D. and J. B. Offer. 1975. *From Teenage to Young Manhood: A Psychological Study.* New York: Basic Books.

Rigdon, Joan. 1991. "Exploding Myth: Asian-American Youth Suffer a Rising Toll from Heavy Pressures." *Wall Street Journal,* July 10, A1.

Rosenau, P. M. 1992. *Post-modernism and the Social Sciences: Insights, Inroads, and Intrusions.* Princeton: Princeton University Press.

Rue, David. 1993. "Depression and Suicidal Behavior Among Asian Whiz Kids." In *The Emerging Generation of Korean Americans,* ed. H. Kwon and Shin Kim. Seoul: Kyung-Hee University Press.

Sampson, E. E. 1989. "The Deconstruction of the Self." In *Texts of Identity,* ed. J. Shotter and K. J. Gergen, 1–19. London: Sage Publishers.

Thiselton, Anthony C. 1995. *Interpreting God and the Postmodern Self: On Meaning, Manipulation and Promise.* Grand Rapids: Eerdmans.

Uba, Laura. 1994. *Asian-Americans: Personality Patterns, Identity, and Mental Health.* New York: Guilford Press.

Wong, Joseph. 1990. "Bridging the Gap." *About Face* 12 (February): 1–2.

Yep, Jeanette, et al. 1998. *Following Jesus without Dishonoring Your Parents.* Downers Grove, Ill.: InterVarsity Press.

Yu, Elena, Ching-Fu Chang, W. Liu, and M. Fernandez. 1989. "Suicide Among Asian-American Youth." In *Report of the Secretary's Task Force on Youth Suicide,* ed. Marcia Feinleib. Washington: U.S. Department of Health and Human Services.

PART SIX

This Relational Age

CHAPTER 17

FAITHFULLY RELATING TO UNBELIEVERS IN A RELATIONAL AGE

Susan Hecht

Several years ago I went on a short-term mission trip to the Republic of South Africa with a small team of Americans. We were there for six weeks, primarily to do outreach in the Zulu community. The first week in the country was filled with lessons in the history, customs, and culture of the region. We even learned some Zulu phrases and songs.[1]

If you have ever heard or tried to speak Zulu, you know what a challenge it can be for an English speaker. The clicks and other sounds of the language are not easy to pronounce. We did our best to learn some phrases, though, and at the end of the week, we were sent out into a small town to converse with whomever we met. We were obviously strangers in the small Zulu town, and the people there were skeptical and a little suspicious of us. I decided to go into a store with a couple of the other American women to try to speak with the women who worked in the store. At first they were a little aloof. But once we opened our mouths and tried to speak their language, their countenances changed dramatically. They couldn't believe that we, as foreigners, would try to speak their language. Immediately they offered to help increase our vocabulary by teaching us new words. When we left the store, we knew we had made some new friends.

Most people who have traveled abroad know that this is not an unusual scenario. It is often the case that you can strike up a friendship with someone from another country, even though you don't know much of the language. Of course, the more you know of the language, the deeper your friendship can become. However, there is a lot you can learn about people and communicate to them even when you don't speak the same language.

Understanding postmodernism can feel like an overwhelming task at times. It can feel like a cross-cultural experience, and in many ways it is one. An unfortunate result can be frustration or discouragement when we talk about evangelizing postmoderns. It is important to realize, however, that even if we don't know or understand all the philosophy of postmodernism, we can still build relationships with postmodern unbelievers. Despite all that is unclear concerning postmodernism, what *is* clear is that people long for connection with others. From the postmodern perspective, the idea of relationships in the context of community is very important. Although rational, logical arguments alone have lost the strength of persuasion they once had, relational connection, authenticity, and pragmatic answers to life's problems are key elements that can help open the door for the gospel. The context of relationships can provide a persuasive entrée for the gospel to be heard.

The challenge we face as evangelical Christians, however, is that we are at risk of being left out of conversation with unbelievers altogether. As the culture drifts farther and farther from a biblical framework of ethics and morality, Christians are viewed more and more as a fringe group that has nothing of relevance to say to the issues facing our culture today. To some, Christians are not the kind of people you want to get to know.

In *The Culture of Disbelief,* Stephen Carter, Professor of Law at Yale University observes that the commonly held attitude toward the religious is that "people who take their religion seriously, who rely on their understanding of God for motive force in their public and political personalities—well, they're scary people" (1993, 34). The attitude of our culture toward the Christian community seems to be moving in that direction. As those in our culture become less biblically literate and more skeptical of Christians, the challenge to share the gospel with unbelievers increases. We must learn to relate to unbelievers in a meaningful way if we are going to enter into conversation with them about the gospel.

Three dynamics of relating to unbelievers that are important in evangelizing the apathetic to moderately interested unbeliever are (1) creating an environment for spiritual progress, (2) engaging in persuasive interaction, and (3) persuading people from the base of an authentic walk with Christ.

CREATING AN ENVIRONMENT FOR SPIRITUAL PROGRESS

Creating an environment for spiritual progress has to do with connecting with unbelievers in a relational environment that allows them to move from a position of little understanding of God and the Bible to an attitude of openness and interest.

If someone is sitting in a dark room and you flip a switch that floods the room with light, the person in the room will undoubtedly wince and turn away from the source of light with eyes shut tightly. If, on the other hand, you walk into the dark room with a candle or flashlight, the person in the darkness will be attracted to the light.

Sometimes we take a floodlight approach in evangelism. We understand that God is light and that in him there is no darkness. We also understand that unbelievers are separated from God and are in darkness. We feel that we must share everything immediately with the unbeliever. If the person winces and turns away, we conclude they are not ready and we move on to someone else. For someone who has little interest in or understanding of Jesus and the Bible, a gradual approach that will allow for progress to the point of interest in and receptivity to the light of the gospel message may produce a more favorable response.[2]

The context of an ongoing relationship allows the time and opportunity for the unbeliever to ask questions, dispel misconceptions, and grapple with barriers he or she has to the gospel. As we enter into community with unbelievers, we gain a platform for interaction that can foster relationships in which we can help them move toward a consideration of the gospel. Timothy Keller, founding pastor of Redeemer Presbyterian Church in New York City states, "Post-modern people say that it is groups and communities which form values. You cannot give yourself an identity—you don't know who you are except by the group you belong to. All truth and identity are socially constructed, not individually constructed" (1995, 56).

Christians can often be guilty of cocooning or withdrawing into the community of believers to the point that they no longer have connections with unbelievers. Yet the postmodern culture is promoting community as an environment for establishing values. If we are aware of the communities we share with unbelievers and are intentional about building meaningful relationships, we will be able to have significant conversations with them. For example, we may already be in community with unbelievers by participating in the PTA, joining an athletic team, enrolling in a class, or simply living in a neighborhood. We can also create community around a topic of interest. For example, a discussion group on parenting or dating issues, or a holiday celebration could gather people into a community based on common issues or experiences and provide stimulus for meaningful conversation.

ENGAGING IN PERSUASIVE INTERACTION

To enter into the kind of conversation that will foster a progression toward deeper issues and eventually to biblical truth, it is helpful to understand that there is an art and a science to communication. The science of communication is what you have to say. It is the content of what is to be communicated. The art is the style in which you say it. For example, if you are dating someone who has an inflated ego, mere science might say, "You are stuck up!" Art would say, "The problem in our relationship is that we are both in love with the same person." Both statements communicate the same idea, but one is said with art.

There is also a difference between direct and indirect communication.[3] Direct communication is appropriate when the audience you address will readily receive what you have to say. Indirect communication is helpful when your audience will probably resist your point. For example, in Leviticus 19:18 God uses direct communication when he says, "Do not seek revenge or bear a grudge against one of your people, but love your neighbor as yourself. I am the LORD."

In Luke 10:25–37 we see Jesus getting the same point across in an indirect manner to an expert in the law. Jesus tells the man to go and love the Lord with all his heart, soul, mind, and strength and his neighbor as himself. In order to justify himself, the man asks, "And who is my neighbor?" In reply, Jesus tells the story of the good Samaritan. At the end of the story he asks the man which of the three men in the story was a neighbor to the man who fell into the hands of the robbers. He answered, "The one who had mercy on him." Jesus then tells him to go and do likewise. By using an indirect and artful approach, Jesus was able to communicate his point to someone who was hostile to what he had to say. Rather than wincing and turning away, the man got the point that Jesus was making.

Jesus engaged in persuasive interaction with the man. Applying such an approach in evangelism has to do with communicating in a way that fosters understanding, dismantles barriers, and moves toward the gospel. Keep in mind that this is not the only way to approach unbelievers in evangelism. This approach has the apathetic to moderately interested person in mind. It is an approach that is less direct and more interactive in getting to the point of sharing the gospel, but it does not mean that we compromise or weaken the gospel message.

Many people prefer learning by participation rather than listening to someone give a lecture. This is particularly true of those influenced by postmodernism. Postmodernism encourages a participatory epistemology, or a learning-by-doing approach. For example, rather than reading a book in the comfort of their own home about someone else's interpretation of the Holocaust, postmoderns would much prefer to go to the site of a concentration camp; walk through the quarters where the prisoners were kept; see, feel, smell, and hear what they experienced; and then talk with a survivor. They want to engage not only their minds but also their feelings, and indeed their whole beings, in order to learn about the Holocaust. This is not a bad method of learning. If we can provide an environment for participation and discovery rather than one of lecturing to skeptical or apathetic unbelievers, we may be able to lower some of their defenses and get further in our evangelistic efforts.

Another way to lower resistance and encourage interaction is to give unbelievers insight or skills to help them overcome the issues they face. If we demonstrate a genuine interest in helping them and provide practical ways to do so, they will be more open to interaction. Timothy Keller states, "Postmodern people are highly pragmatic, and are used to making choices based on how well an option meets a felt need" (1995, 57). Certainly, biblical wisdom has much to say about living life well and offers very practical ways to do so. Such wisdom is of interest to the postmodern and can help open an avenue of communication.

For many people, however, if you offer to help them, they immediately wonder what is in it for you. They become suspicious of your agenda, and that in turn can fortify resistance rather than dismantle it. If they suspect that your agenda is to convert them, they may reject further interaction. Rather than deny that motivation, we would do better to acknowledge that we have multiple agendas. If we are honest (and being honest means a great deal to people today), yes, we would like to convert them. However, that is not our only motivation. We also want the best for them. We want them to succeed. We are compelled by the love that we have experienced from God. We want them to be able to make an informed decision about Christ. It might also help to explain that our intention is not to force them to believe what we believe, even though we hope they will make the choice to do so.

Some simple principles of persuasion can help guide a conversation or series of conversations with unbelievers in a way that invites participation and avoids lecturing.[4] The first principle is to *investigate where the person is*. I have very little sense of direction, and I get lost a lot. When I ask for directions, the first thing a person needs to know to direct me to where I need to be is where I am located at the time. The same principle applies as we seek to engage unbelievers in conversation in such a way that we can direct them to the gospel.

One way to find out where a person is, either physically or philosophically, is to ask good questions. Asking good questions will help a person gain understanding without causing confrontation. Proverbs 18:2 states, "A fool finds no pleasure in understanding but delights in airing his own opinions." If we air our thoughts and opinions without gaining some understanding first, we will be at a great disadvantage in our evangelistic efforts.

Ask questions that will help you understand issues: How do they view life? What motivates them? What discourages them? What is important to them and why? What problems do they face, and what solutions have they come up with? As you ask questions, listen closely for issues they bring up that may relate to deeper, spiritual issues. Keep those issues in mind as you continue to the next step in the process.

Once you investigate where they are, *evaluate how they got there.* Why do they believe what they believe? Why have they chosen the course they have to solve their problems? If I get lost walking across a college campus, and the person I have asked for directions knows where I am and where I need to be, the next thing the person needs to consider is how I got to where I am. If I am traveling by foot, the directions I need are different than if I am traveling by car. Two sets of directions could get me to the same location, but one would be appropriate, and the other would be of no use to me. The unbelievers we converse with may have come to their conclusions by means of intellectual investigation, personal experiences, the influence of someone they respect or love, or simply by lack of awareness of other options. Knowing which factors have influenced them most significantly can make a vast difference in how we posture our response.

Suppose one day a daughter returned home from college and told her father that she no longer believed that abortion is wrong. As a Christian from a strong, loving Christian home, she knew her father would probably be upset with her conclusion. At that point, the father would have a choice. He could rally all his arguments, support them with biblical principles, and seek to persuade her with sound ethical and moral reasoning. Or he could ask a few questions first to try to understand how she came to her conclusion. Suppose he chose the latter. His daughter explained that a friend of hers had gotten pregnant and her parents would not allow her to get an abortion. Her friend had to drop out of school, and in the eyes of this daughter, her friend's life was ruined because she could not get an abortion. With this understanding of how she came to her conclusion, the father would be able to take a more appropriate and effective approach to direct her to the conclusion he wanted her to embrace.

A third step in the process of persuasion is to *demonstrate understanding*. By demonstrating that we have categories for what unbelievers experience in life, we show that we are fellow travelers who understand at least to some degree what they are going through. As we do so, we gain credibility in their eyes and so do the solutions we offer. If I am lost and ask for directions, I need to have some level of confidence that the person giving me directions knows where I am and where I need to be, otherwise the directions are going to be of no value to me. If that person can relate to where I am, then I will be more receptive to that person's instruction.

If a young woman who is heartbroken over a recent breakup with her boyfriend comes to me for advice, my initial response is to listen, ask questions, and empathize. Until I demonstrate some level of understanding of her plight, any advice I offer will probably be meaningless to her. What she needs is not only intellectual insight but also some level of feeling heard and understood.

Demonstrating understanding is more than simply stating an intellectual comprehension of a situation. It is empathizing as well. It is admitting when there are no easy answers. It is acknowledging the universal longings and desires we share in common. It is recalling the process we personally went through in grappling with issues and not expecting the other person to jump to our conclusions without experiencing some process for themselves. We need to remember that the convictions we hold were not always as clear and obvious to us as they now are. It is also helpful to remember that we are still in process in other areas. We do not have all the answers, and if we appear to have them, we lose credibility and an ability to relate to others.

The final step in persuasion is to *articulate your position*. It is to move the unbeliever in a new direction. Ultimately, our goal is to lead the person to the gospel of Jesus Christ. That presupposes that we know clearly what the message of the gospel is, and we do not compromise it. It also means that we need to present the gospel in terms that the unbeliever can understand. Given the level of biblical illiteracy today, we need to define words like *sin*, and continue to ask questions to determine their level of understanding. We need to be careful at this point not to slip into a lecture mode, but rather to maintain an interactive conversation. Such an approach requires skills on our part that were less critical in years past but are important to communication in a postmodern culture. Those skills must be rooted in the final dynamic of relating to unbelievers: persuading from an authentic walk with Christ.

PERSUADING FROM AN AUTHENTIC WALK WITH CHRIST

For years, experts in the field of communication studies have observed that nonverbal communication accounts for 65 to 93 percent of all communication. In a postmodern culture that is leery of truth-claims and that looks for practical answers to life issues, what people see in our lives will communicate to them as much as, and probably more than, what we communicate to them verbally. We need to communicate the gospel message both verbally and nonverbally and to recognize that inconsistencies in our nonverbal communication can undermine our verbal communication. Authenticity, honesty, and respect are important nonverbal messages to communicate, and those qualities are worked out in our lives as we walk humbly and daily with the Savior. In short, what we communicate nonverbally to postmodern unbelievers can either invite them to look more closely at the relationship we have with Christ or keep them at a distance.

For the postmodern, an intentional yet unrestricted atmosphere of interaction is an effective way to invite communication in a nonthreatening way and to encourage a demonstration of respect and honesty. In his article, "Have You Ever Been X-perienced?" Jim Anderson states,

> We are the first generation to grow up seeing and using computers everywhere in our daily lives. We may not know what they are called, but nearly all of us know how to use hypertext links, whereby when reading some text on a computer, a differently colored or underlined word indicates that we can use the computer's mouse pointer to click on it to see more information on that particular subject. This approach presents information as a web of interconnected elements, rather than as a logical linear sequence. (1994, 7)

A modern approach to education (which the evangelical community has been strongly influenced by) is generally structured, systematic, orderly, defined, and sterile. A postmodern approach is random, relative, dynamic, nonlinear, and messy. Although a random approach can lead to confusion, it does not need to. There can still be a progression of thoughts even when different views are voiced. As a matter of fact, if we can demonstrate that we are comfortable with diverse views and a nonlinear approach, the freedom of exchange can foster trust and openness. Such an approach can also allow postmodern unbelievers to process new information in a way that suits their style of learning.

Allowing freedom to express ideas and struggles is important to postmodern unbelievers. Creating a safe environment means, then, that we need to resist the temptation to correct every comment and settle every issue unanimously by the end of the conversation. Life is not clean-cut to the postmodern, and in many respects that is true. The Christian community is often guilty of simplifying life issues so dramatically that we reduce complex problems to something that is easy to resolve. We need to be willing to admit that we don't have all the answers. At the same time, we should be able to articulate why we are compelled to believe what we believe. There are crucial issues that the Bible is clear about, and those are the issues we can address with confidence and persuasiveness.

The approach to evangelism that I am suggesting involves moving out into the unbelieving, postmodern culture, establishing relationships with unbelievers, and persuading them to consider the gospel message. To engage in such an approach requires wisdom and humility on our part. It is an approach that invites us to be patient students of those we seek to reach, able to guide a conversation with gentleness and respect. It requires us to have a deep and broad understanding of how biblical truth and wisdom relate to everyday concerns, and the skill to be able to bring that truth to light for the unbeliever.

In Colossians 4:5 Paul writes, "Be wise in the way you act toward outsiders; make the most of every opportunity." Proverbs 16:21, 23 encourages us: "The wise in heart are called discerning.... A wise man's heart guides his mouth, and his lips promote instruction." Wisdom requires patience and discernment and has its source in God himself. As we seek to persuade unbelievers from the base of an authentic walk with Christ, they will see clearly the Christ whom we serve and the Christ who is pursuing them. An authentic walk with Christ will also provide us with the wisdom and humility that effective evangelism requires.

As we seek to reach postmodern unbelievers with the message of Christ, we need to consider ways in which we can engage them where they live and not simply expect them to enter the Christian community in order to hear the gospel. We also need to recognize that a context of relationship for communicating that message is increasingly important to a postmodern culture. We will do well to allow people to learn spiritual truth in a way that is participatory and does not assume biblical literacy. A process of persuasion that involves asking questions, listening, and understanding before explanation of the gospel can be very effective in reaching apathetic to moderately interested unbelievers. Perhaps most important of all is presenting an authentic walk with Christ in the context of a relationship with unbelievers and being able to explain clearly, with gentleness and respect, how they can know him, too.

In lectures delivered at Reformed Theological Seminary in Orlando, Florida, R. C. Sproul, dealing with the subject of reaching unbelievers, commented recently that Martin Luther, as a herald of the Reformation, insisted that the church must be profane. It must move out of the temple and into the world. Luther looked to the Latin roots of the word *profane,* which comes from *pro-fanus* (outside the temple). If Christ is not relevant outside the church, he is insignificant inside the church. If our faith is bound to the inner chambers of the Christian community, it is at best a disobedient faith, and at worst, no faith at all. It was again Luther who declared that a new Christian must withdraw from the world for a season, but upon reaching spiritual maturity must embrace the world as the theater of redemptive activity.

Let us not shy away from evangelism in a postmodern culture, but go forth in wisdom, humility, and confidence to make a defense for the hope that is in us.

References

Anderson, Jim. 1994. "Have You Ever Been X-perienced?" *The Gospel and Our Culture* 6 (December): 7–8. Reprinted from *Logos Light,* a publication of Logos House, Inc., Corvallis, Ore.

Carter, Stephen. 1993. *The Culture of Disbelief: How American Law and Politics Trivialize Religious Devotion.* New York: Anchor Books.

Downs, Tim. 1999. *Finding Common Ground.* Chicago: Moody Press.

Keller, Timothy. 1995. "Preaching to the Secular Mind." *Journal of Biblical Counseling* 14 (Fall): 54–62.

CHAPTER 18

THE LIFESTYLE OF THE GREAT COMMISSION

Robert E. Coleman

Thinking of evangelizing postmoderns, I am reminded of a college student going around campus wearing a big lapel button with the letters BAIK printed on it. When someone asked him what that meant, he replied, "That means 'Boy Am I Confused.'"

"But don't you know that confused is not spelled with a K?" he was reminded.

"Man," he replied, "you don't know how confused I am!"

That's how many people may feel when considering the viability of different ways to reach contemporary unbelievers. Certainly there is no want of proposals. But in our effort to find workable methods, let us not overlook the basic directive of the Great Commission to "make disciples of all nations" (Matt. 28:19).

Notice that the command is not to make converts but to make disciples. A disciple is a learner or pupil, an apprentice. Such a person is more than a convert, though turning to the Savior in repentance and faith clearly must take place (Matt. 18:3; John 3:1–36). But disciples do not stop with conversion; they keep moving on with Christ, always learning more of his grace and glory.

Here is the genius of Christ's plan to win all nations, raising up a people in his likeness who will praise him forever. For disciples of Christ grow in his character, and by the same virtue, they develop in his ministry to the world. By making this the focal concern, Jesus assures an ever-enlarging labor force, and in time, through multiplication, workers will bring the good news of salvation to the ends of the earth.

Christ's disciples were only asked to live by the same rule that governed his time among them. That is what the Great Commission is all about. It simply enunciates the strategy implicit in Jesus' own ministry while he was in the flesh. Just as Jesus had ordered his life on earth, now his disciples are expected to follow in his steps.

To understand what this means, we must look closely at the way our Lord made disciples. His pattern of doing it becomes the interpretation of the command. Though our understanding is encumbered with all the limitations of fallen intelligence, it is reassuring to know that in the Son of God we have a perfect teacher. He never made a mistake.

Adaptations of his approach, of course, must be made to our situation. The way Christ worked in his culture nearly twenty centuries ago is not necessarily exactly how he would proceed in our postmodern society. Methods are variable, conditioned by time and circumstances that are continually changing. But principles inherent in his way of life remain constant. They provide guidelines for making disciples where we labor today. I will mention nine, all of which flow together.

1. INCARNATION: BECOME A SERVANT — LOVING PEOPLE WHERE THEY HURT

One does not have to observe Jesus very long to be made aware that he lived by a different value system from that of the world. Renouncing his own rights, he "made himself nothing, taking the very nature of a servant, being made in human likeness" (Phil. 2:7; cf., 2 Cor. 8:9). From the beginning, he established the criteria of a fruitful life.

Jesus came to serve, and in that role he went about doing good. When he saw need, he had compassion and reached out to help (Matt. 9:36). He fed the hungry; he healed the sick; he opened the eyes of the blind; he cleansed the lepers; he bound up the brokenhearted; he delivered the demon-possessed; he raised the dead. And through it all, he held forth the word of life, proclaiming the gospel of the kingdom.

Little wonder that multitudes were drawn to him. People always respond to love when it finds practical expression in ministry, the more so when it is empowered by the Spirit of God. Though his fearless preaching often invoked the disdain of the religious gentry, it was generally received with appreciation by the masses (e.g., Matt. 21:26; Mark 12:12; Luke 20:19). They realized that "he taught as one who had authority, and not as their teachers of the law" (Matt. 7:29). People will listen when they know you care.

The same holds true of skeptics today. To reach them, we must take the servant's mantle. When they know they are loved, we have their attention. In

ROBERT E. COLEMAN

a generation like ours that has lost a sense of objective truth, living by their feelings rather than by faith, this may be the only way to make sense to them initially.

Look around and see how you can meet a need. Take a fresh-baked loaf of bread to your neighbor. Better still, have the family over for dinner. Help the man next door on a work project like fixing a roof or building a room in the home. Tutor a child on a school subject. Visit people in sickness. Be there to help in times of bereavement or when someone is in trouble. There are a thousand things we can do. It's our business to identify felt needs of people around us and try to help.

Unassuming as it may be, this is how our witness becomes credible. Communication usually begins at the feeling level. Don't you like to be around persons who can feel where you hurt? One who is known as a servant will never lack opportunities in evangelism. Soul-winners are first known as shepherds.

Building on this foundation, another principle must be observed, one easily overlooked by persons especially adept at care-giving.

2. Selection: Look for Disciples — Seeing the Answer to Your Prayers

Getting the appreciation of people, while it is a beginning, can be very deceptive. The crowds shouted "Hosanna" the last time Jesus entered Jerusalem (John 12:13), but as he withdrew from the city, tears filled his eyes. He knew that they did not understand who he was, nor did they comprehend the kingdom he had come to establish (Luke 19:41–44). They wanted a messiah who would use his mighty power to overthrow their enemies and satisfy their temporal desires. Good people, usually respectful, they nevertheless were utterly self-serving in their interests. Neither the love of God nor the love of neighbor motivated their actions.

Making the situation worse, the masses had no one to show them the way. They were like aimless sheep without a shepherd (Matt. 9:36). Oh yes, there were many leaders who were supposed to give direction, like the scribes and priests. The problem was that these persons in privileged positions were themselves blind to the truth (Matt. 15:14; Luke 6:39); they did not truly love the people (John 10:12–13).

You can see why Jesus wept over Jerusalem. The multitudes were lost. Confused by their own waywardness and victimized by self-serving religious professionals, they were an easy prey to the beguilement of Satan. When it appeared to them that Jesus would bring in a new era of freedom and prosperity, they were eager to declare his praise; but a few days later, when it was obvious that his kingdom was not of this world, they cried, "Crucify him! We have no king but Caesar" (John 19:15; cf. Matt. 27:22–26; Mark 15:11–15; Luke 23:20–21).

We blink our eyes in dismay, wondering how people can be so callous, so fickle in their allegiance. Of course, to take the side of Jesus openly in the judgment hall of Pilate would have brought retaliation from the chief priests and officers. Under the circumstances, it seemed expedient to play it safe and follow the crowd.

What a commentary on human nature! Understand it, for unless you come to grips with this condition, you will never be relevant to the Great Commission. People must not only hear the gospel of salvation but also learn how to follow Christ in a totally new lifestyle of supernatural grace.

For this to happen, the lost sheep must have shepherds to lead them. Jesus was doing all he could to help, but in the incarnation he assumed the limitation of his body. He could not give attention to all the people. Obviously, unless coworkers—redeemed men and women with the hearts of shepherds—multiplied his ministry, there was no way the waiting harvest could be gathered. This is to be the burden of our prayers (Matt. 9:37–38).

So while ministering to the multitudes, Jesus concentrated on making disciples who could learn to reproduce his life and mission. This priority became more pronounced as his ministry lengthened into his second and third years.

His first disciples were found largely within his home environment in Galilee. In culture, education, and religious orientation they had much in common. To be sure, they were not generally the most socially astute people, perhaps not even the most religious. None of them, for example, appears to be from the levitical priesthood. Yet Jesus saw in these untrained laypersons the potential for turning the world upside down. Though often superficial in their comprehension of spiritual reality, with the exception of the traitor they were teachable. Such persons can be molded into a new image.

This is going to require a long-term approach to reaching the world. Too easily we have been satisfied with short-lived efforts to see multitudes turn to Christ without assuring their discipleship. In so doing we have inadvertently added to the problem in evangelism rather then its solution. We dare not compromise the focus of the Great Commission.

Since this is best accomplished with a few people at any one time, at least in-depth relationships, everyone can do it. You may be sure too that some of those who feel the warmth of your servant heart will want to know more about your Lord.

Notice them. They are the answer to your prayers. Likely many of them will belong to your peer group. That reminds me of a man down in Texas who was

ROBERT E. COLEMAN

arrested for horse stealing. The sheriff gave him the choice of being tried before the judge or a jury of his peers. "Peers," he replied, "who's that?" Whereupon the sheriff explained, "That means someone just like you." "Oh," said the man, "I'll take the judge. I don't want to be tried by a bunch of horse thieves."

Look around you. See the persons with whom you already have much in common, beginning with your family and reaching out from there to neighbors and friends. Within this natural sphere of influence, you will probably have your greatest potential for changing the world.

With those persons who do not yet know the Savior, your relationship becomes a means of clarifying the gospel. The same servanthood pertains to believers needing encouragement and direction in their life. Though you are not the only person involved in their discipleship, for a period of time you may be one of the most significant influences in their Christian growth. How this happens underscores a third principle.

3. ASSOCIATION: STAY WITH THEM — BUILDING A FAMILY-LIKE RELATIONSHIP

As the number of disciples grew, Jesus appointed twelve to be with him in a special comradeship (Mark 3:14). Of course, he continued to relate to others as the fellowship of believers increased through his ministry, but it is apparent that he gave a diminishing priority of attention to those outside the apostolic company. Within this select group, Peter, James, and John seem to have enjoyed an even closer relationship to the Master.

All of this impresses me with the deliberate way that Jesus proportioned his life to persons in training. It also illustrates a basic principle of teaching: the more concentrated the size of the group being taught, the greater the opportunity for learning. In a profound sense, he is showing us how the Great Commission can become the controlling purpose of every family circle, every small group gathering, every close friendship in this life.

For the better part of three years, Jesus stayed with his pupils. They walked the highways and streets together; they sailed on the lake together; they visited friends together; they went to the synagogue and temple together; they worked together. Have you noticed that Jesus seldom did anything alone? Imagine! He came to save the nations—and, finally, he dies on the cross for all humankind; yet while here he spends more time with a handful of disciples than with everybody else in the world.

There is nothing new in this pattern, of course. He is simply incorporating in his lifestyle the dynamic of the family, the foundation for all learning. It was

God's plan in the beginning when he instituted marriage and ordained that the home become the center of religious training. Here in this natural environment with parents, and perhaps even grandparents, and likely with some brothers and sisters, our values are largely formed. Family influences are especially determinative, for good or ill, in the impressionable years of early childhood.

That is why close personal relationships in the church are crucial to evangelism, particularly with persons just starting out with Christ. Like newborns in the physical world, beginning disciples must have spiritual guardians to help them develop. More mature Christians should meet with them as often as they can, inquire about their needs, answer their questions, encourage their witness, and make them feel a part of the family of God.

There is no reason why you cannot get together on a regular basis with a few learners. The more informal and unpretentious the association the better, like playing a round of golf. What a happy way to have some meaningful conversation! The exercise and recreation on the course is just a bonus. Who would ever want to play this game without the joy of fulfilling the Great Commission? For that matter, why would you do anything if you did not have this confidence? What a way to live! Nothing is insignificant; nothing is meaningless. It's all part of the plan.

Such casual activities, of course, do not take the place of formal church services. Both are needed and serve the same purpose of making disciples. But learning comes most naturally in more relaxed family-like settings.

Some of this fellowship can be arranged in small group meetings, periods devoted to corporate times of testimony, Bible study, prayer, and anything else deemed important to the participants. Meeting like this with a few students early in the morning once a week has been one of the most rewarding disciplines of my life for forty years. I am not suggesting that this be your practice, but in some way I hope you have such a blessing. To realize the full potential of association, however, another principle must be applied.

4. COMMITMENT: TEACH THEM TO FOLLOW WHAT THEY BELIEVE — LEARNING BY OBEDIENCE TO PERCEIVED TRUTH

What facilitated the disciples' relationships with Christ and made it so productive was their willingness to follow him. Indeed, that is what made them his disciples. He did not ask them to recite a creed or kneel at an altar; he simply invited their obedience (Matt. 9:9; Mark 2:14; Luke 5:27; John 1:43, 46; cf., John 18:19). Faith in Christ was evidenced by following him.

ROBERT E. COLEMAN

This does not mean that the disciples quickly understood everything the Lord said. Far from it. Take as an example their inability to grasp the deeper truths of the Lord's vicarious ministry. The disciples really did not comprehend the necessity of the cross until after the resurrection, even though Jesus had spoken of his death many times. Yet Jesus patiently endured their human failings because they were following him, willing to walk in the truth they did understand.

Obedience to Christ was thus the very means by which those who were with him learned more truth. He did not ask the disciples to follow what they did not know to be true, but no one could follow him without coming to learn what was true (John 7:17; 8:31–32).

What made them want to obey was their love for Jesus. "If you love me," he said, "you will obey what I command" (John 14:15; cf. 14:21, 23–24; 15:10). Putting this in perspective, he added, "My command is this: Love each other as I have loved you" (John 15:12).

Absolute obedience to the will of God, of course, was the controlling principle in the Master's own life. Calvary was but the crowning climax of his commitment. Having already accepted the cross in advance (Acts 2:32; Rev. 13:8), Christ took each step on earth in conscious acceptance of God's eternal purpose for his life.

Just as he found his blessedness in doing the Father's will, so his followers would find theirs. From the standpoint of strategy, however, it was the only way that Jesus could mold their lives by his word. A father must teach his children to obey him if he expects them to be like him.

We must learn this lesson again today. There can be no dillydallying around with the commands of Christ. If we have learned even the most elemental truth of discipleship, we must know that we are called to be servants of our Lord and to obey his Word.

One might ask why there are so many professed Christians stunted in their growth and ineffectual in their witness. Is it not because there is a general indifference to the commands of God? Certainly if we are to make any impact on this indulgent generation, the obedience of the cross must become more evident. Though postmoderns reject claims of theological certainty, they are not blind to sacrificial love when they can see it.

Is it not time that the expectations of the church are spelled out in terms of true Christian discipleship? If this seems too much to ask of the whole congregation, at least we can make it a requirement with those few learners that God has brought into our lives and, like Jesus, instill into their faith the meaning of obedience. For this commitment to realize its potential, another principle must be in operation.

5. DEMONSTRATION: SHOW THE APPLICATION— THE PRACTICAL NETWORKING IN LIFE

Following Christ, the disciples observed the way he planned for his disciples to live. His life was the object lesson of his doctrine. By practicing before them what he wanted them to learn, they could see its relevance and application.

For example, there was his habit of prayer. Surely it was no accident that Jesus often let his disciples see him conversing with the Father. They observed the priority of this spiritual discipline and the strength it gave to his ministry. Inevitably the time came when they asked him, "Lord, teach us to pray" (Luke 11:1). Having awakened their desire to learn, he could teach them how. Notice that in this beginning lesson, he did not preach them a sermon or assign them a book to read; he gave them an example (Luke 11:2–4; cf. Matt. 6:9–12).

In the same way, he taught his disciples the importance and use of Scripture, the meaning of worship, stewardship of time and talents, social responsibility, and every other aspect of his personal life. At the same time he was showing them how to care for the needs of people, to bear their sorrows, to care for their griefs, while seeking their ultimate welfare in the gospel. Evangelism was so woven into his daily experience that it did not seem contrived or programmed. It was a way of life.

Through it all, what is most significant is that he was demonstrating how to make disciples. When finally he gave them the Great Commission, there was no confusion in their minds about its meaning. They had been discipled, and reflecting on their own experience, they knew exactly what to do.

Those of us seeking to disciple people must be prepared to have them follow us, even as we follow the Lord (1 Cor. 11:1). We are the illustration of our teaching (Phil. 3:17f.; 1 Thess. 2:7–8; 2 Tim. 1:13). They will do those things they see and hear in us (Phil. 4:9). Let us be sure that the example they see reflects the mission of Christ to seek and to save the lost. They will get the idea as they watch us befriend sinners, win their respect, confront them with the cross, and lead them to decision. Most clearly your burden will come through as you pray together.

Giving this kind of leadership, of course, puts us on the spot. Persons whom we let into the inner working of our lives will see our shortcomings and failures. But let them also see a readiness to confess our sins when we understand the error of our ways. Let them hear us apologize to those we have wronged. Weaknesses need not impair discipleship when there is transparent sincerity to follow Christ. An honest exposure may tarnish our halo, but, in seeing our humanness, others may more easily identify with our precepts. Furthermore, if we learn from our failures, as abundant as they are, there is no end to the lessons we will derive.

Yet, as we know, more than a demonstration is needed in learning. There comes a time for action, which introduces another principle.

6. ASSOCIATION: GET DISCIPLES INVOLVED IN MINISTRY — EVERYONE FINDING HIS OR HER PLACE

Jesus was always preparing his disciples to carry on this work. So as they were able to assume some responsibility, he gave them things to do suited to their gifts and talents. First duties were small, unassuming tasks, like providing food and shelter for the group. Since Jesus was unmarried and had no house of his own, it was natural for him to accept their hospitality graciously (Matt. 8:20; Mark 1:29; Luke 8:3). What a beautiful way to help some people get involved where they were already qualified! As far as I can find, our Lord never turned down an invitation to dinner. I was glad when I discovered that!

After a while he began to have the disciples more actively assist in his ministry. They were enlisted, for example, in baptizing persons who responded to his preaching (John 4:2). In another setting, he had them distributing food to hungry people that had come to hear him teach (Matt. 14:13–21; 15:29–38; Mark 6:30–44; 8:1–9; Luke 9:10–17; John 6:1–13).

The work assignments increased with their developing self-confidence and competence. Before long they were sent out to do much the same kind of work that Jesus was doing—healing, teaching, and preaching the gospel (Matt. 10:1–10; Mark 6:6–9; Luke 9:1–3; cf., Luke 10:1–16).

Lest they forget the priority of training leadership, however, he stipulated that above the public ministry they were to search out "worthy" persons to spend time with wherever they went (Matt. 10:11–15; Mark 6:10, 11; Luke 9:4, 5). They could work across the community all day, but in the evening they were to return to the house of those people interested enough in their mission to offer hospitality. In effect, the disciples were instructed at the onset to build a relationship with a few promising disciples and prepare them to follow up their ministry after they were gone. If no one could be found with a desire to learn of Christ, then they were to shake the dust off their feet and move on to another village.

We do not have the luxury of going through the motions of evangelism when no one wants to be discipled. I wonder what would happen if we really took this to heart? Can you imagine the changes that would come in our church priorities?

The Great Commission involves the whole church. Everyone can do something. I am reminded of a riding academy in West Texas that advertises that they have a horse to suit every taste. For fat people, they have fat horses; for skinny people, they have skinny horses; for fast people, they have fast horses; for slow people, they have slow horses. And for people that don't know how to ride at all, they have horses that have never been ridden before.

Well, I don't know what your taste is, but when it comes to the Lord's work, there is a horse you can ride. More to the point, there is a horse that every member of the body of Christ can ride. As a leader, it's your business to help each follower find the right horse. Certainly they can share their faith, though you may need to help them do it with greater ease and clarity. With your assistance they also can get started in a follow-up ministry with some new believer needing personal encouragement and ongoing discipleship.

Many of the programs of the church also afford opportunities for service. Early assignments can be in areas where new believers are already equipped, perhaps helping in the nursery or driving a bus. As they grow in grace and knowledge, they may assume leadership roles in the Sunday school or in youth activities, eventually becoming deacons and elders of the congregation. Some may receive a special call into vocational church work as pastors or missionaries.

Whatever form the ministry takes, be it structured or informal, whether in the church or out in the marketplace, it fits into God's plan for making disciples. When the Great Commission is seen as a lifestyle, everything you do has this potential. Nothing is insignificant; nothing falls outside the work of helping a few learners fulfill their roles discipling the nations. This brings another principle into operation.

7. SUPERVISION: KEEP CHECK ON THEIR PROGRESS— BUILDING A SENSE OF ACCOUNTABILITY

Jesus would get back with his disciples after some attempt at ministry to see how things went (Mark 6:30; Luke 9:10; 10:17). Checking on their assignments, asking questions, responding to their queries, he was making them responsible for what they learned. "From everyone who has been given much, much will be demanded" (Luke 12:48). What is more, experiences the disciples were having in their work became illustrations for him to teach some new or deeper truth (e.g., Matt. 15:37–16:12; 17:14–20; Mark 8:10–21; 9:17–29; Luke 9:37–43; 10:14–24). It was on-the-job training all the way.

Problems were dealt with when they came up, which was quite often. The disciples were far from perfect, and their spiritual immaturity was constantly

ROBERT E. COLEMAN

coming out. In one instance, James and John wanted to call down fire on the heads of some disrespectful Samaritans (Luke 9:51–56). When Jesus saw their impulsiveness, he rebuked them. But he also seized the occasion to emphasize again the saving purpose of his mission: "You do not know what kind of spirit you are of, for the Son of Man did not come to destroy men's lives, but to save them" (Luke 9:55–56).

Here, as throughout their training, the disciples were pointed to the redemptive purpose of Christ's coming into the world and to their function in continuing that mission. Though their progress was painfully slow, Jesus patiently kept them moving toward his goal. He did not ask more from them than they were capable of giving, but he did expect their best, and this he expected to improve as they followed him.

To me the most awesome aspect of Christ's concern for his disciples' growth comes out in his prayers. John 17 is the greatest example. Have you noticed how most of the prayer turns to these men given to him out of the world (John 17:6–19)? He prays for their protection from the evil one; he prays that they might have his joy in doing the will of God; and as they are sent into the world on a mission like his own, he prays that they will be sanctified even as he sanctifies himself. Nothing must be allowed to distract them from the work to which they are called, for "through their message" the world will come to believe on him (John 17:20ff.).

Think of it! Though he knows that in a few hours they will forsake him, even that his chief spokesman will openly deny him, yet his love will not let them go. He believes in them when they cannot believe in themselves. This is the test of a real shepherd. However weak and faltering his disciples may be, Jesus cherishes for them the highest that he knows in spiritual communion, "that the love you have for me may be in them and that I myself may be in them" (John 17:26).

Jesus is teaching us never to limit what he wants to accomplish in and through his disciples. Following that example, those persons entrusted to us need continual nurture. Innumerable things can happen to sidetrack the best of intentions, and unless these matters are faced realistically, young disciples can easily become defeated. Ask them how they are coming along. Sharing out of your experiences may encourage greater openness as well demonstrate your own accountability.

Probably the most deceiving problems in human relations come out when the ego is offended, giving rise to various expressions of self-centeredness like pride or bitterness. Where these fleshly traits are recognized, they must be brought to the cross. Rebuke will not be resented when offered in love if we build self-esteem in believers through constant commendation of every evidence of progress in the developing priesthood.

Though we are perceived to be the leaders, let us make it clear that Christ is the authority and keep the focus on him. Avoid any authoritarian role of a master guru. Jesus alone commands. In subjection to him, discipler and disciples learn together.

In this joint experience of growth, I have come to see that the Great Commission is more than our Lord's plan to reach the world; it is his way to assure the sanctification of his church. You cannot sincerely lead another person to learn more of Christ without being discipled yourself in the process. It all comes back to prayer as we bear one another's burdens to the Lord of the harvest, and so fulfill the first evangelism command of Christ (Matt. 9:38). Keeping this future destiny in view brings out another principle.

8. REPRODUCTION: EXPECT THEM TO REPRODUCE THE LIFESTYLE — THE VISION OF MULTIPLICATION

Life inevitably reproduces its own kind. Careless persons who let the cares of this world choke the word of God will reap the harvest of their foolish ways. On the other hand, those living in conformity to Christ develop the qualities of his life and ministry.

Jesus' parable of the vine and the branches is a beautiful illustration (John 15:1–17). Jesus likens himself to the vine and the disciples to the branches. The branches are conveyors of the life in the vine, and when properly functioning, they produce a harvest. Any branch not fulfilling its purpose is cut off by the watchful gardener. Even producing branches are pruned by the gardener in order that they may be more fruitful. "This is to my Father's glory," Jesus explained, "showing yourselves to be my disciples" (John 15:8).

When fruitbearing is seen in this larger context of producing Christlikeness—first in ourselves and then in others—practically everything Jesus did and said points to this truth. The Great Commission simply brings the principle into focus, phrasing it in terms of disciple making.

The disciples were taught to live with the harvest always in view. "Open your eyes and look at the fields," he said, noticing the men coming to hear him in Sychar. "They are ripe for harvest" (John 4:35). The disciples could see what he meant and could also appreciate its spiritual application when he added, "Even now the reaper draws his wages, even now he harvests the crop for eternal life" (John 4:36). Whether disciples sowed or reaped, Jesus wanted

Robert E. Coleman

them to realize that their work had an impact on eternity, ultimately culminating in the gathering of the nations at the throne of God.

The key to the final harvest centers in the quality and supply of laborers
obeying the mandate of Christ. It does not matter how few their numbers are
in the beginning, provided they reproduce and teach their disciples to do the
same. As simple as it may seem, this is the way his church will ultimately triumph. I know of no other plan.

Our Lord did not come in his incarnate body to evangelize the world; he
came to make it possible for the world to be saved through his atoning sacrifice. But on his way to Calvary, he made sure that his followers were equipped
by strategy and vision to gather the harvest.

He has given us a model that every believer can follow. Making disciples
is not a special calling or a gift of the Spirit, it is a lifestyle—the way Jesus
lived, and now the way he commands his people to follow.

As persons close to you come to realize how they fit into this strategy, you
can dream with them about their place in the harvest. It will be fun talking
about how God will use their unique personalities and gifts in ways beyond
your own. It's the kind of conversation parents have with their mature children before they leave home.

The time comes when they are so occupied in their own work that your
relationship takes on a different quality. Though you are not needed as before,
a bond of love remains, perhaps even deepens. As they move on, others will
take their place, and the process begins again. With each succeeding spiritual generation, anticipation of the harvest grows, looking joyously to the day
when disciples will be made of all nations and there will be a reunion in the
sky. However, there remains yet one principle to understand, apart from which
everything I have said to this point would come to naught.

9. Impartation: Trust Disciples to the Spirit of Christ—The Promise of the Great Commission

It is the Holy Spirit who puts it all together. What God administers as the
Father and reveals as the Son, he accomplishes as the third person of the Holy
Trinity.

We are introduced to the Spirit in the first chapter of Genesis, as he creates
the cosmos (1:2), and later breathes life into the creature God has made in his
image (Gen. 2:7). When persons turn to their own way, it is the Spirit who
seeks to bring them back and effect reconciliation with God. Throughout the
Old Testament he can be seen at work making a nation to be his witness in a

fallen world (Isa. 43:10; 44:8; 49:6). Though Israel fails in her calling, a day is envisioned when one would come on whom the Spirit would rest (Isa. 11:2; 42:1; cf. John 3:34).

Just as the prophets had said, in the fullness of time the Holy Spirit overshadowed the virgin so that she conceived and gave birth to the only begotten Son of God (Matt. 1:18, 20; Luke 1:35). Thereafter, the Spirit directed Jesus during the days of his incarnate life. Everything he said and did was in the strength and demonstration of the Holy Spirit (Luke 4:18–19).

Jesus taught that by the same mighty power, persons who believed on him would partake of his life and ministry. He would guide them into truth (John 16:13); he would help them pray (John 14:12–13; 16:23–24); he would give them utterances to speak (Matt. 10:19–20); he would enable them to do the very works of Christ, even "greater things than these" (John 14:12). Through it all, the Spirit would glorify the Son (John 16:14). That supremely is his ministry—to lift up Christ—and as he is revealed, men and women are drawn to the Father.

It is not difficult to understand why Jesus told his disciples to tarry until they were empowered by the Spirit (Luke 24:49; Acts 1:8). How else could they ever make disciples who develop in his likeness? In their own wisdom and strength they were helpless. Only as Christ was with them, filling them with his presence, could they do his work. Recall his promise, "And surely I am with you always, to the very end of the age" (Matt. 28:20). We see how this begins to unfold at Pentecost (Acts 2:4). The witness of the church now becomes the acts of the Holy Spirit.

Just as it was then, so the same is true today. It is the Spirit who incarnates Christ in us, reversing the self-centered values system of this world so that we begin to live as servants. It is he who draws out disciples, planting in their hearts the desire to learn; our part is to respond to his initiative. The same Spirit forms the body of believers, the church, even in our daily associations with one or two followers. Through his infusion of love our faith comes alive in obedience. By his indwelling we become a demonstration of what he teaches. The indwelling Counselor calls us to ministry and disperses gifts for service. He supervises our growth in grace—reproving, encouraging, enlightening, helping in prayer—always leading on to something better. Finally, it is the Spirit who brings forth the harvest. From beginning to end, making disciples is the work of Almighty God. We are merely the instrument through which he works.

Evangelizing postmoderns, as with anyone else, depends on the Spirit's possession of the sent ones. Just as these first disciples needed a heavenly endowment, so do we. The power from on high, by whatever name it is called,

ROBERT E. COLEMAN

must be a reality in our lives, not as a distant memory, but as a present experience of the reigning Christ. Hindrances that obstruct his lordship must be confessed, and in complete dependence upon the Spirit of Christ, we need to let him have his way in our lives. Though we can never contain all of him, he wants all of us—to love him and adore him with all that we are and hope to be.

The issue in evangelism centers finally in the enduring fruit of our labors. It does not matter how many we enlist for the cause, but how many become workers in the harvest. If we produce this lifestyle in a few, others will follow; if we do not develop this leadership, others have nothing worth following.

Where do you want your life to count? Though the way Jesus made disciples does not promise immediate gratification, we are not living primarily for the present. Our satisfaction is in knowing that in generations to come, our witness will still be bearing fruit in an ever-widening circle of disciple makers to the ends of the earth and to the end of time.

CHAPTER 19

AUTHENTIC CHURCH-BASED EVANGELISM IN A RELATIONAL AGE

Ron Bennett

Evangelism! Nothing can bring terror, guilt, or just plain perspiration to the average Christian quicker than the topic of evangelism. Ask people what they associate with the word *evangelism* or *evangelist* and you get answers such as "pushy," "used-car salesman," "televangelist," "door-to-door salesperson," "Crusades," and so forth.

I have observed that there are three effective ways to get your heart rate up to the healthy aerobic level. One is to jog for thirty minutes. Another is to lose sight of your two-year-old toddler while shopping in a blown-glass retail store. The third is to raise the subject of evangelism. On hearing the word, most people look for exit signs, feign headaches, or remember appointments that were never made.

The church that takes evangelism seriously usually schedules some event that will bring in a well-known speaker who proclaims the gospel at a church men's breakfast or women's luncheon or couple's potluck. Only a few members actually invite their neighbors (most don't know their neighbors), so the audience is made up of regular church attendees with a few relatives who are in town for the weekend. Those who come enjoy seeing their church friends again for the third time that week. George Barna reports that in spite of the one quarter trillion dollars annually spent on ministry by the church in America, only one in eight church members feels prepared to share their faith. And only 2 percent of the gross annual revenues received by a typical church is allocated to evangelism (1995, 84).

Frequently when I ask church leaders about their plan for evangelism, I am told of their strategy of hiring a pastor of evangelism. One senior pastor said, "Our evangelism will take off when we can afford to hire someone gifted in evangelism who will set the pace for the rest of us." This is code for "I hope to get this monkey off my back and get back to the teaching that I love."

Gifted in evangelism! I have met some who may be so gifted, but not many. Most evangelism seminars that I have attended were taught by those gifted in evangelism. I have gone away feeling inadequate, guilty, and frustrated. I try for a few days to act like them, but eventually I return to the real me and the seminar notes return to the shelf.

In workshops I have given on the subject, I frequently ask for a show of hands of those who think they are gifted in evangelism. In one seminar, seven out of the seventy said they were. Out of those seven, four had not shared their faith with anyone in the past two years. Of the remaining three, two had shared their faith only once. The response is never higher than 10 percent, and that from a crowd that is interested in the subject.[1] Actually, I find that most people don't want to be gifted in evangelism. Moreover, most people don't even want to sit next to people who are gifted in evangelism! Regardless of the percentage of gifted evangelists in any church, there are not enough to build a strategy around. They are an inadequate model. We need models that connect with the other 90 percent of the body if we are to impact our world for Christ.

I have found that evangelism for most Christians comes, not out of giftedness, but out of relationship. It first comes from a dynamic relationship with Jesus Christ. It is instructive to me that when Jesus called his disciples he said, "Follow me, and I will make you fishers of men." It is in the following that we begin to fish. He did not begin by recruiting these men to fish. The fishing finds its natural place as we follow the Master, the one who is himself fishing and who invites us to come alongside to join him in the heartbeat of God.

The second relationship that bears on evangelism is involvement in a personal way with lost people. Matthew tells us that as Jesus walked, talked, served, and touched lost people, he was moved with compassion (Matt. 9:36–38). As long as people are just out there—projects, nameless faces, or mere statistics—we are comfortable in our isolation. But when the person takes on a name, becomes a friend, or moves into our area of concern, then we feel compassion and press through the discomfort to share the love of Christ.

IDENTIFYING YOUR AUDIENCE

One of the first things a church needs to do when developing an outreach strategy is to discover the profile of those it is trying to reach. "One size fits all" may work for socks, but not for people. Others have written regarding the profile of the unchurched. Strobel's *Inside the Mind of Unchurched Harry and*

Mary (1993) and Barna's *Frog in the Kettle* (1990) are excellent resources to help us understand how certain unchurched people think and feel.

At the risk of oversimplification, I'd like to suggest three broad categories of people that the church needs to understand: (1) the lost within the church, (2) the lost who will visit the church, and (3) the lost who won't come to the church. Each of these categories demands its own focus. Each presents its unique challenges and opportunities. Their primary point of commonality is being spiritually dead. Beyond that, they are very different.

The church will always contain those who are lost. No matter how structured a screening device for membership, there will always be some who have the right answers but who lack a personal relationship with Christ. Jesus told a parable regarding the mix of tares and wheat in the kingdom. One day God will judge and separate the authentic from the counterfeit (Matt. 13:24). In the meantime, depending on the personality and history of our church, we must address the lost condition of those who are inside the church structure. George Barna concludes from his research that half of those who attend Protestant churches on a typical Sunday morning are not Christians (1995, 38).

Lost people in the church are often difficult to reach since they are comfortable in the culture. They are comfortably confused, and we are carelessly content. Churches need to give serious planning to help the lost within the church think clearly about their own faith in Christ.

The second category is the lost who are currently unchurched but who will visit a church. They are possibly "prechurched"; that is, they have a church reference point from the past. They may have attended as a child, but they concluded that church was irrelevant to their adult life and left it behind like the high school letter jacket. Often the prechurched are motivated to return to church when they become parents and are seeking help in establishing a moral foundation for their children. They think, "I don't need this religion, but my kids do. I can make it, but I am worried about my kids. After all, a little religious morality can't hurt."

Another reason the prechurched may be willing to give church a try again is that life has not worked out as they thought. Marriage, job, finances, and relationships have been disappointing. It seems as if the dream has crumbled, and they are out of solutions. Perhaps church is different now than it was when they were young. Many of these people will return to a church similar to the one in their past. They hope that something has changed and that this time there are real answers to life issues. These people carry a casual biblical worldview. God is in their framework, though he is distant and impersonal.

RON BENNETT

Wives are often the ones most sensitive to the need of reconnecting with church and God. They tend to take the initiative in bringing the family to church. So Christian leaders argue that recognizing who is taking the lead is critical for a church when it is developing its strategy for reaching this group. The church nursery and children's classes are one major factor in whether these people will return. If the kids enjoy the experience, if the environment is upbeat, friendly, and attractive, then maybe these people will return.

Many churches are intentionally orienting their Sunday morning services to meet the needs of this group of people. These churches refer to themselves as seeker-oriented, seeker-targeted, or seeker-sensitive. Willow Creek near Chicago has been a flagship for this strategy. Others have positioned their traditional worship services to minimize the obstacles the seeker has to climb over to return to the church environment.

A seeker-sensitive Sunday morning service is one strategy to reach this group of people, but it is not the only one, nor is it the one that will fit every church. For many churches, the Sunday worship service will not be a key part of their outreach strategy. For these churches, Sunday morning is a worship time for the family of God. Outsiders are welcome but not a priority. Many of these more traditional churches have adapted their adult classes to evangelize seekers. Others have developed their small group program to be the entry point. Regardless of a particular strategy, a church needs to address how it is going to reach this significant category of prechurched people.

Another challenge for the church today is the group of lost people who for whatever reason will not come to the church. They may have an interest in God or spirituality, but they have consciously decided that church, as they understand it, is irrelevant. It doesn't fit their worldview. In their minds, even if there are spiritual answers to life's big questions, they won't be found in the organized church.

For this group of people it doesn't matter how big a loudspeaker you use, how large a marquee you put up, or how large an ad in the paper—they are not coming to your church meeting. These people are like hikers and campers lost in the mountains while the church operates in the valley. Many of these people are second-generation lost in the mountains. They have never been to the valley with churches. Their friends do not even get married in churches.

A few years ago a movie was made about a young couple and their baby who were lost in the mountains. On their way to Idaho, Jim and Jenny Stolpa attempted to cross the mountains in northern California during a heavy snowstorm. When the highway patrol closed the interstate, they left it and took an alternative route.

Eventually they became snowbound. Stranded on a lonely road fifty miles from the nearest town, they had no provisions and no means of communication. After four days of waiting in their truck for help, they gave up hope of being found. Checking a map, they decided to walk eighteen miles across country with their baby in search of a road that might lead to help. After walking all day and night in deep snow, they found no sign of a road.

Meanwhile the parents had aggressively marshaled all the resources at their disposal to help search for their children. Police, forest service, and news media personnel were all part of a team effort of search and rescue. Regardless of the technology and personal energy of this committed group of people, they were frustratingly ineffective. They were limited for two major reasons. One was lack of knowledge of where to look in the thousands of miles of mountainous terrain. The other was the continuous winter storms making aerial and ground reconnaissance impossible.

Back in the mountains, Jim and Jenny had now been snowbound for six days. Their last desperate plan was for Jim to set out alone, leaving Jenny and the baby in a small cave. Jim hoped to backtrack to their abandoned truck and from the truck walk the fifty miles to the nearest town.

On the eighth day of their ordeal, as Jim was stumbling down a lonely road, a rancher out checking his cattle found him. Dehydrated and frostbitten, Jim was taken to the mountain cabin and eventually to a hospital. Before Jim was driven down to a local hospital, the rancher got a faint description of the route Jim had taken. With a few of his friends, he set out in a blizzard to find Jenny and the baby. Jim's sketchy description, combined with the knowledge of a local ranger, provided the clues for a miraculous rescue.

This story is a picture of what is required to reach people who are trapped in the mountains. Lost people in the mountains cannot come to the valley. They are trapped in the snowdrifts of secularism, skepticism, and narcissism. Owing to foolish choices or unfortunate circumstances, they are hopelessly trapped and separated from the rescue efforts of those who live in the valley.

Valley people are for the most part unaware of or disinterested in the fate of the lost people in the mountains. They are too busy doing healthy valley things that take their time and energy. Some hear of the lost people in the mountains and try to help. Some bring blankets and set up aid stations. Some write articles and make videos of the dangers of mountain travel. Some actually try to fly over the mountains and drop supplies.

If the church is to reach those trapped in the mountains of our society, it must take a different strategy. It will take the ranchers and rangers who are personally acquainted with the mountains to reach these lost people. It will take teams of search parties that are courageous and equipped to travel into the mountain region.

Expanding Your Paradigm

Expanding from Event to Process

The first-century church certainly did not view evangelism as an event, even though the church was launched in Jerusalem through the big event of Pentecost. Those who witnessed the harvest of Peter's preaching did not duplicate his model. Major events can be tremendously helpful in bringing people to personal faith, but consistent and persistent evangelism consists of many small events and encounters.

The seminal metaphor used in the New Testament for evangelism is the agrarian model of raising crops. Successful farming is not confined to the harvest, as climactic as it is. Each phase of the process is critically important and involves care and planning. The farmer cultivates and sows with the same intensity as he harvests. The farmer also knows that different seasons and stages require different tools. No farmer in his right mind would drive a combine through the field twelve months out of the year.

I find great encouragement in Paul's message to the Corinthians: "The man who plants and the man who waters have one purpose, and each will be rewarded according to his own labor" (1 Cor. 3:8). I imagine we will be surprised when one day God evaluates the labor and elevates both the sowers and the cultivators to the gold medal stand.

Expanding from Individuals to Community

Evangelism training, when done at all, is usually directed toward training individuals to share their faith. Certainly every believer needs to know how to share his or her own faith story and explain the gospel. Christians should also understand the major stages of the evangelism process and have some basic tools to use. Ideally, however, evangelism is a function of the body of Christ, with division of labor and utilization of diverse gifts. An individual rarely accomplishes the whole process of evangelism in isolation. When reading Luke's report on Philip's encounter with the Ethiopian, I wonder how many people were involved in this stranger's journey to faith in Christ. Whom did he encounter at the temple on his recent visit? Where did he first develop an interest in the Jewish monotheistic faith?

Not only does the Holy Spirit use a variety of individuals in the process of evangelism, but he uses the dynamic of community life to enhance the process. The gospel of John gives us the powerful principle that love within the Christian family is proof of the reality of our faith in Christ (John 13:34–35). How will this love be evident without exposing seekers to the reality of Christian community?

Jesus enlarges on this principle in his prayer in John 17. The unity of believers will point outsiders to the reality of Christ. We cannot measure the power that comes from establishing loving relationships within the body and exposing seekers to it. Its absence, on the other hand, may explain much of the lack of effectiveness in evangelism found in today's church.

EXPANDING FROM ON CAMPUS TO OFF CAMPUS

The early church found much of its success through its involuntary centrifugal force (Acts 8). The movement was outward. It was a go-to strategy starting from Jerusalem (Acts 1:8). Peter's audience in Acts 2 was an exception rather than the norm. That audience, rather exceptionally, was the result of the centripetal force of people being drawn into the religious center, the temple. Peter capitalized on this gathered audience and appealed to its religious heritage with a message that touched their collective consciousness.

The Jewish mentality from the Old Testament was primarily centripetal. It was a come-to strategy. Build a grand temple, demonstrate the moral and civil laws of God, and the nations will notice and come to look. The temple structure was even designed to welcome and accommodate the Gentiles who were seeking God. When Christ came, he changed the direction of missions forever. Evangelism is now a go-to strategy.

When looking at the evangelism strategy of most churches, I find little that is planned off campus or outside the walls of the church. One inward pull is simply the building. So much of a church's resources have gone into the structure that we feel it's a shame not to use it. It becomes an issue of stewardship. Jim Peterson points out in *Church without Walls* that we still operate in the church today as though we lived in a society that is largely rural and illiterate; our method is "come to and listen" (1992, 118). The early church penetrated their culture and beyond with mobile and flexible forms. As James Rutz points out, "Until Constantine, there was no such thing as a church building or 'Christian' architecture'" (1992, 55).

Another inward force is comfort. The church environment is home to us, and we feel others would surely feel the same way. The fact that the unchurched would find coming to our church building unattractive, intimi-

RON BENNETT

dating, awkward, or just weird is a difficult pill to swallow. After all, we are such nice people.

As a couple trying to relate to neighbors and unchurched friends, we have found that even our home is not the first place to begin a relationship. If we invite new people over, it is usually for a cookout in the back yard, not for a dinner inside our home. The initial place is often a local restaurant that is neutral ground. Our church is not neutral ground for the unchurched. Planning evangelistic activities on campus creates an unnecessary barrier for many we are trying to reach. Our strategy needs to include locations that are neutral, common, and natural to the unchurched. We need to ask, "Where would the unchurched feel comfortable?" Rather than our own comfort being primary, we need to apply the attitude of a servant and missionary and remove unnecessary barriers to sharing the message.

EXPANDING FROM GIFTED TO GIFTS

When the more verbal and public spiritual gifts such as preaching and teaching dominate, evangelism becomes more an event than a process. Those with the more private, nonpublic gifts conclude that they can't do evangelism or are not needed. However, viewing evangelism as a process makes all the gifts relevant. We need a team, a community of people, if we are to be effective. Since no one person embodies all the gifts, we discover a new freedom to work as part of a whole, each one using his or her gifts in the process. The more we focus on reaching the lost, the greater the need for those with the gifts that offer mercy, touch, and relationships. These gifts demonstrate the love of Christ to a postmodern world. As we work together, we can capitalize on strengths and find freedom to serve in the way God has wired us.

My wife, Mary, discovered this dynamic a few years ago when we moved to the Kansas City area. She met Linda, a cosmetics consultant who was concerned about reaching her lost friends. They discovered complementary gifts and teamed together. Mary used her gift of teaching, while Linda used her gift of hospitality to set up some small group Bible discussions on relevant issues for women. Linda recruited, and Mary led the discussions. Together they were able to do what neither could do alone.

EXPANDING FROM DECISIONS TO CONVERSIONS

In our eagerness to see success, we often record external displays of forms rather than working and waiting for reality. We are eager to measure and report the baptisms, prayers, or number of response cards that accompany our event-oriented evangelism. However, since it is true that only God knows the hearts of people and that only God brings conversion, we will always labor with some degree of uncertainty.

There is a place for response indicators and evangelistic invitations as part of the evangelism process, but too often we are content with an external act rather than an internal response of the heart. When the gospel is not clearly understood, the result can be people who make a decision but want nothing to do with following Christ.

A pastor called me the other day and asked for help with people who had come forward in his church but did not want to follow Christ or connect with the church. "We don't have trouble getting decisions," he said, "we have trouble getting disciples." Talking further, I wondered if the problem was more in the evangelism than in the follow-up.

In his book *Follow Me* (1996), Jan Hettinga raises the issue that the gospel is not only a gift to be received but a new leader to follow. In a culture that is increasingly biblically illiterate and holding a truncated view of God, we need to take the effort and patience to help people understand the complete gospel, not just a part of it. People need to understand the gospel and not just be exposed to it.

EXPANDING FROM LOCAL TO KINGDOM

The church has often limited evangelism by its territorial mentality. We have been more concerned in building up our local congregations than in expanding the kingdom. Often it is unintentional and is a by-product of an intense mission focus, but the results are the same. We tend to look at lost people and our commitment to them based on whether they will fit into our church or system. Many times our hidden or not so hidden agenda is to get people to join our group as a condition of getting them into God's kingdom.

Early in my ministry, I focused so much on making disciples that I would tend to ignore lost people when I felt they wouldn't connect with me through the discipling process. Subtly we evaluate the merit of relating to lost people based on the likelihood that they will come to our church or join our group. We tend not to become involved if they are already in a church or show little interest in our group.

EXPANDING FROM "PASS-THROUGH" TO PENETRATION

My initial training in evangelism was on a university campus. Our strategy was to expose as many people to the gospel as we could. We found those interested in seeking God and spent additional time with them. With 40,000 people on campus and Jesus' statement "I tell you, open your eyes and look at the fields! They are ripe for harvest" (John 4:35) fixed in our minds, we looked for the harvest. We even had the harvest figured out statistically. If you shared the gospel with ten people, one would become a Christian.

The sheer size of the mission field and the fact that 10,000 new students showed up every year created endless opportunities. I developed friendships with those interested in the gospel. We sponsored debates on the topic of God and held rallies where professors and athletes shared their testimonies. We saw hundreds of students come to Christ. It was exciting, and it fit the culture. Our strategy was to sow broadly, reap the reapable, and move on.

The apostle Paul usually displayed a similar pass-through strategy. In his case, he would pass through a city, preach the gospel, reap a harvest, set up a church, and move on. His calling and motivation were to preach the gospel where it had never been preached. Nevertheless, when he instructed the early church in evangelism, he did not teach believers to emulate his method or calling. Primarily he taught them to penetrate right where they were. "Live it out where you are" was his theme.

There are settings where a pass-through strategy is still valid. The church, however, exists in a penetration environment. Buying homes is still part of the American dream. Regardless of the mobility of American culture, we still live in our communities with a sense of permanence.

When I graduated from college, I went to work for Boeing Aircraft in Seattle. I was assigned to an electronics section that was working on the 747 jumbo jet. I realized quickly that the ten people in my section were not part of a pass-through system. We would be working closely for a number of years. If I used a strategy of sow broadly, reap the reapable, and move on, it would be a lonely tenure.

The church often promotes a pass-through strategy in the context of community. This results in a lack of relationships with lost people and a sense of isolation—almost a fortress mentality. It is easy for lost people to escape the influence of a pass-through strategy. All they have to do is turn down the invitation to the pass-through event. "No thanks" and they are safe! It is difficult, however, to escape the influence of a penetration strategy of love, relationship, and service.

EXPANDING FROM ENEMIES TO BROKEN PEOPLE

How we view lost people will largely determine our approach. When lost people are seen as a threat, we become defensive and retreat. When we view them as the enemy, we either go to war or withdraw.

My early training in evangelism often referred to the process of evangelism as going to war. We were in a battle and invading Satan's territory. Prayer was critical as we needed the full armor of God. So far so good. But sometimes we would casually refer to lost people as the enemy whom we were out to capture. The lost were rebels who needed to be conquered.

Later I stopped to look at how Jesus described lost people. What I discovered was a whole new way of viewing those outside of Christ. Rather than an enemy to conquer, I began to see them as broken and in need of healing, as captives in need of liberation, and as blind in need of sight. Jesus announced his mission in his home town by reading from the book of Isaiah. He referred to people as blind, captives, and downcast (Isa. 61:1–3). At other times he referred to them as sick needing a physician or as sheep needing a shepherd. Paul refers to lost people as the dead needing life and the blind needing sight (2 Cor. 4:3–4). There is certainly nothing threatening about those descriptions. Rather than creating hostility in me, they create compassion. When someone is sick or lost or blind, I can understand why they act the way they do. Rather than feeling defensive, I feel empathy.

DEVELOPING YOUR PROCESS

During the medieval period of European history, wealthy land owners built castles for security and protection. Ideally the castle was surrounded by a moat as the first level of defense. A drawbridge could be lowered from the castle gate to allow access to those considered friendly. The second level of protection was the wall itself. The higher and thicker the wall, the better. A main gate served as a concentrated point of access. The final point of protection was the tower. The tower was the residence of the royal family, and to get to the monarch, you had to get to the tower.

Our lives are much like this feudal picture. We each are rulers of our castle. The flag that flies over our castle is the flag of ego or self. Self-rule or independence from God is at the heart of our identity. Christ represents a new flag, a new leader, and a new allegiance. Evangelism is the process of bringing a new flag to the heart of the castle. The goal of evangelism is to lower the flag of self and raise the banner of Christ. Anything less is an incomplete gospel.

The process of discipleship is the working out of the implications of coming under new leadership, the leadership of Christ. Discipleship is working out the meaning of a new alliance into the daily activities and structures of castle life. It is the process of acquiring new values, beliefs, and behaviors that will govern castle living. God's kingdom is made up of rulers and their castles that have been brought under a new sovereign leadership. A new federation is formed of castles that make up a vast empire.

Evangelism is the process of gaining access to the tower of the castle. Access is gained only as the barriers that form the natural defense are overcome. The first barrier, like a moat, is the emotional defense. The second barrier, the castle wall, is the intellectual defense. The final barrier, the tower, is the volitional defense. Of course, an attack on a real castle tackles the barriers one by one, whereas that is not usually the case in evangelism. Still, the analogy may be useful. Evangelism is the process of bringing the gospel of Christ through these barriers. Each barrier is part of an individual's castle system.

When we think of evangelism as a process and focus on the strategies for overcoming these barriers, we have two approaches. One is to attack in a military posture: break down the walls, bash in the gate, and overpower the defense. The other is to relate to the ruler of the castle in such a way that he or she will let down the drawbridge, open the gate, and allow access to the tower.

The process of evangelism involves overcoming these three main barriers: emotional, intellectual, and volitional. The emotional barrier—the moat—is overcome by building a bridge of love that touches the hearts of people. It is the relational component. The bridge we build must be strong enough to bear the weight of truth. The bridge must overcome isolation, suspicion, fear, and hostility.

The intellectual barrier—the castle wall—is overcome as we gain access to the mind with truth. The gate to the wall is open as interest is created and questions answered. Access through the intellectual wall is not information disseminated but truth understood.

The volitional barrier—the tower—is overcome as the will is surrendered and a new authority is recognized. Repentance is the about-face of self to Christ. It's a change of direction, radical and revolutionary. A new flag is raised in place of, not alongside, the old one.

BRIDGING THE EMOTIONAL MOAT

The choice of the bridging material used is critical to the success of bridge building. Only in fairy tales can bridges be made of straw and string. In real life, bridges are made of steel, concrete, and wood. The solid stuff in relationships is trust, respect, and credibility. Trust means we are approachable, respect means we are believable, and credibility means we are authentic. Although these three may be gained in a matter of moments, it usually takes time.

Bridges built without these materials are doomed to fail. Bridges built with them allow access and bear the weight of truth. In process evangelism, we may build the bridges that others cross later with the load of truth. In process evangelism there are no insignificant contacts. As ambassadors, we are either building bridges or raising barriers.

As we relate to people during our day, we may not share the gospel, but we can build bridges. Every encounter with lost people, whether spontaneous or planned, is the chance to enter the evangelism process by building bridges. Shopping at the local Wal Mart takes on new significance when we see ourselves as bridge builders for Christ. The clerk is not an animated scanning operator but the ruler of a castle that needs a bridge. The auto mechanic is not an inconvenience but an opportunity for construction. Bridge building means we will still be their friends even if they reject our Christ.

Most of us can smell a hidden agenda. We are suspicious and alert. Picture yourself working in your yard on Saturday morning. It's great day to be out, and you are attacking the yard with a vengeance. Suddenly you are aware of two young men riding up your drive on bikes. They are wearing white shirts and black ties and appear very friendly. They approach you with a cordial greeting and offer you some literature on morality and family values.

How are you feeling at this moment? Suspicious? Cautious? Annoyed?

They proceed to invite you to a pancake breakfast at their church next Saturday morning at seven. There will be a speaker on the family, and it's free. They also would be glad to pick you up. Would you come?

Now how are you feeling? Eager? Open? Anxious to get back to yard work? If you are like most, you smell a hidden agenda. Yet too often we are they! In a postmodern culture, people are increasingly suspicious, cautious, and defensive. Bridge building is critical to the evangelism process.

There are two practical steps we can take to build bridges across the emotional barriers. The first is to *identify our God-given networks*. Who are the people we relate to naturally? Evangelism is not a matter of going someplace to start but of simply recognizing where God has placed us.

There are five places to look:

Where we work
Where we live
Where we play
Our family
Divine appointments

Each of these environments gives us contact with people for whom Christ died. As we look into each network, we should be asking the question, "Whom is God placing on my heart for heaven?" Not every person in my workplace will respond to me or I to them. Not every person in my neighborhood will click with me or develop common ground. But it's the place to begin looking.

Some of the best advice I received on evangelism came from a Navigator staff member as I was beginning my career as a military intelligence officer in the U.S. Army and was being assigned to Fort Devins for additional training. I was anticipating six months with a class of fellow officers. Ron's advice was, "Don't try to relate to the whole class. Just ask God to help you connect with two or three who have similar interests." That advice has worked in each new environment I've been in.

Since I am on staff with a Christian organization and work mainly with church leaders, I have not found my work environment a huge source of non-Christian relationships. So I major on my neighborhood. You, however, may find the marketplace to be key to your relationships. For others their extended family may provide natural relationships that open the opportunity for bridge building.

Take some time to pray through your natural networks. Make a list of those three or four people that God seems to put on your heart. If you are part of a small group or lead a small group, encourage others to develop a list of people and begin to pray for them.

The second step is to *interact*. Using the principle of common ground, begin to relate around those activities that you have in common. If you don't hold things in common, you probably will not be a bridge builder.

It is at this step that we need to apply the *principle of intentionality*. Rather than waiting for opportunities to develop passively, we need to take the initiative naturally. Intentionality means we set up the neighborhood block party, we invite our officemate to a baseball game, and we offer to keep the neighbor's kids so they can have a weekend away.

Intentionality works its way out as we pray for specific people, as we relate on common ground, as we meet real needs, and as we share our lives authentically. Bridge building cannot be done without contact and touch. This kind of involvement takes time, sacrifice, and priority.

How do we add more activities to an already busy schedule? One solution is through the *principle of consolidation*. Rather than creating separate activities for evangelism or bridge building, we simply integrate it into what we already do.

Jim worked in an office with thirty other people. As we talked about who was on his heart for heaven, he thought of four or five. The problem was that they lived in different parts of the city and his only contact with them was at work. Jim's young family and a heavy work schedule left little time for new activities. I asked Jim what he did for lunch, since it was one thing he had in common with those on his list. It didn't require a special evening, and it looked like Jim was good at it!

Jim said that lunch was his time to catch up on paper work. The office emptied out, and he could focus without interruption. It was an efficient use of time since he could eat lunch and fill out forms without being bothered. As we talked further, he saw how with a little adjustment he could consolidate activities. He started going to lunch with one of the men on his list once each week.

Bridge building also allows for the *principle of pliability*. This means that people are more receptive to spiritual issues at special times. The ground is either too wet or too dry. When it's wet, it is sticky and forms clumps that are hard to remove from shoes, shovels, and kids. When it's dry, it is like hardened concrete. I have found since moving to this area that there is a short window of time when I can work with this soil—usually about two hours in the late spring and two hours in the fall. It's a small window, and it never comes on the same date each year. Last year I was traveling during the pliable windows and had to wait another year before I could put a post into the ground.

People are like the clay. We can never predict when the heart will be sensitive to spiritual things. It may be a result of a job layoff, an illness, or a soccer championship. As we are involved in building bridges, we remain connected. This allows us to take advantage of those plastic moments when people are most pliable.

ENTERING THE INTELLECTUAL FORTRESS

Entrance to the intellectual fortress is gained when the person willingly explores truth. The objective is to help bring understanding to spiritual truth. Confrontation with truth does not always result in understanding; it may create resistance and hostility. Even when Jesus presented the truth during his ministry, some understood it, while others became hostile.

Entering the intellectual fortress can be thought of in two additional stages. The first is to *introduce spiritual topics*. In this stage we are bringing truth to life issues, getting to a value level through felt needs. This stage of dialogue takes us from news, weather, sports, and kids to values and truth. If we are not comfortable talking about life values, we will not be comfortable sharing the gospel. This open door involves sharing biblical truth on life issues. It can be formal or informal, planned or spontaneous. Like Christians, non-Christians are also trying to put life together. Often they are doing the best they can with what they have. Life issues provide a great opportunity to build credibility for the gospel as people discover that the Bible is actually relevant for life today. Michael Green writes in *Evangelism through the Local Church,* "Not many people are brought to Christ via the route of the intellect, though some are. Vital though the intellect is, most people are won when they sense Christ coming to touch broken places and torn feelings in their lives" (1992, 224).

The second stage of entering the mental fortress is to *invite people to discuss the gospel* and its related issues from the Bible. Ultimately we must introduce seekers to Jesus, his claims and teaching. Process evangelism creates the environment for investigation.

As we equip people in the process of evangelism and especially in the skill of investigation, we need to provide a variety of tools that can be used. Ashker's *Jesus Cares for Women* (1987) and my *Design 4 Discovery* are two resources produced by the Navigators that stimulate discovery and investigation for seekers. Both can be used individually or in a small group context.

CLIMBING THE VOLITIONAL TOWER

The third barrier is the will. The focus of this barrier is persuasion and coming to personal faith. Whether we call it new birth, conversion, or personal faith, it is the point where God by grace through faith creates new life.

It is helpful to think of this process in two stages as well. The first is to *illustrate.* In the illustration stage the gospel is presented in summary form so that it can be easily grasped and understood, and then it is illustrated.

After Jesus had been demonstrating who he was to the disciples, he stopped and gave a quiz. "Who do people say the Son of Man is?" His second question was more personal, "Who do you say that I am?" (Matt. 16:13–15). Their understanding was still incomplete, but they had come to some important conclusions. As we stop and summarize the gospel to people, it gives them a chance to clarify what they now believe. It can also help them put the pieces together as the Holy Spirit brings conviction and faith.

In a visually oriented culture, a word picture is often helpful. An illustration like "The Bridge" that has been used in various tracts and training courses is an excellent example of a summary presentation that is visual. Christians need a variety of tools to use in presenting the gospel. Most of us will have one favorite tool with which we are most comfortable and which we will use most often. Developing an expanding box of tools, however, allows us to treat seekers individually. "When all you have is a hammer, you'll treat everybody like a nail."

Illustrating the gospel in a visual and summary form leads naturally to the second stage of *inquiry.* Inquiry is the step of asking a seeker where they are in their journey. It is giving them the opportunity and the incentive to take the next step. The next step may be to repent and receive Christ by faith. It is at this point that we can help people move another step closer to Christ. Inquiry can be as simple as asking, "In the light of what you have just seen in this illustration, where would you say you are in your journey to God?"

There are only three responses that people have to the gospel. We need to know how to recognize and handle each of them. The three responses are illustrated by the diverse reactions to Paul on Mars Hill (Acts 17:22–34).

One group responded by sneering. They thought Paul was crazy or the message was strange or both. They were not ready to buy into what he was saying. At the very least, they needed more time and exposure. Both the emotional and intellectual barriers needed to be penetrated.

A second group said, "We will hear you again concerning this." They were wildly curious but not convinced. They were seekers who needed more investigation and discovery. When people are at this stage of coming to Christ, we need to create the opportunity to explore the issues of the gospel. We need to spend time overcoming the intellectual barriers by helping them investigate truth.

The third response was belief. "Some men joined him and believed." God opened their hearts. They believed or wanted to believe. Helping these people formulate their decision by praying is an exciting moment in process evangelism. Often, however, when we are involved in evangelism, seekers come to faith along the journey and do not tell us until later. Larry had been studying the Bible with his seeker friend Bob over a period of months when he began to notice a change. Instead of referring to "what you believe" and "your Bible," Bob began referring to "us" and "our" Bible. Upon further inquiry, Bob referred to a time weeks earlier when he had prayed on his own following one of their discussions.

Bringing Christ to the heart of the castle is authentic evangelism. Fruitfulness in evangelism is helping people move one step closer to faith in Christ. Knowing where people are in their journey and being equipped with the skills and tools to take the next step is the role of every ambassador of Christ. Training people in this role is the job of the church and its leadership.

MAXIMIZING YOUR ENVIRONMENT

Three relational environments support the process of evangelism. These three environments form a comprehensive strategy for leaders to develop effective outreach through their church. The three main relational environments are individual, small groups (teams), and corporate or large groups.

Most evangelism training is done to support individual efforts. We train people how to work through the three barriers on their own. In the agrarian metaphor, they learn how to cultivate, sow, and harvest—on their own. A variety of resources are available to use. For example, the *Contagious Christian* and *Living Proof* video series are both helpful in preparing people for individual evangelism.[2]

Individual effort is certainly a key part of evangelism, but it is grossly inadequate in the light of the paradigm shifts mentioned earlier and the postmodern culture in America. To be comprehensive and biblical, we need to involve other dynamics as well.

The small group or team dynamic is another critical form that needs to be developed in a church strategy. Many churches are using small groups for nurturing and caregiving. They have experienced the benefits of a small group of people focused on a common objective. The same benefits result as teams are used in evangelism. Teams allow for community and individual gifts to be utilized effectively. Teams allow people to exercise their strengths and benefit from the strengths of others. They also foster accountability.

A team approach to evangelism is simply two or more people uniting in the common task of evangelism. As a team, they relate to the lost through the process of bringing Christ to the heart of the castle. As a team, they work to overcome the barriers of emotion, intellect, and will. Rather than an individual modeling the Christian faith, the team becomes the model as well as the individuals within it.

I believe Jesus knew the power of the team as he formed the twelve disciples into an identifiable band focused on mission. Even in their early training, Jesus sent them out not as individuals but as pairs. Paul deployed teams as he took the gospel to the Gentile world. If we are to reach a postmodern culture that is increasingly isolated from the church, we are going to need teams of people.

One church developed such a plan when some men in the church discovered they shared a common talent and interest in fixing cars. As they discussed how to use their talent as a team for evangelism, they asked the church leadership to put them in contact with needy people in the community that could benefit from their service.

On Saturday mornings this team would volunteer to fix cars for single moms, widows, or other needy persons in the community who came to them through the church network. It was a practical way of expressing the love of Christ to meet real needs. Most of these men would never feel comfortable teaching in front of a small group, but they could connect with people using their automotive talent. They purposely drove their mission toward lost people in the community as they saw how they could be key in the initial phase of the evangelism process.

After reading the book *Conspiracy of Kindness* (Sjogren 1993), another church formed a team to do yard work in the community. They focused on new people in the community who were just unpacking. They offered to rake, mow, or trim to make the move a little less hectic; there was no cost, no strings, no agenda other than showing the love of Christ in a tangible way. The ideas are endless once people begin to see how teams of people can begin to build bridges over the emotional moat of people's lives.

Working through the intellectual fortress can also be done with a team. Small group discussions on relevant issues like marriage, children, finances, and stress can be done as a team in the marketplace, neighborhood, or church. Recovery groups have been used as an effective environment for seekers to experience community and answer real-life issues. In the context of a caring small group, community seekers can move from spiritual felt needs to the gospel.

In Columbia, Missouri, some businessmen have used the team effectively to enter the intellectual fortress. Even though the men are involved in separate Bible studies during the week, they meet together monthly for a Discovery Forum at a businessman's home. Each team member brings his or her seeker friends to meet others and discuss relevant issues from the Bible. In this environment those who are skilled in teaching and leading discussions use their strength, while those who are gifted in hospitality add their part. As the team works together, seekers are exposed to the dynamic and unity of Christ's body.

The small group is also effective in the volitional phase of evangelism, where the gospel is presented and seekers are encouraged to respond to it or at least identify where they are in their journey.

Teams come in various forms. Baseball is one of America's favorite team sports. Watching and sometimes coaching my son's team, I have seen the boys develop from a group of nine individuals wearing the same colored shirt, kicking dirt and watching airplanes, to a cohesive unit of sometimes skilled players. The team has grown in knowledge, attention, and skill.

This past winter my son signed up for a new adventure—a wrestling team. Both of these sports use the term *team;* both have coaches, players, and rules; but what is meant by the term *team* is very different in the two sports. In baseball each team member plays a complementary defensive position, but in wrestling, each team member does the same thing. In baseball, team members play their positions together at the same time. In wrestling, they compete alone while team members watch. When a wrestler is on the mat, there is no one backing him up. There are cheers from the crowd and instructions from the coach, but a wrestler is alone—on a team.

Outreach teams can look like baseball teams, wrestling teams, or even track teams. A baseball team is a single-focus team. They hold everything in common. They have a common mission, audience, activities, and location. In my early ministry on the university campus, we developed single-focus teams. We had students who lived in the same dorm, ate in the same dining hall, went to the same classrooms, and cheered for the same sports team. Our ministry outreach focused on the same group of people. They were on the same schedule and attended the same activities. We would plan outreach ski events over semester break when everybody had vacation at the same time.

A single-focus team can have great impact when life parameters are widely shared. This type of team can focus on the same company, the same neighborhood, or the same social club. This team has common relationships, interests, and activities.

Another form of team is more like the wrestling team. Each team member ministers on his or her own schedule. They share a common mission and strategy and even activities, but they labor with a different audience and location. This type of team can train together and even perform at the same time. They can have the same coach and wear the same colored jersey. Yet each player functions independently.

A few years ago I had the privilege of working with Bob Jacks, who has successfully modeled evangelism through a wrestling-type team. Bob and his wife Betty call their team concept "Your Home a Lighthouse" (Jacks 1997). In their model, a team of people band together around a common mission and strategy. They set up the common activity of a monthly Bible study for non-Christians. One of the couples acts as the host and another is the discussion leader. Everybody invites and brings friends to this common event. People who come may not know each other initially. They may know only the person who invited them. The group can be diverse in backgrounds and interests. They may come from the neighborhood or from across town. It is an example of a wrestling-type team that can be used in evangelism.

A third type of team is the track team. In my senior year in high school we had recently moved to a new town. I had been on football teams and wrestling teams but never on a track team. The school was small and track was not very popular, so anyone who showed up without crutches could wear a uniform. I was not fast enough to run track, but I discovered if I stood in one spot and turned around fast enough, I could throw the discus. I made the team! I found out that a track team is a very different form of team.

At practices I never saw the whole team. Some were out running around the city, others were in the gym lifting weights, and others were running laps on the track. The only time we were all together was on the bus and for the yearbook picture. Even the meets were different. We did our event at different places at different times. Events were held simultaneously and with different audiences. We didn't even show up at the meet at the same time. It was a diverse, scattered team. Yet it was a team.

The track team form is effective when little is held in common. There is a common mission and strategy but little else. Locations, audiences, and activities may all be different. A team of this form is the most flexible but the most difficult to train and lead. This type of team is more effective with experienced people who need little coaching, training, and accountability. It works well when the team members have very diverse audiences and networks, when common activities are unlikely and schedules are complex.

Developing teams for evangelism takes planning, effort, and creativity. But once people experience the benefit of working as a team, regardless of its form, they will never be content to minister without it.

The third relational dynamic is the corporate or large group form. This includes the typical city crusade or church evangelistic event where a speaker is brought in to share the gospel. The fruitfulness of this event largely depends on the rest of the matrix. When the other dynamics are not in place or working, then the large event is usually more sterile.

MINING YOUR VEINS — WORKING SMARTER NOT HARDER

One of the great challenges in evangelism is keeping the gospel mobile. The church has tended to institutionalize methods that were once successful. They worked in the past, so we continue to use them regardless of their effectiveness. When we are ineffective, we conclude that we must not be working hard enough. Perhaps, the thinking goes, we need to pray more and have more faith.

The principle of working smarter not harder can be a help to churches in evangelism. "If the ax is dull and its edge unsharpened, more strength is needed but skill will bring success" (Eccl. 10:10). This principle applied to evangelism could be called mining the veins.

RON BENNETT

A few years ago we took our family camping in the Rocky Mountains of southern Colorado. One of the highlights was four-wheeling in the back country where we could get close to old silver mines from a not-too-distant past. High above the timberline, we viewed peaks sprinkled with the tailings of abandoned mining operations. Often the mine entrance was only evident by the unnatural pile of yellowish rock. As I looked at the various locations, I wondered why a prospector would start digging in that particular spot. When there were thousands of acres of mountain terrain, why did he dig there? Why did he choose that mountain peak and not the one further over?

I suppose there were some indicators that were obvious to the keen eye of the prospector but irrelevant to my untrained eye. Literature on the area told how prospectors would begin digging with some initial success. As they began digging, their hope was to hit a vein of silver deeper within the mountain. The initial success would yield even greater riches as they hit the mother lode. The crusty old prospector was not interested in creating a myriad of mine entrances so that a later generation of tourists would be impressed. He wanted silver and lots of it. He wanted the mother lode, not exercise. Locating and following the vein was his strategy.

Evangelism has its own mining-the-vein strategy. It is instructive to observe that when Levi left his office and followed Jesus, he didn't end up in the temple. Jesus responded to Levi's invitation to a backyard barbecue and got more than kosher hot dogs and diet Coke. Jesus got access to a network of trapped mountain people, people deep within the mountain—a rich vein waiting to be mined. It was so radical and politically incorrect that the disciples were unable to explain Jesus' behavior to the religious spectators.

Jesus followed the vein of relationships that started with Matthew. Matthew was the mine entrance, but his friends were the mother lode. Jesus' method as well as his message penetrated a culture within a culture. Through Levi, Jesus saw another generation of lost people. His mobility and flexibility allowed access to a hidden group outside the reach of the traditional forms.

A few years ago my wife and I were discipling a group of couples who were beyond our socioeconomic and religious comfort zones. It was one of those divine encounters that only God could create. We had responded to their invitation to hold a Bible study in their homes. At first we were cautiously accepted by the group, but eventually we gained their trust and respect. We were elated after months of personal contact to be invited to a retirement party with their friends. A whole new network of people was made accessible because we had been willing to follow the vein.

The church has had the debilitating tendency to take the initial silver discovery and bring it back down the mountain rather than keep digging in the same location. The result is a lot of tunnel entrances without much silver. The more comprehensive we are in our strategy of process evangelism, the more adept we will become at following the vein.

References

Ashker, Helene. 1987. *Jesus Cares for Women*. Colorado Springs: NavPress.
Barna, George. 1990. *The Frog in the Kettle*. Ventura: Regal Books.
_____. 1995. *Evangelism That Works*. Ventura: Regal Books.
Bennett, Ron. n.d. *Design 4 Discovery*. Colorado Springs: NavPress.
Green, Michael. 1992. *Evangelism through the Local Church*. Nashville: Nelson.
Hettinga, Jan. 1996. *Follow Me*. Colorado Springs: NavPress.
Jacks, Bob, and Betty Jacks. 1997. *Your Home a Lighthouse*. Colorado Springs: NavPress.
Petersen, Jim. 1992. *Church without Walls*. Colorado Springs: NavPress.
Rutz, James. 1992. *The Open Church*. Auburn, Me.: The SeedSowers.
Sjogren, Steve. 1993. *Conspiracy of Darkness*. Ann Arbor: Vine Books.
Strobel, Lee. 1993. *Inside the Mind of Unchurched Harry and Mary*. Grand Rapids: Zondervan.

PART SEVEN

Experiences and Strategies

CHAPTER 20

FINDING GOD AT HARVARD

Reaching the Post-Christian University

Kelly Monroe

Rather than arguing about the superiority of Christianity over world religions, I would rather put forth a light that is so lovely that all would be drawn into his presence.

—*Madeline L'Engle*

I would like to take a narrative approach to this subject, so it might be helpful if I begin with the context of my own experience. I am the daughter of a psychology professor, whom I love. He was a doctoral student at the University of Chicago and then a professor at Ohio State University. Like his colleagues in the 1960s and 70s, he renounced any childhood faith and absorbed the religion of behaviorism and atheism, assuming a mechanistic and therefore, it seems to me, a low view of being human. These scholars assumed that we were not created by a good and loving God who has, for us, a future and a hope. Truth, according to this worldview, is to be invented more than it is to be discovered.

Growing up in this world, I also saw what later seemed to me a high degree of conformity and fearfulness in the academic world. Higher education often seemed illiberal inasmuch as students were not welcomed into the wide spectrum of ideas, including the message of the gospel itself.

The theories professed in classrooms and therapy sessions did not seem to work in real life. Not receiving the love of God, my parents could not love each other. Our family, like other families in that department, disintegrated. The center could not hold. And I saw that proud and false thinking, unhinged from Christ and a Christian ontology, ended in brokenness and sorrow, whereas humble and truthful thinking ended in love, wholeness, and joy. Though I had few words for this at the time, the feeling of loss ran deep. God began in me a longing for himself.

These problems of brokenness and alienation are not found just in the academic world. I've seen this at the U.S. Olympic Training Center, where self-worth is derived from performance measured in milliseconds. We see it in the cities, where some kids are killing each other, and in the suburbs, where some kids are killing themselves.

As a teenager I knew that if there *is* real hope out there it must be big enough for the challenges we face. I knew that the well must be deep and the water must be good. I felt that this hope would be down to earth. True to life. Flesh and blood.

When high school friends shared the gospel with me, I realized that nothing was too good to be true and that truth was not an abstract and disembodied concept but a Person, who is still with us each moment by his Holy Spirit.

Ten years ago I came as a visiting student to Harvard. Though I met no Christians at the Divinity School where I was doing research and thesis writing, I did meet believers in isolated pockets of the university. God began to knit us together as a community.

I also discovered, in a treasure hunt while writing a brief history of evangelical Harvard, that the college's earliest motto was *In Christi Gloriam*—For Christ's glory. Likewise, Yale was later founded on *Lux et Veritas*—Light and truth. And Dartmouth was founded as *Voces Clamantium in Deserto*—A voice crying in the wilderness.

Similarly, Stanford, Duke, Wellesley, Columbia, Mount Holyoke, Tufts, the colleges in Cambridge and Oxford, Yen Si in Korea, St. Xavier in India—among many others—all were inspired by Jesus Christ.

Do we now call these schools post-Christian? Do we call them secular? Some now call them pre-Christian, given the loss of even academic references to the Garden, the Flood, the cross, the gospel. How do we describe these places in which it is possible for students to graduate in English literature and art history without ever having read the Bible?

Do we call these schools Christian but dormant because good seeds have been planted and are buried deep beneath the surface, usually invisible, as seeds are, but still alive and potentially fruitful? Perhaps they're waiting for sunshine and water and good soil and tender loving care.

You've likely pondered these questions as well. Most important, what does Jesus think of these schools that were once dedicated to him so future generations of students would find life in him? What happened to them and in them to cause their decline? How do we learn from all the ways the Philistines have stopped up the wells of the living water that makes education truly liberal and liberating? That makes education more about transformation than information?

KELLY MONROE

Beyond some critique, I'd like to spend most of this essay exploring God's faithfulness and power to reinvigorate, to redeem, to re-create. I want to learn from Martha in John 11, when Jesus finally arrived in Bethany, four days after her brother, Lazarus, had died. She ran out to greet him on the outskirts of the village. No doubt she was disappointed, probably weeping. She said, "If only you'd been here, my brother wouldn't have died. But even now, I know you can do all things." I love that—"even now, you can do all things."

The founders of Princeton, for the first 150 years while it was called the College of New Jersey, dedicated their school with these words: *Vitam Mortuis Reddo*—I restore life to the dead. "Even now," said Martha, "I believe you can do all things." Even now, you are the resurrection and the life. Post-Christian universities need people of faith to say to Christ, "Even now you can do all things," particularly when the picture is bleak.

Let's take as a case study America's first college, Harvard. The earliest by-laws read: "Let every student consider well the main end of his life and studies is to know God and Jesus Christ, which is eternal life (John 17:3), and therefore to lay Christ in the bottom as the only foundation of all sound knowledge and learning. Seeing the Lord giveth wisdom, everyone shall seriously by prayer and in secret, seek wisdom of Him."

Likewise, a 1789 Massachusetts law instructed Harvard professors "to impress on the minds of youth committed to their care the principles of piety and justice and a sacred regard for truth; love of their country, humanity, and a universal benevolence; sobriety, industry and frugality, chastity, moderation and temperance, and those other virtues which are the ornaments of human society." Today, many students do not even know the meaning of these words, much less the one who could bear this fruit and character in them.

As you know, it is not just schools inspired by and dedicated to Jesus, but also countless homes warmed by the love of him; countless hospitals and orphanages; the music of Bach, Handel, Mendelssohn, Michael Card, Rich Mullins, and Fernando Ortega; the paintings of Rembrandt, Michelangelo, and Bruce Herman; the poetry of Hopkins, Rosetti, Luci Shaw; the resistance of Bonhoeffer, the Huguenots, Corrie ten Boom; the environmental stewardship of John Muir, founder of the Sierra Club, whom God healed of blindness to tell of the wonders of his creation.

Jesus Christ inspired the founding of the Red Cross and other relief organizations around the world. He inspired the abolition of slavery and apartheid and of sati in India. He inspired those who began child labor laws in many countries, and disease vaccination programs for polio in the Amazon River Basin.

Harvard's founders put the word *Veritas* (Truth) on their shield. This Truth was neither an abstract concept nor a social construct of those in power. The founders understood that Veritas is a Person. He is the Life Giver. The life of the party. The Author who enters the Play. He is a revolution of tenderness for the least, the last, and the lost. For all of humble heart. For sinners like me.

His is a brilliant mind that could cut to the heart of the scholars. He is one who taught from simple things of earth: seeds, birds, water. One who willingly died for us, exchanging his wholeness for our brokenness. He is the Truth who defeated death by rising from it. He is the Word who finally became flesh.

Today, Veritas is no longer equivalent to Jesus Christ at Harvard. In fact, his name has been deleted from the motto. When Billy Graham asked our former president, "What is the biggest problem among college students?" the president answered, "Emptiness." In fact, in the past five years we know of ten suicides, one after murdering her roommate. Two seniors embezzled one hundred thousand dollars raised by their dorm for children with cancer. And the *Harvard Gazette* proudly reports that "secularism is taught in every classroom."

Though many good deeds are also done here, students have begun to question the secular spirit of the age. They have begun to rethink the "century of despair" following Nietzsche's pronouncement that God is dead. Last year the Christian fellowship T-shirt read, "Nietzsche is dead." It was signed, "God." I believe that there is a new hunger for a new century.

THE BOOK

Much of our story is found in the epilogue and throughout the book *Finding God at Harvard*.[1] When I arrived there in 1987, as I have already said, I met no Christians at the Divinity School, which is a very lonely place for Christians. However, I began to meet believers in otherwise isolated pockets of the university, or as one person said, the "multiversity connected only by a central heating system."

I met Christians in astrophysics and philosophy and business, believers in the math and botany and law and public health departments, and on and on. And God began to knit us together as a community as the idea of university—unity in diversity—took hold once again. Allow me to read a short section from our book to describe this.

For the first time since coming to Harvard, I felt joy. The reach of this gospel amazed me. Musicians, physicists, historians, architects, and athletes sharing the goodness of God in friendship, the life of the mind. Life. We discussed our research. We considered our vocation as our calling from God. The place, as Frederick Buechner said, where our deep joy meets the world's deep hunger. Like many retreats to come, this was the time for hours of beach soccer and ultimate frisbee, Bible study, laughter, prayer, and the confluence of old and (for me) new friends. The retreat marked a turn of seasons. Woodsmoke-scented cool air. Autumn leaves changed the season of the observers, though we sensed the promise of spring. Just as ours was a time out of time to prepare for a world which, we believed, would soon become alive to us.

This was my introduction to an iconoclastic subset of graduate students out of Harvard's ten thousand who seemed more interested in making a life than in making a living. They are attracted to Jesus because Jesus knows that our danger is not in too much life, but in too little. They come from many countries to integrate great ideas with life and service. Truth for the art of life. They are people, as Charles Malik says, "of being."

This community is orchestrated by God via a servant-leader with IVCF named Jeff Barneson. Jeff kindly invited me to work with him, and I became like a cyclist drafting off his rear wheel and energy. Our graduate Christian fellowship became a kind of symphony where different sounds come together in beauty and harmony and coherence.

To use yet another metaphor, the fellowship is an extended family that is counter-culturally more invested in service than in power. We began to find ways to be together, such as worshiping in the middle of Harvard Yard on Easter. God was gathering coals for a fire.

Mission trips and community service in North America and Latin America provided opportunities to build small businesses, reform prisons, and construct churches and schools and medical clinics. So we've had ten summers during which God was enlarging our hearts for the poor, helping us to see our own poverty apart from him, and expanding our imagination for service. In various ways we began asking the Holy Spirit how to be the body of Christ in the world. How to be his eyes, his feet, his hands. Some are even asking how to become poor with the poor.

As well as regular Bible studies, mission trips, ski trips, and rock climbing, we have raised internal discussions about the use of fetal tissue in biology labs and about the disappearance of endowments and gifts intended for students wanting to grow in faith. We have hosted conferences on racial reconciliation and on the dynamic role of the church for human rights in Eastern Europe and South Africa.

So we have seen God build a community centered in worship, service, and the project (now a book), *Finding God at Harvard*. Often people stare at this book in disbelief and ask, "Can I find that in any fiction section?" I'll just say that this book is not theory, but testimony.

In the book, we wanted to go beyond the genre of critique and analysis to actual witness in the middle of a hard place. We wanted to break through the insecurity and sterile academic language, which is the mode of expression within the secular academy in general, and actually to learn to speak in honest human language. James Houston says we need to become postintellectuals—that is, real human beings being saved by grace, who can speak the language of the mission field but are not limited to it.

So this was a seven-year project, a sort of coming together, and very much a coming out of the closet, if you will, of alumni and professors and students. I'll just give you a few examples.

Many of you know Nicholas Woltersdorff from Calvin and now at Yale in philosophy. He writes not merely a modern abstract essay on theology and the problem of evil but of his own personal crisis of faith—he writes of the unimaginable loss of his son in the mountains of Austria. He speaks of a God who suffers along with us. And if Truth is a Person, then we need such personal accounts of him, rather than rarified essays on theodicy.

Or there is the story by Glenn Loury, an economist and ethicist, who wrote very bravely to say that while teaching ethics at the Kennedy School at Harvard, he was addicted to drugs, committing adultery, and repeating to himself that "life has no meaning, life has no meaning." Again, this was while he was teaching ethics to graduate students, many of whom would soon go on to Washington to influence our country. And then someone shared the gospel with him. He shared how Jesus came that we would have life and have it abundantly, and that when the Son sets us free, we are free indeed. The story ends with Glenn Loury's account of being born again.

There is the story of Robert Coles, who won a Pulitzer Prize for his work on children in crisis. It is the story of a self-important Harvard M.D./Ph.D. who went to New Orleans in the early 1960s and encountered a mob of adults waiting on a corner outside an elementary school. "Oh, this is interesting," he thought. The mob was protesting and ranting and raving, and he decided to stop and see what was happening.

They were waiting for a little six-year-old African-American girl named Ruby Bridges. Perhaps you have seen Norman Rockwell's painting of her being escorted to school by federal marshals (the local police were on the side of the mob). Ruby was among the first to be racially integrated into the all-white school system in New Orleans. As a response, the other parents took their children out of the school for the entire year; but Ruby's parents both worked two jobs cleaning for white folks, so she was the only child in the school for an entire academic year. Just Ruby and her teacher. And the mob, every morning and every afternoon, was there to greet Ruby as she walked to and from school.

Being a good academician, Robert Coles said, "Hey, I bet I could get a grant to study this little girl." And so he did, from the American Psychiatric Association, to see how she would respond to this persecution. And he couldn't understand why she seemed to be sleeping well and to be quite sane given the circumstances.

One morning he watched her approach the school. He saw her stop, in her little white dress and with bows in her hair, and talk to this mob of people, which she had never done before. When she came into the classroom, Robert Coles said, and I'll paraphrase, "Ruby, I noticed that you were talking to those folks today."

Ruby said, "No, sir. I've never spoken with them."

And he said, "Well, I'm sure I saw you speaking with them just now."

She said, "No. Well, maybe it was that I was late today, and I usually say my prayers for them before I come to school, but today I was a little late, so when I heard them I just stopped then, and I just wanted to talk to God about them today."

"Well, Ruby, you're saying that you pray for these people?"

"Yes, sir. Every day and every night with my parents and on Sunday in church."

"Now, Ruby, why should you be praying for them?"

"Well, sir, I guess I think maybe they need praying for, don't you?"

"Yes, Ruby. You've got me there. . . ." he said, and he went on with this psychiatric interview. Finally he said, "Ruby, what do you say when you pray for these big white people?"

And she said, "Well, my minister told me that when Jesus was here they gave him a lot of trouble. They used to call him names, kind of like what they call me, and they used to say they were going to kill him, kind of like what they say to me, and that, well, before they did actually kill him, he said some things back to God. So that's what I say too."

"What's that, Ruby?"

"I say 'Father, forgive them, because they don't know what they're doing.' I say it every morning and every night and on Sundays. Except today I was late, and so I forgot until I remembered. That's all I was doing."

Well, this was a six-year-old girl who couldn't read or write her name yet, nor could her parents, but they had whole chapters of Isaiah and Proverbs and the Psalms memorized. These are the world's finest people—meek, to use a biblical word—teaching a self-important Harvard M.D./Ph.D. on his way to getting a Pulitzer Prize about grace and about dignity, about forgiveness that breaks the cycle of evil in the world.

Robert Coles said, "You know, at Harvard I got straight A's on all my moral philosophy exams, but I never knew the name of the woman who cleaned my dorm room for four years." So he learned a lot from Ruby about the art of life and about the extraordinary grace and dignity of what look to be very ordinary people.

Last, I'll mention the story of Harold Berman, who taught at Harvard Law School for thirty-seven years and is now at Emory. He wrote somewhat of an academic essay on the nature of Judeo-Christian versus pagan scholarship for the book. I thanked him and explained that, more than theory, this was a personal book about our own journeys and faith. I asked, "Could you add something of your own story to this?" And he said, "Well, let me think about it." A few weeks later I received this addition in the mail:

> In my own case, the truth that set me free first appeared to me at the outbreak of World War II when I was 21 years old. [He is Jewish.] I was in Europe where I had been studying European history for a year. While I was in Germany Hitler announced on the radio that Germany had invaded Poland. It was literally the outbreak of the World War, and many of us fled for France. I thought that Hitler's invasion of Poland would lead to the total destruction of human civilization. I felt as one would feel today if all the major powers were to become involved in a full-scale nuclear war.
>
> I was shattered, in total despair. There, alone on that train, Jesus Christ appeared to me in a vision. His face reminded me of one of the Russian icons that I would later see, heavily scarred and tragic. Not suffering, but bearing the marks of having suffered. I suddenly realized that I was not entitled to such despair, that it was not I, but another, God Himself, who bore the burden of human destiny and that it was rather for me to believe in Him even though human history was at an end.
>
> When the train arrived in Paris that morning, I walked straight to the Notre Dame Cathedral and I prayed a personal prayer to God for the first time in my life. My wife, who is Protestant, asks me how I could have become a believer in Christ without having read the Gospels. My answer is that that is how the first disciples became believers. Truth is a person. And so this experience of amazing grace not only made me a Christian believer against my will and against my heritage, but also freed me from that pride and illusion of intellect which is the besetting sin of academic scholarship.

KELLY MONROE

THE VERITAS FORUM

In 1992, three years into the writing of this book, we gathered the writers and tried a sort of live version of the book called the "Harvard Veritas Forum" at the law school. The idea was to create a space, a forum, where every question could be asked about the possibility of truth in relation to Jesus Christ, reviving the original idea of *Veritas* as a Person in whom all of life coheres and is endowed with meaning.

We expected a hundred people, and seven hundred people came. The ethos of the forum was not a defense of Christianity but an exploration of life in relation to Jesus. The Veritas Forum as it has developed is not combative but is rather a sort of coming alongside of the students' questions, most of which are no longer allowed in their classrooms, by the way (which is also why Christian colleges and universities are much more liberal in the best sense). There are questions like the occasional, "Why do my socks disappear, and where do they go?" and, "Why does the parking patrol always find my car?" (which you'll understand if you come to visit us in Cambridge) as well as questions like, What are our origins? What is it to be human? Do faith and science conflict? What about chaos and entropy and evolution? How can I trust that the Bible is accurate?

"How can human love last?" Beneath that question is a broken heart, and if truth isn't a Person whose nature is love, then there is no answer for that question, and then there's no hope for our society or for our own hearts.

"If God is love, why do I suffer?" "Why is Christian faith based on a blood sacrifice? That seems so primitive!" "Aren't all religions equal?" (To that last question, the speaker answered, "Yes, except in matters of creation, human worth, God's love and power, caring for the poor, hope, happiness, and human destiny of heaven and hell.") And then there is maybe my favorite question, "Why does beauty mean something?"

Writers can answer from their own struggles and discoveries rather than with theoretical and abstract answers. And then the skeptics and others come along with something to contribute, perhaps a good question. They feel welcome; this is a place of hospitality, a space where the word *hospital* is for healing, for dialogue—a place where we feel like we all need each other in this journey together.

To me, what's intriguing about this is not that it's something new. I think the church has always been asking questions about truth. This is what you all are doing all the time, so I feel a little silly telling you what you probably already know. But it's countercultural for us in academia.

What is intriguing about the Veritas Forum is the apologetic of community and the unity and beauty of truth in relation to Jesus. In other words, there might be a thousand people at the Veritas Forum looking at a panel of these writers on stage—fourteen or fifteen of them in a conversation with this large group in which any question is fair game. And students and faculty are scratching their heads and thinking, "There's an astrophysicist, a philosopher, an historian; there's a mother of four, a grandmother, a painter—why do they all agree with each other? How often do three Harvard people ever agree with each other about anything? That's not how you publish a dissertation or gain tenure. You say something new, whether or not it's true.

"And yet why do all of these agree with each other on the very basic nature of reality? And why do they seem to love each other and students? Why do they seem joyful even though they suffer? Why do they sing together?"

Again, we want to fan into flames not the multiversity, but the university, which reunites disciplines and cultures and generations. We want to see the gospel as the only fabric of real integrity and the starting point for the living of life.

Whether in Bible studies, in the book *Finding God at Harvard,* or in person at the Veritas Forum, this symphonic apologetic is intriguing and constructive. It is simply the extended family of Christ shining together in love and in the brilliance of Jesus. Like a symphony, a theme emerges as we are together. We begin to see a unity to Truth, the beauty of Truth, within the diversity of cultures, disciplines, and generations.

Madeleine L'Engle said, "Rather than arguing about why Christianity is superior to other world religions, I'd rather put forth a light that is so lovely that all in its presence would be drawn to it." This is what we hope the Veritas Forum and the Christian presence on every campus can be to freshly inspire every generation of students.

These are real people with real hunger, questions, and suffering, found by a real God. The great adventure now is to love him with our hands and feet, with our whole hearts, souls, strength, and minds.

As I travel I see a hunger in students everywhere. I see minds that want to be awake. I hear a holy inkling when at an Indigo Girls concert there is an eruption of cheers each time they sing the lyrics, "I will not be a pawn to the prince of darkness any longer."

By God's grace, and with sense of humor, the Veritas Forum has indigenously emerged in more than fifty universities involving approximately one hundred thousand students at schools including Stanford, Cal Berkeley, Cal

KELLY MONROE

Santa Barbara, Michigan, Virginia, Florida, New Hampshire, Texas A & M, Yale, and Princeton. I now am privileged to be a part of the Veritas Forum as it emerges at other universities. I don't think it's a new idea but a new name and a new kindness of God to do this one more time. And it's just like him to be faithful to every generation in various ways.

Looking back, I have to ask myself, "How do we burn brightly without burning out?" These have been very trying years for me, as for many of you. In the past year God has shown me that I was not living enough in his ecology. I was not drawing from the vine and often became exhausted. I was brokenhearted for failing to love a dear friend well enough in daily and concrete ways. I was consistently humbled.

I have fewer answers than I did several years ago. What I do know is that it is not enough to tell the truth. The Truth became flesh and dwelt among us. Let's not convert him back to only words again. He now, first and foremost, wants to live within us as his new and better temples. Words or no words.

I ask myself, Am I striving to live for Christ? Or am I dead, and Christ is living in me? Do I imitate him only out of my limited strength, or have I invited his Spirit to indwell and enthuse me as his new and better temple?

When Jesus gave up his spirit on the cross, at that moment the curtain of the temple tore in two (Matt. 27:51). Why? Perhaps only in part so that we could enter the holy of holies by way of a better priest. And maybe also the Holy Spirit was itching to bust out of there all along. Maybe he was sick and tired of a cold, stone temple and wanted a better home, finally clean by the blood of the lamb.

Perhaps this is why Paul says to the believers in Ephesus, "Did you believe only with your minds, or did the Holy Spirit get inside of you?" (Acts 19:1, *The Message*). Likewise, Paul later writes to the same church:

> For this reason I kneel before the Father . . . that out of his glorious riches
> he may strengthen you with power through his Spirit in your inner being, so
> that Christ may dwell in your hearts through faith. And I pray that you . . . may
> have power, together with all the saints, to grasp how wide and long and high
> and deep is the love of Christ. . . . Now to him who is able to do immeasurably
> more than all we could ask or imagine, according to his power that is at work
> within us, to him be glory in the church and in Christ Jesus throughout all
> generations, for ever and ever! Amen. (Eph. 3:14–21)

And so we sing, "Lord prepare me to be a sanctuary, pure and holy, tried and true. With thanksgiving, I'll be a living sanctuary for you."

Through the pain of mistakes and exhaustion, God is renewing my life and my hope for new life everywhere. Today our privilege, and our constant challenge, whether we're in a postmodern or a traditional culture, is to revive the knowledge of truth as a Person—as the Life Giver, as the relentless Lover—and to nurture a community that is filled with him.

We need him, and we need each other as we learn to abide in grace and Truth—the person of Jesus Christ. We keep our eyes fixed on Christ. We remain in him as our first love—and we will remain a light that is so lovely that others will be drawn into his warmth, his beauty, and his truth that raises the dead to new life because only his love is stronger than death. *Vitam Mortuis Reddo*. Even now.

I will end by quoting from the epilogue of *Finding God at Harvard*.

> In my search for God at Harvard I expected to find something new. Something beyond Jesus. But instead, I have found more of him. I have begun to see how the pure light of God's truth refracts and falls in every direction with color and grace. I found the memory of this truth in the color of crimson, in the ivory yard gates, and in the symbols on the college seal. I began to see him in the work and eyes of fellow students, in rare books, in a friend's chemistry lab, in recent astrophysical abstracts, and in the lives and legacies of founders and alumni who, whether living or beyond this life, would befriend and teach us. . . .
>
> I have only about three notes to contribute, but I join in. We sing while hanging drywall with Habitat for Humanity in Boston and while ski-hiking Tuckerman Ravine. We sing while quilting in Cambridge and while building a school for kids with polio in the rain forest of Peru. We sing while riding low in the back of a dusty pickup truck across war-torn El Salvador. We sing at the weddings and funerals of friends. The Lord is our song, and so we sing.
>
> With the eyes to see we find a great cloud of witnesses to which we all belong. We sing with them, warmed by the knowing that all manner of things shall be well one day. We remember the prophet Jeremiah, to whom the Lord said, "Do not say that 'I am only a youth.' Be not afraid, for I am with you to deliver you." And so we find courage in ages past, the age to come, and this age which, by grace alone, is ours. (Monroe, 1996, 359–60)

References

Monroe, Kelly. 1996. *Finding God at Harvard*. Grand Rapids: Zondervan.

CHAPTER 21

MINISTERING IN THE POSTMODERN ACADEMY

Walter L. Bradley

As our culture has moved from a modern to a postmodern view of truth and life, it has become necessary to adjust our approach to reaching out to non-Christians. Otherwise, we will be providing answers to questions that the average non-Christian does not have. In Jim Engel's classic book *What's Gone Wrong with the Harvest* (1975), he says that evangelism should not be thought of as simply sharing the gospel. For persons who already believe there is a God and are aware of their sinfulness and separation from God, the good news of God's love and forgiveness in Christ is the appropriate evangelistic activity. However, for the modern or postmodern person who doubts the existence of God or the idea that objective truth about God is available from God in history, the presentation of the gospel will fall on deaf ears, or worse yet, will become a stumbling stone.

If we picture people on a continuum from −10, which represents atheism, to −6, which might represent an open-minded agnostic, to −1, which represents a seeker, and on to +1, a new believer, and +5 as a person at some stage of discipleship and spiritual maturity, then effective evangelistic activities (for −10 to −1) and effective discipleship activities (for +1 to +10) will depend on where the person is on this continuum. To effectively reach out to people in our sphere of influence, we must get to know them sufficiently well that we may determine where they are along the belief continuum and then reach out to them in a way that is appropriate.

The planned and unplanned opportunities described in this paper are appropriate for people who are classical atheists or agnostics, or who are postmodernists who believe all religious truth is subjective and personal. This includes about 80 percent of all faculty and at least 50 percent of all students at Texas A&M University.

UNPLANNED OPPORTUNITIES TO MINISTER
TO THE POSTMODERN ACADEMY

When I was appointed head of the mechanical engineering department of sixty-five professors in 1989, I began to have the opportunity for much more personal interaction with faculty in our department who worked in divisions other than my own. A faculty member named Clay asked for an appointment with me to discuss his request for a one- to two-year leave of absence, and I suggested that we have lunch at the faculty club. He explained that Gail had finished her degree in veterinary medicine and had gotten a job at the zoo in Portland, Oregon, and he wanted to go with her. As we visited, I asked him about his and Gail's relationship, how long they had been married, and if they had any children. He responded with some discomfort that he and Gail were not married but had lived together for six years. While this was known to some people in the department, he had apparently not wanted to share it with me, anticipating my disapproval since he knew I was an evangelical Christian. How would you have responded to such an opportunity?

I thought a response indicating my Christian disapproval not only would be not very helpful to Clay but would reinforce his stereotype about evangelical Christians and his desire to keep a safe distance from them. Instead, I responded by telling Clay that I could understand how a person who did not believe in a God of revelation who had given specific guidance about how we should live our lives would find such an arrangement to be perfectly sensible. I indicated that society today seemed to affirm such alternative lifestyles. I went on to share that if indeed the Bible was the Word of God, then such an arrangement would prove to be unsatisfactory in the long run, however satisfactory it seemed to be in the short run. He seemed relieved by my response and immediately asked me to tell him more about why I thought the Bible was the Word of God and therefore should be used as a moral compass to get through life. We spent the rest of our lunch hour discussing this fundamental question, which was much more fruitful than arguing about whether he should or should not live with Gail out of wedlock. Until our friends accept the authority of Scripture, the primary questions to be discussed have to be those of God's existence and transcendence.

Clay subsequently read C. S. Lewis's *Mere Christianity* (1943), and we had some very fruitful discussions. About a year after moving to Oregon, Gail, who unbeknownst to Clay was a bisexual lesbian, left him for a female lover. It was for this reason that she had been reluctant to marry Clay. My lunchtime prophecy was, unfortunately, all too accurate.

WALTER L. BRADLEY

A second example of an unplanned opportunity to minister in the post-modern academy is of a colleague, a Hindu from India, who invited me to attend a presentation by a well-known Indian swami. My first reaction was to decline, thinking that I would not be interested or edified by listening to an Indian swami. However, it dawned on me that if I hoped to get others to come to my activities, I needed to reciprocate. If I wanted others to pursue truth honestly, I also had to be willing to be open to the ideas of others—not to accept them uncritically, but at least to listen with an open mind. I attended the lecture (probably as the only non-Hindu present) and was surprised to hear a message very much in the vein of the power of positive thinking, without giving a relationship with God any prominence in the presentation. On my invitation, I wrote a short note indicating how much I appreciated the invitation, that I found the message interesting, but that I was surprised that it was practical, psychological advice with very little spiritual content. My friend responded by indicating that he totally agreed and asked if we could have a lunch together to discuss this further. Subsequently, I had the opportunity to have lunch with him and another Hindu faculty member from our department, during which time I shared very clearly why I thought that a personal relationship with God was much more crucial to human happiness than the power of positive thinking. It was a very special opportunity that I would never have had if I had not gone to listen to a program my Hindu colleague helped to sponsor. This experience has persuaded me that one of my best opportunities is to respond positively to the invitations of my non-Christian friends to attend their programs and then give them my critique.

A third example of an unplanned opportunity to deal with postmodernism came during a panel discussion at a Veritas Forum program at Arizona State University. The evening panel discussion was meant to bring together non-Christian and Christian scientists to discuss the relationship between Christianity and science. A non-Christian physicist on the panel began by claiming that there was absolutely no relationship between science and religion, since science was based on empirical observations and Christianity was based entirely on blind faith. His claim was basically that science produced Truth that was objective and empirically validated (or modern), while Christianity was based on truth that was subjective and personal (or postmodern). These were, in his mind, mutually exclusive types of truth. He further argued that scientific theories could be overturned by new observations but that faith-based beliefs were never tested and rejected. He was quite surprised when I replied that I would reject my Christian beliefs if compelling evidence became available that it was indeed not true. I added that even the apostle Paul said that if the resurrection had not actually occurred, then Christians were to be the most pitied of all men because they had believed a lie. I concluded by adding that the only valid reason to believe in Christianity is that it is true. If there was not good evidence for the existence of God and the deity of Christ that could be further confirmed by subjective personal experience, then I would not be a Christian. He seemed truly astonished that I and the other two Christian scientists on the panel were rejecting his simplistic stereotype of Christian faith being based on blind faith.

A fourth example of an unplanned opportunity to minister to people whose thinking is clearly postmodern came in December of 1997, when the churches in our community united to offer the videotape *Jesus* to our community as a Christmas present. These were distributed door-to-door by people from the participating churches. Much to our surprise, there was a very negative editorial in our local paper, supported by additional letters accusing the local Christian community of being insensitive to, and intolerant of, the religious beliefs of others in the community, even invoking the Holocaust as the consequence of such intolerance by Christians.

I wrote a letter of response in which I quoted John Stewart Mill's classic essay on tolerance. I noted that tolerance was not the uncritical acceptance of all points of view as equally valid (postmodernism), but rather the practice of forbearance toward others with different beliefs and the engagement in civil discussion of our differences with the shared purpose of the pursuit of truth. The editorial had seemed to want all discussion of differences to cease, with everyone accepting all religious beliefs as equally valid and with the tag of intolerance being used to bludgeon everyone into acquiescence.

If we pay attention, we will find many such opportunities to minister to people whose postmodern way of thinking has clearly blinded them to the pursuit of all truth, especially religious truth. If we do not respond clearly and forcefully to these attacks by the cultural elite and others, we will soon be completely marginalized, and the Christian truth-claims will be ignored as irrelevant rather than judged on their merits.

PLANNED OPPORTUNITIES TO MINISTER
TO THE POSTMODERN ACADEMY

In this section I want to share several approaches that I use each year to provide a forum for meaningful dialogue that addresses universal questions about life, meaning, and relationships with God and each other. The discussion/dessert series has been very effective in providing such a forum for faculty and graduate students, while the "Friday Night at the Movies" has been an effective forum for undergraduate students. Veritas Forums and lunchtime discussion groups built around stimulating books are alternative venues for students or faculty.

DISCUSSION/DESSERT SERIES

The discussion/dessert series idea originated with Search Ministries in the early 1970s. Originally designed to provide a beginning point for dialogue with professional people who often had serious questions and stereotypical views of Christianity and Christians, it has proven to be very successful for a general audience as well as for the campus community, especially faculty and graduate students.

A group of five or six singles or couples agree to cohost the discussion/dessert series for one night each week for four consecutive weeks. Formal invitations are printed (computer-generated ones are fine, but the format is formal), and each host single or couple invites at least five friends who would have some worldview other than Christianity. The invitation indicates that the four evenings will consist of open-ended discussions of issues related to God and life, with illustrative questions such as, "If God is all loving and all powerful, why do bad things happen to good people?" printed in the invitation. These are distributed in person rather than mailed and usually provide an opportunity for invited persons to raise questions or concerns they might have as they consider coming.

The discussion begins with finger food and informal visiting from 7:30 to 8:00 P.M. to provide a buffer for late arrivals and to give the guests and hosts a chance to get better acquainted before the formal discussion begins. The discussion monitor calls the discussion to order at 8:00 P.M., explaining that an alarm clock is being set for 8:59, at which time the formal discussion will end and the dessert buffet provided by the hosts will be available. He or she then asks what question the group would like to use to launch the discussion. One of the guests suggests a question of interest, and the open-ended, freewheeling discussion begins. The goal of the discussion is to have a free exchange of ideas, to get different points of view on the table, and to stimulate the thinking of all the people present. It is important that it not degenerate into a debate with winners or losers, which would dampen the spirit of true inquiry and search for truth that is essential for the series to be a success. When the alarm goes off at 8:59, the discussion is usually at some very interesting point, and the discussion monitor must insist over the objections of the participants that formal discussion is finished for the evening but informal discussion over dessert is certainly permissible and desirable. Needless to say, the formal discussion is just a catalyst to many small informal discussions, which often continue until midnight. With a host group of six couples, we usually average about thirty to forty people per night.

The beauty of this program is that it breaks down entirely the social taboos that prevent us from discussing the most important issues of life, keeping conversation on politics, sports, shopping, or other superficial but safe topics. Once the ice is broken, such discussions naturally come up not only at the discussion/dessert programs but also at work or in the neighborhood with guests who have attended the series. It stimulates interest in this much higher level of communication and personal interaction, and it establishes dialogue between the people who share this discussion/dessert series together.

FRIDAY NIGHT AT THE MOVIES

We have found that movies are an interesting and enjoyable way to stimulate a discussion of the bigger questions of life, the so-called universals. Undergraduate students might not function so easily in a discussion/dessert series because they have not given as much thought to the more fundamental philosophical and spiritual questions of life. However, a movie that clearly frames such questions can provide the needed catalyst for a very lively discussion. Movies that we have found to be very useful include *Crimes and Misdemeanors* by Woody Allen (1991), *Citizen Kane* by Orson Wells (1940, and recently voted the best movie of all time), *Out of Africa* (1986), and *Chariots of Fire* (1983). It is not necessary that the movie selected give Christian answers; it must only frame some very important question in a clear and stimulating way. For example, *Crimes and Misdemeanors* addresses the question of whether it is possible to have moral structure to the universe if there is not a God. *Citizen Kane* is very much like the book of Ecclesiastes, considering whether happiness can be found in success, power, and material wealth alone.

When we have such programs for students, we normally invite them over for pizza and sodas. We ask three questions, show the movie, and then return to the three questions to begin our discussion. The three questions we typically use are:

1. What important question does this movie raise?
2. What answer to this question does the movie give?
3. Do you agree or disagree with this answer? Why or why not?

The discussion often moves from the question raised by the movie to other important questions about life. The discussion usually lasts for at least one hour after the movie and provides a unique opportunity for students to take off their masks and talk about the fundamental issues of life, meaning, and purpose.

WALTER L. BRADLEY

For the modern college student, the problem of postmodernism is compounded with the preoccupation with trivia. These carefully selected movies quickly get our discussions beyond trivia and get the students thinking about the fundamental truths on which, whether or not they are aware of it, they will build their lives.

VERITAS FORUMS AND LUNCHTIME DISCUSSION GROUPS

The Veritas Forums[1] are programs with outstanding speakers who address issues of truth in the academy from a Christian perspective. These programs provide a special opportunity for faculty and students to invite their friends and colleagues to stimulating lectures intended to provoke people to reconsider their ideas about truth, particularly the truth-claims of the Christian faith. I have found that such special programs are useful to catalyze ongoing conversations with friends and colleagues, both students and faculty.

To continue these discussions after the most recent Veritas Forum held at Texas A&M University in the fall of 1997, I invited five faculty friends to a lunchtime discussion around the book *The Journey* by Peter Kreeft (1996). This book addresses in a very clever and entertaining way the various philosophical objections to belief in objective truth. I gave each person a copy of the book, and invited them to read the first chapter, "To Journey or Not to Journey," and then decide whether to join our lunchtime discussion for four weeks. All but one agreed, with the group growing to eight when my guests invited their friends. It took closer to ten weeks to go through the book at the pace my group went, but it is better to ask for a short commitment initially. After finishing this book, the group decided they wanted a quick overview of the truth-claims of the various world religions, which we obtained from www.leaderu.com. We also discussed Mortimer Adler's book *Truth in Religion* (1990), which considers which if any of the major world religions might be objectively true. We read separately Kelly Monroe's book *Finding God at Harvard* (1995) to balance the objective, cognitive approach we had been taking with some personal experiences, which are important to validate the Christian truth-claims even if they are weak as stand-alone arguments. This naturally led us to the critical question of who Jesus was, and we are now doing a study of the gospel of John to address that question. It has been a very interesting journey.

SUMMARY

My experiences have persuaded me that it is indeed possible to have meaningful encounters and dialogues with postmodern college students and faculty members. I need to be prayerfully sensitive to unplanned opportunities that arise and creative in the planned activities I use to provide a comfortable platform on which to engage my postmodern friends. These can lead to some wonderful ongoing discussions with people through which my life and theirs are enriched. Hopefully, these discussions will help them find the ultimate truth in a relationship with Jesus Christ, who is the way, the truth, and the life.

References

Adler, Mortimer J. 1990. *Truth in Religion*. New York: Macmillan.
Engel, Jim. 1975. *What's Gone Wrong with the Harvest?* Grand Rapids: Zondervan.
Kreeft, Peter. 1996. *The Journey*. Downers Grove, Ill.: InterVarsity Press.
Lewis, C. S. 1943. *Mere Christianity*. New York: Macmillan.
Monroe, Kelly, ed. 1995. *Finding God at Harvard*. Grand Rapids: Zondervan.

CHAPTER 22

EXAMPLES OF EFFECTIVE EVANGELISM

Andrea Buczynski

I heard a story recently that captures much of what I've observed about taking the gospel to university students. A student named Ryan was sitting in his dorm room at the University of Northern Colorado one morning, when a staff member with Campus Crusade for Christ stopped by and completed an evangelistic survey, followed by a *Four Laws* presentation. By many of our standards, that is considered a successful appointment. However, we found out later that when the staff guy left the room, Ryan promptly tossed *The Four Spiritual Laws* into the wastebasket with a shrug of his shoulders.

A few minutes later Mark, from down the hall, walked in. Seeing the booklet in the wastebasket, he said, "What's this doin' in here?"

Ryan replied. "Oh, some guy came by to talk to me about God, and well, you know, I pitched it."

"Well, at least let me have the booklet," Mark responded. "I really believe this stuff, and you should start thinking about it."

That started a long conversation, which ended with Ryan's deciding to join his friend at one of our meetings that evening.

The campus director at Northern Colorado remembers talking to him that night: "I was doing a talk on the glory of God. Ryan listened intently, and at the end of the time he came up to me and said, 'You know, I really got a lot out of your talk.'"

A few days later Ryan was walking aimlessly through a grocery store when he felt a tap on his shoulder. He turned to see the grocery clerk, who said to him, "Can I help you? Are you lost?" With a stunned look on his face, he shot back, "Lost? Lost? How did you know I was lost?" It was just a couple of days later that he knelt down in the center of the student union and gave his life to Christ.

Ryan's story illustrates several things we've been observing on campus. First, many students don't know much of the Bible, and it seems irrelevant to them. They don't understand God as personal or sin as real. It doesn't affect them. Although many have genuine spiritual hunger, they are unaware of the claims Christ made about himself or what a relationship with him would mean to them. Second, logical reasoning doesn't provide adequate answers to the questions they are asking. A presentation by itself doesn't connect the relevancy of the gospel to their lives. When they can talk with peers and hear how God is working in others' lives, the truth takes on fresh meaning. It becomes relevant. When they come into a meeting and see believers worshiping, extending love and grace to one another, and hearing the truth taught, they see the reality of the gospel and experience it in a different and more believable way. Third, students without relational connections to a group of believers have a harder time getting into a discipleship process. When students are exposed to the gospel in a group setting, they are developing friends in a whole new context. Their attraction to the life of the body of Christ is motivation to return, and they get continued exposure to the gospel. When a student does come to Christ in that context, he already has friends who can help him in the discipleship process. Creating opportunities that link the truths of the Bible with students' lives, that meet them where they are, and that allow for the best possible follow-up has become a challenge.

These are just a few observations being made by Christian workers on college campuses across the country. They compel us to ask questions about how we can effectively bring the gospel to students. We're looking at effectiveness in three ways: getting the gospel out to the largest possible audience, seeing students trust Christ, and involving new believers in the discipleship process.

Not all students are philosophically postmodern; however, most are culturally postmodern. There is a greater level of biblical illiteracy among students now than there was a decade or two ago. Because of that, we are asking ourselves how we can provide lost students with multiple exposures to the gospel—both to its content and to its reality in the lives of believers. If there is a tremendous respect for another's experience and if the apologetic for this age is the reality of Christ in the life of the believer, then how can we expose more people to that real life? There seems to be a greater need for dialogue; discussion is a prerequisite for learning. If this is so, how can we include more interaction in our evangelistic settings?

As we have considered many of these questions, we have realized the need to innovate and adapt our methods in order to be effective. I would like to be clear that innovation is simply the means to accomplish the end of effectively communicating the gospel. In some places in the country, a more traditional approach works. One can still sit down with a student, share the Four Spiritual Laws, and see the student trust Christ. In other parts of the country, a more common response would be like Ryan's. Yet over and over again, we see the spiritual hunger of students and their responsiveness to the gospel once it is understood.

Innovation resulting in increased evangelistic effectiveness across the country has been in six areas: multiple exposures campus-wide; multiple exposures in small groups; interactive group experiences; presenting both sides of the story; the power of testimony; and training strategy.

MULTIPLE EXPOSURES CAMPUS-WIDE

"Every Student's Choice" is a media campaign designed to raise awareness of biblical issues and the gospel message. Students hear many messages about how to live while they're on campus, and we would like the biblical perspective to be part of that stream. The campaign covers eight topics: relationships, sex, alcohol, the resurrection of Christ, the birth of Christ, comparative religions, homosexuality (there is another way out), and racism.

At West Virginia University the comparative religion campaign "Do All Roads Lead to God?" created a furor on the campus. For two months, letters to the editor of the school paper kept in front of students the idea that Christ is the only way to God and created many opportunities for Christian students. Not only did they have to take a stand before their peers, but they also had many great opportunities to explain the "hope that was within them." Different versions of this idea have been tried in other places. A couple of staff members have written their own columns in the school newspaper. Bruce McCluggage at Boise State and Andy Wineman at Colorado School of Mines have each attempted to prod the thinking of students by regularly presenting Christian viewpoints on different topics. At one of the Ivy League schools, student leaders have published their own ads on the topic of their choice and signed them. At West Chester State University in Pennsylvania, staff and students produced a newspaper twice a year, filled with helpful information for the start of the semester as well as with articles related to student issues and testimonies.

Another means of exposing a greater portion of the campus to Christ has been Freshmen Survival Kits. Each kit includes a New Testament from the American Bible Society, a video testimony of a student who is living with AIDS, Josh McDowell's book *More Than a Carpenter* (1994), a CD from Christian artists, and other items. When a freshman receives the kit, she has the gospel in four different formats in her hands. We ask for an opportunity to discuss and get feedback at a later time. Another plus to the kit is that the exposure is not limited to a single point in time. It's not uncommon to hear the music from the CD bouncing off the dorm walls or for students to pick up the Bible later in the year when life gets a little difficult. A more limited version of this idea has been book distributions: McDowell's *More Than a Carpenter* (1994), *Mere Christianity* (1952) and *The Screwtape Letters* (1970) by C. S. Lewis,[1] and *Finding God at Harvard* (1995), edited by Kelly Monroe.

Typically every Campus Crusade for Christ group has some sort of weekly meeting. This has become another avenue for exposing students to the gospel. Over the years the most common setting for these meetings has been a classroom with the chairs arranged theater-style. Until a few years ago, that worked. But remember that "interaction" has become an increasingly high value for this generation. A classroom just doesn't seem to cut it. One student said to her campus director, "Who would want to come here? I have chemistry here at 8:00 in the morning. I don't really want to be here at 8:00 at night with that as a reminder." In the meantime, a church had given the local Campus Crusade ministry the use of an old building, in reality just a big empty hall. She suggested, "We've been having our socials there. Why don't we just do our meeting there?" They filled the place with small tables and chairs, painted the walls dark blue, and created more of a coffeehouse atmosphere. That change was one of the things that enabled the students to invite their friends. It was a cool place to come and hang out. It was the same music and biblical teaching, but the environment had become very important.

The need for a more relational setting has become apparent, but at the same time, the need for truth to be proclaimed and to be taught well is equally important. At Baylor, using a similar coffeehouse type setting, the CCC staff taught through the gospel of Mark this year. Despite a straightforward approach to the truth, roughly 10 percent of their audience every week are skeptical nonbelievers who keep coming because they do feel loved. Students are responding to people who extend love and grace to them and who are authentic in their beliefs.

MULTIPLE EXPOSURES: SMALL GROUPS

Three new ideas have surfaced using small groups. The first is evangelistic dinner parties. At Princeton students invited their friends to have dinner once a week for five weeks. During and after dinner they would discuss different topics related to the gospel: the big picture of the Bible; the historicity of the Scriptures; the problem of evolution; the life, death, and resurrection of Christ; and Jesus as the only way to God. During these weeks, the person who brought them followed up with the guest students. Books and other resources were made available to the guests.

The second idea is focus groups, pulling together a group of non-Christians to hear what their beliefs are on a set of basic questions. At the end of the time, the hosts share their biblical viewpoint and invite the guests to participate in an investigative Bible study.

The third idea has been using a more open discipleship structure based on the cell-group concept. Students are great at bringing their friends with them wherever they go. This flexibility in the group system allows students to invite friends to something on a regular basis. Content is geared to the group as a whole, but newcomers are always welcome.

Interactive Group Experiences

The participation of the hearers really enhances whatever topic is being presented. For people to process truth and understand it, they have to be involved. I've often seen students not able to understand something until they sit and talk about it themselves. This participation can be facilitated in a variety of ways: discussing the topic with others, being physically involved, or using a question-and-answer format, allowing the audience to determine the flow of the time. At the University of Alabama, sororities and fraternities have gotten together to discuss views on relationships, using a "Life Skills" Bible study. The topic catches their interest, the discussion gets them thinking, and the study gives them practical answers that help make the truth relevant. The gospel is presented in follow-up conversations.

Both Sides of the Story

With access to students becoming tighter on most campuses, presenting multiple points of view gives an opportunity to draw students with many different viewpoints. One of the most effective outreaches has been the debate with Dr. William Lane Craig and a number of atheist professors. Because both points of view are represented, roughly twice as many people come. An interesting twist on a debate format was recently tried at Baylor. They presented the debate, but then they had a discussion group afterward. The several hundred people attending were broken down into small groups to interact on a set of questions. The moderator encouraged those interested in the topic to check out a web site for more information.

A couple of students at Indiana University produced a play based on *Between Heaven and Hell* by Peter Kreeft (1982). They presented dialogue between John F. Kennedy, Aldous Huxley, and C. S. Lewis, who all died the same day but had different beliefs about the afterlife. It was well received on campus and was presented in philosophy classes as well.

THE POWER OF TESTIMONY

This generation, being more visual and participatory, responds very well to stories. One of the students who has had a significant ministry across the country has been a twenty-one-year-old former student named Steve Sawyer, a hemophiliac who contracted AIDS through a transfusion when he was young. When his health began to suffer a few years ago, he decided he didn't really need a degree to do what he wanted to do with his life—tell people about Christ. In the past several years over 17,000 students have heard his story, and more than 3,000 have indicated decisions for Christ. When he speaks about living with a terminal illness without bitterness, the joy of Christ on his face and his sincere love for those who don't know Christ are winsome. Students want what he has. They want to be able to survive life with that kind of joy. And while not many of them are sitting there with AIDS, many of them are sitting there with some kind of pain that they are facing. They want to have the same kind of hope that Steve has found in Christ.

We've seen it with other students in a variety of settings. Students won't question someone else's experience. With that in mind, some of our staff are looking at ways of combining testimony with some transition questions at the end to get the other person's point of view.

TRAINING STRATEGY

One of our concerns in training students in evangelism is to develop people who are both willing and able to connect with the lost. For students who have recently come to Christ, this is usually not a problem. However, many who came to Christ as children are ill at ease relating to non-Christian students. For them, both the motivation and the skills of evangelism have to be acquired.

A few things are evident. Until students have tried to share Christ, they aren't especially open to specific training. Giving them that experience is critical to helping them discover where they are uncomfortable. Because they are uncomfortable initiating, their understanding and internalization of God's heart for the lost is critical to seeing them step out in faith. Listening skills help them respond to the unbelieving student. Servant-type evangelism (doing small tasks like emptying wastebaskets or handing out cookies or drinks during exam study times) exposes them to the reality of being lost and builds compassion in their hearts. Beyond that, they still need the basics of communicating the gospel clearly.

Despite some of the challenges that a postmodern culture presents on campus, students are hungry for the real thing. When they see it, they recognize it and want it. All across the country, students have been coming to the Lord in increasing numbers every year. We're creating a climate for learning about how to reach out to people in this culture, but we haven't really yet established the means for sharing what we're learning with each other.

We know that it will take the entire body of Christ working together to reach every student. We have a lot of questions: How can we share what we're learning about being effective? How can we build a network to help each other out? Who are the people with resources or tools with similar heart to reach the campus? What is the balance between formal, campus-wide outreach that produces filtered contacts and sharing Christ with friends? How will we continue to gain access to a changing audience?

The bottom line is that we want to see students like Ryan come to Christ. This past year Ryan met a guy on his floor who had never been to church and was looking for spiritual answers. Ryan led this student to Christ and brought him to the meeting. Afterward, this young man said that what he heard confirmed the decision he had made. Because God is all about drawing people to himself, we continue to be very hopeful and thankful for what the Lord is doing in the midst of some shifts in our culture.

References

Kreeft, Peter. 1982. *Between Heaven and Hell*. Downer's Grove, Ill.: InterVarsity Press.

Lewis, C. S. 1952. *Mere Christianity*. London: Fontana.

_____. 1970. *The Screwtape Letters*. New York: Macmillan.

McDowell, Josh. 1994. *More Than a Carpenter*. Wheaton, Ill.: Tyndale House.

Monroe, Kelly, ed. 1995. *Finding God at Harvard: Spiritual Journeys of Thinking Christians*. Grand Rapids: Zondervan.

CHAPTER 23

GENERATING HOPE

A Strategy for Reaching the Postmodern Generation

Jimmy Long

Although I've been involved in campus ministry for twenty years, I originally entered seminary planning to become a pastor. While I was at seminary, I asked numerous pastors about their vision for their churches. I asked them what prevented them from accomplishing their vision. Frequently they answered that they didn't have enough strong lay leaders in their churches. So I saw God encouraging me to go into a ministry like InterVarsity to raise up leaders for the church. For twenty years I saw myself as a coach of a baseball farm system team. We prepared people for a lifetime of ministry.[1]

I see my next ten to twenty years in ministry a little differently. My goal will be to continue to strengthen the church but in a different manner. As I see the postmodern societal shifts influence students, and as I work as an elder in my local church, my focus is changing. Instead of preparing these young adults to enter into churches, I see my role as preparing the church to receive these postmodern young people. The process of the church receiving these folks includes welcoming them, meeting them where they are, understanding who they are, leading them into the fellowship, helping them to grow, and eventually giving the leadership of the church to them. This is a mighty task before us. I think it's a task God desires for us to be involved in for the next twenty years.

I started this journey about ten years ago at Christmastime when I was getting ready to give a talk to a group of students. Although I'm not very good at small talk, I casually asked the person sitting next to me if she was going home for Christmas. I'd not met Joan before, and I later learned that she was not a Christian. Since it was two weeks before Christmas, I thought this was an easy question. I expected her to say yes or share her travel plans if she was not going home, but instead she burst into tears. At that moment I was introduced as the speaker and had to proceed to the lectern and begin my talk. I didn't have a chance to talk to her, and I felt bad about it during my whole talk. I don't remember anything I said, but after it was over I went over to her and said, "Joan, I obviously touched a nerve that I did not mean to touch." She answered that it was okay and then went on to say, "I don't know where my home is. You see, ten years ago when I was ten years old my parents got a divorce, and now each of my parents has been divorced again. So where is my home?"

Joan's story caused me to begin to think through the changing culture and ask how God wants us to change our ministry to be able to make an impact on it. So I began to grapple with some of these ideas. One of the things that came across my path fairly quickly was a cartoon that I think typifies a lot of people in a postmodern world. The cartoon shows a young person obviously in the first week—or maybe, because his room is so neat, the first day—of dorm life. He really wants to fit into the campus world, so he is laboring over the decision of which shirt to wear. The logo on one shirt says "Just Do It" and on the other, "Just Say No." The caption reads, "Some days it took hours to get dressed." This confusion is an example of the things we are struggling with. Students are confused, people who are postmodern are confused, and we who are ministering among them are confused. How do we make sense of what's going on?

When I went to college at Florida State in the late 1960s, I went with the idea that I wanted to be a meteorologist. I wanted to be one of those wild people who flew into hurricanes to help tame them. I stayed in meteorology for two or three years until I hit differential equations, and though I was passing the class, I didn't enjoy it at all. I still have a love for meteorology, and my family will attest to my tendency to immerse myself in the details of the daily weather report.

I'm convinced now that I'm as much in the midst of a hurricane in ministry as I would literally have been if I had continued in the career track of meteorology. Let me try to describe what I think is happening in society today by using a hurricane analogy. In a hurricane there are two wind patterns. There is the wind pattern around the hurricane that is semicircular. These winds of one hundred plus miles an hour are the ones that we think about the most because they are the ones that cause the most damage. Typically tornadoes come out of this pattern as well as the feeder bands of rain. The second wind pattern is the steering mechanism of the hurricane.

A couple of years ago Hurricane Fran hit the coast of North Carolina. I had just put my wife on a plane to Florida to visit her relatives. I reassured her that the brewing storm was not going to hit us because we were in the middle of the state and away from the coast and the forecasted hurricane path. My daughter and I watched the news coverage as Hurricane Fran hit the coast. We were familiar with the place it was hitting and wondered what the damage would be there. We went to bed confident that the storm would follow the coastline north and then out to sea. About one o'clock in the morning my daughter woke me and suggested that we move downstairs. I asked why and then realized I was hearing strong winds blasting our house. The hurricane was coming our way. Instead of following the coast, the storm had come straight across the state toward Raleigh, Chapel Hill, and Durham. It hit us very hard. We had not considered that the second wind pattern, the steering mechanism of the hurricane, would change so dramatically. The steering mechanism takes the hurricane where it's going next. It's actually the most important part of the storm to study, but we don't think about it a lot because of the impact of the feeder bands and the winds right around the eye. The steering mechanism is what I want to use to describe what is going on today in our culture.

From 1988 to about 1993 I began to ponder how this new generation, Generation X, was affecting how we ministered. I wondered about the differences between my generation, the Baby Boomers, and Generation X. As I wrestled with this generational transition, I began to realize that something in the explanation was missing. We were spending too much time studying the transition from the Baby Boomer Generation to Generation X. We spent so much time studying this transition because it was all around us like the feeder band wind pattern of a hurricane. I saw some of the changes affecting my generation as well as the next generation. I saw that some of the changes were not just generational but societal. I began to realize that we were in the midst of a greater transition than simply a generational transition. It was a transition from the Enlightenment (or more lately called modernism) to postmodernism. If we didn't understand the interplay between the two and eventually didn't concentrate on postmodernism and the interplay with the postmodern culture, then we were going to miss out on the most important transition. The transition to postmodernism is like the steering current wind pattern of a hurricane. It is steering society into a major new paradigm.

What we see in postmodernism is a major change. It's probably the sixth or seventh major change since the time of Christ. David Bosch, a South African theologian who died very suddenly about seven years ago, wrote a book called *Transforming Mission* (1991). In this book he identifies different societal paradigm shifts since the time of Christ and the influence each of these shifts had on ministry and especially missions in each of those arenas. He called this last paradigm shift ecumenism. Today most of us would call it postmodernism. As we look at history, we can identify transitional changes that have lasted for two or three hundred years. As God's people we need to see these changes as unique opportunities. This transition into postmodern culture is one of those unique opportunities for ministry.

One of my favorite books of the Bible is Habakkuk. One reason I enjoy the book is that it is a dialogue between Habakkuk and God. I'm not an emotional person, and I grew up in a family that is not emotional. This book helped me understand that it is okay to share my emotions with God. Habakkuk is also a book that helps us understand a significant transitional time in the history of Israel. Before this time the Israelites thought Jerusalem, and especially the temple, could never be destroyed. Habakkuk realizes that this destruction of the temple is going to happen. He cries out to God. He asks God how he can allow injustice to happen in Israel. In verse five of chapter one, God comes back to Habakkuk and says, "You would not believe, even if you were told [what I am going to do]." He then describes how he is going to use the Babylonians. He doesn't even tell Habakkuk that they are going into captivity and all that is going to happen there. I don't think Habakkuk could have dealt with that much change.

Some of us will have difficult times dealing with what God is going to be doing in our own culture in the coming years. However, we need to try to understand what God is doing. I'm convinced that as in Habakkuk's time, God is giving us doors of opportunity for the gospel. I want to concentrate less on postmodernism as a philosophical movement and more on postmodern culture. I think God has given us, in this transition from the Enlightenment to postmodernism, some doors of opportunity for the gospel to be preached and lived out and for people to come to know Jesus. Let me share some of these ideas.

TRENDS IN THE SHIFT TO POSTMODERNISM

If somebody gives you a definition of postmodern, by definition it is not a definition of postmodern. It's a *modern* definition of postmodern, because postmodernists would say that postmodern can't be defined. They are probably right. I would like to describe three trends in this shift from the Enlightenment to postmodernism.

One trend is a shift of focus *from the autonomous self to tribalism*. This transition into tribalism or community involves people needing other people. In the 1950s and 60s when I was growing up, except perhaps in the hippie movement, people were more concerned about themselves and had little desire or need for community. Those of us who grew up with television in the

1960s remember that the most watched show for the longest time was the last episode of the series *The Fugitive*—one person against the world, trying to solve life by himself. When I was a student at Florida State, my favorite song was Art Garfunkel's "I Am a Rock, I Am an Island." The song did not have great spiritual insight, but it reflected how I felt. I was by myself. In contrast to that time, people today gravitate toward other people.

We see the evidence of this gravitation on television. In the show *Friends,* the most copied television show of the 1990s, the six characters in the show have become a community for one another. Even some of the lyrics of the theme song illustrate this community or tribalism:

> So no one told you life was going to be this way.
> Your job's a joke, you're broke, your life's DOA. . . .
> I'll be there for you like I've been there before.
> I'll be there for you cause you're there for me too.

Both the theme song and the show reflect a sense of community or of coming together.

For Christians, people desiring to come together in community is primarily good because God has created us to relate not just to ourselves and to him, but to relate to him and to each other. He created us to live in community. This renewed desire for community is one of the doors of opportunity for the gospel to be proclaimed and lived out. We will look at implications for ministry a little later.

A second attribute of postmodern culture is the movement *from basing decisions on truth to basing them on preferences.* On the surface this looks bad for Christians because we're committed to truth. But the truth of the late Enlightenment was never God's truth. People lived like there was a dome around the world. There was no intervention from above, no transcendence, so all the world and truth had to be described by what could be seen and observed. At least in postmodernism this pattern is breaking down. There is transcendence, there is discussion about spirituality, and many people are basing their lives on spirituality. We are all aware that there are tons of weird stuff out there. But at least there is an openness to spiritual ideas and experiences, something that was not as evident during the late Enlightenment. People are more open to listening to Christians talking about God because they are more open to spiritual influences in their lives.

The final characteristic of postmodern culture is a movement *from belief in human progress to hopelessness.* In the Enlightenment, when people were committed to human progress, they mistakenly saw the world as continually getting better. They saw little or no need for God. In postmodern culture, however, there is a pervasive sense of despair. People are crying out for help and are hoping that there is more to life than what they are presently experiencing.

These are the doors of opportunity for the gospel. In the movement to community or tribalism we see people searching to live as they were created to live, in community. In the movement into preferences, we are players in the game again because we can talk to people about spiritual things and they don't ignore us. In the movement from a sense of human progress to a sense of hopelessness we see a third door of opportunity, the opportunity to provide God's hope.

How do we do ministry in this context? First we need to be people who come with the message of hope.

THE MESSAGE OF HOPE

One of the things I'm convinced of is that as we preach and teach and disciple, we need to emphasize hope. People are searching for hope today and cannot find it. We are looking for it all over the place. I find it interesting to see the impact the movie *Titanic* has had within society. A recent cartoon shows a line of people getting ready to see *Titanic*. The older couple in the front of the line says, "I hear the scenes of the ship sinking are spectacular." The younger people behind them exclaim, "The ship sinks? Thanks for ruining it for us!"

Like the two boys in the cartoon, we are all looking for hope today. People in this first postmodern generation have seen their dreams and heroes die. Whether it's Princess Di or Kurt Cobain, all their heroes are dead. An author for *Rolling Stone* described Kurt Cobain as a savior of this generation, but he wasn't Jesus and he couldn't save the generation. The author went on to say, "There is no Mommy and Daddy, no great Savior coming down to walk us through the millennium. There is no Savior."

A number of years ago Arthur Levine wrote a book called *When Dreams and Heroes Died* (1980) about how the heroes for this generation have all died. He used the *Titanic* as an example because he said this coming generation is a generation that is on the *Titanic*. They know the ending, but they want to go first class on the journey. Like people on the *Titanic*, their hopes are dashed. We Christians know the ending of the movie *Titanic* and we know the ending of the world. We need to be people who give others that message of hope.

We need to be people who speak more and more from Revelation 21 and 22; we need to give a sense of what God is doing and will do. We need to give people hope in the midst of their present pain and suffering.

About seventeen years ago the InterVarsity Christian Fellowship student group had a massive outreach at UNC-Chapel Hill. We brought Billy Graham in for a week and had over thirty thousand people, including fourteen thousand college students, come to hear him. The title of the outreach was *Reason to Live*. If we were going to do the outreach now in the late twentieth or the early twenty-first century, we would need to change the title. We would call it *An Offer of Hope*. The speaker would use some of the same passages of Scripture but would offer a message of eternal hope to a people that have no hope.

THE METHOD: A LOVING COMMUNITY

If the message is one of hope, what is the method of proclaiming the message? I think the method is the context of community. One of my InterVarsity staff friends who works with graduate students describes a loving community this way: "The greatest apologetic for Christianity is not a well-reasoned argument but a wildly loving community. Our Lord did not say they will know us by our truths, as important as that is; truth is very important, but they will know us by our love." So the starting point as we minister in a postmodern culture is the message of hope, and the method to proclaim the message is a loving community.

People are searching for a place to belong. A few years ago my son, who enjoys listening to rock music, told me about a song from a group that most of you may not have heard, *Soul Asylum*. Their song, I think, typifies what people are looking for today. It expresses the theme of looking for a place to belong: "I want to live with you in the fifth dimension in a dream I've never had; but because I just can't live like this in a world like this I just want to kiss goodbye. . . . I am so homesick, but oh, that's not so bad because I'm homesick for the home I never had."

A loving Christian community is the beginning context of an effective ministry in a postmodern culture. Joan, the person I mentioned earlier, stayed involved in the InterVarsity group on campus and was brought into the community. Her small group was her community. This small group loved her and cared for her. They began to help her open up and share herself with others. They talked about Jesus and how Jesus could meet her. They helped her see her sin and rebellion against Jesus and to understand the need for the cross of

Christ in her life. By the end of the year she became a Christian and started sharing and being involved in this loving community.

THE MODE OF TRANSMISSION: STORY

If the community is the context for the gospel, the mode of transmission is story. Story is the starting point for narrative evangelism. We place our story in the context of God's story. When I arrived at Chicago's O'Hare Airport today, I was exhausted. I had driven a thousand miles in the last three days, setting up two camps, registering five hundred students, and speaking a couple of times before I left to fly out here to Trinity Evangelical Divinity School. I was picked up in a limousine because of my role here as a speaker. (I was glad it wasn't a real limousine, because that would have been embarrassing.) But it was a nice car with a driver whom I will call Jane. Although I was tired, I began asking Jane a few questions, and in the twenty-minute drive from O'Hare to Trinity, I listened to her life story.

Jane told me that she is twenty-five, is engaged to be married, and has a six-year-old son. She is estranged from her family. Her father is both a workaholic and an alcoholic. He never showed emotion. She had an okay relationship with her mom, but her mom was rather flighty and really wasn't available for her. Her mom wanted to be her friend and not her mother. For a long time the daughter liked that, but then she realized that she needed a mom. She needed some guidance. Neither of her parents ever said they loved her, so she basically didn't connect emotionally with her family. She got involved in a relationship that didn't go well. She became pregnant and had a child. Now six years later she's engaged to be married to somebody who is thirty-five and has his own ten-year-old child. She is determined to marry only once.

When Jane dropped me off, she thanked me for hearing her story. She said that she had driven two other groups of people to the conference and when she got to the point where she mentioned having a six-year-old child but not being married, the conversation kind of dropped.

If we are going to work within a postmodern culture, we can't be shocked by stories like this. This is a fairly mild story compared to some of the things you're facing within your church or with the people around your church, or that we're facing on the college campus. We need to be people who will listen and allow people to share their stories. Then we need to help them place their story into the larger context of God's story. One of my prayers is that Jane drives me back to the airport tomorrow. And if she does, I think now I have the right to be able to share God's story with her as we head back to the airport. I might not get a chance to do that, but somebody else will along the way in her life. Because I listened to her story, someone will be able to share with her how her story fits into the larger gospel message.

I have a professor friend at UNC-Chapel Hill who is not a Christian. We've developed a good friendship. For about four years in a row I was invited to come in and dialogue with him and his students on the authority of Scripture. By the fourth year our dialogue was not having the same impact it had in previous years. The next fall he called and said he had a movie he wanted me to see. He wanted the entire class to watch it, and then he and I would dialogue in class about it. The movie was called *Jesus of Montreal*. I actually had seen it about six months before. It is not a Christian movie. We showed it to the class, and my professor friend and I had a dialogue about how the life the lead character portrayed in the movie paralleled the story of Jesus in the Bible. We looked at both the movie story and the Jesus of the Bible. In our dialogue we eventually reached the same point that we had in past classes where I had presented a more classical debate on the authority of Scripture. However, the result was more powerful for students because we are in a different culture today. The students could easily dialogue about the historical Jesus by first starting with the portrayed story of Jesus in the movie. My conversations with students afterward were far more fruitful. In the end we did talk about truth, we just did not start there—we started with story. Since students today do not believe in truth—they only believe in preferences—we get to the truth through story.

We need to live the truth out in our own lives, our own story. As I talk to Christian college students, I remind them that one of the hard things now is that you can't just talk the talk—you've got to walk the walk. On campus or in the community, people will look at your life—not just how you refrain from doing things, but what you *do,* especially in terms of caring for people. So in our churches, in our work at IBM, in our Mother's Morning Out programs, or in factories at break time, we need as Christians to be people who are modeling the truth in our lives. I call this living out the gospel "embodied apologetics." As we live out the gospel, people start seeing that we are different. Our lives and our story intrigue them. They become more open to sharing their story with us. Then we have the right to share God's story with them.

Although I think people still can become Christians through large evangelistic meetings, I think fewer people will. Although I think people still can become Christians in a setting where the gospel is shared with them one time, I think fewer people will. For more people, becoming a Christian is going to be a longer process. The good news is that if we do it right, these people will be Christians for life because they are making a radical change, not just a one-minute decision for some type of after-life insurance policy.

THE MANDATE: THE GREAT COMMANDMENT

If the method is a loving community and the mode of transmitting the gospel is the story, what is the mandate? For the longest time we have used the Great Commission as our mandate for being a witness to the gospel of Jesus Christ. However, I think in a postmodern culture the Great Commandment, not the Great Commission, should be our mandate. Although we end up at the same place, we start at a different place. We witness because God first loved us. Our response to his love is to love God and love our neighbor. God calls us to be a people of love, to care for others. We will still be discipling and teaching, but embodied apologetics says we start with a community and we start with a mandate of love. I can assure you that for people who are postmodern, the Great Commandment can initially be a more compelling mandate than the Great Commission.

For Christians who struggle with the whole area of tolerance, the Great Commandment is a challenge. In this era of tolerance we find it difficult to talk about Jesus to our neighbor in our apartment complex or the person who sits by us in our job or in the classroom. We have been duped by society and by Satan to view tolerance as a high value today. Instead of being a high value, I would say that tolerance, as currently defined, is a very low value. We need to get over the tolerance wall that prevents us from being witnesses for Christ. A number of years ago G. K. Chesterton said, "Tolerance is a virtue of the man or person without convictions."

"I'll tolerate everything" is very postmodern. I prefer this, you prefer that, that's okay. In a recent book, Don Posterski, a vice president for World Vision of Canada, said that "rather than taking people seriously, tolerance treats people superficially. Instead of conveying [that] who you are and what you believe is to be valued, tolerance says I will endure you. I will tolerate you is just another way of saying I will put up with you. In doing so the [implied] message is I will not take you seriously" (Posterski, 1995, 138).

In his book *The Future of the Church,* Douglas John Hall writes, "Tolerance too easily reflects a decision to simply look past people allowing them to have their beliefs. It may be good enough legally and politically for the pluralistic society but it is not good enough for the one who did not say tolerate your neighbor but love your neighbor" (1989, 57). As we think about being witnesses in a postmodern culture, we've got to come to grips with tolerance. We need to help people see that tolerance is a very low value compared with the high value of love. The type of love that God calls us to be involved with is tough love.

What Jane the limousine driver needed from her mom wasn't to be a good friend; she needed love from her mom. But the love that she needed from her mom was a love that is really a deep love, a tough love that helps her to see right and wrong. We have a fifty-pound dog named Missy whom we love dearly. Missy still has a very independent nature—partly because we have a large back yard and we allow her to roam at will. But when we take her on a walk, I use a choke collar. So if Missy moves into the traffic, I just pull her back. Is that a harsh thing I'm doing to her? Yes, in one way it is, but it is a loving thing I'm doing to her. When we talk about love, it is not an ooey gooey feeling of allowing people to do what they want, but it is a deep love as a parent loves a child, as a leader loves parishioners, as we love our friends. Part of what defines a good community is that the people care deeply for one another and spend time together.

The most crucial way to live out love within the church or campus ministry is through formal and informal small group communities. I was part of a group of people within the InterVarsity staff team in 1981 who wrote a book called *Small Group Leaders Handbook*. The book described the four components of a small group—nurture, worship, community, and outreach. In 1995 I led the team that wrote *The Small Group Leaders Handbook, The Next Generation*. What we learned during the fourteen intervening years is that small group components are not equal. In the 1990s and beyond, to be an effective small group, the central component is biblical community. We also learned that effective small groups aren't things you do for an hour and fifteen minutes. If they are really going to be effective, they become like a family. This means that how we place people in small groups, whether it is in campus ministry or a church context, is very important. Presently we are struggling with how to put people together in small groups who already have some relationship with each other so they can continue that relationship. We are trying to decide how to encourage these small groups to continue beyond a one-year commitment. We are also learning how to leave the small groups open as an extended community to bring other people into the community.

If we are going to minister within a postmodern context both to people who are Christians and to those who are not, we need to provide community, an intimate place for people to be cared for. In many cases a small group or a social event is the entry level into the church or into a campus group.

JIMMY LONG

For somebody who is postmodern to become a Christian isn't primarily an intellectual ascent; it's a leaving, a divorce from their previous community. One of the Campus Crusade staff at UNC-Chapel Hill was recently sharing with me about his relationship with a person involved in an anti-Christian group on campus. The person he had been befriending finally came to an understanding of what prevented him from becoming a Christian. It was not an intellectual stumbling block but an emotional one. If he were to become a Christian, the hardest thing would be for him to leave his community.

How do we help non-Christians in this dilemma? First, we, along with other Christians in our Christian community, need to enter into their community. We need to get to know not only the person we are witnessing to but also other people in that community. We also need to bring them into our Christian community. Slowly, over time, we get to know them and they get to know us. They begin to see that although they may be leaving one community, they are going to a better community. It's a lot like the leaving and cleaving of marriage. So for a postmodern person what is most critical is not a change of intellectual thought but a change of community. It's a change of allegiance—not just to Jesus, but to a group of people—and it's going to take longer to happen.

One of the things we are doing in InterVarsity is changing our purpose statement. A key expression in our new purpose statement is "witnessing communities." Traditionally when you think about witness, you think about outreach; when you think about community, you think inward. We think of witness as something you do—you proclaim something—and community as something you relate to. But in a postmodern culture if we are going to be effective ministers and witnesses we need to become a witnessing community.

Communities not only are for Christians but also are entry points for non-Christians. Our witness should flow from the life of the community. Part of our witness is to show people the gospel lived out among God's people. The book of Acts is a word picture of a witnessing community. Jesus says in Acts 1:8, "You will be my witnesses." He does not give us a choice. However, Luke spends chapters 2 through 6 talking about the community, the witnessing community. In Acts 2:47 he says that "they enjoy[ed] the favor of all the people. And the Lord added to their number daily those who were being saved." It was from the community that witness took place.

Part of our witness is bringing people into community. How does this happen? I want to leave you with something that is in process. I describe it as a journey.

THE POSTMODERN CONVERSION PROCESS

Some of us have been wrestling with what a postmodern conversion process looks like. Let me share with you some preliminary observations. First of all, people start out with a discontentment of life. There is confusion over meaning and longing for relationships. I am very thankful that 90 percent of people who live in a postmodern culture are already there. They are discontented with life even though they might have a great job. They are confused over meaning because of preferences. They are longing for relationships because God has created them for community even though they do not realize it.

Next they have contact with Christians. We enter into their community, and they enter into our community. Then they become converted to the community. They start coming to our church or to small groups at our church or to our campus groups, and we are excited about that. They may even start experiencing God in worship as part of the worshiping community. However, what will happen (if we aren't careful) is that they will be converted only to the community. They will graduate and/or move someplace else and will be converted to another community that may not have anything to do with Christ.

The Baby Boomer generation was first converted intellectually. We intellectually knew that Jesus was Savior and Lord, but a lot of times we never got to the heart or the emotions of it. This generation most likely will become Christians initially through the heart or just become converted to the Christian community. However, we need to make sure they are converted not only to the community but to the King of the community, Jesus Christ. And that's where biblical revelation needs to be coming through all of the time. It can be done in a preaching context, and it can be done in an individual or small group context, but it needs to be done. Then, as people grow in commitment to Christ and are contributors to the community in the body of Christ, they become part of the witnessing community.

I would like to conclude by sharing with you the conclusion from my book *Generating Hope: A Strategy for Reaching the Postmodern Generation*: "Many Christians see this postmodern generation as a hopeless cause. But I think that the opportunity for revival is greater today than it has been in the last forty years. . . . As we approach the 21st century this postmodern generation is struggling to survive the confusing changes that surround them. They feel hopeless. Are we ready to offer them God's hope? . . . God is calling us to be a people of hope who offer this gospel of hope to a generation without hope" (1997, 211).

References

Bosch, David. 1991. *Transforming Mission*. Maryknoll, N.Y.: Orbis.

Hall, Douglas John. 1989. *The Future of the Church: Where Are We Headed?* Toronoto: United Church Publishing House.

Levine, Arthur. 1980. *When Dreams and Heroes Died*. San Francisco: Jossey-Bass.

Long, Jimmy. 1997. *Generating Hope: A Strategy for Reaching the Postmodern Generation*. Downers Grove, Ill.: InterVarsity Press.

Posterski, Don. 1995. *Ture to You: Living Our Faith in a Multi-Minded World*. Winfield, B.C.: Wood Lake Books.

CHAPTER 24

WILLIAM CAREY REVISITED

Going after Every College Student

Mike Tilley

William Carey is known as the father of modern missions. But when he talked about the Great Commission in 1786, ministers in England replied by saying, "Sit down, young man. If God wanted to reach the heathen, he could do it without you." In response, Carey wrote a treatise called *An Enquiry into the Obligations of Christians to Use Means for the Conversion of the Heathens*. It was William Carey who later said, "Expect great things from God; attempt great things for God."

As we face the task of evangelizing postmoderns in our day, we can take two lessons from William Carey. First, he believed that the church needed to bring the gospel to every person. Second, he was not a fatalist—he believed that God uses means to accomplish the spread of the gospel.

As I discuss the topic of going after every college student, I speak not only to those who are in college ministry but to all who have a vast scope of responsibility and few resources. I would like to take a case study approach and share an insider's view of an organizational process that was undertaken in light of the vision of reaching every student for Jesus Christ.

FACING REALITY

What will it take to reach every college student in the United States? I first began to face this question when I was asked to join the national team of Campus Crusade's U.S. campus ministry. In 1991 we began to face two hard realities.

First, college students had changed since the 1960s. When I got involved in Campus Crusade as a freshman at Virginia Tech in 1971, we would share our faith with five people and one would indicate a decision to trust Christ.

MIKE TILLEY

By the late 1970s we shared the gospel with twenty people to see one decision. Students had changed, and some of the classic approaches to evangelism that had worked in the 1960s did not seem as effective. We call it postmodernism today, but we felt a more hardened soil throughout the 1980s.

Second, we were only positioned to reach a small percentage of America's fourteen million college students. True, we were active on three hundred campuses in 1991, but there were over two thousand beyond our reach. Someone checked with other parachurch ministries and estimated that only 30 percent of America's students were within reach of the gospel in any given year. That left ten million students who were not hearing about Christ. This does not mean that there was no church nearby—it just means that no one had plans to reach the ten million in a language they could understand. Beyond this, we were practically sitting on the sidelines as demographic studies showed a dramatic increase in the percentage of ethnic students.

REVOLUTIONARY CHANGE

In 1991 Steve Sellers, director of Campus Crusade's campus ministry, became deeply burdened with the importance of giving every student the opportunity to hear about Jesus Christ. Many of us rolled our eyes at the thought ("Let's get real"), but Steve was convinced we should move ahead in faith. He had been paying attention to reality when it came to the decline of our ministry, and he concluded that revolutionary change was needed. While such an organizational change process involved great risk, he believed that it was riskier not to change. We were past the point of sticking our collective heads in the sand and believing our press reports.

The first step was to reorganize our U.S. campus ministry around what we called the comprehensive scope of our mission. By this we meant taking the Great Commission and Acts 1:8 seriously. Since our call was to college students, we wanted to be in a position to give every student a chance to hear. So Steve set up a "staffed campus" ministry to strengthen our classic approach of placing teams at major universities. Then new teams were formed to focus on other areas: a Catalytic team to lead U.S. expansion to two thousand new campuses; an Intercultural Resources (ICR) team to lead a contextualized ministry to ethnic students; and a Worldwide Student Network (WSN) to lead in the area of pioneering international ministries.

The next step was to undertake a far-reaching direction-setting process. We met as a national team to define our mission and core values. While such a process can at times be perfunctory, we really wanted to hold our feet to the fire on mission and values. This became our mission statement: To turn lost students into Christ-centered laborers. While the statement seems innocuous, it powerfully focused us on lost, unreached students.

When arresting the slide of an organization, it's easy to change organizational structure and words on paper, but it is far more difficult to change values. Our team adopted three core values: faith, effectiveness, and development. While our stated value was faith, we felt that too often we were merely being faithful. While our stated value was effectiveness, too often we were content with busyness. And while our stated value was development (of our staff and students), our actual value was often our happiness. Faith involved dependence on God and trusting him to work powerfully as we moved into the future. Effectiveness meant letting go of out-of-date strategies and adapting to a changing student culture, especially in the area of evangelism. Development meant nothing less than developing a new generation of leaders. In developing leaders, we wanted to give attention to issues of character and integrity along with other essential areas of spiritual leadership.

GOD DOES USE MEANS

At this point some might ask, "Why burn time and energy on organizational issues and strategy? Why not just pray?" I believe that there are always three factors at work in any Christian effort that makes a lasting, genuine impact for Christ. These three factors can be observed in any church or Christian organization, from William Carey to Willow Creek, from Young Life to Campus Crusade, from Chicago to Shanghai.

First, foundational to any biblically successful Christian movement is the work of God's Spirit. We see a beautiful picture of this work in the ever-deepening river of Ezekiel 47 bringing healing to the nations. When Jesus promised the power of the Holy Spirit in Acts 1:8, this promise was the fountainhead of the expansion of the gospel in the book of Acts. Throughout church history God has moved in the lives of individuals and nations, and God has mightily used the prayers of his people. We are rightly concerned about the challenge of evangelizing postmoderns, but think of where God is moving today. National and ethnic walls are coming down. We are seeing unprecedented partnerships in the body of Christ. Spiritual interest is increasing. In the 1997–98 school year, hundreds of students pledged their allegiance to Christ in response to the call of fellow students who had signed the Millennial Pledge. God is even sovereign in the events going on around us. As William Carey said, let us "expect great things from God."

Second, any biblically successful Christian effort involves human leadership. Think of Moses, Nehemiah, and Paul. Think of Bill Hybels, Billy Graham, and Bill Bright. There is a leadership factor in any ministry. Part of my work involves the launching of Metro Teams to reach the large numbers of college students in America's major cities. It makes a big difference to get the right Metro director. When that person has a God-given vision, a sense of ownership for the mission of reaching the city, and the character to lead, we often see the vision become reality. That's why we invest a lot of time and money in leadership development. We have a school of leadership; a clear framework of what it takes to lead; and a process for development that involves education, exposure, experience, environment, and evaluation. God burdened Nehemiah to rebuild the wall of Jerusalem and used him to mobilize the people and implement a plan to do it. Nehemiah said, "The God of heaven will give us success" (Neh. 2:20). And then he got to work.

Finally, I believe that any biblically successful work has a strategy. Too often Christians set up a false dichotomy between trusting God and strategy. But if strategy were of no consequence, we would be fatalists. We would not even have a conference on evangelizing postmoderns. We need to pray and trust God, then on Monday morning we have to wake up and have some kind of approach. We may prefer a kind of spiritualized fatalism because it insulates us from responsibility, but God wants us to use our sanctified common sense. It is right to understand a culture in order to reach it. It is right to become "all things to all men." It was right for Nehemiah to strategically place people along the wall and to implement a plan to finish the work. "Expect great things from God; attempt great things for God." Strategy gives legs to the vision.

A "CATALYTIC" MINISTRY TO GO AFTER EVERY COLLEGE STUDENT

What will it take to reach every college student? As part of Campus Crusade's change of 1991, I was asked to form a Catalytic team to focus on this issue. Our mandate was to pioneer five to seven new strategies for expansion and to give leadership to the reaching of every college student that was beyond the reach of our two hundred staffed campuses. This team would be comprised of ten regional directors, each of whom would trust God to raise up sufficient leaders to plant two hundred new campus ministries per region—two thousand across the United States.

We dreamed of an expansion effort that would be pioneering in nature. As Paul said in Romans 15:20, we wanted to go "where Christ was not known."

We dreamed of an effort that would breed innovation. Since "necessity is the mother of invention" it was clear that the magnitude of the task would require creativity and resourcefulness. It was energizing to have the freedom to dream of new strategies. Think of how God has used the *Jesus* film. What might be the next idea? Beyond pioneering and innovation, we dreamed of radical cooperation with churches and with the rest of the body of Christ. The magnitude of the task was too great for Campus Crusade—we needed a network of ministry alliances who would brainstorm around one question: What can we do together to reach every student for Jesus Christ? Finally, we dreamed of prayerful expectation. We wanted this effort to bring glory to God, and we wanted to be able to look back and say, "This is something God did." So we committed ourselves to move ahead in prayer.

As we prayed and moved ahead, we were compelled by certain powerful biblical texts. Looking at Genesis 15:1–6, we saw that Abraham's offspring would be as great as the stars of the heavens. God had a plan for salvation history, and our work was not just about the revitalization of an organization; it was about our participation in God's plan. Verses like Mark 1:38, Acts 1:8, and Romans 15:20 fueled our desire to reach every person. The book of Acts became our manual for expansion as we sought to plant new campus ministries.

New Opportunities and New Strategies for Going After Every College Student

The biblical passages cited above remind us that it is *desirable* to reach every college student. We do not need to roll our eyes at such a seemingly impossible vision. God can do it, and we must expect great things from him. But the vision is not only desirable, it is becoming feasible. Thanks to the work of God in our present day, we can seize opportunities (what some call *kairos* moments—see Col. 4:5) and formulate strategies to be effective for the glory of God. Here are some of the strategies, tied to opportunities, that are beginning to bear fruit:

1. *Student LINC:* We've discovered that near every campus, God already has the people to reach that campus for Christ. For example, any Christian college student might wish to begin a ministry on campus. That student can call 1–800–678–LINC and get help in developing a new ministry. A trained staff member can coach student leaders from ten to fifteen campuses using the telephone, e-mail, or personal visits.

2. *Metro Teams:* A team of staff going after every campus in a city can develop a citywide movement by forming a student leadership team on every

campus. We've placed teams in the top twenty cities in the United States, and we're seeing progress from Boston to Atlanta to St. Louis to Chicago to Los Angeles to Seattle. These teams are catalytic in that they partner with indigenous resources and are not staff-intensive. The Atlanta Metro ministry now has four hundred students involved from fifteen campuses.

3. *Church partnerships:* If we want to launch two thousand new campus ministries, could it be that many of those campuses have a church nearby? Why not help those churches form vital college ministries to reach every student? As trust relationships are formed, we've found that we can accomplish more together than we can apart, and God gets the glory.

4. *Broad sowing strategies:* Sometimes we call these exposure or coverage strategies. Imagine changing the climate of a campus by using thought-provoking or humorous posters or newspaper ads. Or imagine a gift bag for every freshman on campus that includes a Bible, a music CD, the book *More Than a Carpenter* by Josh McDowell, and other helpful information. Local leaders distributed 160,000 of these Freshman Survival Kits in 1997–98.

5. *High touch relationships:* The postmodern student is yearning for community, relationships, and authenticity; and that's the kind of life the Bible talks about in Acts 2:42–47. So on each campus we trust God for a transformational community where lost students are changed by the gospel, where believers are changed as they get into small groups and experience grace and truth, and where the campus and world are influenced by laborers who are sent out.

6. *Internet strategies:* Someone has said, with only a little hyperbole, "What the Roman road was to Paul, what Gutenberg's printing press was to the Reformation, the internet is to us." I used to discount the notion, but no more. I've been made a believer by godsquad.com—a web site designed to help student leaders of campus ministries. Take the student who has a Bible study on Monday night. On Monday afternoon she can download a series on Philippians and take it to Kinkos to make copies. The Godsquad web site also has a weekly e-zine, helpful articles and other resources, and all sorts of tips for effective evangelism. And as breakthroughs are made by anyone in the area of evangelism, these can be shared with everyone on the web site.

These are just some of the strategies that God is using to make it possible for us to evangelize postmoderns and to go after every college student. The amazing thing is how God goes before us and how he seems to multiply our efforts. Often we feel like the disciples when they were faced with the challenge of feeding five thousand people, but God multiplied the five loaves and two fish that they offered to Jesus. We plant, we water, but God gives the growth (1 Cor. 3:6). In the case of our efforts in Campus Crusade, we realize that God is using other ministries as allies in the same cause, as fellow workers in God's harvest.

We dream of a day when every student will have the opportunity to say yes to Jesus Christ and get involved in the body of Christ. We know that God uses our prayers, a growing army of spiritual leaders, and the creativity of his image-bearers to accomplish the task. We know that God can slay the Goliath of postmodernism and even use the changes in the student culture for a great advance of the gospel. Let us unite our hearts and our prayers and say with William Carey, "Expect great things from God; attempt great things for God."

CHAPTER 25

EVANGELIZING POSTMODERNS USING
A MISSION OUTPOST STRATEGY

Don Bartel

How do we go about launching, developing, and sustaining a gospel movement among postmoderns? That's a little bit different question than those asked about church planting or church growth or church dynamics. It's the kind of question that a missionary has to ask. How do we get the gospel out in an understandable way and see it propagate from person to person, social network to social network, and group to group?

THE SITUATION IN AMERICA TODAY: A MISSION FIELD

A George Gallup survey says that more than 44 percent of all American adults eighteen and over are unchurched; that is, they haven't gone to church in the last six months or more. That would be 78 million adults.

Kennon Callihan, who has been a church consultant for about thirty years, describes some characteristics of this unchurched culture this way. There are four elements. First, by and large persons live life as though the church does not substantially matter. Second, most people are not seeking out churches on their own initiative; that is, they are not looking to go to church. Third, the church is not among their major values. And fourth, unchurched people do not necessarily view the church as harmful or hurtful; it is simply viewed as not particularly relevant or helpful. Callihan concludes that "the day of the churched culture is over, the day of the mission field has come" (1990, 13). He is looking at a reality that is emerging in the mainstream of our culture and in our society.

One of my friends, Jack, an unbeliever who is in an investigative Bible study with me, puts it this way: "My friends wouldn't come if it's churchy, and I wouldn't come either." This is a simple reflection of where a lot of people are today. Twenty years ago Dr. Ralph Winter made this comment: "Are we in America prepared for the fact that most non-Christians yet to be won to Christ will not fit readily into the kinds of churches we now have? Present-day Americans can wait forever ... for the world to come to Christ and join them, but unless they ... go out after these people and help them found their own churches, evangelism in America will face and is already facing steadily diminishing returns" (1981, 302–3). He was saying that people are culturally far enough away that they won't be comfortable coming to where we are; we have to go to them. He was talking about planting churches that fit these kinds of people. In the nearly twenty years since then, the cultural shift has been still more rapid and radical.

A Philadelphian decided to go into farming. He moved out to the Midwest and decided he was going to raise chickens. He bought five hundred fertile eggs and went off to his property. Two weeks later he came back and bought another five hundred. The clerk said, "What are you going to do with all those chicks?" The farmer replied, "I don't have any chicks. I can't figure out if I planted them too deep or not deep enough." If we are talking about church planting in a context that requires gospel planting, it is just like that little story. It is the wrong picture for what needs to take place. We are talking about how you plant the gospel and see it remain pure and mobile in our culture.

In the book *The Power of Stories,* Leighton Ford says, "North America is now the largest mission field in the English-speaking world and the 200-million-plus 'secular' North Americans make the United States and Canada the third largest mission field in the world—after China and India. . . . In a real sense, we are back in Apostolic times. We are in a missionary situation in our own countries, just as the early church was" (1994, 43–44). In *World Evangelization* journal, Os Guinness wrote, "The three strongest national challenges to the Gospel in the modern world are Japan, Western Europe and the United States. Japan has never been won to Christ, Western Europe has been won and lost twice. Though having the strongest and wealthiest churches, America represents the clearest test case of Christian response to modernity" (1993, 8). He is referring to the cultural values we export. This was five years ago. We are now exporting the fruits of modernity, while at the same time that fruit is rotting here and turning to postmodernity.

George Hunter in his book *How to Reach Secular People* says, "Our challenge to reach the undiscipled populations of North America, Europe, and Australia will require as sophisticated a mission strategy as any mission field in the world, today or at any time in history" (1992, 25). What I want to high-

DON BARTEL

light here is that what is needed is not just working harder; it is not even working smarter. We need a mission strategy.

It has been stated that 120 million Americans have no substantial Christian memory. This probably means that they have a grandmother who prays, they know a weird coworker who reads his Bible, but they themselves have no first-hand Christian experience. They may know a few Bible stories, but what they know they got on the streets. They didn't get it from going to church.

There is, however, another side to these developments, a very positive side. Postmodernity has opened up a whole new avenue of ministry that constitutes a great opportunity. In fact, there is a spiritual awakening taking place in America today. It is just that a biblical dialogue is excluded from most of the discussion of spirituality. I can give a case in point.

One of our neighbors is a very well-educated woman who believes she is a reincarnated thirteenth-century artist and a more recently reincarnated American Indian. She takes yoga classes from a Buddhist monk. In line with reincarnation, she believes in Hinduism. She is an unpublished author and writes about the American Southwest. Her religious philosophy of choice is Indian mysticism. Nevertheless, she attends an Anglo-Catholic church because she likes tradition and structure. She likes to talk with me about the Bible. She believes it would be great if we could have a five-way dialogue with an Indian chief, a Buddhist monk, a Hindu priest, a Catholic priest, and me. As you can see, she is very eclectic in her religious outlook. Even when she talks about Christianity, she is not talking from a biblical point of view. She is typical of many around the country.

In the Northwest there is a lot of New Age spirituality, in the Southwest a lot of Indian religion, in the Southeast a lot of merely formal religion devoid of much personal meaning, and in the Northeast a lot of secularism. But many people are interested in spiritual things, and this provides a window of opportunity for us in the next few years, because they won't stay in this transition period forever. They will land on something, and once they land, it will be much more difficult to reach them.

Now how does the church fit into this? Healthy, growing, mission-minded churches typically have strong core programs for discipling, for training, for education, for youth. They typically have strong outreach programs, foster personal evangelism, sponsor outreach events, and reach people and draw them into the church. They have a strong program of supporting vocational missionaries. But there is sometimes a blind spot in their vision. They need to begin thinking about how they are going to train their lay people to become informal missionaries in their own contexts.

A LAY MISSION MOVEMENT

God is raising up many people with a passion for reaching the lost. God is mobilizing his people now to step out and become lay missionaries. Everywhere I go I find people who have this burden, this calling. But when you ask them, "How is it going?" there are five common responses.

First of all, they will say something like this: "We know how to share the Bridge to Life and the Four Spiritual Laws; we have been to Evangelism Explosion. We can give a personal testimony, and we reach some people that way, but there are a lot of people out there with whom we are just not communicating. What they are really saying is, "I need to learn to think like a missionary."

The second thing they say is, "Our time is too limited and our gifts are too narrow. We can't do this job alone. We've been taught to pray together, to worship together, to study the Bible together, but when it comes to evangelism, I feel alone." What they are saying is that they need a team of some sort working together.

Third, they commonly say, "When we are among the lost, we do not feel very prepared. When we did ministry in the context of the programs of the church, we had lots of support and encouragement, but as soon as we step outside this framework, we don't feel supported. We don't have a portable community that we can take with us in this mission field that we have chosen." What they are saying is that they need a sense of community to hold them up in the context in which they're ministering.

Fourth, they say, "It's war out there! We feel spiritually weak; we need to learn to pray more effectively; we need to have more people praying for us; we need the same kind of empowerment support that we give our vocational missionaries." They need spiritual empowerment.

And finally, they say, "There are few tools, resources, and materials to help us in this task. Most of the materials that are out there are geared for another context or they are geared for a vocational missionary level."

THE NAVIGATORS' RESPONSE: THE MISSION OUTPOST

Hearing those five common responses, several years ago the Navigators said they were going to try to respond. The outcome is the "mission outpost," which is simply a group of people who have banded together for the purpose of taking the gospel to the lost.

I want to highlight three things about a mission outpost. First, it is a group of people. It is not an individual, isolated effort. It doesn't have to be a highly trained group of people. Second, it is a group of people who have banded together to collaborate in the ministry. And third, they have come together for the purpose of taking the gospel to the lost.

What are these mission outpost teams going to do? They are going to be reaching, discipling, and equipping people in their own context. We are not going to reach people and pull them out of their natural social and relational environments, but we are going to leave them there and deliver to them all that they need for the purpose of reaching the people in their own sphere. When you pull people out of their natural spheres, they lose their ability to reach the people with whom they are already connected.

The harvest is plentiful, but the laborers are still few. The opportunity today is great compared to the number of lay people who are prepared and mobilized to respond to this need. The gap between the need and the resources is great.

Let us consider the five responses we detected among lay believers.

THINKING LIKE A MISSIONARY

What does it mean to think like a missionary? First, it means we need to understand the gap between our own world and the world of our neighbor. We who have grown up in a church environment have inadvertently imbibed a whole lot of church culture. The church culture and the mainstream of American culture have so diverged that we need to become resensitized to where mainstream America is.

Second, thinking like a missionary means developing the skills to connect with people in relevant and sensitive ways. It doesn't just happen naturally. It takes some intentionality, and there are some simple skills that can be helpful.

Third, thinking like a missionary means taking the initiative to love people. If we tell people we want them to become evangelists, a lot of people are just frozen in their tracks. But if we tell them to love and serve their neighbors, they can take initial steps and then build the bridge of trust across which the gospel can flow more naturally.

Thinking like a missionary also means being empowered by prayer to reach unbelieving friends and neighbors. This includes the prayer of the group; the prayer of the church to support them; learning to be effective in prayer, spiritual warfare, worship—all the dynamics of prayer.

What this does is put a little group of people working together in a posture of being lock-pickers in the hearts of people in America.

TEAMING WITH OTHERS

People need to be teamed together with an intentional focus. Let me tell you about one mission outpost team that I was a part of so you can get a flavor of what we mean by teaming together.

In this particular outpost there were three couples and myself, so there were seven people total. We didn't have common relationships that overlapped, so one of the things we had to do was develop a set of common relationships so that we had a common sphere in which to minister. We did that through a number of things. In the case of two of the couples, the men were twin brothers, so one obvious thing was to become involved in family dynamics. I went to birthday parties and that kind of thing. One of the couples said that they had a lot of unbelieving friends that they would like for us to get to know, so they invited their friends from five different spheres—his work, her work, his fraternity brothers, and so on. From these five groups they invited eighty people, and forty of them came. We talked about all those people and prayed for them before they came, so we had some name recognition and some understanding of each of the people who were coming.

When they walked in the door, they saw people they knew, so they initially huddled into five little groups. The host couple stayed mobile, but the other five of us split up into the five groups and just began talking and entering into natural informal conversation. If I found somebody and thought that Dave would really get along with this person, I would go get Dave out of his group, plug him in there, and I'd go where Dave was. All night we just crisscrossed among these five groups. Two things happened. First, when people were leaving, they said, "Wow, what great friends you have." They were basically referring to the five of us, because we were the most mobile there. Second, they said, "We would like to get to know them a little better." We followed up that large party with smaller dinner parties with the host couple and the people where the relational connection was, and had evenings on a much smaller scale. We did that for the purpose of building relationships for the gospel. That is just one example of teaming together. There are many others.

LIVING IN COMMUNITY

Teamwork focuses on the task. Community focuses on the nature of the relationships. This is the place where reaching postmoderns is very critical. Postmoderns need and want community. They don't know how to get it, and they are not good at it. We need to demonstrate it and live it out where they can see it, because they will find it very attractive. Our problem is that we are very individualistic as a whole culture, and entering into community is not something we do well either.

By community I mean a set of relationships where you can live out the "one anothers" in the Bible: love one another; exhort and encourage one another; and so forth. The particular group that I just referred to spent a number of months working through relational matters in the group. I remember telling my wife one night, "I'm not sure I want to go tonight; it might just be too painful." But once we had worked through the relational issues, it created a dynamic that was very attractive. Two of the men are actually closer to me in many ways than my two brothers are. Working through those relationship issues is critical.

We need to demonstrate to the broader public that what the Bible talks about really is true. Peoples' lives can be transformed; people can be changed; brokenness can be put back together; wholeness and healing can take place. We give meaning and identity to people in the context of community because they have a place to belong. These are the deeply felt needs that many people have that are not immediately addressed in a sermon or a Bible study, but a group of people that are living vibrantly together demonstrate how those needs might be met.

This type of community is a safe place. People are afraid to let down their guard, and therefore they can't get better. As my friend Jack said, "If it's churchy [his definition of not a safe place], I can't come and be myself. I'm expected to be somebody else." If you create a safe place, then first of all, people will be honest. Second, they will be transparent, which means they will go to deeper levels of intimacy and self-revelation. Finally, they will be vulnerable. They will say, "I will let you help me. I want you to help me change." When you have gotten to that point, you have gotten to a safe place. When that dynamic takes place, we will find ourselves being healed and made whole, and we will be very attractive to anyone who is sniffing around for that kind of thing. So community is one of those very critical elements in a mission outpost team that relates to postmoderns.

THE POWER OF PRAYER

I don't know that I need to say a lot about the power of prayer. I assume that we are committed to prayer. What is clear is that we need intercession. As soon as we step out into this evangelistic ministry, we will be attacked. Satan wakes up. He takes notice, and it truly is war out there.

PRACTICAL HELPS

In the Navigators we have tried to produce some practical, user-friendly tools designed so that the typical layperson can take them home and use them.

The first is *Coaching Notes for Mission Outpost Teams*. This booklet goes along with a training seminar that provides tools and exercises to help a person gather a group, secure a commitment to a common vision, work together with appropriate leadership, pray together with power, and go to the lost. All of the materials are built around adult learning principles so that they take into consideration that the people who are coming into this process have experiences that are relevant to the task at hand. It draws on the resources of the community of people, this team, to solve their own problems.

A second booklet, *Thinking Like a Missionary,* is a Bible study with guided exercises. It has five sessions. It takes a group—whether it's a Bible study group or a prayer group—and launches it into engaging with people to learn from them as a missionary would. It ends with a commitment to pray for those people by name.

The sequel to this booklet is called *Living Like a Missionary*. It's not enough to think like a missionary. We have some encumbering lifestyle issues, such as busyness, that will prevent us from being able to engage in the mission adequately if we do not give them up.

Another resource we've developed is a *Case Study Portfolio*. This tool is designed to help break through the issues that are hindering a group. This portfolio contains case studies that cover aspects of a mission outpost from start to fruitfulness. The case studies refer to real people and real situations, though we have changed the names and places so no one will know who they are. The case study describes an issue that the group is confronting and ends without describing the solution. As a group you work through the case study and come to some conclusion. This allows you to grapple with real issues in the safety of your own living room. You identify the issues, you go to the Scriptures to resolve them, and then you implement what you discover in your own context.

An enjoyable teaching tool that we have developed is the *Mission Outpost Board Game*. The pieces move around and cover four different phases—thinking like a missionary, teaming with others, living in community, and going to people. Prayer is built into each of those phases. We used this game with all of our community staff last summer. They played the game for three hours and had a great time. When it was over, they couldn't believe the three hours were gone.[1]

MISSION OUTPOST STRATEGY: ESSENTIAL ELEMENTS

The mission outpost is not a comprehensive strategy; it is only the first step. Step one in the process is to establish mission outposts that effectively

Don Bartel

reach the lost. But then we need to have a pathway that goes from where we are to the desired destination.

Step two is to build up the people of God in the context of community. The seeds of that community are planted in the mission outpost. They don't begin to grow and bear fruit until you start reaching people and they begin joining your community or forming a community of their own. The key is building people up in their own context. This kind of community has to be a healing community because the people that you are going to reach are broken people.

The third step is to train mission outpost leadership in order for the process to continue on to new networks of people.

References

Callihan, Kennon L. 1990. *Effective Church Leadership: Building on the Twelve Keys*. San Francisco: Harper and Row.

Ford, Leighton. 1994. *The Power of Stories*. Colorado Springs: NavPress.

Guinness, Os. 1993. "Reflections on Modernity: Eleven Thoughts to Ponder." *World Evangelization* 18 (December): 8.

Hunter III, George T. 1992. *How to Reach Secular People*. Nashville: Abingdon.

Winter, Ralph. 1981. "The New Macedonia: A Revolutionary New Era in Mission Begins." In *Perspectives on the World Christian Movement*, ed. Ralph Winter and Steven C. Hawthorne, 302–3. Pasadena: William Carey Library.

CHAPTER 26

THE GOSPEL FOR A NEW GENERATION

Keith A. Davy

As postmodernism's influence permeates our society, its impact on evangelism is becoming apparent. This influence is particularly noticeable in evangelistic outreach among the younger generations.

When speaking of today's young people, whether high school or college-age youth or young adults, it is important to observe that we are in a time of generational transition. Throughout the 1990s much attention was given to the study of Generation X (or the Busters). Now, as the Busters advance in age, attention is turning toward Generation Y (or the Millennials). The college campus today has a mix of both generations as they have been popularly defined and described. Generation X has moved into adulthood. However, reality is never so neatly packaged with clearly defined boundaries between successive generations. Instead, the generations are more like the waves at sea, each cresting yet flowing into one another in the troughs. At the time of this writing, it is easier to speak of the "younger generations" than to differentiate between Generations X and Y.

Those involved in evangelism among the younger generations are encountering widespread biblical ignorance. During 1998 more than eight thousand students were informally interviewed in evangelistic encounters as a part of a nationwide research project known as QuEST.[1] One question presented students with this scenario: "Your best friend comes to you and says, 'I want to become a Christian, but I don't know how.' What would you tell your friend? Assume your friend wants you to answer the question, not be sent to a priest, minister or someone else." The most common responses suggested that going to church or encouraging some religious practice was the answer to becoming a Christian. Only 14 percent of the students interviewed, including professing Christians, mentioned Jesus in their answer.

KEITH A. DAVY

These findings suggest that the majority of students today think of Christianity as a religion, not a relationship. Becoming a Christian involves adopting a religious belief or practice, but it has little to do with Jesus or a personal relationship with God. This is one example of the growing disparity between the worldview of the witness and that of his or her audience. Today's evangelist cannot assume the audience will share common understandings of key biblical concepts or the definitions of terms. It is a post-Christian audience.

Yet there is also evidence of a significant spiritual openness among today's youth. It is assumed by many that students on the whole are not interested in God. Yet in QuEST interviews, when students were asked to rate their desire to know God personally[2] on a scale of 1 to 10, 39 percent rated their desire to know God as a 10. The statistical average was a 7.8. It would be a mistake to assume that this spiritual openness translates to an openness toward the gospel or interest in Christianity, however. Often students assume that Christianity is irrelevant to their lives. After all, they say, it is merely a religious choice or lifestyle. Perhaps worse, it is an offense to their worldview, especially in matters of tolerance.

Of course, many other significant characteristics of the younger generations create the context for evangelism today, not the least of which is the pervasive influence of media and pop culture. Tolerance, pluralism, and a deeply personal or experiential basis for truth have been embraced. Worldviews are built from the smorgasbord of ideas, with choices made by preference or hunger rather than by a coherent search for truth. Together these realities underscore the challenges faced in evangelism at the beginning of a new century.

As awareness of postmodernism has grown among leaders in evangelism, all dimensions of outreach are being reexamined. There are significant issues related to *pre-evangelism,* that is, what prepares us for significant gospel interactions in this culture. Not enough has been said regarding *re-evangelism,* or the process of ongoing discussions and interactions that serve to reinforce the gospel. It is beyond the scope of this chapter to examine the breadth of these and related issues. Here we will focus on the message of the gospel and the means we use to communicate it to these generations. In addressing these issues, care must be taken to maintain our faithfulness to the gospel message while seeking relevant ways of communicating it to our audiences.

It would be presumptuous to suggest one definitive solution to the issues mentioned. No doubt there will be a wide array of answers provided in the future. Our explorations will be framed by two questions: (1) What influence should our postmodern culture have on the shape of our gospel presentation? and (2) What will effective gospel presentations look like for the younger generations?

The first question provides a framework to understand the issues. The second suggests a path that may lead us further in the search for new solutions.

WHAT INFLUENCE SHOULD OUR POSTMODERN CULTURE HAVE ON THE SHAPE OF OUR GOSPEL PRESENTATION?

Recent writings have underscored the complex relationship between the gospel and culture.[3] Careful consideration must be given to this relationship to ensure that we have a firm foundation for our gospel presentations. A clear understanding of the gospel is essential to protect the integrity of our message. A growing understanding of the culture increases the ability to adapt that message appropriately to the audience.

THE DYNAMIC CONTENT OF THE GOSPEL MESSAGE

The beginning point for our discussion must be the gospel itself. Our quest will be simplified by a clear grasp of the essence of the gospel coupled with a broad understanding of the fullness of the gospel.

By "the essence of the gospel" I am referring to that core of gospel truth, all of which is essential and must be communicated in gospel presentations regardless of form. The essence of the gospel is that which is left when the gospel is boiled down to its irreducible minimum. Anything less and you no longer have the gospel. While the exact definition of the gospel's essence is open to discussion,[4] we can get close enough to guide our evangelistic enterprises.

The writings of both Paul and Luke provide us with complementary insights into the essence of the gospel. In 1 Corinthians 15:1–6a, Paul provides this summary of the gospel's essence:

> Now, brothers, I want to remind you of the gospel I preached to you, which you received and on which you have taken your stand. By this gospel you are saved, if you hold firmly to the word I preached to you. Otherwise, you have believed in vain. For what I received I passed on to you as of first importance: that Christ died for our sins according to the Scriptures, that he was buried, that he was raised on the third day according to the Scriptures, and that he appeared to Peter, and then to the Twelve. After that, he appeared to more than five hundred of the brothers at the same time.

Luke records Jesus as saying, "This is what is written: The Christ will suffer and rise from the dead on the third day, and repentance and forgiveness of sins will be preached in his name to all nations, beginning at Jerusalem. You are witnesses of these things" (Luke 24:46–48).

KEITH A. DAVY

From these two passages, the essence of the gospel can be organized around the answers to five questions:

1. Who is Jesus? Both statements identify him as the Christ, a title packed with all the theological significance of the promised Messiah.
2. What has he done? Paul said that he had died, was buried, and rose again on the third day. Luke records that he will suffer and rise from the dead on the third day. The death and resurrection of Jesus, the Christ, are the essential works of the gospel.
3. Why did he do it? Paul states that Christ died for our sins. Luke records that forgiveness of sins would be preached. The essential outcome of the gospel is forgiveness of sins.
4. How do we know? For Paul, the confirming evidence is found both in Old Testament prophecy ("according to the Scriptures") and the eyewitnesses to the resurrection. Luke also refers to both in the phrases, "this is what is written" and "you are witnesses of these things." Prophecy and eyewitnesses of the resurrection are the essential proofs.
5. How are we to respond? Paul begins his discussion with a reference to the Corinthians' faith in verses 1 and 2. Jesus stated that repentance would be preached to all nations. The essential response to the gospel involves repentance and faith. These are, of course, integrally connected in our salvation response.

These same five elements can be detected throughout the biblical presentations of the gospel despite the varied contexts. They are embedded in the accounts of Jesus' life, death, and resurrection in the four Gospels, as well as in the apostolic messages in Acts. There is a principle here that must guide those in reaching the younger generations: *There is a core of gospel truth that neither culture nor context can alter.* This gospel truth must be faithfully and clearly articulated. It is the foundation of our faith.

But there is more to the gospel than its essence. The four canonical Gospels (Matthew, Mark, Luke, John) faithfully present the essence, but they do so with greater detail and fullness. What influenced these writers' selection of truth as they wrote their Gospel accounts? Each was influenced in part by the cultural context to which the Gospel was written. To a primarily Jewish audience, Matthew presented the good news of the kingdom of God. Jesus is proclaimed as the king and promised Messiah, grounded in references to Old Testament prophecies. John, however, emphasizes different gospel themes. He presents Jesus as the Son of God, the life for all men and women, using Jesus' signs and discourses as evidence. Each author selected gospel truths under the inspiration of the Spirit to bring about the highest level of understanding for the intended audience.

But the gospel's fullness is not limited to the historical accounts. Jesus opened the disciples' minds to "all that is written about me in the Law of Moses, the Prophets and the Psalms" (Luke 24:44–45). The Old Testament is filled with gospel truth, as are the epistles. Romans is a presentation of the gospel truth in its theological fullness. Therefore, when properly understood, the gospel is not an initial message about Jesus presented at the time of salvation from which one then graduates to other truths for Christian living. In one sense, the whole New Testament is gospel truth unpacked.[5]

From the fullness of the gospel, the themes will be found that will speak powerfully and relevantly to the younger generations just as they have to each cultural context. If the biblical writers were to record a modern Gospel for today, what themes might they use to build their account of the life, death, and resurrection of Jesus? If Paul were to speak to this generation, what gospel truth might he emphasize "to win as many as possible?" (1 Cor. 9:19). Consideration of these questions could lead us to powerful new presentations.

Our initial conclusion can now be stated: *The postmodern cultural context must not be allowed to influence the faithful and clear presentation of the gospel's essence. But the culture will significantly influence our selective use of the gospel's fullness, including the themes and supporting truths.*

This understanding of gospel communication requires us to carefully consider the audiences to whom we speak in order to faithfully and effectively contextualize the message.

THE DEFINING CONTEXT OF THE POSTMODERN MASSES

Today's young are a postmodern generation. Not all would espouse a pure postmodern philosophy, rejecting reason on the basis of epistemology. But many have become practical postmoderns, drinking from the wells of a pluralistic and relativistic culture. What then will characterize the gospel presentations that will effectively reach this new postmodern generation? Four characteristics can serve as initial guides.

First, the gospel presentations must be *culturally relevant.* Much has been written about the philosophical underpinnings of the thought patterns of this generation. But there are also more popular characteristics. This generation is media savvy, cyber literate, adult in experience if not in maturity, experiencing a remote-control reality, feasting on a smorgasbord of options, and living for the now with no guarantees for the future. Our presentations of the gospel must succeed at capturing the heart and attention of this generation. For example, eternal life (as theologically important as it is) is not a common subject of thought or discussion among today's students, who are far more focused on the present than what appears to them a distant future. The gospel must speak to their experience to capture their attention. Sophisticated technology may aid in capturing their attention, but by itself it may not succeed in capturing their hearts. Evidence suggests that relational authenticity will have the greater power, for the most effective technologies fail to meet the deepest needs of the heart.

This suggests a second characteristic: new gospel presentations must be *relationally oriented*. Every generation has its relational styles. The younger generations appear, among other things, to be a generation of relational processors. Decisions are often made with the influence of the individual's small group or social cluster. While the impact of broken families and damaged relationships are often observed, relationships remain a defining characteristic and a high value. This hunger for community has many implications for Christians engaged in evangelism. The love this generation seeks is most fully experienced in relationship with God and in healthy relationship with other believers. Many students respond to the communal or relational aspects of the gospel. The witness of the corporate body of Christ is a powerful apologetic for the young adults who observe it. Inclusion into the people of God is an important gospel theme for this generation.

Third, the diversity within the younger generations will require *adaptability* in our presentations. A plethora of ideas and values have streamed into the vacuum created by the demise of the once dominant worldviews—Christian and modern. This diversity is evidenced in the varied philosophies, lifestyles, interests, and ethics. Diversity also characterizes this generation's spiritual pilgrimages and proximity to the gospel. Some are part of the "fields white for harvest." Others are a hardened soil. Some will move through the spiritual process quickly. For others it is a long and arduous journey. This diversity affects our ability to communicate clearly. Our approaches to personal evangelism must be flexible in order to meet the need of the individual, so our gospel must be adaptable as well.

Fourth, our presentations of the gospel must have *spiritual power*. Spiritual realities do not change with the generations. This generation, like all before it, is spiritually blind (2 Cor. 4:4), subjected to spiritual bondage (Eph. 2:1–3), and involved in spiritual battle (2 Cor. 10:3–5). Only the gospel itself has the power to break through these spiritual realities. It is the power of God for the salvation of all who believe (Rom. 1:16). Thus, the power must be rooted in the gospel itself and not in our presentations.

In summary, as gospel presentations are shaped for this new generation, they must be culturally relevant, socially sensitive, personally adaptable, and spiritually powerful. But what means will prove effective in communicating such a presentation?

THE DISTINCT COMMUNICATION OF VARIOUS EVANGELISTIC MEANS

A biblical and historical study of gospel presentations sheds interesting light on the subject of means. Though there has been more uniformity in gospel presentations during the twentieth century,[6] both the Bible and history demonstrate that a variety of means can be used to effectively package the gospel for communication. Within the New Testament we see evidence of at least six major categories of such means.

First, some presentations of the gospel were *theologically structured*. This was the case for Peter on the Day of Pentecost (Acts 2:14–36). Peter's message portrayed the historical Jesus of Nazareth as the crucified Lord and Christ, using Old Testament prophecies to explain the gift of the Spirit, the resurrection, and the exaltation of the Christ.

At other times, the presentation of the gospel was primarily *testimonial*. Paul presented the gospel through his personal life story to King Agrippa (Acts 26:1–32). The Samaritan woman shared her experience with her villagers, leading them to encounter Jesus (John 4:39–42).

The gospel was also presented through *historically shaped* accounts. Consider the historical shape of the Gospels themselves. Or Paul's message at Psidian Antioch (Acts 13:16–41), which traced salvation history from the Exodus to the Christ.

Paul's message in Acts 17:22–31 was a *philosophically driven* presentation, appropriate to the Greek philosophers gathered in the Areopagus. Here Paul presented biblical truth without biblical references. In fact, the only quotes Luke records come from pagan philosophers.

The parables of the kingdom are examples of gospel truth presented through a *narrative* or story form. The historicity of the parable is not assumed. Yet the truth of the gospel was presented in this powerful and popular medium, and the crowds came to listen. Those with ears to hear heard and believed (see Matt. 13; Mark 4:33–34).

Finally, some gospel interactions were completely *conversational*. Jesus did not make a presentation to Nicodemus (John 3:1–21) or to the Samaritan woman at the well (John 4:7–26). He carried on conversations with

KEITH A. DAVY

both. Indeed, those conversations were guided to the end that they might believe Jesus to be the Christ. But they were conversations nonetheless.

While these are not mutually exclusive forms, they do illustrate the variety of legitimate means that can be used to communicate the gospel. Which means will be the greatest prospect for effective communication with this generation? Traditional gospel presentations have been primarily theologically shaped (*The Four Spiritual Laws,* for example). They will continue to have a significant place in evangelism. But more attention is being turned toward the power of story,[7] by which most refer to life story or testimony. Other means need to be investigated as well. Indeed, one possibility is a mix of means, as will be seen in the example that follows. Each biblical means proved effective in a different ministry context. And so it will be in our day. This postmodern generation will not hear the gospel through one means or form alone. We must explore each of these and many more besides.

WHAT WILL EFFECTIVE GOSPEL PRESENTATIONS LOOK LIKE FOR THE YOUNGER GENERATIONS?

As already implied, no one approach will be the final answer. The campus ministry of Campus Crusade for Christ has launched multiple initiatives to meet the challenges of today. The Research and Development team (R & D) is spearheading many of these creative projects in an effort to accelerate the fulfillment of the campus ministry's mission of turning lost students into Christ-centered laborers among the sixty million college students worldwide.

As part of the effort, we are rethinking the importance of personal testimonies. The scripted and memorized testimonies of the past are giving way to more spontaneous and flexible life stories. Conversational experiences, such as the informal interviews initiated through QuEST, are being used more frequently. Older tools, such as *The Four Spiritual Laws,* are being updated into more relevant formats.[8] Microfiction is being considered as a potential means of communication similar to modern-day parables. Other media, including music, video, and the internet, are proving effective as well.

During the second half of the twentieth century, transferable gospel presentations like *The Four Spiritual Laws,*[9] Steps to Peace with God,[10] and *The Bridge of Life*[11] have been commonly used. These presentations have proven fruitful in the past. As the culture continues to change, will transferable gospel presentations continue to be effective? If so, what changes will characterize them? Five characteristics are emerging as vital for effective gospel presentations among the younger generations. The following discussion will illustrate each characteristic with the use of Life@Large, a current R & D project.[12]

The history of Life@Large begins in January 1998 when a team of R & D staff, communication specialists, and a campus ministry director assembled in Raleigh, North Carolina, to develop new evangelistic resources. As ideas were evaluated, the first project approved involved the development of a gospel presentation that would enable students to conversationally present the gospel within the story line of salvation history. The prototype of this tool, called The Ultimate Pursuit, was presented at the "Telling the Truth: Evangelizing Postmoderns" conference in May 13–15, 1998. As the project progressed, its name was changed to Life@Large.

1. COMPREHENSIVE GOSPEL PRESENTATIONS

As our culture becomes increasingly biblically illiterate, it is necessary to provide a framework of the biblical worldview. Individuals can, of course, genuinely encounter Christ without grasping all the broader strokes of the biblical worldview. Yet the gospel makes sense when it is understood within its broader context. Jesus' death on the cross is most fully understood, not simply in the light of one's personal guilt, but against the backdrop of humanity's fall. Likewise, God's love is more fully grasped when God is understood as the personal and sovereign Creator, and we as his creatures in rebellion.

The cultural waters have also been muddied by the pervasive influence of the Christian culture. Superficial exposure to Christendom has made essential truths of the gospel sound like clichés to this generation of young people. Despite the profound implications of a statement like "God loves you," many today do not hear its significance or sense its power. When these misperceptions are coupled with the influence of spiritualism or other worldviews, foreign concepts are imported into this generation's understanding of gospel terms. The most obvious example is their view of God. To begin a discussion with "God loves you" can leave unanswered the critical question of "Which God?" or "Who is God?" Is it the infinite and personal Creator of the Bible or the impersonal force of the movies that pervades the cosmos? Since the Spirit's power is most operative when the gospel's truths are most clear, this generation needs to hear the gospel in context.

The challenge, of course, is creating a simple means of communicating the gospel through the biblical story line in a manner that will connect with the hearts and minds of the younger generations. The task is not easy. The presentation must be not only culturally relevant but also biblically sound. It will not only communicate the gospel to unbelievers but also shape, in part, how the next generation of Christian students understands the gospel.

Life@Large has been developed around seven primary themes of salvation history. Together they serve as an introduction to the plot line of the Bible for the biblically illiterate and trace major turning points. The themes are:

Intimacy, which explores God's creation of humanity.

Betrayal, which exposes our fall and its consequences.

Anticipation, which introduces the Old Testament promise of the Savior.

Pursuit, which considers the life of Jesus, the Promised One.

Sacrifice, which focuses on Jesus' death and resurrection.

Invitation, which announces God's gracious offer to us in this age.

Reunion, which looks ahead to the judgment and eternal life in the age to come.

Others may prefer to highlight other significant turning points in the gospel story or to express these themes in different terms.[13] The goal of *Life@Large* is to provide the younger generations with an overview of the gospel in its context so that its power may be released and their faith will be firmly founded on a scriptural understanding of life. The text of *Life@Large* was reviewed and edited numerous times to ensure that the message communicated not only the biblical themes but also a biblical balance.

During the field test, one Harvard student shared *Life@Large* with a Jewish friend from her childhood. Afterward, she wrote in a field journal, "First we 'talked' through it over the phone and then we had an e-mail dialogue about it and her reactions to what it was saying for a week and then we talked again. The first time we talked about it she said she wanted it to be true, but didn't know if it was. Then when we talked a week later, she said that she knew it was true. We prayed over the phone and she accepted Christ. No one had ever told her that God loves her regardless of how 'good' she is and that was what had the greatest impact on her. The parts about man's sinfulness were difficult because she already felt guilty and knew she was doing things she shouldn't be and thought that all Christianity would offer her was condemnation. 'God did not send His Son into the world to condemn it, but to save it' (on panel 4) really interested her and struck her." What God used to prepare this student to receive his Word is beyond our knowing. But the power of the gospel was experienced as it was shared within the broad context of the biblical story line. Similar stories are emerging across the nation.

2. CONVERSATIONAL RESOURCES

A survey of contemporary evangelistic resources illustrates that most are designed to be a simple but carefully controlled presentation of the gospel.[14] When used according to their design, they are like a well-mapped ride in a car—they take you to where you are going (the call for a decision) by the quickest available route (a few brief explanations coupled with appropriate verses, but normally few questions.) The strength of these presentations is that the gospel is communicated clearly and concisely.

But many involved in evangelism today, especially among this new postmodern generation, have found that fewer individuals are willing to sit and listen to a presentation. Young people today want to be active participants, not passive listeners. They want to interact, question, and reflect. When the individual is engaged in a relationally safe environment, significant time can be spent in the conversational give and take. This type of dialogue can provide a positive environment in which the spiritual decision process can occur. Such conversations can foster greater understanding and remove many roadblocks to faith.

In many ways, evangelism among the younger generations reflects the question raised in the title of Ronald Johnson's book, *How Will They Hear if We Don't Listen?* (1994). The key to conversational evangelism is the art of asking questions and listening. In the past, evangelism training often discouraged or postponed questions and discussion until after the presentation was completed. At times the questions remained unanswered even then, for the perceived goal of the presentation had been reached with the call to decision. Given postmoderns' bent toward conversation, is it possible to allow significant discussion without becoming sidetracked from communicating the gospel?

Unlike traditional evangelistic tools, *Life@Large* is designed to serve as a conversational guide, not a presentation. On a city tour, a guide knows where you will go. But along the way you are able to pause, explore, and enjoy. In a similar way a *Life@Large* conversation is designed to pause and explore the other person's life, thoughts, and experiences. Questions like "What troubles you most about life?" and "Who or what has been the most significant influence in your spiritual pilgrimage?" allow elements of the unbeliever's life story to be told. These insights are then woven together with the themes and verses from God's story. Rather than a presentation, *Life@Large* becomes a true conversation.

Often in the traditional evangelism paradigm we discover *what* a person is through the conversation—that is, he or she is an unbeliever. But too often

Keith A. Davy

we fail to discover *who* a person is—that is, their story. That failure often leaves uncovered the insights that could provide valuable bridges in helping them discover the relevance of Christ in their lives. Brian was an adult stockbroker who had spent much of his life in and around church. He admitted that he was now moving away from God. The turning point of the conversation with Brian came in the third concept (Anticipation) when he was asked, "Have you ever experienced God? If so, how?" After a long pause for reflection, Brian responded that despite his years in and around religion, he had never experienced God in any real sense. His own words brought him face to face with the reality of an existence separated from God.

In another conversation Michael, a twenty-five-year-old college sophomore, answered the same question: "No, I've never experienced God. But once I had an experience with the devil." He went on to describe a spiritual encounter with an evil being. These are not simply interesting facts for conversation but are important glimpses into lives of people. These insights provide the context for understanding the other's spiritual journey and our role within it.

3. AN EMPHASIS ON LIFE STORIES

Guiding a conversation from the casual and mundane to a significant conversation about the Christ often involves breaking a spiritual sound barrier. Fear and uncertainty keep many believers from ever doing so. The conversational bridge to many transferable evangelistic presentations has been the audience's interest in spiritual issues ("Would you like to know God personally?" or "Can I show you how you can be sure you have eternal life?"). Others have relied on the identification of certain felt needs to which one can relate the gospel (loneliness, anxiety, etc.). Such approaches will no doubt continue to connect with a segment of our society. But many individuals today have not openly expressed an interest in spiritual issues (especially in the Christian viewpoint), nor are they willing to consider Christ as the answer to their felt needs. Any approaches that will prove effective at communicating with our audience, no matter their interest or need, must connect with them on a different basis. Their life story may provide a more universal bridge.

Life@Large has been designed to connect with any individual by expressing a genuine desire to hear and understand his or her story. That interest is the key to unlocking often closed doors and is greeted by their willingness to share their thoughts and experiences in appropriate and safe conversations. Rather than approaching the individual with our message ("Could I show it to you and see what you think of it?"), *Life@Large* expresses our interest in them ("Every person has a story—a life story. What's yours?"). Each person's story is significant. By weaving their life story together with the story line of the Bible, unbelievers share about themselves as much as they are comfortable. At the same time, they are considering the themes of the Bible's story line and adding to their understanding of the gospel.

It is common in evangelistic encounters for an unbeliever to raise his or her disbelief in the Bible as an objection to considering its message. *Life@Large* anticipates and neutralizes that concern by first asking, "How much exposure have you had to the Bible?" and "What is your present attitude toward it?" These answers serve as the beginning point for hearing their story while they explore the story of the Bible.

Students using *Life@Large* have frequently made comments like, "It was very conversational. . . . He said they were great questions that really made him think and allowed him to express what he was feeling." A Harvard student wrote this comment after sharing with a friend who considered Christianity too exclusive and forceful. After a student from the University of Texas shared with a friend who had had very little exposure to the Bible, he wrote: "I really feel that the questions and Scripture really helped me understand where he was coming from. . . . He said he appreciated the deep conversation we had and thought it helped him understand Christianity." In the initial field test, students used *Life@Large* to guide conversations with 123 unbelievers. Thirteen indicated decisions to receive Christ through prayer as a result of the discussion. But equally encouraging were the descriptions Christians gave of the positive discussions with those who were skeptics and agnostics. *Life@Large* did not lead to their conversion, but it appeared to be a step forward in their spiritual decision process. They expanded their understanding of the gospel's story while feeling that they themselves were better understood through sharing their stories. The objective is therefore met by fostering ongoing dialogue about the gospel rather than arriving at a conversational impasse.

4. ADAPTABLE APPROACHES

As noted previously, there is great diversity in the audience we seek to reach in evangelism today. Individuals are unique and so are our conversations with them. A conversational approach requires an evangelistic resource that is adaptable to the individual and the situation. Some individuals are good listeners; others want to talk. Some like to reflect on a subject beforehand; others want to process out loud. Some want a brief summary; others love to talk for hours. An effective evangelistic approach will allow for such diversity. A conversational approach can do so.

KEITH A. DAVY

But diversity is not limited to conversational styles and preferences. It is also seen in the spiritual understanding and openness of the audience. As already noted, the witness today cannot assume that the audience already understands key concepts. Yet they might. Is it possible to approach evangelism in a way that is adaptable to the spiritual interest and process of the individual? The life-story emphasis of *Life@Large* appears to provide that freedom. The individual's story is treated with respect through the believer's willingness to listen and understand, yet it is challenged by the biblical message. Furthermore, in the field test of *Life@Large,* particular attention was paid to the individuals from other world religions and from various ethnic backgrounds. As the student testers recorded these conversations, the outcomes of both groups were very positive.

Diversity is a characteristic not only of our audience but also of us as witnesses. We are at different stages of maturity and experience. Many believers have never engaged an unbeliever in a significant conversation about their faith and feel uncomfortable doing so. Others have shared their faith as a way of life. Again, a conversational approach can be used by all. But how can we effectively resource such conversations?

Life@Large was created as an approach that can be used by any believer, including those who have little training or experience in evangelism. Though one's comfort and ability will grow with experience, anyone can use the tool after a short orientation of about fifteen to twenty minutes. What makes this possible is the ease of the approach. Sharing each panel is as easy as speak, look, and listen. In guiding the conversation, one first speaks, that is, reads or explains the theme with a brief introductory paragraph. Then the friend or acquaintance is asked to look, that is, to look at and read to themselves (or aloud) the selections from God's Story (usually three verses from the Bible related to that theme). By reading the verses themselves, they participate and the Bible speaks directly to them. A follow-up question is simply "What does it say?" At this point, the objective is to have them accurately observe what the Bible is saying (not interpret it.) The message and its implications will be clear as it is accurately observed. The final step is to listen. By asking the discussion questions from Your Story, the believer is able to explore the experiences and thoughts of the unbeliever. This is the basic conversational approach.

But the tool is flexible and can be used in a number of other ways. A summary of the Bible's story line has been written in narrative form on the back of *Life@Large*. It can be read in about seven minutes by the friend or acquaintance on his or her own before the conversation. With that preparation accomplished, the believer can simply guide the conversation with the questions, seeking to understand the friend and helping clarify the message. Conversations with *Life@Large* have lasted from twenty minutes to two and a half hours among students. Yet a person can share the essence of it in ten to twelve minutes by limiting the presentation to introducing all seven themes and using the verses and questions only on the two major turning points—the Betrayal (our problem) and Sacrifice (God's solution).

The message of *Life@Large* can also be used without the printed resource. Michael had an early experience with Catholicism but had been an atheist for most of his life. Now in his midtwenties, he was rethinking spirituality. His views were being shaped by the popular spirituality in modern media. I had the privilege of tracing the themes of *Life@Large* for him, using only my Bible and pen and paper. After seeing it all, Michael responded, "I've always had questions but have never known who to ask. As you began to show me the Bible, I knew that I was hearing the truth." Before the conversation concluded, Michael bowed in prayer and placed his trust in Jesus as his Savior and Lord.

Sarah, an Orlando high-school student, used *Life@Large* as the basis of two talks, one with her cross-country team and another at a meeting with the choir. The choir meeting was built around the theme of "The True Meaning of Christmas." Her presentation started, "You can't know the true meaning of Christmas if you don't understand the bigger story of which it is a part." She then used the themes, verses, and a few of the questions from *Life@Large* to explain the story, relating it to Christmas along the way. Five classmates indicated decisions to receive Christ as a result of the presentation. A veteran youth worker said afterward, "That may be the clearest gospel presentation I have ever heard."

Life@Large can be a flexible evangelistic resource that will speak to this new postmodern generation in a variety of settings and with a variety of approaches. Again, *Life@Large* isn't the ultimate tool. Its value is in illustrating what can be done in reaching the younger generations.

5. VISUALLY SOPHISTICATED DESIGNS

We are communicating with a visual generation. TV, movies, and the world wide web have saturated their experience with images. While interpersonal conversations appear to be the most important element in personal evangelism, any physical medium that supports the conversation must be carefully designed. Its visual appearance can make a significant difference to this generation. To be effective, the design must do more than capture the attention or entertain the audience. Each element should be chosen for what it will visually communicate and the effect it will produce.

KEITH A. DAVY

As the prototype of *Life@Large* was presented at the "Telling the Truth: Evangelizing Postmoderns" conference, a graduate student trained in fine arts and involved in evangelism among other graduate students raised his hand. He exclaimed, "This is the first evangelistic tool I have ever seen that I think even has a chance to communicate to our visually sophisticated generation." When Christian messengers embrace the importance of visual communication, such statements will no longer be made.

Through the testing of *Life@Large*, the prototype has been significantly altered to a more subtle design. The print media of *Life@Large* is not a traditional booklet or tract. Tracts are foreign to students' experience. Therefore, *Life@Large* utilizes an unfolding pamphlet design to subtly convey the unfolding nature of the Bible's story line. Photos are tied to key concepts throughout, but they are muted in color. The desire is to support but not dominate the interest of the audience. The faces in *Life@Large* represent the spectrum of ethnicity and age, honoring the pluralistic mood of our culture. Color is used to create a hierarchy of information and to emphasize the critical turning points. Every element is given attention in design.

There are, of course, multiple styles that will effectively communicate. What communicates today may look outdated tomorrow. But Christian communicators must recognize the importance of these visual elements for this generation and produce resources accordingly. A generation that is bombarded with hundreds of media messages daily ought to have the gospel spoken to them through media with which they are most comfortable.

These five characteristics—comprehensive gospel presentations, conversation resources, adaptable approaches, an emphasis on life stories, and visually sophisticated designs—can be applied in many ways to evangelism messages and resources. *Life@Large* represents only one possible application. Despite the enthusiasm it has generated, it is not the final answer in communicating the gospel to the younger generations. Its greatest value may be to simply raise the bar so that future attempts in evangelism resources will go higher in both biblical integrity and communication effectiveness. Both are essential for this and every generation.

References

Carson, D. A. 1996. *The Gagging of God.* Grand Rapids: Zondervan.

Dodd, C. H. 1936. *The Apostolic Preaching and Its Developments.* New York: Harper and Row.

Ford, Kevin Graham. 1995. *Jesus for a New Generation*. Downers Grove, Ill.: InterVarsity Press.

Ford, Leighton. 1994. *The Power of Story*. Colorado Springs: NavPress.

Hunsberger, George R., and Craig Van Gelder, eds. 1996. *The Church between Gospel and Culture*. Grand Rapids: Eerdmans.

Johnson, Ronald W. 1994. *How Will They Hear If We Don't Listen?* Nashville: Broadman and Holman.

Ladd, George E. 1993. *A Theology of the New Testament*. 2d ed. Grand Rapids: Eerdmans.

Newbigin, Lesslie. 1986. *Foolishness to the Greeks*. Grand Rapids: Eerdmans.

_____. 1989. *The Gospel in a Pluralist Society*. Grand Rapids: Eerdmans.

Poe, Harry L. 1996. *The Gospel and Its Meaning*. Grand Rapids: Zondervan.

PART EIGHT

Closing Plenaries

CHAPTER 27

THE URGENCY OF THE GOSPEL

Ajith Fernando

One of the many challenges the Christian witness faces in this postmodern era relates to the question of motivation to evangelism. Traditionally, Christians have been motivated to evangelism through their belief that the gospel is absolutely true and is the only hope for salvation. However, the aptness of thinking in such categories as "absolutely true" and "only hope for salvation" is being questioned by today's pluralistic thinking. The postmodern mood is thus hostile to the idea of urgency as it is portrayed in the Bible. In this paper we will look into the meaning and causes of biblical urgency by examining the biblical texts describing urgency and seeing how the postmodern mood challenges them.

HARD TRUTHS THAT FOSTER URGENCY

There are situations described in the Bible in which God's people were motivated to action through a realization of what we may call the hard truths of the gospel. The realization that people without God are lost and headed for judgment had a strong influence on them. Paul expresses this with great feeling as he ponders the lostness of the Jews in Romans 9:1–4. First he declares the urgency of what he is going to say: "I speak the truth in Christ—I am not lying, my conscience confirms it in the Holy Spirit" (v. 1). Then he expresses his feelings about the lostness of the Jews: "I have great sorrow and unceasing anguish in my heart" (v. 2). Then he describes how this stark truth is able to motivate him to great heights of commitment: "For I could wish that I myself were cursed and cut off from Christ for the sake of my brothers, those of my own race, the people of Israel" (vv. 3–4a). In the next chapter he tells how he desires the salvation of the Jews: "Brothers, my heart's desire and prayer to God for the Israelites is that they may be saved" (10:1). What we see here is a description of urgency derived from the fact of the lostness of the Jews. This becomes a direct motivation to evangelism. Jude 23 describes evangelism as snatching people from the fire and saving them.

Some of the great leaders in the history of the church express a similar urgency derived from the fact of the lostness of persons apart from Christ. The seventeenth-century Scottish preacher Samuel Rutherford once told a person, "I would lay my dearest joys in the gap between you and eternal destruction."[1] Hudson Taylor said, "I would have never thought of going to China had I not believed that the Chinese were lost and needed Christ." D. L. Moody told an audience in London, "If I believed there was no hell, I am sure I would be off tomorrow for America." He said he would give up going from town to town spending day and night "urging men to escape the damnation of hell."[2] William Booth said he wished that his Salvation Army workers might spend "one night in hell" in order to see the urgency of their evangelistic task.[3]

The reality of judgment, of course, adds urgency to our message. Several times in the Bible the prospect of judgment becomes a means of warning people to the end that they would turn to God. Peter Toon lists thirty-one passages (not counting parallel passages) in the Gospels that contain warnings of hell (1986, 29–46). Often these warnings are given in evangelistic contexts (e.g., Mark 8:31–38).[4]

Judgment has never been a popular message, and that is so today. Religious pluralism is the dominant philosophy influencing religious life in both the East and the West. Pluralism emphasizes the essential equality of religious systems and seeks through that to unify people of different faiths. The doctrine of judgment speaks of an eternal division of the human race into those who are saved and those who are lost.

Many who think about the afterlife prefer to think of heaven rather than of hell. Perhaps that is the reason why in the recorded statements of Jesus there are more references to hell than there are to heaven. This may also be the reason why in the Bible there are more references to the wrath of God than to the love of God. It is so easy to lull ourselves into forgetting these truths and thinking positive about our future destiny. A poll done for *Newsweek* magazine by the Gallup organization in December 1988 found that 77 percent of Americans believe there is a heaven, and 76 percent think they have a good or excellent chance of getting there (13 April 1989, 43).

One of the key features of the postmodern era has been its emphasis on the subjective and experiential aspects of life. In response to this, many churches have majored on entertainment in their programming as part of their

AJITH FERNANDO

effort to reach people in this culture. In an environment where entertainment is a primary motivation in programming, it is easy to neglect the hard truths of the gospel, because they are not usually attractive or entertaining. If one generation neglects a difficult doctrine, it is quite possible that the next generation will reject it. Having not been regularly exposed to this difficult truth, people will find it difficult to accommodate it in their worldview, their approach to life and religion. The result will be a loss of urgency in the church.

THE COMPULSION OF TRUTH

In the Bible we often see urgency arising from the fact that what is being proclaimed is the truth that God has given to humanity. This is seen vividly in the prophets, who were compelled by what may be called "the burden of the Lord." Amos cried, "The lion has roared—who will not fear? The Sovereign LORD has spoken—who can but prophesy?" (Amos 3:8). Just as fear is the anticipated response to the roaring of a lion, prophesying is the anticipated response to the speaking of the Lord.

The compulsion of the message is well illustrated in Jeremiah's complaint to God after he has been humiliated by the chief officer of the temple. He has been beaten and kept in the stocks overnight. Following his release, he accuses God of having deceived him and describes his humiliation (Jer. 20:7–8). Then he ponders the possibility of abandoning his ministry. He says, "But if I say, 'I will not mention him or speak any more in his name,' his word is in my heart like a fire, a fire shut up in my bones. I am weary of holding it in; indeed I cannot" (v. 9).

Truth has a way of burning in our hearts, as the disciples who met Christ on the road to Emmaus found out. They exclaimed, "Were not our hearts burning within us while he talked with us on the road and opened the Scriptures to us?" (Luke 24:32). This is knowledge on fire, and it produces an urgency that expresses itself in the proclamation of the gospel.

A major reason for this knowledge to be on fire and thus produce urgency is the conviction that it is the truth. In Romans 1:14–16, another urgency passage, Paul describes his sense of indebtedness to proclaim the gospel to all people, resulting in an eagerness to preach the gospel in Rome (vv. 14–15). Then he gives his reason for this eagerness: "[For (*gar*, not translated in the NIV)] I am not ashamed of the gospel, because it is the power of God for the salvation of everyone who believes" (v. 16). A conviction of the power of the gospel has given rise to urgency.

A report in the *London Daily Mail* during one of Billy Graham's early campaigns in England, explains this urgency that comes from a conviction that the gospel is the truth. It said, "He has no magnetism; he has no appeal to the emotions. His power—and power he has—is the indivisible conviction that he knows the right way of life."[5]

Some months ago when I was traveling by train to a Buddhist village where we were having a ministry, I sat next to a Buddhist government officer. When he realized that I, a Christian worker, was traveling to a Buddhist village, he asked me a question that is in the minds of many Buddhists in Sri Lanka: "Why do you Christians want to convert Buddhists to Christianity? This is causing so much disruption to our society today. Can't you help them to be better Buddhists, while you attempt to be better Christians?" I told him that we believe this world was created by a supreme God, and that seeing the mess the world was in, this God has provided an answer to the world's problems. Then I told him that we have found out what this answer is, and after finding it out, we must share it with the people of our land. I said that we would be selfish if we did not do that. He may not have been happy with my response, but I think he at least understood why we preach the gospel to non-Christians.

POSTMODERNISM'S LOSS OF CONFIDENCE IN THE VALUE OF OBJECTIVE TRUTH

A basic feature of postmodernism militates against what we have said about urgency coming out of the objective truthfulness of the gospel as God's unique answer to the human dilemma. People say that truth is subjective and personal, not objective and absolute. Therefore they say, "You have your truth, and I have mine. Don't be arrogant and say that your truth is the only truth for me." In such an environment there can be no urgency to proclaim the message to the whole world. Those committed to evangelism with conversion in view are considered hopelessly out of step with the way society is moving.

This is a vast topic, and it requires a separate treatment. Let me say here that while people may not be interested in objective truth, they are not incapable of thinking in objective categories. The ability to respond to and appreciate objective truth is part of our human nature, and while we may suppress it for a time, sooner or later we will realize its value. In fact, when people recognize the chaos that results from living without objective, unchanging foundations, they may start looking afresh for the certainty that comes from building one's life on a firm foundation. Recently there are indications of a worldwide reaction to the uncertainty of pluralism and to the subjective approach to truth. Examples of this trend are the growth of Islam in the West; the growth of Buddhist, Hindu, and Islamic fundamentalism in the East; and the growth of groups like the Mormons and Christian churches that emphasize strict adherence to principles, like the

Boston Church of Christ. The church, then, is faced with the great challenge of demonstrating to Christians and the world that objective truth is still relevant, attractive, and indispensable.

THE LOSS OF THE VALUE OF WORDS IN CHURCH AND SOCIETY

As we with urgency pursue the ministry of the Word in this postmodern generation, we are faced with a problem that is related to postmodernism's loss of confidence in the value of truth. This is the fact that words have lost their value in both the church and society. Carl F. H. Henry begins his massive six-volume work on *God, Revelation and Authority* with a chapter titled, "The Crisis of Truth and Word." In it he says, "The breakdown of confidence in verbal communication is a feature of our times." He points out that "preference for the nonverbal is especially conspicuous among the younger generation who increasingly surmise that words are a cover-up rather than a revelation of truth; that is, words are used to conceal, distort and deceive" (1976, 24). This trend has reached its apex in the postmodern hermeneutic known as *deconstruction,* associated with names like Jacques Derrida,[6] where "absolute relativism prevails [and] objective truth is intolerable and non-existent" (Henry 1997, 38).

Many factors have contributed to this cynicism regarding the capacity of verbal communication to convey objective truth. One factor, of course, is the trend away from objectivity that is a key feature of postmodernism. Another is that people have used words wrongly in both church and society. In the church we often find preachers stretching truth beyond its boundaries by exaggerating to make a point effectively. The point may get through, but the long-term effect is that words lose their value. The same thing happens when those who preach do not practice what they preach. Sometimes we find preachers being dogmatic about nonessentials or things that are not clearly taught in the Scriptures, such as the applying of teachings of the end times to today's situation. Perhaps because of the confusion and uncertainty that has characterized the revolt from the authority of Scripture, some Christian leaders have felt that they must always present what they proclaim with utmost authority. But we must remember that our commitment is to truth and not to a given system of belief. If we are not certain about the truth on a given issue, we are not afraid to admit our uncertainty. If we have communicated something that we later find to be untrue, our passionate commitment to truth is such that we are willing to be publicly corrected.

In society too there is a devaluing of words. In advertising we have seen people passionately proclaiming the praises of trivial things like used cars. We have used superlatives like "the greatest" and "amazing" so loosely that they have lost their value. The word *awesome,* once used primarily for God, is now used for trivial things like ice cream and clothes. Evil but powerful leaders like Adolf Hitler and Jim Jones have, through the passionate use of words, caused people to do things of which they are now ashamed. Is it any wonder then that there is a fear of urgency, especially urgency that is expressed in words?

In such an environment we face the intellectual challenge of addressing the philosophical basis of the subjectivism that characterizes postmodernism and undermines the place of language. We need evangelists and apologists for objective truth. But because this is a generation that is more impressed by experience than by rational arguments, we have the equally important challenge of restoring the value of words by demonstrating it in our lives and ministries. We need proclamation that is faithful to the Scriptures and also attractive, relevant, and convincing. But such proclamation must not try to elicit a response by the unethical use of imposition, manipulation, or other unworthy forms of communication.[7] The right message must be communicated in the right way. We need communicators of truth who practice what they preach both at home and at church. In short, we need to help restore a respect for language in people's minds by demonstrating that it can be a reliable, essential, relevant, and desirable form of communication if used in the proper way.

TRUTH AND THE CONTEMPORARY PURSUIT OF PLEASURE

The emphasis on truth can be attractive to our pleasure-seeking generation too. Biblical Christians committed to truth have been caricatured as dour people whose commitment to orthodoxy makes them so serious and scrupulous about doctrinal details that they are not fun to be with and thus are unattractive to this generation. According to the Bible, however, truth is capable of producing great pleasure. So the psalmists spoke often about delighting in the Word of God or the law.[8] C. S. Lewis reflects on this phenomenon in his book *Reflections on the Psalms.* After looking at different reasons for such delight, he concludes, "Their delight in the Law is a delight in having touched firmness; like the pedestrian's delight in feeling the hard road beneath his feet after a false shortcut has long entangled him in muddy fields" (1958, 62). A similar thing happens today when people find the truth in Jesus after having struggled with the confusion caused by the array of competing voices in the pluralistic supermarket of faiths.

Gordon Haddon Clark described this joy of truth in a statement that his student at Wheaton College, Carl F. H. Henry, heard him say in class: "A satisfactory religion must satisfy. But satisfy *what* and *why?* The Greek mysteries satisfied the emotions; brute force can satisfy the will; but Christianity satisfies the *intellect* because it is *true,* and truth is the only everlasting satisfaction."[9]

The idea that objective truth is pleasurable may be alien to the postmodern mind that seeks satisfaction through subjective experiences and through liberation from the constraints caused by submission to objective truth. Owing to the strong influences of our sensate culture upon us, our minds are often unable even to understand how truth could be pleasurable. But this is so, and we are challenged to demonstrate this to our generation through the proper handling and use of the truth.

One of the answers to the crisis caused by the loss of belief in the pleasure of truth is for the church to demonstrate this pleasure. But we seem to have been influenced by the postmodern mood so much that we are afraid to focus too much on truth in the church's program. Instead, we seek to entertain people through the subjective factors that the world says are pleasurable. I would go so far as to say that entertainment has replaced urgency as a primary means of attracting people to the gospel. Therefore, we do not strive to let the truth shine forth in all its glory, an enterprise that calls for dedication and hard work. Instead, the hard work goes to producing an entertaining program. We often find that Christian worship is characterized by an entertaining and technically excellent program of music, drama, worship, and sharing, followed by a ministry of the Word that is comparatively inferior and unimaginative. As music, drama, and sharing is done to the glory of God, it should be done well. But so also with the ministry of the Word.

As a result of this focus on entertainment, people come to worship looking to have an entertaining time. Songs and stories and humor are chosen so that the people might be entertained. In the process, truth is subordinated to an inferior position. So today when many Christians inquire about the value of a worship service they ask, "Did you enjoy the worship there?" But what they mean is, "Did you get an emotional lift from the spiritual entertainment provided there?"

I am not against the use of entertainment in Christian programming. I work for Youth for Christ, and entertainment forms an important part of our programming. But entertainment is always a servant of truth. It may be used to win a hearing for the truth by attracting people to the church. It may be used to communicate truth. But it must never overthrow truth from its supreme place in the Christian agenda. So when we plan a worship service, we may consider the entertainment value of a given item, but the deciding factor on whether to use it is how it agrees with and/or communicates the truth. In this way we preserve the primacy of truth and maintain an environment conducive to fostering the urgency that springs from the truth.

SUBJECTIVE TRIGGERS OF URGENCY

When it comes to religion, postmodernists place much stress on subjective experience. The subjective has a high place in biblical religion. In fact, there is a subjective side to biblical urgency too.

URGENCY THROUGH EXPERIENCING THE TRUTH

One subjective trigger of urgency is our experience of the truth. Peter and John are examples of this when, after they are commanded not to speak to anyone in the name of Jesus, they tell the Sanhedrin: "For we cannot help speaking about what we have seen and heard" (Acts 4:20). The woman of Samaria expresses this when she tells the people, "Come, see a man who told me everything I ever did" (John 4:29). In fact, this is implied in the use of the word *witness* to describe evangelism. What we share is what we have personally witnessed to be true. And one of the ways we know is to experience it in our lives. Hebrews 2:3–4 gives several factors that affirm the truth of the gospel:

- The preaching of Jesus: "This salvation, which was first announced by the Lord"
- The confirmation of eyewitnesses: "was confirmed to us by those who heard him"
- Miraculous signs: "God also testified to it by signs, wonders and various miracles"
- The experience of gifts: "and gifts of the Holy Spirit distributed according to his will"

The last two of these evidences are experiential in nature. Certainly the first two are more basic, for they give the objective realities on which the experience is based. But experience does lend weight to our case and add to our urgency.

E. Stanley Jones, an American missionary to India, tells the story of a young preacher who said, "I've been perjuring myself. I've been preaching things not operative within me. I'm through with this unreality. I'll give God till Sunday to do something for me. And if he doesn't do something for me before Sunday, someone else can preach. I won't." He took Saturday off as a day of retreat, and God met him. He went into the pulpit a new man. That Sunday the congregation got the shock of their lives. They had a new minister! The congregation found themselves seeking what their young minister had found. A contagious urgency had been triggered by an experience of the truth he proclaimed (Jones 1963, 149).

URGENCY THROUGH IGNITING TRUTH BY THE HOLY SPIRIT

Another subjective trigger of urgency is the igniting of the truth in our hearts by the Holy Spirit so that this truth is transformed into knowledge on fire. Then we become like Stephen, whose opponents "could not stand up against his wisdom or the Spirit by whom he spoke" (Acts 6:10). In another of his urgency statements, Paul says, "For Christ's love compels us" (2 Cor. 5:14). Elsewhere Paul had said that this love has been poured into our hearts by the Holy Spirit (Rom. 5:5). The word translated "compels" (*sunecho*) in 2 Corinthians 5:14 basically means "to press together, constrain." As Colin Kruse explains, "It is the pressure applied not so much to control as to cause action. It is motivational rather than directional force" (1987, 122). So urgency comes to us through love, which is, in turn, endowed by the Holy Spirit.

We often forget what follows Paul's statement about being compelled by love in 2 Corinthians 5:14, even though it is part of the same sentence and the same verse in our Bibles. Paul goes on to say, "because we are convinced that one died for all, and therefore all died." The expression "because we are convinced" is the translation of one word *krinantas,* an aorist participle that means "having judged." The main verb is "compels" (*sunechei),* and this participle modifies it. This shows that the compulsion of love is intimately associated with our conviction regarding the gospel. We know the gospel is true. The next verse gives the implication of believing that Christ died for all: "And he died for all, that those who live should no longer live for themselves but for him who died for them and was raised again" (v. 15). What Christ has done must be experienced by all. The love of Christ in us combines with the conviction that what Christ did is efficacious and necessary for all people, and it produces an urgency that motivates us to ministry.

In our preparation for ministry, then, we seek to ensure that we have both the conviction of truth and the fullness of the Spirit from which love comes. Prayer is what enables us to get in tune with God and thereby open ourselves to the fullness of the Holy Spirit. An African-American preacher described his preparation for the pulpit in three steps. He said he "read himself full" and "thought himself clear" and "prayed himself hot" (Sangster 1958, 90).

God's servant will grapple with God until there is a conviction that God's Spirit has filled him or her with an anointing for the ministry to be discharged. This desire for God's fullness is illustrated in a story that Dr. Martyn Lloyd-Jones liked to tell. An old preacher in Wales was invited to preach at a Christian convention in a little town. The people had assembled, but the preacher had not come. The leaders sent a maid back to the house where the preacher was staying to tell him that they were waiting for him and that everything was ready. The girl went and came back saying, "I did not like to disturb him. He was talking to somebody." They said, "That is rather strange, because everybody is here. Go back and tell him that it is after time and that he *must* come." So the girl went back, and again she reported, "He *is* talking to somebody." "How do you know that?" they asked. She answered: "I heard him say to this other person who is with him, 'I will not go and preach to these people if you will not come with me.'" The leaders responded saying, "Oh, it is all right. We had better wait" (Lloyd-Jones 1958, 88).

THE TYRANNY OF TECHNOLOGY

The final challenge to biblical urgency that we will examine is what we might call the tyranny of technology. While technology is not evil in and of itself, it can so entangle people that they will find it difficult to switch to the sphere of the Spirit and truth from which urgency comes. Technology can make us technicians, but it will not make us Spirit-filled theologians. In fact, unrestrained absorption in technology may hinder us from becoming Spirit-filled people with knowledge on fire. Let us see how this happens.

Through the marvels of technology, the Christian publishing industry has been able to serve the church with an amazing variety of Bible study aids and study Bibles in printed form and in the form of computer software. These tools are advertised as being able to take the sweat out of Bible study. But when it comes to handling the Word of God, sweat can be thrilling! As we grapple with God's truth and prayerfully meditate on it, we will find ourselves encountering the God of the Bible. The resulting enrichment gives rise to urgency.

This is not to say that technology is unhelpful. We can use it to save time so that we are freed to think and meditate and pray. But it is possible to linger with technology without giving ourselves to diligent study, thinking, and prayer. We may go on and on playing at the computer or surfing the internet without switching off from the technology mode and entering into the theology mode. This is one of the commonest examples of the tyranny of technology today, and it fits in with an aspect of our fallenness—the aspect that makes us prefer to fill up the void in our lives with human activity (work) rather than waiting upon God in humble submission.

When we enter the theology mode, we should still be active, but it is the activity of one who is humbly submitted to God. Here we seek to understand the truth; to meditate on it; and to apply it reverently, obediently, and prayerfully to our lives and to the lives of those we serve. In this way we graduate

AJITH FERNANDO

from being technicians to being theologians. The result is a vibrant relationship with God and his truth. The truth grips us and passion returns so that we are filled with urgency over the gospel. We must, then, develop the art and the discipline of switching off amidst the rush of life and the potential tyranny of technology so that we linger prayerfully and meditatively with the truth.

Today's minister finds it very difficult to set aside long segments of time for study. I am grateful for a piece of advice I heard when I was a student at Fuller Theological Seminary. John Stott was visiting the seminary, and a time was arranged for the students to ask him questions. Someone asked him about his study habits. He replied that the minister in earlier times was able to dedicate the whole morning for study, but that this is difficult to do in today's society. Therefore he had learned to use whatever short times he could find at different times of the day for study. We first need to believe in the priority of truth in the life of the minister. Then out of that conviction, we start looking for opportunities to give ourselves to the study of the Word. It is amazing how opportunities will present themselves to the one who looks diligently.

Sri Lanka is embroiled in an ethnic conflict between the majority Sinhalese and the minority Tamils. There is a militant group, the Tamil Tigers, whose cadres often strike in the city of Colombo with bombings and other devices aimed at disrupting the life of the city. Because of this, Tamil youth are often arrested by the security forces on suspicion of being terrorists. Among those arrested are Youth for Christ volunteers and staff. As a Sinhalese, I often go to the police station to vouch for them and secure their release. The process may take as much as five to six hours, and I always take my books along. One day, following a bombing, I was in a police station seeking the release of two of our volunteers. I was studying the book of Galatians. Beside me was a person who had been injured in the bomb blast and another who had come to complain about her husband, who had assaulted her. As I studied Galatians, I suddenly realized that the police station may be a better place to theologize than even my study room at home. I was surrounded by people whose experience vividly demonstrated needs that the gospel must meet. My point is that if we wait for the ideal time for study, it may never come. We must develop the discipline of using whatever time we can find for this priority activity.

URGENCY AND INCONVENIENCE

Let me mention briefly that urgency is what propels us to bold ventures beyond what we would call our comfort zone. In 1 Corinthians 9:16 Paul expresses his urgency with great intensity: "I am compelled to preach. Woe to me if I do not preach the gospel!" Shortly after that, he talks of the way he deprives himself of his rights and becomes a slave to all, so that more people will come to Christ (vv. 19–23). In this passage is found the statement, "I have become all things to all men so that by all possible means I might save some" (v. 22b). Earlier he has said how he becomes like a Jew, like a Gentile, and even like a weak person so that he may reach those types of people (vv. 20–22a). Such is his commitment to the gospel.

Fostering commitment that is willing to pay the price is one of the results of urgency. We realize that the gospel cause is so important that we are willing to pay a price on account of it. One of the characteristics of postmodernism is the unwillingness to pay the price of commitment to causes outside of us. A church that focuses primarily on entertaining its people will have large numbers of people who come primarily in search of entertainment. On the other hand, when the majestic truthfulness of the gospel is given due place in the program of the church, it will produce the type of urgency that issues in costly commitment.

URGENCY AND FRESHNESS

Urgency, then, is intimately connected to the fact that the gospel is true. When we accept this fact and add to that a vibrant experience of Christ and an intimate tie with the Holy Spirit, we will find that the truth begins to burn within us and to cry out for release. This fire will help us persevere in ministry amidst all the problems we face. Perseverance in ministry is an important subject, given the fact that burnout in the ministry and dropping out of the ministry has reached epidemic proportions today. I am convinced that one who is fed with the Word and filled with love from the Holy Spirit can go on and on ministering with freshness and urgency. Did not the psalmist say, "The law of the LORD is perfect, reviving the soul" (Ps. 19:7a)?

A pastor left the ministry so burnt out and discouraged that he even left his library behind in his last church. When his successor went through this library, he found that, while many of the books the former pastor had acquired at the start of his ministry were on the Bible and theology, his later books were mostly on practical topics. Had he retrogressed from the theologian mode to the technician mode? It could be that he had neglected feeding his soul and thus had lost the fire that would keep him persevering in ministry. Susan Pearlman, a leader in Jews for Jesus, once told me, "Burnout takes place when the wick and not the oil is burning." The oil that propels Christian ministry is the Word of truth and the love that comes from the Spirit.

The British preacher Gypsy Smith preached the gospel from the age of seventeen until he died at sea at eighty-seven on his way to America for a preaching mission. Someone asked him the secret of his freshness and vigor even in his old age. Smith replied, "I never lost the wonder." When we are filled with a perception and an experience of the wonder of the gospel, urgency will be our hallmark.

References

Carson, D. A. 1996. *The Gagging of God: Christianity Confronts Pluralism*. Grand Rapids: Zondervan.

Erickson, Millard J. 1993. *Evangelical Interpretation*. Grand Rapids: Baker.

Fernando, Ajith. 1994. *Crucial Questions about Hell*. Wheaton: Crossway.

Gaebelein, Frank E., ed. 1980. *The Letters of Samuel Rutherford*. Chicago: Moody Press.

Gundry, Stanley N. 1976. *Love Them In: The Life and Theology of D. L. Moody*. Grand Rapids: Baker.

Henry, Carl F. H. 1976. *God, Revelation and Authority*. Vol. 1: *God Who Speaks and Shows: Preliminary Considerations*. Waco, Tex.: Word.

————. 1986. *Confessions of a Theologian: An Autobiography*. Waco, Tex.: Word.

————. 1997. "Postmodernism: The New Specter?" In *The Challenge of Postmodernism: An Evangelical Engagement*, ed. David S. Dockery, 34–52. Grand Rapids: Baker.

Jones, E. Stanley. 1963. *The Word Became Flesh*. Nashville: Abingdon.

Kruse, Colin. 1987. *The Second Epistle to the Corinthians*. TNTC. Grand Rapids: Eerdmans.

Lewis, C. S. 1958. *Reflections on the Psalms*. New York: Harcourt, Brace and World.

Lloyd-Jones, D. Martyn. 1958. *Authority*. London: Inter-Varsity Fellowship.

Sangster, W. E. (1958) 1976. *Power and Preaching*. Grand Rapids: Baker.

Toon, Peter. 1986. *Heaven and Hell*. Nashville: Thomas Nelson.

Wirt, Sherwood E. 1997. *Billy*. Wheaton: Crossway.

CHAPTER 28

ATHENS REVISITED

D. A. Carson

I would like to think that most of us have become convinced of the primacy of what might generically be called worldview evangelism. In the recent past, at least in North America and Europe, evangelism consisted of a fairly aggressive presentation of one small part of the Bible's story line. Most non-Christians to whom we presented the gospel shared enough common language and outlook with us that we did not find it necessary to unpack the entire plot line of the Bible. A mere quarter of a century ago, if we were dealing with an atheist, he or she was not a generic atheist but a Christian atheist—that is, the God he or she did not believe in was more or less a god of discernibly Judeo-Christian provenance. The atheist was not particularly denying the existence of Hindu gods—Krishna, perhaps—but the God of the Bible. But that meant that the categories were still ours. The domain of discourse was ours.

When I was a child, if I had said, "Veiled in flesh the Godhead see," 80 percent of the kids in my school could have responded, "Hail the incarnate deity." That was because Christmas carols like "Hark, the Herald Angels Sing" were sung in home, church, school, and street. These kids may not have understood all the words, but this domain of Christian discourse was still theirs. Young people at university doubtless imbibed massive doses of naturalism, but in most English departments it was still assumed you could not plumb the vast heritage of English poetry if you possessed no knowledge of the language, metaphors, themes, and categories of the Bible.

In those days, then, evangelism presupposed that most unbelievers, whether they were atheists or agnostics or deists or theists, nevertheless knew that the Bible begins with God, that this God is both personal and transcendent, that he made the universe and made it good, and that the Fall introduced sin and

D. A. Carson

attracted the curse. Virtually everyone knew that the Bible has two Testaments. History moves in a straight line. There is a difference between good and evil, right and wrong, truth and error, fact and fiction. They knew that Christians believe there is a heaven to be gained and a hell to be feared. Christmas is bound up with Jesus' birth; Good Friday and Easter, with Jesus' death and resurrection. Those were the givens. So what we pushed in evangelism was the seriousness of sin, the freedom of grace, who Jesus really is, what his death is about, and the urgency of repentance and faith. That was evangelism. Of course, we tilted things in certain ways depending on the people we were addressing; the focus was different when evangelizing in different subcultural settings—in the Bible Belt, for instance, or in an Italian-Catholic section of New York, or in an Ivy League university. But for most of us, evangelism was connected with articulating and pressing home a very small part of the Bible's plot line.

In many seminaries like Trinity, of course, we recognized that missionaries being trained to communicate the gospel in radically different cultures needed something more. A missionary to Japan or Thailand or north India would have to learn not only another language or two but also another culture. No less important, they would have to begin their evangelism farther back, because many of their hearers would have no knowledge of the Bible at all and would tenaciously hold to some worldview structures that were fundamentally at odds with the Bible. The best schools gave such training to their missionary candidates. But pastors and campus workers were rarely trained along such lines. After all, they were doing nothing more than evangelizing people who shared their own cultural assumptions, or at least people located in the same domain of discourse, weren't they?

We were naive, of course. We were right, a quarter of a century ago, when we sang, "The times they are a-changin'." Of course, there were many places in America where you could evangelize churchy people who still retained substantial elements of a Judeo-Christian worldview. There are still places like that today: the over-fifties in the Midwest, parts of the Bible Belt. But in the New England states, in the Pacific Northwest, in universities almost anywhere in the country, in pockets of the population such as media people, and in many parts of the entire Western world, the degree of biblical illiteracy cannot be overestimated. One of my students commented a week ago that he was walking in Chicago with his girlfriend, who had a wooden cross hanging from a chain around her neck. A lad stopped her on the sidewalk and asked why she had a plus sign for a necklace. The people whom we evangelize on university campuses usually do not know that the Bible has two Testaments. As Phillip Jensen says, you have to explain to them the purpose of the big numbers and little numbers. They have never heard of Abraham, David, Solomon, Paul—let alone Haggai or Zechariah. They may have heard of Moses, but only so as to confuse him with Charlton Heston.

But this analysis is still superficial. My point is not so much that these people are ignorant of biblical data (though that is true) as that, having lost touch with the Judeo-Christian heritage that in one form or another (sometimes bowdlerized) long nourished the West, they are not clean slates waiting for us to write on them. They are not empty hard drives waiting for us to download our Christian files onto them. Rather, they have inevitably developed an array of alternative worldviews. They are hard drives full of many other files that collectively constitute various non-Christian frames of reference.

The implications for evangelism are immense. I shall summarize four.

First, the people we wish to evangelize hold some fundamental positions that they are going to have to abandon to become Christians. To continue my computer analogy, they retain numerous files that are going to have to be erased or revised, because as presently written, those files are going to clash formidably with Christian files. At one level, of course, that is always so. That is why the gospel demands repentance and faith; indeed, it demands the regenerating, transforming work of the Spirit of God. But the less there is of a common, shared worldview between "evangelizer" and "evangelizee," between the biblically informed Christian and the biblically illiterate postmodern, the more traumatic the transition, the more decisive the change, the more stuff has to be unlearned.

Second, under these conditions evangelism means starting farther back. The good news of Jesus Christ—who he is and what he accomplished by his death, resurrection, and exaltation—is simply incoherent unless certain structures are already in place. You cannot make heads or tails of the real Jesus unless you have categories for the personal/transcendent God of the Bible; the nature of human beings made in the image of God; the sheer odium of rebellion against him; the curse that our rebellion has attracted; the spiritual, personal, familial, and social effects of our transgression; the nature of salvation; the holiness and wrath and love of God. One cannot make sense of the Bible's plot line without such basic ingredients; one cannot make sense of the Bible's portrayal of Jesus without such blocks in place. We cannot possibly agree on the solution that Jesus provides if we cannot agree on the problem he confronts. *That is why our evangelism must be "worldview" evangelism.* I shall flesh out what this means in a few moments.

Third, not for a moment am I suggesting that worldview evangelism is a restrictively propositional exercise. It is certainly not less than propositional;

the Bible not only presents us with many propositions, but it insists in some cases that unless one believes those propositions one is lost. The point can easily be confirmed by a close reading of the gospel of John. For all its complementary perspectives, it repeatedly makes statements like "Unless you believe *that* . . ." One really ought not be forced to choose between propositions and relational faith any more than one should be forced to choose between the left wing of an airplane and the right. At its core, worldview evangelism is as encompassing as the Bible. We are called not only to certain propositional confession but also to loyal faith in Jesus Christ, the truth incarnate; to repentance from dead works to serve the living God; to life transformed by the Holy Spirit, given to us in anticipation of the consummated life to come; to a new community that lives and loves and behaves in joyful and principled submission to the Word of the King, our Maker and Redeemer. This massive worldview touches everything, embraces everything. It can be simply put, for it has a center; it can be endlessly expounded and lived out, for in its scope it has no restrictive perimeter.

Fourth, the evangelist must find ways into the values, heart, thought patterns—in short, the worldview—of those who are being evangelized but must not let that non-Christian worldview domesticate the biblical message. The evangelist must find bridges into the other's frame of reference, or no communication is possible; the evangelist will remain ghettoized. Nevertheless, faithful worldview evangelism under these circumstances will sooner or later find the evangelist trying to modify or destroy some of the alien worldview and to present another entire structure of thought and conduct that is unimaginably more glorious, coherent, consistent, and finally true.

All of this, of course, the apostle Paul well understood. In particular, by his own example he teaches us the difference between evangelizing those who largely share your biblical worldview and evangelizing those who are biblically illiterate. In Acts 13:16–41, we read Paul's evangelistic address in a synagogue in Pisidian Antioch. The setting, a synagogue, ensures that his hearers are Jews, Gentile proselytes to Judaism, and Godfearers—in every case, people thoroughly informed by the Bible (what we would today call the Old Testament). In this context, Paul selectively narrates Old Testament history in order to prove that Jesus of Nazareth is the promised Messiah. He quotes biblical texts, reasons his way through them, and argues that the resurrection of Jesus is the fulfillment of biblical prophecies about the Holy One in David's line not seeing decay. From Jesus' resurrection, Paul argues back to Jesus' death and its significance—ultimately, the forgiveness of sins and justification before God (vv. 38–39). Paul ends with a biblical passage warning of fearful judgment against skepticism and unbelief. Here, then, is the apostolic equivalent to evangelism among churchy folk, biblically literate folk—the kind of people who already, at a certain level, know their Bibles.

In Acts 17:16–34, however, one finds the apostle Paul evangelizing intelligent Athenians who are utterly biblically illiterate. Here his approach is remarkably different, and has much to teach us as we attempt to evangelize a new generation of biblical illiterates.

[16]While Paul was waiting for them [Silas and Timothy] in Athens, he was greatly distressed to see that the city was full of idols. [17]So he reasoned in the synagogue with the Jews and the God-fearing Greeks, as well as in the marketplace day by day with those who happened to be there. [18]A group of Epicurean and Stoic philosophers began to dispute with him. Some of them asked, "What is this babbler trying to say?" Others remarked, "He seems to be advocating foreign gods." They said this because Paul was preaching the good news about Jesus and the resurrection. [19]Then they took him and brought him to a meeting of the Areopagus, where they said to him, "May we know what this new teaching is that you are presenting? [20]You are bringing some strange ideas to our ears, and we want to know what they mean." [21](All the Athenians and the foreigners who lived there spent their time doing nothing but talking about and listening to the latest ideas.)

[22]Paul then stood up in the meeting of the Areopagus and said: "Men of Athens! I see that in every way you are very religious. [23]For as I walked around and looked carefully at your objects of worship, I even found an altar with this inscription: TO AN UNKNOWN GOD. Now what you worship as something unknown I am going to proclaim to you.

[24]"The God who made the world and everything in it is the Lord of heaven and earth and does not live in temples built by hands. [25]And he is not served by human hands, as if he needed anything, because he himself gives all men life and breath and everything else. [26]From one man he made every nation of men, that they should inhabit the whole earth; and he determined the times set for them and the exact places where they should live. [27]God did this so that men would seek him and perhaps reach out for him and find him, though he is not far from each one of us. [28]For in him we live and move and have our being.' As some of your own poets have said, 'We are his offspring.'

[29]"Therefore since we are God's offspring, we should not think that the divine being is like gold or silver or stone—an image made by man's design and skill. [30]In the past God overlooked such ignorance, but now he commands all people everywhere to repent. [31]For he has set a day when he will judge the

D. A. CARSON

world with justice by the man he has appointed. He has given proof of this to all men by raising him from the dead."

[32]When they heard about the resurrection of the dead, some of them sneered, but others said, "We want to hear you again on this subject." [33]At that, Paul left the Council. [34]A few men became followers of Paul and believed. Among them was Dionysius, a member of the Areopagus, also a woman named Damaris, and a number of others. (Acts 17:16–34)

I have organized the rest of what I have to say under four topics: the realities Paul faces, the priorities he adopts, the framework he establishes, and the nonnegotiable gospel he preaches.

THE REALITIES PAUL FACES

Apart from their obvious biblical illiteracy—these Athenian intellectuals had never heard of Moses, never cracked a Bible—three features of this culture are striking.

First, the Roman Empire was characterized not only by large-scale empirical pluralism but also by government-sponsored religious pluralism. The Romans knew that a captive people were more likely to rebel if they could align religion, land, and people. Partly to break up this threefold cord, the Romans insisted on adopting into their own pantheon some of the gods of any newly subjugated people, and they insisted equally strongly that the newly subjugated people adopt some of the Roman gods. In any potential civil war, therefore, it would be quite unclear which side the gods were helping—and this policy of god-swaps strengthened the likelihood of imperial peace. It also meant that religious pluralism was not only endemic to the Empire but was buttressed by the force of law. After all, it was a capital offense to desecrate a temple—any temple. But let no temple and no God challenge Washington—I mean Rome.

Second, like us, Paul was dealing not with people who were biblically illiterate and therefore had no worldview, but with people who vociferously argued for various competing and powerful worldviews. Two are mentioned in the text: Epicurean and Stoic (v. 18). In the first century, *philosophy* did not have the fairly esoteric and abstract connotations it has today, connected with minor departments in large universities. It referred to an entire way of life, based on a rigorous and self-consistent intellectual system—close to what we mean by worldview. The ideal of Epicurean philosophy, Epicurean worldview, was an undisturbed life—a life of tranquility, untroubled by undue involvement in human affairs. The gods themselves are composed of atoms so fine they live in calmness in the spaces between the worlds. As the gods are nicely removed from the hurly-burly of life, so human beings should seek the same ideal. But over against this vision, as we shall see, Paul presents a God who is actively involved in this world as its Creator, providential Ruler, Judge, and self-disclosing Savior.

Stoic philosophy thought of god as all-pervasive, more or less in a pantheistic sense, so that the human ideal was to live life in line with what is ultimately real, to conduct life in line with this god/principle of reason, which must rule over emotion and passion. Stoicism, as someone has commented, was "marked by great moral earnestness and a high sense of duty." Against such a vision, the God that Paul presents, far from being pantheistic, is personal, distinct from the creation, and is our final judge. Instead of focusing on "universal reason tapped into by human reasoning," Paul contrasts divine will and sovereignty with human dependence and need. In short, there is a massive clash of worldviews.

Of course, there were other Greek and Latin worldviews. There is no mention here of the sophists or of the atheistic philosophical materialists such as Lucretius. What is clear is that Paul here finds himself evangelizing men and women deeply committed to one fundamentally alien worldview or another.

Third, no less striking is the sneering tone of condescension they display in verse 18: "What is this babbler trying to say?"—this "seed picker," this little bird fluttering around picking up disconnected scraps of incoherent information, this second-class mind? Others remarked, "He seems to be advocating foreign gods." Of course, as it turns out, some of these people become genuinely interested in the gospel. The tenor of condescension is unmistakable, however, when an alien worldview feels secure in its thoughtless majority.

These, then, are the realities Paul faces.

THE PRIORITIES PAUL ADOPTS

The most immediate and striking response of the apostle Paul to all that he witnesses in Athens is an intuitively biblical analysis: he is "greatly distressed to see that the city was full of idols" (v. 16). Paul might have been overwhelmed by Athens' reputation as the Oxford or Cambridge or Harvard of the ancient world (though universities per se did not then exist). He might have admired the architecture, gaping at the Parthenon. But Paul is neither intimidated nor snookered by Athens; he sees the idolatry. How we need Christians in our universities and high places who are neither impressed nor intimidated by reputation and accomplishment if it is nothing more than idolatry!

D. A. CARSON

The apostle sets out, then, to evangelize. He aims at two quite different groups. As usual, he attaches a certain priority to evangelizing Jews and God-fearing Gentiles, the churchy folk, the biblically literate people; he reasons in the synagogue "with the Jews and the God-fearing Greeks" (v. 17a). He has a theological reason for this priority that we cannot examine here, but in any case we must never forget to evangelize such people. Second, he evangelizes the ordinary pagans who have no connection with the Bible: he evangelizes day by day in the market place, targeting anyone who happens to be there, most of whom would have been biblically illiterate (v. 17b). He does not wait for an invitation to the Areopagus. He simply gets on with his evangelism, and the invitation to the Areopagus is the result (v. 18).

These, then, are his priorities: God-centered cultural analysis, and persistent evangelism of both biblical literates and biblical illiterates.

Perhaps I should add that there is at least one fundamental difference between Paul's situation and ours. When Paul evangelizes biblical illiterates, he is dealing with people whose heritage has not in recent centuries had anything to do with biblical religion. So when they react negatively to him, they do so solely because, from their perspective, his frame of reference is so alien to their own. They are not rejecting him in part because they are still running away from their own heritage. That is the additional problem *we* sometimes face. We sometimes deal with men and women who have adopted a worldview that is not only at several points profoundly antithetical to a biblical worldview but also self-consciously chosen over against that biblical worldview. That opens up some opportunities for us, but it raises some additional barriers as well. However, we cannot probe these opportunities and barriers here. It is enough to observe the priorities that Paul adopts.

THE FRAMEWORK PAUL ESTABLISHES

Here it will be helpful to run through Paul's argument from 17:22 to 17:31. Before I do so, however, I want to make three preliminary observations.

First, it takes you about two minutes to read this record of Paul's address. But speeches before the Areopagus were not known for their brevity. In other words, we must remember that this is a condensed report of a much longer speech. Doubtless every sentence, in some cases every clause, constituted a point that Paul expanded upon at length.

Second, if you want to know a little more closely just how he would have expanded each point, it is easier to discover than some people think. For there are many points of comparison between these sermon notes and, for instance, Romans. I'll draw attention to one or two of the parallels as we move on.

Third, there is a fascinating choice of vocabulary. It has often been shown that many of the expressions in this address, especially in the early parts, are the sorts of things one would have found in Stoic circles. Yet in every case, Paul tweaks them so that in his context they convey the peculiar emphases he wants to assign to them. In other words, the vocabulary is linguistically appropriate to his hearers, but at the level of the sentence and the paragraph, Paul in this report is saying just what he wants to say; he is establishing a biblical worldview.

Now let us scan the framework Paul establishes.

First, he establishes that God is the creator of "the world and everything in it" (17:24). How much he enlarged on this point we cannot be certain, but we know from his other writings how his mind ran. The creation establishes that God is other than the created order; pantheism is ruled out. It also establishes human accountability; we owe our Creator everything, and to defy him and set ourselves up as the center of the universe is the heart of all sin. Worse, to cherish and worship created things instead of the Creator is the essence of idolatry.

Second, Paul insists that God "is the Lord of heaven and earth and does not live in temples built by hands" (v. 24). The sovereignty of God over the whole universe stands over against views that assign this god or that goddess a particular domain—perhaps the sea (Neptune), or tribal gods with merely regional or ethnic interests. The God of the Bible is sovereign over everything. This teaching grounds the doctrine of providence. Because of the universality of his reign, God cannot be domesticated—not even by temples (v. 24). Paul is not denying the historical importance of the temple in Jerusalem, still less that God uniquely disclosed himself there. Rather, he denies that God is limited to temples, and that he can be domesticated or squeezed or tapped into by the cultus of any temple (which of course threatens popular pagan practice). He is so much bigger than that.

Third, God is the God of aseity: "he is not served by human hands, as if he needed anything" (17:25). *Aseity* is a word now largely fallen into disuse, though it was common in Puritan times. Etymologically it comes from the Latin *a se*—"from himself." God is so utterly "from himself" that he does not need us; he is not only self-existent (a term we often deploy with respect to God's origins—the existence of everything else is God-dependent, but God himself is self-existent), but he is utterly independent of his created order so far as his own well-being or contentment or existence are concerned. *God does*

D. A. CARSON

not need us—a very different perspective from that of polytheism, where human beings and gods interact in all kinds of ways bound up with the finiteness and needs of the gods. The God of the Bible would not come to us if, rather whimsically, he wanted a McDonald's hamburger; the cattle on a thousand hills are already his.

Fourth, the truth of the matter is the converse: we are utterly dependent on him—"he himself gives all men life and breath and everything else" (v. 25b). This strips us of our vaunted independence; it is the human correlative of the doctrines of creation and providence.

Fifth, from theology proper, Paul turns to anthropology. He insists that all nations descended from one man (v. 26). This contradicts not a few ancient notions of human descent, which conjectured that different ethnic groups came into being in quite different ways. But Paul has a universal gospel that is based on a universal problem (cf. Rom. 5; 1 Cor. 15). If sin and death were introduced into the one human race by one man such that the decisive act of another man is required to reverse them, then it is important for Paul to get the anthropology right so that the soteriology is right. We cannot agree on the solution if we cannot agree on the problem. But Paul's stance has yet wider implications; there is no trace of racism here. Moreover, however much he holds that God has enjoyed a peculiar covenant relationship with Israel, because he is a monotheist, Paul holds that God must be sovereign over *all* the nations. Did he, perhaps, develop some of the lines of argument one finds in Isaiah 40ff.? If there is but one God, that God must in some sense be the God of all, whether his being and status are recognized by all or not.

Sixth, for the first time one finds an explicit reference to something wrong in this universe that God created. His providential rule over all was with the purpose that some would reach out for him and find him (v. 27). In short order Paul will say much more about sin (without actually using the word). Here he is preparing the way. The assumption is that the race as a whole does not know the God who made them. Something has gone profoundly wrong.

Seventh, although it has been important for him to establish God's transcendence, Paul does not want such an emphasis to drift toward what would later be called deism. The God he has in mind "is not far from each one of us" (v. 27). He is immanent. Paul will not allow any suspicion that God is careless or indifferent about people; he is never far from us. Moreover, the apostle recognizes that some of this truth is acknowledged in some pagan religions. When Greek thought (or much of it) spoke of one "God" as opposed to many gods, very often the assumption was more or less pantheistic. That structure of thought Paul has already ruled out. Still, some of its emphases were not wrong if put within a better framework. We live and move and have our being in this God, and we are his offspring (17:28)—not, for Paul, in some pantheistic sense, but as an expression of God's personal and immediate concern for our well-being.

Eighth, the entailment of this theology and this anthropology is to clarify what sin is and to make idolatry utterly reprehensible (v. 29). Doubtless Paul enlarged this point very much in terms of, say, Isaiah 44–45 and Romans 1. For he cannot rightly introduce Jesus and his role as Savior until he establishes what the problem is; he cannot make the good news clear until he elucidates the bad news from which the good news rescues us.

Ninth, Paul also introduces what might be called a philosophy of history— or better, perhaps, a certain view of time. Many Greeks in the ancient world thought that time went round and round in circles. Paul establishes a linear framework: creation at a fixed point; a long period that is past with respect to Paul's present in which God acted in a certain way ("In the past God overlooked such ignorance"); a now that is pregnant with massive changes; and a future (v. 31) that is the final termination of this world order, a time of final judgment. The massive changes of Paul's dramatic now are bound up with the coming of Jesus and the dawning of the gospel. Paul has set the stage so as to introduce Jesus.

So here is the framework Paul establishes. He has, in fact, constructed a biblical worldview. But he has not done so simply for the pleasure of creating a worldview. In this context he has done so in order to provide a framework in which Jesus himself, not least his death and resurrection, makes sense. Otherwise nothing that Paul wants to say about Jesus will make sense.

This is the framework Paul establishes.

THE NONNEGOTIABLE GOSPEL PAUL PREACHES

We read again verse 31: "For [God] has set a day when he will judge the world with justice by the man he has appointed. He has given proof of this to all men by raising him from the dead." Here, at last, Jesus is introduced.

I want to emphasize two things. First, it is extraordinarily important to see that Paul has established the framework of the biblical metanarrative before he introduces Jesus. If metaphysics is a sort of big physics that explains all the other branches of physics, similarly metanarrative is the big story that explains all the other stories. By and large, postmodernists love stories, especially ambiguous or symbol-laden narratives. But they hate the metanarrative, the big story that makes all the little stories coherent. But what Paul provides is the biblical metanarrative. This is the big story in the Bible that frames and explains all the little stories. Without this big story, the accounts of Jesus will not make any sense—and Paul knows it.

For instance, if in a vague, New Age, postmodern context, we affirm something like "God loves you," this short expression may carry a very different set of associations than we who are Christians might think. We already assume that men and women are guilty and that the clearest and deepest expression of God's love is in the cross, where God's own Son dealt with our sin at the expense of his own life. But if people know nothing of this story line, then the same words, "God loves you," may be an adequate summary of the stance adopted by Jodie Foster in her recent film, *Contact*. The alien power is beneficent, wise, good, and interested in our well-being. There is nothing whatever to do with moral accountability, sin, guilt, and how God takes action to remove our sin by the death of his Son. The one vision nestles into the framework of biblical Christianity; the other nestles comfortably into the worldview of New Age optimism. In short, without the big story, without the metanarrative, the little story or the little expression becomes either incoherent or positively misleading. Paul understands the point.

Second, what is striking is that Paul does not flinch from affirming the resurrection of Jesus from the dead. And that is what causes so much offense that Paul is cut off, and the Areopagus address comes to an end. Paul was thoroughly aware, of course, that most Greeks adopted some form of dualism. Matter is bad, or at least relatively bad; spirit is good. To imagine someone coming back from the dead in bodily form was not saying anything desirable, still less believable. Bodily resurrection from the dead was irrational; it was an oxymoron, like intelligent slug or boiled ice. So some of Paul's hearers have had enough, and they openly sneer and end the meeting (v. 32). If Paul had spoken instead of Jesus' immortality, his eternal spiritual longevity quite apart from any body, he would have caused no umbrage. But Paul does not flinch. Elsewhere he argues that if Christ has not been raised from the dead, then the apostles are liars, and we are still dead in our trespasses and sins (1 Cor. 15). He remains faithful to that vision here. Paul does not trim the gospel to make it acceptable to the worldview of his listeners.

For Paul, then, there is some irreducible and nonnegotiable content to the gospel, content that must not be abandoned, no matter how unacceptable it is to some other worldview. It follows that especially when we are trying hard to connect wisely with some worldview other than our own, we must give no less careful attention to the nonnegotiables of the gospel, lest in our efforts to communicate wisely and with relevance, we unwittingly sacrifice what we mean to communicate.

But suddenly we overhear the muttered objection of the critic. Can it not be argued that Paul here makes a fundamental mistake? Elsewhere in Acts he frequently preaches with much greater fruitfulness, and in those cases he does not stoop to all this worldview stuff. He just preaches Jesus and his cross and resurrection, and men and women get converted. Here, a piddling number believe (v. 34). In fact, Paul's next stop in Greece after Athens is Corinth. Reflecting later on his experiences there, Paul writes to the Corinthians and reminds them, "For I resolved to know nothing while I was with you except Jesus Christ and him crucified" (1 Cor. 2:2)—doubtless because he was reflecting with some sour-faced chagrin on his flawed approach in Athens. So let us be frank, the critics charge, and admit that Paul made a huge mistake in Athens and stop holding up Acts 17 as if it were a model of anything except what not to do. The man goofed: he appealed to natural theology; he tried to construct redemptive history; he attempted to form a worldview when he should have stuck to his last and preached Jesus and the cross.

I sometimes wish this reading were correct, but it is profoundly mistaken for a number of reasons. (1) It is not the natural reading of Acts. As Luke works through his book, he does not at this point in his narrative send up a red flag and warn us that at this point Paul makes a ghastly mistake. The false reading is utterly dependent on taking 1 Corinthians in a certain way (a mistaken way, as we shall see), and then reading it into Acts 17.

(2) What Paul expresses, according to Luke's report of the Areopagus address, is very much in line with Paul's own theology, not least his theology in the opening chapters of Romans.

(3) Strictly speaking, Paul does not say that only a "few" men believed. He says *tines de andres*, "certain people," along with *heteroi*, "others." These are in line with other descriptions. The numbers could scarcely have been large, because the numbers in the Areopagus could not have been very large in the first place.

(4) Transparently, Paul was cut off when he got to the resurrection of Jesus (vv. 31–32). But judging from all we know of him—both from a book like Romans and from the descriptions of him in Acts—we know where he would have gone from here.

(5) That is entirely in line with the fact that what Paul had already been preaching in the marketplace to the biblically illiterate pagans was the "gospel" (v. 18).

(6) At this point in his life Paul was not a rookie. Far from being fresh out of seminary and still trying to establish the precise pattern of his ministry, on

D. A. CARSON

any chronology he had already been through twenty years of thrilling and brutal ministry. Nor is this Paul's first time among biblically illiterate pagans or among intellectuals.

(7) In any case, 1 Corinthians 2 does *not* cast Paul's resolve to preach Christ crucified against the background of what had happened to him in Athens. He does not say, in effect, "Owing to my serious mistakes in Athens, when I arrived in Corinth I resolved to preach only Christ and him crucified." Rather, in 1 Corinthians Paul's resolve to preach Christ crucified is cast against the background of what Christians in Corinth were attracted to—namely, to a form of triumphalism that espoused an ostensible wisdom that Paul detests. It is a wisdom full of pride and rhetoric and showmanship. Against this background, Paul takes a very different course. Knowing that believers must boast only in the Lord and follow quite a different wisdom (1 Cor. 1), he resolves to preach Christ and him crucified.

(8) In any case, it would be wrong to think that Paul has no interest in worldviews. Writing after 1 Corinthians 2, Paul can say, "We demolish arguments and every pretension that sets itself up against the knowledge of God, and we take captive every thought to make it obedient to Christ" (2 Cor. 10:4–5). The context shows that Paul is not here interested so much in disciplining the individual's private thought life (though that certainly concerns him elsewhere) as in bringing into obedience to Christ every thought structure, every worldview, that presents opposition to his beloved Master. In other words, Paul thought "worldviewishly" (if that is not too monstrous a neologism). That is clear in many of his writings; it is clear in both 2 Corinthians 10 and in Acts 17.

(9) Finally, the first line of Acts 17:34 is sometimes misconstrued: "A few men became followers of Paul and believed." Many have assumed Luke means that a few people became Christians on the spot and followers of Paul. But that reverses what is said. Moreover, Paul has not yet given much gospel—in precisely what sense would they have become Christians? It is better to follow the text exactly. Following Paul's address, no one became a Christian on the spot. But some did become followers of Paul. In consequence, in due course they grasped the gospel and believed; they became Christians. This is entirely in line with the experience of many evangelists working in a university environment today.

A couple of years ago I spoke evangelistically at a large meeting in Oxford. So far as I know, no one became a Christian at that meeting. But sixteen students signed up for a six-week "Discovering Christianity" Bible study. A few weeks after the meeting, the curate, Vaughan Roberts, wrote me a note to tell me that eleven of the sixteen had clearly become Christians already, and he was praying for the remaining five. In other words, as a result of that meeting, some became "followers of Don," as it were, and in due course believed. That is often the pattern when part of the evangelistic strategy is to establish a worldview, a frame of reference, to make the meaning of Jesus and the gospel unmistakably plain.

In short, however sensitive Paul is to the needs and outlook of the people he is evangelizing, and however flexible he is in shaping the gospel to address them directly, we must see that there remains for him irreducible content to the gospel. That content is nonnegotiable, even if it is remarkably offensive to our hearers. If it is offensive, we may have to decide whether it is offensive because of the intrinsic message or because we have still not done an adequate job of establishing the frame of reference in which it alone makes sense. But the gospel itself must never be compromised.

SOME CONCLUDING REFLECTIONS

I offer three concluding reflections. First, the challenge of worldview evangelism is not to make simple things complicated but to make clear to others some fairly complicated things that we simply assume. This can be done in fifteen minutes with the sort of presentation Phillip Jensen and Tony Payne talk about earlier in this volume. It might be done in seven consecutive expositions running right through the first eight chapters of Romans. It might be done with the six months of Bible teaching, beginning with Genesis, that many New Tribes Mission personnel now use before they get to Jesus. But it must be done.

Second, the challenge of worldview evangelism is not primarily to think in philosophical categories, but it is to make it clear that closing with Jesus has content (it is connected with a real, historical Jesus about whom certain things must be said and believed) and is all-embracing (it affects conduct, relationships, values, priorities). It is not reducible to a preferential religious option among many, designed primarily to make me feel good about myself.

Third, the challenge of worldview evangelism is not primarily a matter of how to get back into the discussion with biblically illiterate people whose perspectives may be very dissimilar to our own. Rather, worldview evangelism focuses primarily on *where the discussion goes*. There are many ways of getting into discussion; the crucial question is whether the Christian witness has a clear, relatively simple, straightforward grasp of what the Bible's story line is, how it must give form to a worldview, and how the wonderful news of the gospel fits powerfully into this true story—all told in such a way that men and women can see its relevance, power, truthfulness, and life-changing capacity.

NOTES

Chapter 1

1. As quoted in the *Chicago Tribune*, 20 September 1893. Quoted in Johnson 1985, 106.

2. From "Auguries of Innocence," first published in 1863.

3. Paul Johnson, *The Intellectuals* (New York: Harper and Row, 1988), 246.

Chapter 2

1. Reported by Joyce Barnathan and Steven Strasser in *Newsweek,* 27 June 1988.

Chapter 3

1. This expression, which comes from Berger 1967, refers to the set of factors that together help to make a belief or practice appear plausible to a particular group of people within a particular context.

2. Good introductory discussions of religious pluralism, written from various perspectives, can be found in Clendenin 1995; D'Costa 1986; Knitter 1985; Netland 1991.

3. Another way to put this is to say that all restrictivists are particularists, but not all particularists are restrictivists (see Okholm and Phillips 1996, 19–20). For restrictivist views, see Piper 1993, chap. 4; Richard 1994; Nash 1994; Geivett and Phillips 1996. Evangelical particularists who distance themselves from restrictivism, but who nevertheless have not embraced the inclusivist paradigm, include John Stott (Edwards and Stott 1988, 320–29; Stott 1985, 83); McGrath 1996; Erickson 1975, 1996; Packer 1990, 123; and Clendenin 1995.

4. Representative statements of inclusivism can be found in D'Costa 1990; Dupuis 1997; Küng 1976; Pinnock 1992, 1996; Pannenberg 1993.

5. The term *pluralism* itself is ambiguous. It may refer simply to the undeniable fact of religious diversity—people do indeed embrace different religious perspectives. This is obvious and noncontroversial. But the sense in which we are using it here goes beyond mere recognition of the fact of diversity to embrace a particular view about the relationship between the major religions—namely, an egalitarian and democratized perspective that sees a rough parity among religions concerning truth and soteriological effectiveness.

6. For his account of his theological pilgrimage see Hick 1982, chap. 1; and Hick 1996, 29–42.

-400-

TELLING THE TRUTH

7. Later discussion of pluralism by Hick include his volumes for 1993, 1994, and 1995.

8. The contemporary attraction of pluralism is sometimes said to be due to the cultural shift from modernity to postmodernity. Much, of course, depends upon what is meant by the terms. The discussion of modernity and postmodernity—including whether such a distinction is at all helpful—is enormously complex and need not detain us. Our concern here is with the broad intellectual and social patterns shaping the present realities, not with the debate over labels and categories.

9. Good introductions to globalization theory include Waters 1995; Robertson 1992; and Beyer 1994.

10. Turner 1994, 186. For similar perspectives see Berger 1992; Beyer 1994; Bruce 1996.

11. Social theorists such as Peter Berger maintain that this is an inevitable result of modernization. See Berger 1979, 1–31.

12. See Netland 1994, 91; see also Newbigin 1989; Carter 1993.

13. Most informal pluralists, of course, are unfamiliar with Hick's work and most likely would not identify themselves as pluralists.

14. Printed in *The Butler Collegian* (5 February 1998), 4–5. *The Butler Collegian* is a student newspaper published in conjunction with the journalism department of Butler University, Indianapolis, Indiana.

15. This view is also pervasive in the university. Most religious studies courses, for example, examine religion from a sociological and anthropological viewpoint with little consideration of the truth claims implicit in religious beliefs. An interesting example of this can be seen in a five-year study conducted by the National Endowment of the Humanities regarding how religion should be taught in the university. Ninian Smart, professor of religious studies, spoke for a majority of the faculty when he said, "Our field has nothing to do with an ultimate truth-claim, but is solely concerned with the understanding and explanation of the data of human religiousness" (quoted in Beuscher 1989, 36–38).

16. Probably the best summary of Hick's views is in Hick 1989. For some introductory critical evaluations, see Nash 1994; Okholm and Phillips 1996, 60–80; Johnson "John Hick's."

17. See Halverson 1996 with its helpful charts and summaries.

18. Carson 1996 argues this point persuasively.

19. For an excellent discussion of the place of tolerance in a multicultural and multireligious society, see Gaede 1993.

20. At one level Hinduism is very accommodating and even pluralistic in its orientation toward other religions. Nevertheless, in the final analysis most Hindus believe that the ultimate reality is *Brahman.* This truth-claim is incompatible with many forms of theism. Furthermore, Hindus believe that each person is caught in an endless cycle of birth, death, and rebirth (*Samsara*). This contradicts the belief of Muslims, for example, that a person lives one life and then stands in judgment before *Allah.*

21. For further discussion of the nature of religious truth, see Carson 1996, 57–370; Netland 1991, 112–50; Nash 1994, 53–68; and Adler 1990.

NOTES

22. It is also worth noting that these three expressions of informal pluralism share a common feature: they ignore, grossly distort, or subtly deny the factuality of religious truth-claims.

23. Obviously there is a sense in which religious traditions do meet psychological and social needs. This partial truth often makes this assumption difficult to overturn. Another reason this assumption is difficult to overturn is the pervasive influence of this thinking in the academic community. This view dates back to the work of early psychologists like Sigmund Freud and sociologists like Max Weber who viewed religions as complex social institutions and attempted to explain religious phenomena without reference to the transcendent.

24. Campbell's discussion of Jesus' ascension in the PBS series *The Power of Myth* is a vivid example of this. "For example, Jesus ascended to heaven. The denotation would be that somebody literally ascended to the sky. That's literally what is being said. But if that were really the meaning of the message, we would have to throw it away, because there would be no such place for Jesus literally to go.... But if you read 'Jesus ascended to heaven' in terms of its metaphoric connotation, you see that he has gone inward—not into outer space but into inward space, to the place from which all being comes, into the consciousness that is the source of all things." In response, Bill Moyers asks, "Aren't you undermining one of the great traditional doctrines of the classic Christian faith—that the burial and the resurrection of Jesus prefigures [*sic*] our own?" Campbell responds, "That would be a mistake in the reading of the symbol. That is reading the words in terms of prose instead of in terms of poetry" (see Campbell 1988, 67–68).

25. For further discussion of criteria related to the evaluation of religious claims, see Netland 1991, 151–95; Holmes 1983; Mitchell 1973; Nash 1992.

26. Informal pluralists influenced by postmodern thinking may object that all judgments—scientific, historical, or religious—are subjective and relative. Carson (1996, 107) has correctly observed that much postmodern thought depends on a false dichotomy: either we know something objectively and exhaustively, or we are lost in a sea of relativity. It is often helpful to point out this false antithesis to pluralists.

27. Much has been made of several surveys that suggested a large percentage of Americans (as many as 36.8% from a Gallup poll done in January of 1994) believed it was possible the Holocaust never happened. (The data from Gallup's survey were cited by Smith [1995, 269–95].) This conclusion, however, may be unwarranted. More recent studies indicate that "less than 2 percent [of Americans] are consistent and committed deniers." Furthermore, "most uncertainty and doubt about the Holocaust result from general historical ignorance and not from the absorption of the neo-Nazi party line" (Smith 1995, 269–95).

28. For further critique of this assumption, see Johnson "Do All Paths."

29. Keith gives a lecture on university campuses entitled "Comparative Religions: Do All Paths Lead to the Same Destination?" He developed this program both to address informal religious pluralism among college students and to open a hearing for the gospel in a religiously diverse environment. The point of the program is *not*

to prove that Christianity alone is true but to show that all religions cannot be true at the same time. He begins by comparing five religions (Buddhism, Christianity, Hinduism, Islam, and Judaism) in order to demonstrate that these traditions make conflicting claims. Next, he attempts to answer the question, "How does one evaluate these traditions?" with four points: (1) each of these religions makes truth-claims that contradict the truth-claims of other religions; (2) based on the law of noncontradiction they cannot all be right; (3) we must distinguish sincerity of belief from truthfulness; and (4) we must carefully distinguish matters of taste from matters of truth. Finally, he applies these criteria to the various religions and closes by describing how, in principle, Christianity could be *eliminated* because it provides criteria by which its truth-claims can be evaluated.

Chapter 4

1. For Rorty, and for many others, epistemology has been at the center of philosophy, especially in its modern period. Therefore if epistemology fails, all of philosophy as it has been pursued fails as well.

2. Actually the idea that we have a privileged access to the content of our own minds goes at least as far back as Augustine's *Contra Academicos* written about A.D. 386. It was not until Descartes, however, that this privileged access to the content of our own minds became the foundation for an entire theory of knowledge.

3. The fact that it is always the case that there will be more than one theory that is adequate to any given set of evidence has been called (by Quine and his followers) the *underdetermination of theory by evidence*.

4. Berlin 1978, 22. Gutting (1994, 2) makes this observation.

5. Foucault 1972, 30. I cite the translation in Fink-Eitel 1992, 3.

6. Foucault 1984c, 90. It may seem strange for a postmodern to compare his project with an Enlightenment thinker's. Foucault recognizes that his kinship with Kant is far from comprehensive. It consists in an ethos: "[T]he thread that may connect us with the enlightenment is not faithfulness to doctrinal elements, but rather the permanent reactivation of an attitude—that is of a philosophical ethos that could be described as a permanent critique of our historical era" (Foucault 1984a, 42).

7. Foucault asserts this in reference to a slightly more narrow point but would not shy from affirming it as generally as I apply it here.

8. No one familiar with today's universities will fail to recognize them as the theater of this Foucauldian struggle to rewrite the rules of the game and deploy them to advantage. New winners and losers have already emerged: some voices are privileged, other disqualified. There has been a carrying over of affirmative action into epistemology. If a group has been oppressed, it cannot be gainsaid. To challenge such voices, state the new rules, is censurable racism, sexism, or atavistic bigotry. The battle for the rules of the game is well underway, and those groups savvy to the struggle have stolen a march on the other players.

9. "The Masked Philosopher," *Le Monde* (April 6, 1980), cited in Gutting 1994, 207.

10. Cited in Gutting 1994, 152. I suppose the genealogy of this lie would trace its origins back to the promise of the serpent in the Garden.

NOTES

11. This is a reference to the story about some of Aristotle's students who, upon hearing his definition of a man as a "featherless biped," plucked a chicken and threw it over the Academy wall, thus providing an excellent counterexample.

12. This point is pressed in a fine article by Bernstein (1994, esp. 299).

13. This is the marvelous concluding line from Gutting 1989, 288.

14. Foucault (1984a, 47) identified as the crucial conundrum "the paradox of the relations of capacity and power." Again: "How can the growth of capabilities be disconnected from the intensification of power relations?" (48). The very question Foucault poses could serve as a suitable opening for an evangelistic address. One might take the narrative of Genesis 4 and illustrate Foucault's paradoxical predicament by the line of Cain and the only answer by the line of Abel.

Chapter 6

1. Two classic examples of Sydney's biblical theology approach are Graeme Goldsworthy's *Gospel and Kingdom: A Christian Interpretation of the Old Testament* (Exeter: Paternoster, 1981), and his *According to Plan: The Unfolding Revelation of God in the Bible* (Leicester: InterVarsity Press, 1991).

2. *Two Ways to Live: Know the Gospel, Share the Gospel.* This is published by Matthias Media, P.O. Box 225, Kingsford NSW, Australia. E-mail: *sales@matthiasmedia.com.au* Web: www.matthiasmedia.com.au. Matthias Media has also published a tract version of *Two Ways to Live* that Christians can buy and give away, as well as a one-hour evangelistic Bible study based on the outline.

Chapter 8

1. Cited in Phillips 1997, 261.
2. For a response, see Griffiths 1991.
3. Cited in Seamands 1964, 77.
4. Hick 1980, 8; cited in Phillips 1997, 261–62.
5. Roszak 1977, 225; cited in Groothuis 1986, 21.
6. Quoted in Groothuis 1986, 21.
7. See esp. Psalms 19 and 119.

Chapter 9

1. Douglas Bush, ed., *Milton: Poetical Works* (Oxford: University Press, 1966), (1.242–55), 218.

2. Reported in *Newsweek* (July 10, 1955): 8.

Chapter 10

1. Gautama Buddha and Confucius may have been historical persons, but their systems of thought are independent of their personal existence. If one could prove that Gautama Buddha never lived, Buddhism itself would not thereby be destroyed. The same is true for Confucianism with respect to Confucius. But if one could somehow prove that Jesus is not an historical figure, Christianity would be utterly destroyed.

2. D. A. Carson in personal letter to author dated 12 March 1998.

3. Barna 1991; quoted in Carson 1996, 23.

Chapter 11

1. Martin Luther, from the margin of the Luther Bible, as quoted by Moo 1996, 218.

Chapter 12

1. Cited in "A Postmodern Scandal," *World Magazine* (21 Feb. 1998).

2. Report of the Henry Jackson subcommittee, cited in Bailey 1968, 65.

3. From Luther's commentary on Galatians, as cited in Stott 1986, 345.

4. From Martin Luther's *The Freedom of a Christian*, as cited in Dillenberger 1961, 60.

Chapter 13

1. For more detail to fill out this brief account, see Horn 1971, and Barclay 1977.

2. For a helpful analysis of the biblical theology of worship, see Peterson 1992.

Chapter 16

1. Many of the presentations at the conference addressed postmodernism as a philosophical reality or as a hermeneutical problem to be addressed by the church. Our contribution examines postmodernity as a social reality with which the church must engage.

2. See chapter 15, where Charles Gilmer, an African-American workshop speaker at the conference, also argues that postmodernism has had a relatively minor impact on the African-American community on the whole.

3. Books such as Rosenau's *Post-modernism and the Social Sciences* (1992) describe how various academic disciplines are being affected by postmodernism.

4. *Christian Scholar's Review* 25 (June 1996) offers a number of articles that examine the relationship between postmodernism and multiculturalism and how Christians should assess and respond to these movements.

5. For example, see Celek and Zander 1996; Long 1997.

6. In this paper we will use the term *self-identity* rather broadly so that it also incorporates ethnic, religious, vocational, and gender identities.

7. For further reading on this critical topic, we recommend *Following Jesus without Dishonoring Your Parents: Asian-American Discipleship* (Yep et al. 1998).

8. In fact, many American social psychologists argue that a critical aspect of self-identity formation is one's independence and separation from parents (e.g., Offer and Offer 1975; Lidz 1968).

9. See Denzin 1989; Sampson, 1989; Gergen 1992.

10. Recognizing that racial reconciliation and unity in diversity are important biblical values, IVCF is encouraging Asian-American chapters to be more proactive about entering into meaningful fellowship relationships with other Christian groups on their campuses and to participate in many multiethnic training events and outreach programs.

11. Inouye 1984; Fong 1990, 91–96; Lin 1996, 43–50; Yep et al. 1998. Some scholars, however, observe that even Western culture, as it is shifting away from modernity, is gradually becoming more shame-based, e.g., Giddens 1991.

NOTES

Chapter 17

1. I am grateful to my colleagues at the Communication Center who have been instrumental in shaping and sharpening my thought on this topic.

2. I am indebted to Timothy Oliver for this insight.

3. For a discussion of art and science, and direct and indirect communication, see Downs 1999, 61–72.

4. I am indebted to Tim Muehlhoff for his model of persuasion and his insights on Proverbs that have influenced my thoughts.

Chapter 19

1. Barna (1995, 73) found that only 12 percent of those who do evangelism feel that they have a gift for it.

2. Both series are available from Zondervan Publishing Company.

Chapter 20

1. Kelly Monroe, ed. 1995. *Finding God at Harvard*. Grand Rapids: Zondervan.

Chapter 21

1. The original idea was developed by Kelly Monroe and financially supported by Jerry and Adelle Mercer of Columbus, Ohio. These forums have become annual events at many universities across the country.

Chapter 22

1. *The Screwtape Letters* first appeared during World War II as a series of articles in *The Guardian,* now defunct, and was subsequently revised and published in a variety of editions. The edition referred to here is merely one of them.

Chapter 23

1. A more extensive discussion of material in this chapter can be found in Long 1997.

Chapter 25

1. These materials, which are produced for us by Creation Resources, an internal group within the Navigators, are available by calling (614) 263–8954. For training seminars throughout the year, call (719) 594–2255.

Chapter 26

1. QuEST (an acronym for Questions Exploring Students Thinking) is a research-based outreach sponsored by the Research and Development office of Campus Crusade for Christ. QuEST uses informal student interviews to gather useful research information and to provide students with a basis for interaction about spiritual issues.

2. The intent of this question was to shed light on the student's level of desire to know God. Their answers certainly cannot be taken to indicate their desire to know the God of the Bible. At best they can serve to indicate the students' level of desire to know whatever God they conceive, whether that is the God of the Bible or not.

3. Consider the writings of Leslie Newbigin (1986; 1989) and the Gospel and Our Culture Network his writings spawned. Hunsberger and Van Gelder (1996) provide a helpful introduction to the issues. Also helpful is Poe (1996).

4. Consider the search for the apostolic *kerygma* suggested by Dodd (1936, 38–45) as well as the many works of others who followed his lead. Ladd (1993, 364–78) has a helpful summary. See also Poe (1996).

5. For an excellent exposition of the gospel, see "The Gospel of Jesus Christ: An Evangelical Celebration" (*Christianity Today*, June 14, 1999) or at www.christianity.net/ct/9T7/9T7049.html.

6. See Johnson (1994).

7. For example, see L. Ford (1994) and K. Ford (1995).

8. Campus Crusade for Christ is testing an updated campus version entitled *Knowing God Personally* in the spring of 2000.

9. Produced by Campus Crusade for Christ, Inc. (1965, 1994).

10. Produced by Billy Graham Evangelistic Association.

11. Produced by the Navigators (1969).

12. For information regarding *Life@Large*, contact Research and Development, Campus Crusade for Christ–2500, 100 Lake Hart, Orlando, FL 32832 (1-407-826-2500). *Life@Large* is available through Integrated Resources at 1-800-729-4351.

13. For a fuller discussion of the story line, see Carson (1996).

14. *The Four Spiritual Laws* serves as a good example of a presentation. There is one transitional question asked between the first and second laws. The next questions occur at the end of the fourth law, where a response to the gospel is sought. As a whole, *The Four Spiritual Laws* is intended to serve as a clear presentation of the gospel, not a discussion. Many who use the tool will effectively adapt it to a more conversational style, but that is not implicit in its design.

Chapter 27

1. Cited in Gaebelein 1980, 22.

2. Cited in Gundry 1976, 97–98.

3. For a fuller discussion, see chapter 13, "Lostness as a Motivation for Evangelism," in Fernando 1994.

4. For a fuller discussion, see chapter 12, "Why Should We Talk about Judgment?" in Fernando 1994.

5. Quoted in Wirt 1997, 47.

6. For evangelical descriptions of deconstruction, see Erickson 1993, 102–4, 110–14; Carson 1996, 72–79.

7. See my essay, "The Uniqueness of Jesus Christ," chapter 8 in this volume.

8. See especially Psalm 119, where the word *delight* appears nine times in connection with the Word of God.

9. Quoted in Henry 1986, 67 (italics Henry's).

INDEX

SUBJECT

Subject Index

INDEX OF MODERN NAMES

Index of Modern Names

SCRIPTURE INDEX

SCRIPTURE INDEX